East West Central

East West Central
Re-Building Europe, 1950–1990

Edited by Ákos Moravánszky, Torsten Lange,
Judith Hopfengärtner, Karl R. Kegler

Ákos Moravánszky, Karl R. Kegler (Eds.)

Re-Scaling the Environment

New Landscapes of Design, 1960–1980

East West Central
Re-Building Europe
1950–1990
Vol. 2

Birkhäuser
Basel

Editors
Prof. Dr. Ákos Moravánszky
Department of Architecture, ETH Zurich, Switzerland

Prof. Dr. Karl R. Kegler
Department of Architecture, Munich University of Applied Sciences, Germany
karl.kegler@hm.edu

Translation from German into English ("On Bees and Bolts"): Gillian Morris, D-Berlin
Editors' proofreading: Alan Lockwood, PL-Warsaw
Publishers' proofreading: Alun Brown, A-Vienna
Project and production management: Angelika Heller, Birkhäuser Verlag, A-Vienna
Layout and typography: Ekke Wolf, typic.at, A-Vienna
Cover design: Martin Gaal, A-Vienna
Printing and binding: Holzhausen Druck GmbH, A-Wolkersdorf

Library of Congress Cataloging-in-Publication data
A CIP catalog record for this book has been applied for at the Library of Congress.

Bibliographic information published by the German National Library
The German National Library lists this publication in the Deutsche Nationalbibliografie; detailed bibliographic data are available on the Internet at http://dnb.dnb.de.

This publication is also available as an e-book (ISBN PDF 978-3-0356-0823-6).

P.O. Box 44, 4009 Basel, Switzerland
Part of Walter de Gruyter GmbH, Berlin/Boston

Printed on acid-free paper produced from chlorine-free pulp. TCF ∞

Printed in Austria

ISBN 978-3-0356-1015-4 Volume 1
ISBN 978-3-0356-1016-1 Volume 2
ISBN 978-3-0356-1017-8 Volume 3
ISBN 978-3-0356-1014-7 Set Volume 1–3

9 8 7 6 5 4 3 2 1

www.birkhauser.com

Contents

III Practices and Agencies 197

Appendix 307

Ákos Moravánszky

Foreword

East West Central: Re-Building Europe

The Iron Curtain stood for the static immutability of the status quo. "From Stettin in the Baltic to Trieste in the Adriatic, an iron curtain has descended across the Continent" – Winston Churchill told his audience in a famous speech on March 5, 1946. Like most metaphors, the term Iron Curtain has imprinted itself into the perception of reality and was associated with the fortified border, erected to block the movement of people and information between East and West. Architectural historiography followed suit, presenting the history of modernization and modernism in Europe from a perspective determined – and limited – by this political boundary. The imagery produced by the dissolution of the Soviet Union: the "fall," the "lifting" or the "raising" of the curtain, the "breaching" of the wall, is a sign of confusion – regarding not only metaphors, but also underlying assumptions, methods and categories of architectural historiography.

Writing in the 1920s, art historian Erwin Panofsky famously referred to the perspective as a symbolic form. By this he meant that representing reality by means of a cohesive set of rules and symbols would give shape to a specific worldview. The exchange of views between cultures can therefore be studied using examples of visual representations, based on differing concepts of the relationship between observer and reality. When Panofsky gave his seminal lecture on Western perspective, Russian philosopher-physicist-inventor-priest Pavel Florensky wrote a study on the "reverse perspective" used in icon painting. He compared it to Renaissance representations of space in order to point out the differences between the two types of visual representation and their respective philosophical and theological underpinnings.

The exchange of glances as expressed in the German word *Blickwechsel* is a suggestive image: we are invited to switch between the viewpoints of the observer and the observed, so that our image of the world is suddenly no longer taken for granted. The metaphor of the Iron Curtain, however, suggests that after WWII the boundary between the two halves of Europe was hermetic and impermeable, even to the gaze. Western and Eastern Europe regarded each other as their own dark "others": communism and capitalism, divided by the Iron Curtain, were the "Twin Empires" on the mythical map of Europe. Yet, the perfect symmetry of the image eschewed the evidently more complex reality. As an image, the Iron Curtain was able to trigger both Western fear and desire, but actually it was far from being impenetrable. Rather, the Iron Curtain's semi-permeability, which turned it into an osmotic membrane, refuted the supposed symmetry of the East-West division. Contrary to the widespread identification in the West with the concept of Western Europe and its corresponding values, the idea of a shared Eastern European identity has never been popular among the inhabitants of this region. Architects in the East were generally very well informed about the latest developments in Western architecture. One could hardly survive as an architect without having browsed the latest issues of *L'Architecture d'Aujourd'hui, The Architectural Review* or the magazines from Scandinavian countries, all of which were available in the libraries of the large state-owned design offices. The optical metaphor, however, held true: images were floating around but remained disembodied signifiers, as they weren't grounded in personal experience. At the same time, travels of architects and professional organizations from the West to the East intensified during 1970s and 1980s. The lessons that participants drew from such exchanges more often than not depended on their respective viewpoints of the perspective.

The discrepancy between the bipolarity of block-thinking and the more complex and heterogeneous civilizational and political reality of Europe has led historians to develop different concepts to describe the historical identity of European regions more adequately than the East-West dichotomy. The term *Mitteleuropa* has never been merely a geographical term. It was a political one as well, just as East and West were connected with distinct political ideas or concepts. With the active support of intellectuals from the United States and England in the 1980s, Central Europe became a program to affirm a particular identity of the region: politically part of the Eastern Bloc, but without losing its Western cultural orientation – a result of the region's specific historical development and its political affiliations before the war. "The phrase, a peculiar one, a hybrid of sorts, hearkened back to the Cold War period; while it reflected a certain deference to the ideas of Milan Kundera and others, it avoided the outright suggestion that the notion of Eastern Europe was outmoded, essentially a fabrication of the age of Stalin, that it brought together in a single category societies that remained significantly different" – wrote Stephen R. Graubard, editor of *Daedalus*, the journal of the American Academy of Arts and Sciences in 1990, in his introduction for the issue "Eastern Europe... Central Europe... Europe." The title suggested a development of concepts: the first term referred to the Cold War period, the second was the "preferred word of certain individuals and groups in the 1960s, 1970s, and 1980s," while the third was the "word of the moment." From the contemporary perspective of more than two decades later, the question about what might be further stages in this progression is at the heart of heated debates.

Ironically, it was exactly the abolishment of state socialism and the new freedom of movement that have lessened the urgency to cross borders intellectually. In 1987, the idea of a joint international exhibition to take place in Budapest and Vienna in 1995 was embraced with much enthusiasm, only to be abandoned in its advanced stage. The "bridges into the future" – the motto of Expo'95 – literally lost their appeal after the Pan-European Picnic in August 1989.

Today, as block-thinking and block-politics are reemerging, the category of the Central promises to be a useful tool for investigating European architecture between two moments of "re-building": the postwar reconstruction and the start of shifting the "curtain" (which is not less "irony" today than before) more and more toward the East. We decided to use the word Central not only because it was a buzzword during the decades that are the focus of our investigation, but because the "thirding" that is implicit in the term opposes a bipolar narrative that regards modernization and globalization as Westernization and regards Eastern European developments as secondary or non-authentic, never questioning the constructs that legitimate these interpretations.

An investigation into issues such as housing, the exporting of knowledge to the Third World, building for education and for leisure between the two re-buildings of Europe would be impossible if one resorted to the narrative of the Iron Curtain. Rather than this dualistic concept, we have to consider among others competitions, cooperation, critical transformation, and knowledge transfer as more adequate frameworks for investigating these more dynamic conditions. The critique of self-serving dichotomizations of cultural phenomena in line with the East/West dispositive (marginal/central, modern/traditional, authentic/copy etc.) does not mean that, in this process of explaining the changing urban and architectural conditions over the course of the last seventy years, the diverse cultural landscape of Europe needs to be flattened.

The re-mapping of the European historiography of the postwar decades is an urgent task in the face of the paradoxical perpetuation of the Cold War discourse. One of the reasons behind its endurance is the imbalance between the ongoing institutionalization of archives of postwar architectural production in Western Europe vis-à-vis the disappearance of archival sources in the East. To lend visibility to the architectural discourse in former socialist countries, it is important to give voice to protagonists and witnesses. The failure to do this would not only reinforce already existing blind spots in the architectural historiography of the postwar period, but would also distort the perception of Western-European architecture culture from the 1960s onward. This includes the concept of the welfare state as being restricted to the Western social-democratic project and posited in contrast to state socialism, rather than recognizing parallel development in the post-Stalinist socialist countries and its architecture revolving around issues of consumption, leisure, mass housing and the emergence of new collective subjectivities such as "users," "inhabitants," or "consumers." Another example could be the reduction of current processes of globalization to their earlier stages, presenting globalization as "Americanization," thus forgetting the multiple, vibrant and heterogeneous processes of the internationalization of architecture and planning practices between socialist and post-colonial countries.

Three international conferences organized by the Chair of Architectural Theory at the ETH Zurich prepared the ground for this re-mapping. The topic of our first East West Central conference in May 2014 was *Re-Humanizing Architecture: New Forms of Community, 1950–1970*. Our intention was to show that the rhetoric of humanism provided an ideal common ground for liberal and socialist positions in the postwar years. With the second conference *Re-Scaling the Environment: New Landscapes of Design, 1960–1980*, held in November 2014, we abandoned the metaphor of the "human scale" as the natural way of viewing the world for a larger, superhuman, geographic or territorial scale. The theme of the third conference in *Re-Framing Identities: Architecture's Turn to History, 1970–1990* in September 2015 shows another overlap by a decade. This does not mean that the themes of humanism and scale disappear; even postmodernism is regarded by some historians as a project of re-humanization. While we investigate these altogether four decades from three different perspectives, the themes of humanism, scale and identity remain relevant categories throughout the entire time period 1950–1990.

We could not have gotten started on this project without the generous and long-term support of the Department of Architecture of the ETH Zurich and its Institut gta (Institute for the History and Theory of Architecture). The Swiss National Science Foundation (SNF) has provided us with financial assistance for the organization of the conferences. The book has been made possible only by the contributions of our authors; we owe them all a debt of gratitude. We would also like to thank the persons and institutions who gave their permission for the illustrations. We owe a considerable debt to everybody at Birkhäuser Verlag who helped in the production of the book; most of all David Marold and Angelika Heller. We also would like to express our gratitude to our student assistants Josephine Eigner and Laure Nashed for their help.

Karl R. Kegler

Introduction

On Systems and System Change

One of the – literally – greatest books in the recent history of architecture was published in 1969. Paoli Soleri's *Arcology. The City in the Image of Man* has the format of an atlas, measuring 60 × 36 cm.[1] To open and file through the book a large library table is needed. However, on the very first page the volume starts with an apparent paradox: "This book is about miniaturization." Soleri (1919–2013) explained this contradiction with a double reference to the notion of scale. In his view contemporary civilization had spoiled space and nature with an absurd "horizontal gigantism" of settlements and infrastructures which caused a progressive destruction of nature, waste of time, waste of energy, resources, coherence, and authentic experience in its jammed horizontal structures. Soleri saw the solution to these challenges in the "intensification" or rather "miniaturization" of human life within dense three-dimensional cities which would reduce spatial and energetic effort by greater efficiency. Such re-scaling of human life by spatial densification would enable every man to reach a much larger variety of objectives within a limited time and distance, and provide a new combination of architecture and ecology – *arcology*. Future man according to Soleri will be an absolute city dweller in three-dimensional structures rising hundreds of meters high but at the same time will live in absolute harmony with nature as an unspoiled landscape will frame the absolute city.

Soleri's 1969 vision of a possible future might look like a fantastic speculation. However, it combines a number of characteristics of the new approaches in architecture, planning and urbanism that are addressed in this volume. This fact may become clearer if the urban vision of Soleri – a collaborator with Frank Lloyd Wright, founder of the commune of Arcosanti in the desert of Arizona, and later author of esoteric books[2] – is compared with another concept of global urban reform of this time: Fritz Haller's study *Integral Urban: a global model* of 1968.[3] Fritz Haller (1924–2012) – architect, successful co-founder of the company USM Haller and propagator of flexible modular designs – is completely unsuspecting of esoteric ideas. His book is opened by an uncompromising sober quote of the psychiatrist and operative social researcher Otto Walter Haselhoff:

> a society which is being moulded by automation and cybernetics, atomic science and space research must consider it an unjustifiable and hardly credulous naivety to hope that just "humane appeal" – that legitimizing reference to one's own care for humanity – is sufficient to master important practical problems. in fact, a modest orientation suffices to show that this principle has never solved the real problems of an epoch.[4]

In this matter of fact style, Haller assesses the present state of the world: "the centers of work, living, and leisure are chaotically intermingled, and a meaningful life in them seems more and more questionable [...] the air is polluted. installations for supply and purification of water cannot be expanded quickly enough to meet the rapidly increasing load."[5] But according to Haller, in the age of space travel even these problems may be solved: "if it is possible to activate and organize the countless intellectual energies necessary for this undertaking, why should it not be possible to form a reasonable living space for society – for this same society which will achieve this fantastic step into the cosmic sphere?"[6]

Just like Soleri's approach, Haller's urban model is a study in scales. Going up from the level of a neighborhood of 3,250 inhabitants as "first order unit *e1*" to the level of towns of more than 61 million inhabitants as "fourth order unit *e4*",[7] Haller interpolated a schematic system of increasing units in which every man on earth would have his equal share of supply, service, transport and living space. Seven years later, in 1975, Haller estimated that a future world population of ten billion people might be accommodated in eighty rationally planned *e4*-level cities which – even with the agricultural areas to feed the residents taken into account – would leave large parts of the earth free for undisturbed nature: "large non-cultivated regions can remain or be re-established as virgin forests."[8]

Scaling as a Method of Design Development

Soleri and Haller may be taken as examples of an approach in planning that combines urban, technological, ecological and systemic aspects with a number of strategies that are characteristic for the architecture of the period of the 1960s and 1970s. With the breaking up of the *Congrès Internationaux d'Architecture Moderne* (CIAM) in 1959 members of Team 10 and other younger progressive architects experimented with design methods that transferred patterns and relations of social space from the small scale to the medium and large level of complex architecture and housing projects. The rhetoric of "great numbers," "no-stop city" (Superstudio) or "megastructures" (Reyner Banham) revealed the advent of new dimensions in architectural thinking. Aldo van Eyck's famous Amsterdam Orphanage, finished in 1960, or the urban extension of Toulouse-Le Mirail (1961–1971) planned by the Paris-based bureau of Candilis-Josic-Woods illustrate a structuralist logic that was inspired by the study of vernacular patterns. At the same time, the years between 1960 and 1980 were a period of a hitherto unknown scale of building production both in East and West Europe. Science, technology and new construction methods based on steel frames and reinforced concrete offered architects and designers hitherto unknown possibilities to conceive and imagine buildings of new scales and typologies. Groups of experimental architects both in Eastern and Western Europe explored such possibilities in unconventional projects, some of them dealing with specific phenomena of modern societies such as mass media or leisure. The hopes that underpinned the implementation of new scales and systems as well as their often conflicting actuality, due to the inertia of material and social realities, triggered the rise of planning and design theory as well as planning systems as new meta-sciences that took on diverse shapes in the East and West.

Global Perspectives

One of the immanent concepts of the era's competing systems and economies in western and eastern Europe was the idea of efficiency; in western economies this target was sought to be met by interventions of the government or other agencies, in eastern economics by centralized large-scale planning. At the same time the new perspectives that were opened by the space programs of the super powers, as well as the impact of design theory, comprehensive planning and new technologies on architecture, helped to generate a vision of the Earth as a space vessel of limited resources – in fact, this thought appears in the very title of Richard Buckminster Fuller's influential *Operating manual for spaceship Earth* of 1969.[9] The encounter of such approaches necessarily had to lead to a debate on how far man's needs could meet with global resources, and as a result, on how to use the capacities of the earth in the most efficient way. Haller's and Soleri's urban visions may be read as tentative answers to this underlying discourse. One of the influential studies that fueled this debate was Constantinos Doxiadis' *Ecumenopolis. The Settlement of the Future* which demonstrated that the prospect of mankind in one way or the other would be life in a world-wide urban network that would cover most of the earth's habitable landscapes.[10] Indeed, it had been Doxiadis' *Ecumenopolis* with its – as Soleri put it[11] – "Map of Dispair" of a widely urbanized earth that had driven Soleri to start working on his *arcology* project. A similar act of awareness led to the establishment of platforms of international cooperation. The International Union of Architects (UIA) or the International Council of Societies of Industrial Design (I.C.S.I.D.) played a leading role in deepening east-west contacts between planners and researchers. The UIA made several attempts to launch a magazine based on East-West-cooperation. Architects from the East and West worked together on international competitions and large-scale projects.

Environmental awareness

Linked with these period discourses is the expansion of architectural concepts to consider the whole environment. Rereading the influential 1972 study *The limits to growth* for the Club of Rome, it is hard to believe that this rather restrained and hypothetical treatise – that in larger parts is a meta-discourse on prognosis itself – would have caused the basic paradigm change in respect to sustainability that is today attributed to it.[12] The impact of the book is linked with the fact that the consequences of industrial development had become clearly visible in the East and the West and hence had led to a new global understanding of ecosystems and access to resources. In addition, the study had been preceded by an almost self-evident belief in growth and development that now was questioned. In architecture and planning, however, signs for a reassessment of the use of nature and natural resources may be traced to much earlier. A larger understanding of manmade reality as habitat including artificial and natural elements is specific for many of the approaches of the 1960s and early 1970s for large scale housing and urban projects. The widespread tasks for such comprehensive planning comprised the design of holiday resorts, the redevelopment of historic urban centers or even the conception of redeveloped former mining landscapes. The awareness for structural and ecological interdependencies generated an increasing criticism toward the transformation of nature as it happened in a yet-unknown scale during these decades. Interdisciplinary encounters of economic planning and sociology with new subjects such as ecology in effect had a profound influence on architecture and urbanism.

Thinking in Systems

The understanding in the period of the 1960s and 1970s of nature as a system that is susceptible to interferences corresponds with a general shift in attention from objects to processes, and the turn to systems and networks as means of scientific and technological progress. The rise of planning and programming as sciences in their own right has much to do with previous experiences of conflict and crisis, with the increasing availability of data processing machines and – maybe most of all – with the competition of Western economies with the programmed economics of state socialism. Planning and programming as means of progress and development were also widely discussed in the West, which may be illustrated by the fact that the introductory quote of Otto W. Haselhoff in Haller's study was taken from one of a whole series of popular science books that discussed the competition and prospect of planning schemes in socialist and capitalist states during the 1960s.[13] Furthermore, in East and West not just certain lines of production but whole cycles of innovation and development were seen as processes that could be programmed by investments in research and education.

In architecture, the ever larger organizational and technical implications of industrialized building production in both East and West challenged the professional identity of architects as artists and individual designers, not only in the context of the large housing programs of the 1960s and 1970s boom-years. The logic of large technological systems and the knowledge bases attached to them was so compelling that in 1973, the West German architect Wolfgang Döring predicted the end of the traditional profile of the architect altogether;[14] in his view the architectural progress of the future would have its place in large specialized development agencies that, based on scientific methods, would plan architecture just like products of mass production. In this regard visionary designers like Soleri or the German architect Richard Dietrich, who in 1969 published an essay on the theory and technology of man-environment-systems,[15] rehearsed as philosophers or futurologists in the field of progress and technology studies predicting a system change from industrial production to the new level of a totally integrated society. Another aspect of the merger of architecture and planning with technology or experimental industrialized building concepts was the discovery of new levels of complexity and interdependence in the design process. Designs of experimental groups of architects were engaged with the application of technical innovations or concepts of architecture that integrated forms of mobility, light-weight construction or prefabrication. These developments went in hand not only with rapid modernization, but also with a rise of utopian ideals and technocratic beliefs about how these processes could be managed efficiently.

Re-Scaling Design and Environment

In the conflicting tension between these basic developments, this volume combines case studies in three main fields of study. In the first part – Technology: New Scales and Projects – Ákos Moravánszky deals with the aesthetics of the scalar sublime as a phenomenon unfolding between technology, planning and media representation of the era. David Crowley studies the prerequisites and implications of the electronic console as interface between man, technology and environment in its specific presence in the art, science and media of eastern and western Europe. Torsten Lange presents the work of the design theorist Horst Rittel and his approaches to the programming of architecture and planning processes. Cornelia Escher traces the work of the *Groupe d'Études d'Architecture Mobile* (GEAM) and its members both in western and eastern Europe with respect to their ideas on large-scale planning. The first chapter is concluded with Mirko Baum's report on the history of and his own engagement in Školka SIAL, a progressive and avant-garde architects' commune in Czechoslovakia that in the early 1970s approched architecture with an original fascination for technology, construction and pre-production.

The second part – Planning, Design and Territory – is opened by Hashim Sarkis' study that links the idea of territorial scale and aesthetics to the work of Le Corbusier on the one hand and his important successors like Kevin Lynch, Vittorio Gregotti, or Constantinos Doxiadis on the other. Kenny Cupers and Igor Demchenko present the still too little known French territorial planning culture of the 1960s and compare it to the schemes of the Soviet planning apparatus. Daniela Spiegel studies the links between planning for tourism and leisure in the German Democratic Republic and the development of specialized building typologies. The section, again, is concluded with the account of a planner and university teacher that was active in the focus period of this volume. Tamás Meggyesi unroles a subtle picture of the contents and hidden agendas involved in the education of urban planners at Budapest Technical University in this period of transition.

The concluding section that is focused on Practices and Agencies in architecture is opened by Ljiljana Blagojević and her analysis of the designs of architect Milan Zloković whose unusual work in cooperation with his children Đorđe Zloković and Milica Mojović combined progressive features of operational and design intelligence at a time when it was unusual for an architect in Yugoslavia to work on private commissions. Erik Sigge deals with the decisive shift of the Swedish National Board of Public Building (KBS) towards a structural approach in building design in the late 1960s, while Andres Kurg examines the professional critique of industrial housing production based on the pattern of the microrayon in Estonia and Tallinn in the later 1970s.

Axel Zutz adds the perspective of a discipline that is related to architecture but seldom perceived as a leading actor in large scale planning processes. In his study on "complex" development projects in Berlin, he demonstrates the great importance of landscape architects for the design of public spaces. The two concluding essays in this section deal with the role of professional institutions for the transfer of knowledge. Andreas Kalpakci treats the activities of the UIA Seminar on Industrial Architecture that from beginning of the 1960s developed an agenda of "total environment," appealing to the professional ethos of architects and strategically using it to bridge the East-West divide in an international institution. Piotr Bujas and Alicja Gzowska analyze and classify professional networks of architects active in Cold War Europe in a field between professional intelligence, innovation, education, exchange, and government control.

New Landscapes

The editors of this volume are greatly indebted to the authors, the publisher, the funding institutions, and all the people that have helped to realize this publication. For the team of editors the project has brought alive a geography of discourse and cooperation covering all of Europe and beyond. Working on such a project with close colleagues that have become friends is a great experience. I vividly remember an afternoon meeting at the Dynamo Café in Zurich close to the river Limmat in summer 2013, when the first ideas for this project took shape. I hope that the work on the questions and processes addressed in this book may continue and that it may help to add some perspective of a greater landscape to everyone dealing with these issues.

Endnotes

1 Paolo Soleri, *Arcology. The City in the Image of Man* (Cambridge Mass., London: MIT Press, 1969). On Soleri's *arcology* see: Karl R. Kegler, "Utopia Babylon. Megastädte als Technikutopien des 20. Jahrhunderts," in: *Die Phantastische Stadt*, ed. Thomas Le Blanc and Bettina Twrsnick (Wetzlar: Phantastische Bibliothek, 2005), 70–111.

2 See: Paolo Soleri, *The Bridge between Matter & Spirit is Matter Becoming Spirit. The Arcology of Paolo Soleri* (New York: Anchor Books, 1973).

3 Fritz Haller, *Totale Stadt: ein globales Modell / Integral urban: a global model* (Olten: Walter, 1968), and *Totale Stadt: ein globales Modell: zweite Studie / Integral urban: a global model: second study* (Olten: Walter [1975]).

4 Haller's translation and notation; Haller is using just the lower case throughout. Fritz Haller, *Totale Stadt* (1968), 6. Haller took Otto Walter Haseloff's quote from "Schicksalsideologie und Entscheidungsplanung," in *Deutschland ohne Konzeption? Am Beginn einer neuen Epoche*, ed. Robert

Jungk and Hans Josef Mundt (Munich, Vienna, Basel: Desch, 1964), 55–94, (p. 65).

5 Ibid. 8 (sic! Again, Haller is using just the lower case throughout).

6 Ibid.

7 This is the case in Haller's study of 1968; in 1975 Haller calculates with 120 million inhabitants for the fourth order unit.

8 Haller, *Totale Stadt* [1975], 92. For a recent analysis of Haller's urban model see: Laurent Stalder, "Raster, Netzwerk, Register. Fritz Hallers Totale Stadt," in *Fritz Haller. Architekt und Forscher*, ed. Laurent Stalder and Georg Vrachliotis (Zurich: gta, 2015), 92–107.

9 Richard Buckminster Fuller, *Operating manual for spaceship Earth* (Carbondale: Southern Illinois University Press, 1969).

10 Constantinos Doxiadis, *Ecumenopolis. The settlement of the future* (Athens: Technological org., 1967): Doxiadis republished the study in 1974 with a more dramatic subtitle: Constantinos Doxiadis and Ioannis Papaioannou, *Ecumenopolis. The Inevitable City of the Future* (New York: Norton, 1974).

11 Soleri, *Arcology*, 2.

12 Donella H. Meadows [et al.], *The limits to growth. A report for the Club of Rome's Project on the Predicament of Mankind* (London: Earth Island, 1972).

13 This series "Modelle für eine neue Welt" was edited by the futurologists Robert Jungk and Hans Josef Mundt, its titles that appeared in 1964 alone comprised: *Der Griff nach der Zukunft. Planen und Freiheit* (Munich, Vienna, Basel: Desch, 1964); *Wege ins neue Jahrtausend. Wettkampf der Planungen in Ost und West* (Munich, Vienna, Basel: Desch, 1964); and Jungk/ Mundt, *Deutschland ohne Konzeption?*

14 Wolfgang Döring, *Perspektiven einer Architektur* (Frankfurt Main: Suhrkamp 1973), 80–83.

15 Richard Dietrich, "Metastadt. Versuch zur Theorie und Technik des Mensch-Maschine-Systems," in *Deutsche Bauzeitung* 1969 no. 1, 4–21.

I
Technology: New Scales and Projects

Ákos Moravánszky

Zooming In: The Powers of Scale, 1960–1980

The shift in discourse from re-humanization in the immediate postwar years to the scalar view of the environment a decade later suggests a radical paradigm change. But the decades of *Re-Humanizing*, 1950 to 1970, which are the focus of the first volume of this trilogy, and those of *Re-Scaling*, 1960 to 1980, the topic of this volume, overlap. We see many efforts in the immediate postwar decades to connect the rhetoric of the human scale with that of a superhuman, geographic or territorial scale. An example of this attempt is the volume *La Découverte aérienne du monde* (The Discovery of the World from the Air), edited by Paul Chombart de Lauwe.[1] Chombart de Lauwe, after graduating in philosophy and anthropology in the 1930s, joined the Allied air forces as a fighter pilot. In 1945, he started research in urban sociology as affiliate of the *Centre national de la recherche scientifique* (CNRS).

In the book, published in 1948, Chombart de Lauwe addressed the issue of the *vision aérenne* both as optical image and a world view (fig. 1). Comparing aerial views of the Moroccan city of Marrakech, two European cities and the American industrial metropolis Cincinnati, he spoke of three concepts of the world. He used a sequence of three aerial photographs of the region of Pont-Saint-Esprit, taken from different altitudes, to explain the thematic differences between them based on the scalar narrative (figs. 2a, b). In the first image, the geographic scale shows the topological significance of the bridge as the place for crossing the river Gard, a focal point in the landscape that regulates the agricultural use of the land. The second image reveals how country roads merge into urban streets, situating the city in its closer environment. Finally, the third photograph explains the disposition of the built structure of the city and the nearby farms.

Chombart de Lauwe stressed in his essay the fact that the familiar,

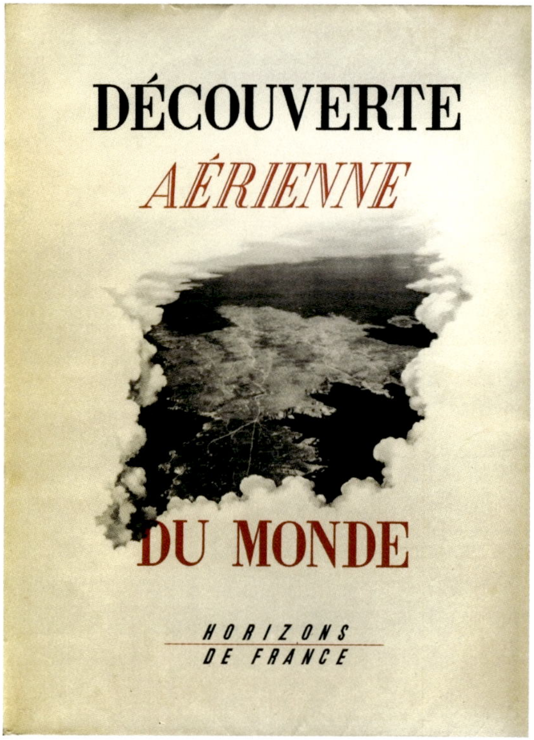

fig. 1 Paul Chombart de Lauwe, ed., *La Découverte aérenne du monde*, Paris 1948, cover.

three-dimensional world that is still perceivable at lower altitudes becomes two-dimensional if we rise higher: buildings collapse into plans and people disappear, particularly in the center of the viewing field. But while flying, we combine such impressions into one synthetic vision, we "know" the world the way the farmer knows his spatial environment. Chombart de Lauwe argues that the view from the airplane allows the integration of images that were once far apart into a single "vision," a world-view of "planetary humanity," which is "integral with the world."[2]

The goals of postwar humanism for which Chombart de Lauwe's aerial vision of humanity might stand were, however, already criticized in the 1950s as too sentimental and vague. The journal *Le Carré bleu,* founded in Helsinki in 1957, supported the goals of Team 10, and distributed the contributions of its members internationally. In the second issue of 1958, editor Aulis Blomstedt published his manifesto "La deshumanización de la arquitectura" (The De-Humanization of Architecture). The French text has a Spanish title, since it is a reference to an essay written by the prolific and influential philosopher José Ortega y Gasset, "La deshumanización del arte" (The De-Humanization of Art), written in 1925. In Blomstedt's view, the term "human" had lost its significance, and became an empty word just like the "social," the "functional"

hotos Ministère des Travaux Publics
Institut Géographique National.

Une même région vue à la verticale à trois altitudes différentes : Pont-Saint-Esprit dans le Gard. Sur la première vue la bourgade se situe dans l'ensemble de son cadre géographique. On voit nettement sa position clef à l'endroit où le pont permet de traverser la rivière, ainsi que la structure agricole du pays. Sur la deuxième on peut en étudier le plan groupé et voir comment les chemins aboutissent aux rues. Avec la troisième enfin, on peut entrer dans les examens de détail, jusqu'au tracé du plan des fermes, la disposition des maisons, etc.

figs. 2a, b Aerial photographs of Pont-Saint-Esprit from Paul Combart de Lauwe, ed., *La Découverte aérenne du monde*, Paris 1948, p. 34–35

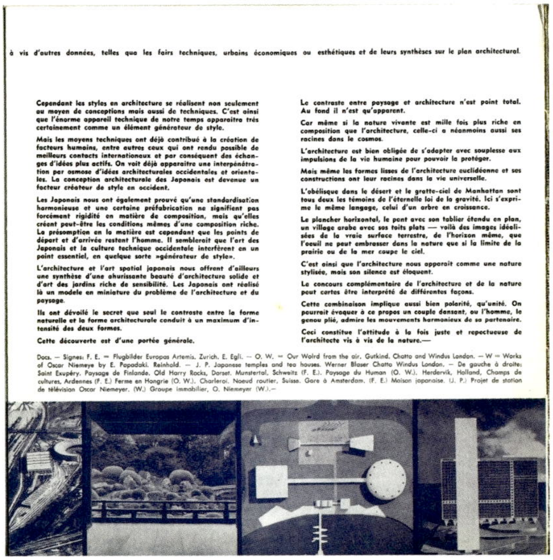

à vis d'autres données, telles qua les fairs techniques, urbains économiques ou esthétiques et de leurs synthèses sur le plan architectural.

Cependant les styles en architecture se réalisent non seulement au moyen de conceptions mais aussi de techniques. C'est ainsi que l'énorme appareil technique de notre temps apparaitra trés certainement comme un élément générateur de style.

Mais les moyens techniques ont déjà contribué à la création de facteurs humains, entre autres ceux qui ont rendu possible de meilleurs contacts internationeux et par conséquent des échanges d'idées plus actifs. On voit déjà apparaitre une interpénétration par osmose d'idées architecturales occidentales et orientales. La conception architecturale des Japonais est devenue un facteur créateur de style en occident.

Les Japonais nous ont également prouvé qu'une standardisation harmonieuse et une certaine préfabrication ne signifient pas forcément rigidité en matière de composition, mais qu'elles créent peut-être les conditions mêmes d'une composition riche. La présomption en la matière est cependant que les points de départ et d'arrivée restent l'homme. Il semblerait que l'art des Japonais et la culture technique occidentale interfèrent en un point essentiel, en quelque sorte »générateur de style».

L'architecture et l'art spatial japonais nous offrent d'ailleurs une synthèse d'une ahurissante beauté d'architecture solide et d'art des jardins riche de sensibilité. Les Japonais ont réalisé là un modele en miniature du problème de l'architecture et du paysage.

Ils ont dévoilé le secret que seul le contraste entre la forme naturelle et la forme architecturale conduit à un maximum d'intensité des deux formes.

Cette découverte est d'une portée générale.

Le contraste entre paysage et architecture n'est point total. Au fond il n'est qu'apparent.

Car même si la nature vivante est mille fois plus riche en composition que l'architecture, celle-ci a néanmoins aussi ses racines dans le cosmos.

L'architecture est bien obligée de s'adapter avec souplesse aux impulsions de la vie humaine pour pouvoir la protéger.

Mais même les formes lisses de l'architecture euclidéenne et ses constructions ont leur racines dans la vie universelle.

L'obélisque dans le désert et le gratte-ciel de Manhattan sont tous deux les témoins de l'éternelle loi de la gravité. Ici s'exprime le même langage, celui d'un arbre en croissance.

Le plancher horizontal, le pont avec son tablier étendu en plan, un village arabe avec ses toits plats — voilà des images idéalisées de la vraie surface terrestre, de l'horizon même, que l'oeuil ne peut embrasser dans la nature que si la limite de la prairie ou de la mer coupe le ciel.

C'est ainsi que l'architecture nous apparait comme une nature stylisée, mais son silence est éloquent.

Le concours complémentaire de l'architecture et de la nature peut certes être interprété de différentes façons.

Cette combinaison implique aussi bien polarité, qu'unité. On pourrait évoquer à ce propos un couple dansant, ou l'homme, le genou plié, admire les mouvements harmonieux de sa partenaire.

Ceci constitue l'attitude à la fois juste et repectueuse de l'architecte vis à vis de la nature.—

Docs. — Signes: F. E. = Flugbilder Europas Artemis. Zurich. E. Egli. — O. W. = Our Wolrd from the air. Gutkind. Chatto and Windus London. — W = Works of Oscar Niemeye by E. Papadaki. Reinhold. — J. P. Japanese temples and tea houses. Werner Blaser Chatto Windus London. — De gauche à droite: Saint Exupéry. Paysage de Finlande. Old Harry Rocks, Dorset. Munstertal. Schweitz (F. E.). Paysage du Human (O. W.). Herdervik, Holland, Champs de cultures, Ardennes (F. E.) Ferme en Hongrie (O. W.). Charleroi. Noeud routier, Suisse. Gare à Amsterdam. (F. E.) Maison japonaise. (J. P.) Projet de station de télévision Oscar Niemeyer. (W.) Groupe immobilier, O. Niemeyer (W.).—

figs. 3a, b Aulis Blomstedt, "Architecture et paysage," *Le Carré bleu* 4 (1959).

or the "organic." These notions failed to reflect the fundamental problem of architecture, the problem of form, Blomstedt maintains: "to make architecture a means to solve the problems of construction first of all with formal means, that is, with geometry."[3]

In the fourth issue of *Le Carré bleu* in 1959, Blomstedt published a paper on architecture and landscape, "Architecture et paysage: Hommage à Antoine de Saint-Exupéry;"[4] (figs. 3a, b) with a title as a tribute to the French writer who had studied architecture and served as a pilot, as had Chombart de Lauwe. A German translation of the article came out as a slim book in 1960[5] (figs. 4a, b). In this text, Blomstedt reflects on the question of the relationship between the larger geographical scale and the human scale. The "daily theater" of human activity is taking place on a stage whose dimensions are expanding dramatically. "Is it really somehow inhuman, to have breakfast (let's say) in

figs. 4a, b Aulis Blomstedt, *Architektur und Landschaft*, Dortmund 1960.

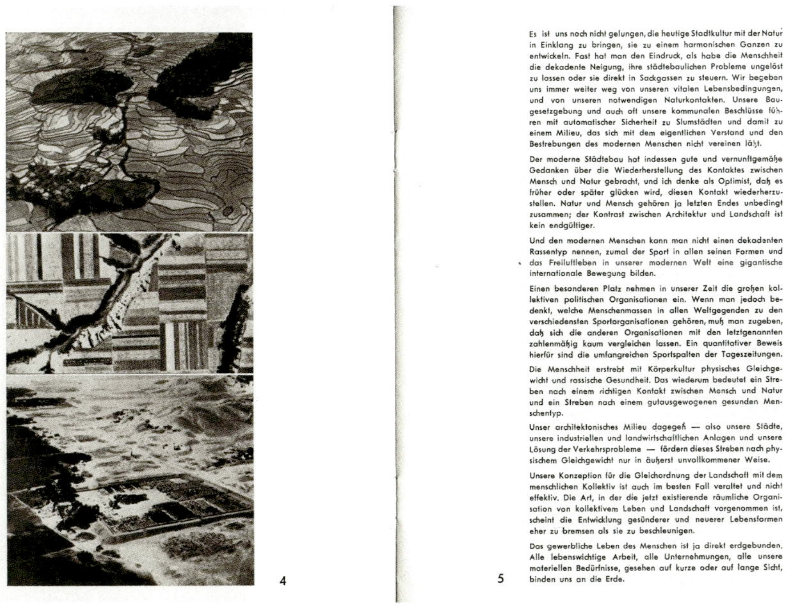

Es ist uns noch nicht gelungen, die heutige Stadtkultur mit der Natur in Einklang zu bringen, sie zu einem harmonischen Ganzen zu entwickeln. Fast hat man den Eindruck, als habe die Menschheit die dekadente Neigung, ihre städtebaulichen Probleme ungelöst zu lassen oder sie direkt in Sackgassen zu steuern. Wir begeben uns immer weiter weg von unseren vitalen Lebensbedingungen, und von unseren notwendigen Naturkontakten. Unsere Baugesetzgebung und auch oft unsere kommunalen Beschlüsse führen mit automatischer Sicherheit zu Slumstädten und damit zu einem Milieu, das sich mit dem eigentlichen Verstand und den Bestrebungen des modernen Menschen nicht vereinen läßt.

Der moderne Städtebau hat indessen gute und vernunftgemäße Gedanken über die Wiederherstellung des Kontaktes zwischen Mensch und Natur gebracht, und ich denke als Optimist, daß es früher oder später glücken wird, diesen Kontakt wiederherzustellen. Natur und Mensch gehören ja letzten Endes unbedingt zusammen; der Kontrast zwischen Architektur und Landschaft ist kein endgültiger.

Und den modernen Menschen kann man nicht einen dekadenten Rassentyp nennen, zumal der Sport in allen seinen Formen und das Freiluftleben in unserer modernen Welt eine gigantische internationale Bewegung bilden.

Einen besonderen Platz nehmen in unserer Zeit die großen kollektiven politischen Organisationen ein. Wenn man jedoch bedenkt, welche Menschenmassen in allen Weltgegenden zu den verschiedensten Sportorganisationen gehören, muß man zugeben, daß sich die anderen Organisationen mit den letztgenannten zahlenmäßig kaum vergleichen lassen. Ein quantitativer Beweis hierfür sind die umfangreichen Sportspalten der Tageszeitungen.

Die Menschheit erstrebt mit Körperkultur physisches Gleichgewicht und rassische Gesundheit. Das wiederum bedeutet ein Streben nach einem richtigen Kontakt zwischen Mensch und Natur und ein Streben nach einem gutausgewogenen gesunden Menschentyp.

Unser architektonisches Milieu dagegen — also unsere Städte, unsere industriellen und landwirtschaftlichen Anlagen und unsere Lösung der Verkehrsprobleme — fördern dieses Streben nach physischem Gleichgewicht nur in äußerst unvollkommener Weise.

Unsere Konzeption für die Gleichordnung der Landschaft mit dem menschlichen Kollektiv ist auch im besten Fall veraltet und nicht effektiv. Die Art, in der die jetzt existierende räumliche Organisation von kollektivem Leben und Landschaft vorgenommen ist, scheint die Entwicklung gesünderer und neuerer Lebensformen eher zu bremsen als sie zu beschleunigen.

Das gewerbliche Leben des Menschen ist ja direkt erdgebunden. Alle lebenswichtige Arbeit, alle Unternehmungen, alle unsere materiellen Bedürfnisse, gesehen auf kurze oder auf lange Sicht, binden uns an die Erde.

Helsinki, and dinner in Rome or Paris?" asks Blomstedt. "A vitally important human contact can bind me to these different places in the course of one day. Is it inhuman if a friend in the US announces his arrival in Helsinki for tomorrow evening? Should I not prepare a warm reception and invite our common friends?"[6]

The basic traits of the landscape were unchanged, the author stressed, but the relationship between landscape and human life is different today. Caused by speed and the rhythm of life, the scale and dimension of the urban had been transformed, with regard to space as well as time.[7] Aerial photography has opened up a whole new visual world and dramatic structures of landscape. But our "routines of urban design" are falling far behind, and it will take time until urban design catches up with this new visual access to the world.[8] Only if we have the courage to draw the consequences of the new "technical realities" can we start to participate in shaping the new human environment.[9]

Concerning architecture, Blomstedt pointed to the traditional Japanese house and garden as a model of harmonic standardization and prefabrication that includes the landscape. In the same issue of *Le Carré bleu*, Finnish architect Reima Pietilä published his manifesto-like "Réflexions rigoristes sur la notion de morphologie" (Rigorist Reflections on the Notion of Morphology), arguing for the development of morphological systems that regulate form on different scalar levels.[10]

Pietilä belonged to a group of young architects gathering around Blomstedt, who worked on a different, less romantic, more "rigorous" concept of man-nature relations than the one proposed by the internationally recognized master Alvar Aalto. Pietilä was at this time associated with a group of artists, writers, sculptors, directors and composers who studied the problem of dimension and the organization of forms. In 1960, the entire third issue of *Le Carré bleu* consisted of Pietilä's "Études de morphologie en urbanisme," zooming in on morphological systems from scale 1:100,000 down to 1:1000[11] (figs. 5a, b, c).

A related idea of an all-encompassing view of the universe, presented in scalar sequences as a visual foundation for a new humanity, had been developed in a book by the Dutch education reformer, Quaker missionary and pacifist Kees Boeke in 1957, entitled *Cosmic View: The Universe in 40 Jumps*[12] (fig. 6). This book consists of a series of drawings, starting with the image of a little girl in front of a school holding a cat in her lap, then the same child from an altitude ten times higher, in the somewhat surreal company of two cars and half of a dead whale. The third image shows a building built by the German military during the occupation but converted to house the Werkplaats Children's Community founded by the author, and so on up the scale to the Milky Way and down to molecules. The journey ends at the nucleus of the atom. Here Boeke reminds us of the dangers and possible benefits of nuclear power: "When we thus think in cosmic terms, we realize that man, if he is to become really human, must combine in his being the greatest humility with the most careful and considerate use of the cosmic powers that are at his disposal."[13] While "primitive man" tended to use this power for himself, the man of today has to learn to live together, caring for each other

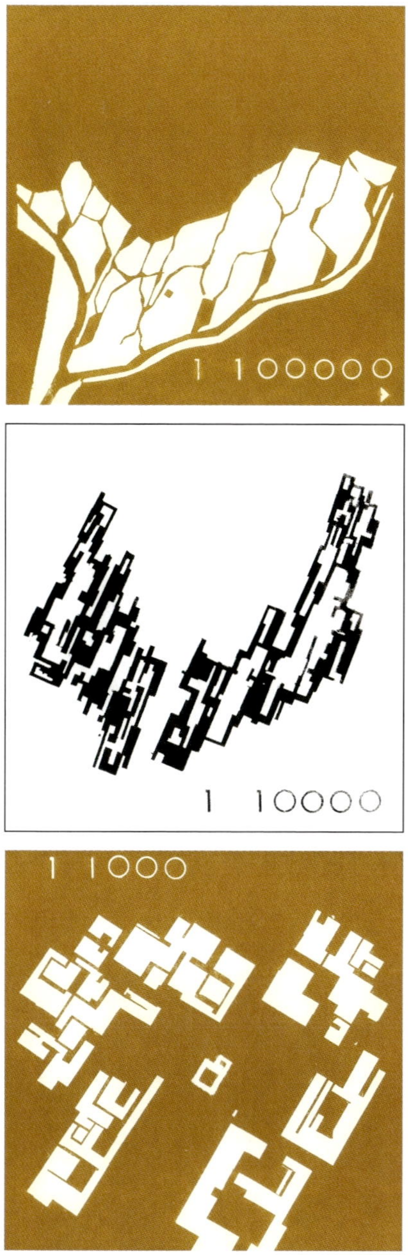

figs. 5a, b, c Reima Pietilä, "Études de morphologie en urbanisme", *Le Carré bleu* 3 (1960).

regardless of nationality, race or creed. "In this education the development of a cosmic view is an important and necessary element; and to develop such a wide, all-embracing view, the expedition we have made [...] may help just a little."[14]

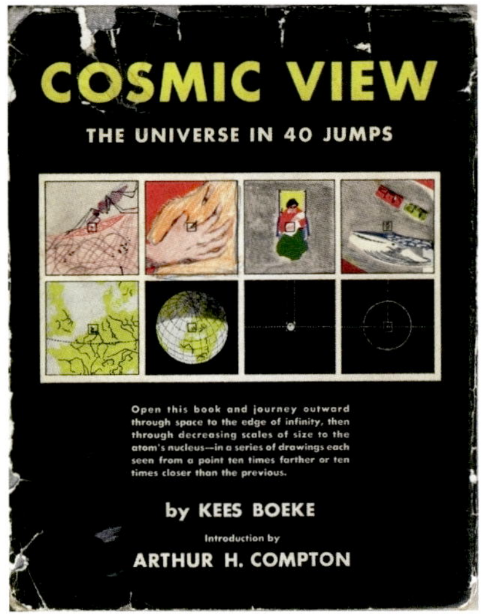

fig. 6 Kees Boeke, *Cosmic View*, New York 1957, cover.

Boeke's book was more than just an inspiration for the film *Powers of Ten*, made by Charles and Ray Eames in 1977. The film starts with the "glow of the distant galaxies," then other images appear: the Milky Way, the earth, Lake Michigan, Chicago, Lake Shore Drive, a picnicking couple, the hand and skin of that man and, finally, a carbon-12 molecule and the proton. The film was later turned into a book[15] (figs. 7a, b, c). Ray Eames stressed in her introduction that "the idea of scale – of what is appropriate at different scales, and the relationships of each to each – is very important to architects. [...] With a constant time unit for each power of ten, an unchanging center point, and a steady photographic move, we could *show* 'the effect of adding another zero' to any number."[16] Of course in reality only a very small section could be really be photographed with a camera mounted on a truck, the rest was a montage of telescopic and microscopic images from diverse sources. In addition, the photographer Alex Funke admits: "in each case we made the imaging more than real through adding, by hand, the details of what might (or should) be there."[17]

The didactic approach of the Eameses, which relied heavily on the powers of a scientific explanation of the universe and its dimensions, looks like a positivistic program when compared with another film from that era dealing with issues of reality to be deciphered by technological means. *Powers of Ten* and Michelangelo Antonioni's film *Blow-Up*, released in 1966, propose two different interpretations of scale. Motivated by environmental thinking, *Powers of Ten* was based on a metric cartography of the universe.[18] In contrast, *Blow-Up* presents shots by Thomas, a fashion photographer in London in the

10^{4} meters

10 kilometers ~ 6 miles

The heart of the city appears, place of home and work for a million people. The whole structure shown here—city districts, parks, harbor—is familiar to them. The conflagration of 1871 burned the city of wooden houses which then lay within this square. Most of the detail shown is newer, though the street and railroad layout survived the fire, as in the future they will outlive most of the individual buildings.

10^{0} meters

1 meter ~ 1 yard

This is the scale of human companionship, conversation, touch. A man is asleep on a warm October day. Around him are necessities and pleasures for mind and body. Between this image and the next frame inward, the size of the image would for once match the size of what it represents. "Of all things man is the measure," wrote Protagoras the Sophist.

10^{-16} meters

0.1 fermi

What will we see, and what will we come to understand, once we enter the next levels?

figs. 7a, b, c Photographs taken from from altitudes of 10 kilometers, 1 meter and 0.1 fermi. Pages from Philip and Phylis Morison and the office of Charles and Ray Eames, *Powers of Ten*, San Francisco 1982.

swinging '60s, as a random sequence of isolated images. Like in *Powers of Ten*, the inaugural scene is a couple in the park – but we find out that a murder is being committed. We don't see the reality merely through the photographer's eye, we are offered a mix of Antonioni's camera views and Thomas' camera shots and their magnifications. It is by the enlargement – the blow up – of one of Thomas' photos in the park that a scene that looks idyllic at first sight is revealed to be a crime. However, the "actual events" in the park cannot be reconstituted. There is no overarching "system," only possible narrations that connect the otherwise incomprehensible array of documents and places.

Thomas wants to clarify what happened and pins up an extremely magnified shot of the corpse – but at the end of the use of technology there is nothing but a blur, which is not unlike the final close-ups in *Powers of Ten* and *Cosmic View*. "What will we see, and what will we come to understand, once we enter the next levels?" asked the Eameses, and Boeke also wondered "Who will say what wonders are hidden beyond the limits of man's investigation today?"[19] For them, the blur was like a theater curtain or a fog that will eventually lift. But Thomas cannot hope for a clearer view, as the more the picture is enlarged, the more it becomes a blur of halftone dots – a message that was received at the time in different ways in Eastern and Western Europe: it is remarkable that while the American, British and Italian posters announcing Antonioni's *Blow-Up* emphasized the voyeuristic aspects of the movie, the Polish and Hungarian ones focused on this issue of scale and representation of reality (or realities), the decomposition of the image.

The Eameses, in turn, had some doubts about whether the image of the universe as presented in their film "transmit at illusion held within human science and human art."[20] But they were however convinced that the development of science and technology would make their little touch-ups to an imagined reality unnecessary: "This is the best we can do today. Tomorrow the view will differ; we hope it will be more penetrating, more inclusive, freer of misconceptions, and more beautiful."[21]

While the smooth, mechanical zooming in of the Eames movie claims to make the world clearer, Antonioni can only offer partial, reversible glimpses: for every moment made visible there is another that becomes invisible. A similar incongruence of mechanic-cartographic and place-based projections had entered the architectural discourse with the emergence of the large territorial scale more than half a century earlier. In the 1920s and 1930s, we see the emergence of competing projections and scalarities. Aerial photographs took over the role of constructed perspectives and bird's-eye views. Freeing architecture from earth's gravity became a topos in both the US and the Soviet Union, and isometric projections became the tools of choice for presenting

fig. 8 M. Iljin, *Naturgewalten und Menschenmacht*. Basel, Zurich 1945. Cover design by Hans Erni.

the architectural bodies floating in space. Georgii Krutikov's flying city was his graduation thesis in 1928, the year when the first five-year plan started in the Soviet Union, pursuing Stalin's policy of collectivization in agriculture and of the electrification and industrialization of the country. In the US, the rhetoric of "New Horizons" connected with the ideals of a consumer society produced similar imagery, culminating in the large-scale regional project of the Tennessee Valley Authority (TVA). This giant project – the first and most important result of President Franklin D. Roosevelt's New Deal policies – started in 1933, five years after the first five-year plan in the Soviet Union. Both grand scalar narratives, the TVA and the Five-Year Plan, had big impacts on public imagination.[22]

Images popularizing the success of five-year plans and the heroism of nature transformation in the Soviet Union were omnipresent themes in Western Europe also; Yuri Gagarin's space flight on April 12, 1961, was seen as a further step upward on this heroic scale. Artists were commissioned to celebrate the success of the five-year plans with their paintings and sculpture, and many focused on and dramatized the contrast between the giant dimensions of the infrastructure and the geographical scale of the building sites in their work. But it would be a mistake to attribute scalar pathos exclusively to ideological dictates in the USSR. Indeed, the Five-Year Plan was in the center of a picture cycle by the Swiss artist Hans Erni, who illustrated *Naturgewalten und Menschenmacht* (Forces of Nature and Human Power) by M. Iljin (Ilya Y. Marshak), published in Basel and Zurich in 1945[23] (fig. 8).

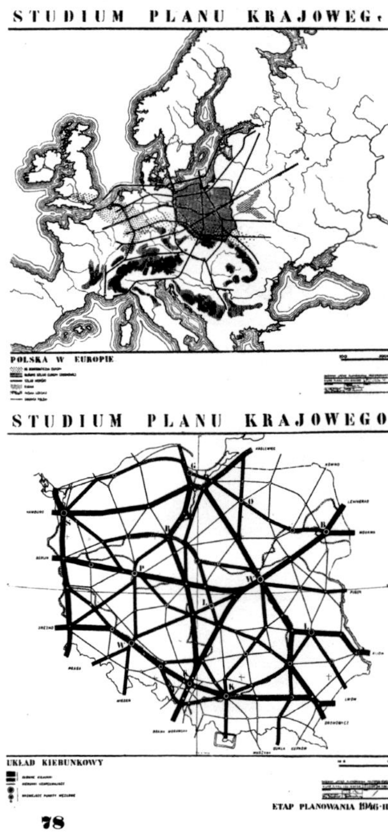

fig. 9 Jan Olaf Chmielewski, Regional plan for Poland (1947). Illustration from the Czech architectural journal *Architekt* 5–6 (1949).

Erni's images show the transformation of the desert that starts with a land survey by a geometer, who – as the explanatory caption stresses – is a woman, helped by two workers and a young boy. Another illustration presents a weather station transmitting data via radio waves, with an isobar temperature map of the USSR.

The aesthetic of the scalar sublime stood in the service of political propaganda; neither Ilyin's book nor the celebration of the TVA "adventure" left any doubts about it. The Swiss artist, architect and designer Max Bill compared the TVA project in his 1945 publication *Wiederaufbau* (Reconstruction) with regional planning in the Soviet Union. Bill's book took Switzerland's central position and neutrality as the basis for an exchange of ideas between East and West.[24] In September 1945, the first exhibition on American architecture opened in Zurich, presenting the example of the TVA project as the "largest example of planning for a peaceful purpose" for an area three times as large as Switzerland, as the author Ernst Friedrich Burckhardt emphasized.[25]

figs. 10a, b Ladislav Žák, *Obytná krajina*, Prague 1947, cover and drawings of the countryside at Posázaví, p. 131.

Ideas of transnational planning emerged in Europe shortly before the postwar continent was divided between the world powers. The Czech journal *Architekt,* for instance, published a Polish project based on a vast Central European economic space between the Soviet Union and France[26] (fig. 9). An exceptional effort to integrate the rural with the territorial scale was Ladislav Žák's book *Obytná krajina* (The Habitable Region), written in 1940–1941 and published 1947 in Prague.[27] In the 1930s, Žák had been a leading architect of Czech functionalism, inspired by ocean liners and airplanes. From 1936, he began documenting country landscapes in Czechoslovakia. He developed a typology and morphology of the natural and built landscapes, and presented proposals for the recultivation of the land. In 1949, in an article published in the journal *Architekt*, Žák coined the term "pan-naturalist socialism" (*pan-naturalistický socialismus*)[28] (fig. 10).

Žák saw no contradiction between the white prisms of Czech purism and the ecological vision of the "habitable region." This is probably the reason why Karel Teige, in his preface to the book, speaks of the "surrealist region," and praises the fact that now a naturalist approach, present in literature and painting, has started to organize the region, "from utopia to science and from science to reality."[29]

Regional planning started in most East European countries immediately after the war, triggered by the increasing centralization of planning and state ownership of the land. Indeed, land reform between 1945 and 1948 was the most important starting point, as the large land estates were divided up, but though this lacked a general concept. Károly Perczel, in charge of the Területrendezési Intézet (TERINT, or the Institute for Territorial Planning) in Hungary, in a longer article explained his intentions to start with the smallest units, small family farms, that had to be connected to small villages then to villages with central functions and so on. The regional-planning authority foresaw that the centrality of Budapest would be weakened by five large regional centers. Although no reference was made to Walter Christaller's theory of the central places, his work on the spatial distribution of agricultural villages was a possible source, directly or indirectly. In Perczel's study "Do We Need a Nationwide Master Plan?" published in the journal *Új Építészet* (New Architecture) in 1946, he stressed the significance of the TVA project.[30] But he also suggested studying a range of other examples, such as Le Corbusier and ASCORAL's *Ville linéaire*. In his "Notes on the Landscape Planning of Hungary," he proposed industrialized strips with roads and linear cities, connecting Hungary with the industrial centers of East and West.

After the political partitioning of Europe into blocs, such plans had to be buried. The "large scale" became a theme, not a method. A curious but characteristic example is the Sputnik observatory in Szombathely, commissioned by the Directorate of the Museums of Vas County in Hungary in 1967 (fig. 11). The building, designed by the architect Elemér Zalotay, is a sculptural object of cast concrete for housing a big photographic camera, which was removed in short order as satellites were watched better by other satellites than from the earth. But the gestures of the building speak in a poetic and somewhat grotesque way about hopes invested in the cosmic scale. Zalotay had proposed a "ribbon house" earlier, a huge slab of apartments of an unde-

fig. 11 Elemér Zalotay, Sputnik observatory, Szombathely, Hungary 1968.

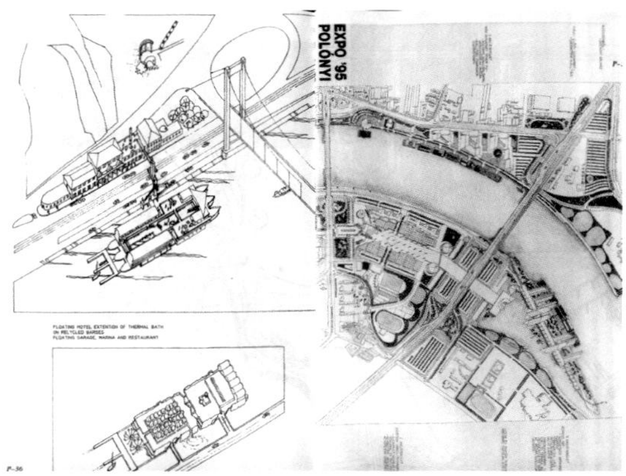

fig. 12 Charles Polónyi in collaboration with a team from Liverpool Polytechnic, Plan for the EXPO '95 in Budapest, 1988.

fined length (from over a half to two and a half miles) for many thousands of inhabitants along the Danube River. This had been conceived as a flexible spatial frame that could be filled by prefabricated units designed by different architects. The project was in the center of intense debates; finally, in 1973, Zalotay emigrated to Switzerland.

Zalotay's "ribbon house" is one of several projects with geo-scalar ambitions; for instance, Croatian architect Vjenceslav Richter's residential slab in Zagreb (*Beogradska ulica*) was developed parallel to his "Heliopolis – Four Dimensional City" theoretical study in 1968, and Mario Fiorentino's kilometer-long Corviale housing block in Rome (1972–1982).

The Danube provided the fluvial scale for Zalotay's ribbon house, and the Danube became the symbol of Central European regional identity, celebrated for instance in Claudio Magris' popular book. Charles Polónyi, the

Hungarian architect associated with the Team 10 and working in the 1960s and 1970s in Ghana, Nigeria and Ethiopia, started an international summer school in Budapest in 1983. In summer 1987, students and teachers – among them Peter and Alison Smithson – were living and working on a boat on the Danube. At this time, planning started for a world exhibition jointly organized by Vienna and Budapest for 1995 (fig. 12). Around 1980, the Central European scale became a concept purged of any similarities with Friedrich Naumann's 1915 program for *Mitteleuropa*,[31] as a way to affirm a particular identity of the region: to be part of the Eastern Bloc politically, but without losing its Western cultural orientation. In Hungary, historian Jenő Szűcs attracted a great deal of attention with his essay "On the Three Historical Regions of Europe," published in 1981. It appeared in France in 1985 as *Les trois Europes* with an enthusiastic preface by Fernand Braudel,[32] which contributed to the book's international success.

The geographic scale and the issue of borders is the theme of a recent version of the "Cosmic View," presented as a project of two Swiss photojournalists, Alban Kakulya and Yann Mingard and titled *East of a New Eden: European External Borders*.[33] Kakulya and Mingard combined data collected by sensors on satellite platforms orbiting at an altitude of more than seven thousand kilometers, with photographs taken at the latitude/longitude coordinates from the satellite dataset. The coordinates link landscapes, border posts, patrols and the faces of refugees. The authors describe their intention as alternating "between the rigors of geopolitics and a personal vision; and though it does not provide any answers, it does, we hope, raise questions in a spirit of openness."[34] As block-thinking and block-politics is the order of the day again, the period between 1960 and 1980, the time of scalar leaps in architectural thinking in East and West, deserves a comparative investigation.

Endnotes

1 Paul Chombart de Lauwe, ed., *La Découverte aérienne du monde* (Paris: Horizons de France, 1948).

2 Original quote: "Cette humanité planétaire est solidaire du monde," ibid., 52. Author's translation.

3 Aulis Blomstedt, "La deshumanización de la arquitectura," in *Le Carré bleu*, 2 (1958), 2–4 (p. 3).

4 Blomstedt, "Architecture et paysage: Hommage à Antoine de Saint-Exupéry," in *Le Carré bleu*, 4 (1959), n.p. (2–6).

5 Blomstedt, *Architektur und Landschaft. Die Landschaft als künstlerisches Gestaltungselement im Städtebau* (Dortmund: Kulturamt der Stadt Dortmund, no year [1960]).

6 Ibid., 7. Author's translation.

7 Ibid.
8 Ibid., 13.
9 Ibid.
10 Reima Pietilä, "Réflexions rigoristes sur la notion de morphologie," in *Le Carré bleu*, 4 (1959), n.p.
11 Pietilä, "Études de morphologie en urbanisme," in *Le Carré bleu*, 3 (1960), n.p. (1–10.).
12 Kees Boeke, *Cosmic View: The Universe in 40 Jumps* (New York: John Day Company, 1957).
13 Ibid., 48.
14 Ibid.
15 Philip and Phylis Morrison and the Office of Charles and Ray Eames, *Powers of Ten: A Book about the Relative Size of Things in the Universe and the Effect of Adding Another Zero* (San Francisco: Scientific American Library, 1982).
16 Ibid., n.p.
17 Ibid., 145.
18 Ibid.
19 Boeke, *Cosmic View*, 32.
20 Morrison, *Powers of Ten*, 15.
21 Ibid.
22 Ákos Moravánszky, "Re-Humanizing Architecture: The Search for a Common Ground in the Postwar Years," in Ákos Moravánszky, Judith Hopfengärtner, eds. *Re-Humanizing Architecture: New Forms of Community*, 1950–1970 (Basel: Birkhäuser, 2016), 23–41.
23 M. Iljin [English transcription: Ilyin; Ilya Y. Marshak], *Naturgewalten und Menschenmacht. Erzählungen von Bergen, Wüsten, Meeren und Menschen* (Basel, Zurich: Mundus, 1945).
24 Max Bill, *Wiederaufbau. Dokumente über Zerstörungen, Planungen, Konstruktionen* (Erlenbach-Zurich: Verlag für Architektur, 1945).
25 E.F.B. [Ernst Friedrich Burckhardt], "Das Tennessee Valley: Beispiel einer verwirklichten Regionalplanung," in *USA baut: Bildbericht der Ausstellung moderne amerikanische Architektur*, ed. Alfred Roth (Winterthur: Verlag Buchdruckerei Winterthur, 1945), 63–67.
26 Jaroslav Kříž, "Štětín – náš přístav," in *Architekt*, 5–6 (1949), 73–79.
27 Ladislav Žák, *Obytná krajina* (Prague: S.V.U. Mánes-Svoboda, 1947).
28 Ladislav Žák, "Otázky krajinného plánování," in *Architekt* 11–12 (1949), 189–196.
29 Karel Teige, "Předmluva: O architektuře a přírodě," in Žák, *Obytná krajina*, 21.
30 Károly Perczel, "Kell-e országos építészeti keretterv?", in *Új Építészet*, 2 (1946), 1–4.
31 Friedrich Naumann, *Mitteleuropa* (Berlin: Reimer, 1915).
32 Jenő Szűcs, *Les trois Europes*, trans. Véronique Charaire, et al. (Paris: L'Harmattan, 1985).
33 Alban Kakulya, Yann Mingard, *East of a New Eden: European External Borders – A Documentary Account* (Baden: Lars Müller, 2010).
34 Ibid., 59.

David Crowley

The Choreography of the Console: Electronic Environments and their Operators

In the late 1950 and 1960s a new kind of non-human actor appeared on the movie screens and televisions around the world. The console – an electronic panel or unit operated with dials, switches or buttons – appeared in numerous Cold War thrillers and science fiction movies, as well as news reports of the command and control centers managing traffic on the street, power stations and space flights. For the film makers who recorded it, the console seems to have been a strangely magnetic and enigmatic object. Immobile and performing seemingly inscrutable tasks in the service of authority, the console – with its flashing lights and illuminated dials, oscilloscopes and monitors – presented a novel site of man-machine interaction and a new conception of the "environment" as a place for the management of information.

Some of these on-screen consoles were fantasies, while others were in operation. But perhaps the distinction between fact and fiction was not important in the technological imaginary of the postwar decades. What was important was the promise of the future that was being made by these electronic interfaces. The command and control room of the military intelligence or the multimedia space of the gallery prefigured ordinary environments "enclosed by images."[1] Designers working for Philips, the Dutch electronics company, for instance, conceived the future classroom as a bank of networked consoles. In the company's 1971 TELL (Teacher-aiding Electronic Learning Links) project, the classroom was to be equipped with a computer, camera and multiple screens "so that the teacher can point at the picture on one of his

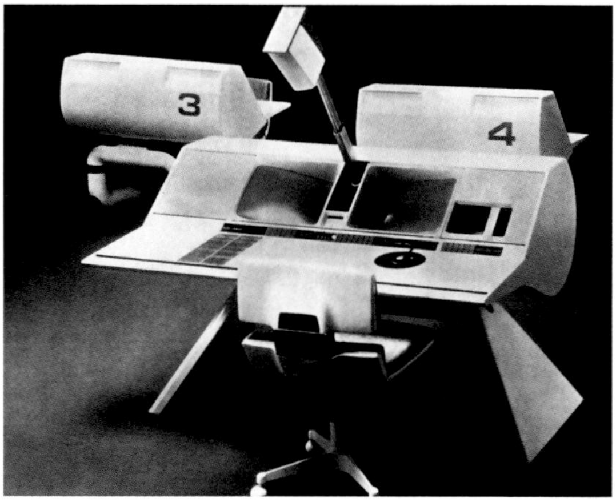

fig. 1 "Teacher-aided Electronic Learning Links" aka TELL, designed by Phillips Design Centre, c. 1970. Courtesy of Phillips.

screens and his finger can be seen on the pupil's monitors."[2] The TELL system envisaged communication as an action in a closed circuit (fig. 1).

To accentuate the promise of perfect communication and automation, such schemes were almost invariably located in smooth, frictionless environments in which the console was a cased object. Cables were hidden from sight, as if revealing a connection to the rest of the world would disturb their symbolic power. The rooms in which they were located were strikingly placeless too, in the sense that their location played little part in their operations. In fact, these consoles often appear in blind rooms; settings without windows in a conventional sense, because the screen or data panel was itself a kind of portal. They afforded remote viewing. And as Cold War defense arrangements seemed to demonstrate, one environment – even an entire hemisphere – could be controlled from another. In eschewing the existential qualities claimed for *place,* such settings were what John Harwood calls "counter-environments" (a term he adopts from Marshall McLuhan). A counter environment is, he writes, "a designed space that is closed off from its surroundings and only linked to like spaces via specific media (e.g., real-time computing) and […] the potential for the control of external environments via an independently conceived logical system […]"[3] Here the scale of an environment could be understood – perhaps for the first time – in terms of the integrating power of networked systems. The gesture of a finger on a keyboard or a hand moving a light pen on a screen in one setting could have immediate effects in others at a great distance or in many places at the same time. Electronic and computer technology was increasingly understood as the means by which the environment – whether at the scale of the home, a factory or the nation – could itself be programmed (fig. 2). Harwood's term perhaps best lends itself to sites of networked power. This was, after all, an age which conceived the doctrine of

fig. 2 Control Center of the Electricity grid for the North-west regions of the USSR designed by Maris Gundars, Soviet Republic of Latvia, 1974–1976. Photograph by Laimonis Stīpnieks.

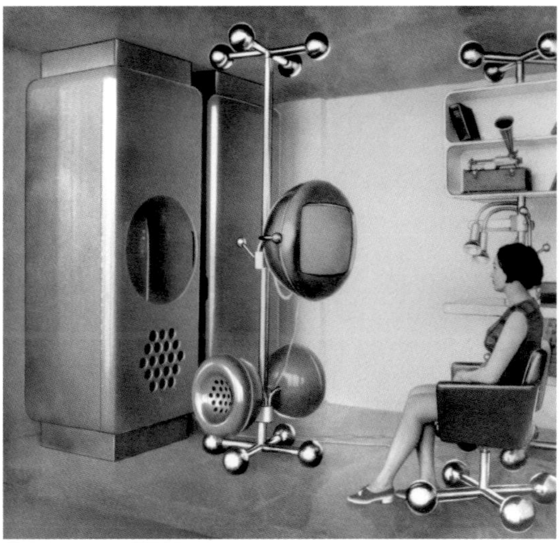

fig. 3 The Domestic Information Machine, designed by E. Bogdanov, V. Paperny, V. Revzin, A. Riabushin and A. Sergeev, USSR, 1972. Photograph from the Vladimir Paperny Archive.

Mutually Assured Destruction. Radar stations on both sides of the Cold War divide and staffed with operators scanning the air for signs of military action were always on; always ready to respond to the threat of attack. But counter-environments could also promise liberty too. The house of the future – a cliché of the era in the East and in the West – invariably featured computerized domestic arrangements. Tom Cubbin, for instance, has drawn our attention to the Domestic Information Machine which was conceived and tested in Soviet Union at the end of the 1960s (fig. 3). Designers working for VNIITE (All-Union Scientific Research Institute of Industrial Design / *Vsesoiuznyi nauchnoissledovatel'skii institut tekhnicheskoi estetiki*) imagined the home as a point in a vast communications network which would connect its users with information. A 1969 report issued by the scheme's creators stressed its benefits over the passive effects of television:

> Such an information service would differ substantially from that which exists today. Currently, the media only transmit practically one type of information which fulfills the basic needs of cultural relaxation and recreation. Mental labor requires the individualization of information. In the future this will become possible and will lead to a significant shift in the cultural and spiritual development of man.[4]

Underlying the thinking of the Domestic Information Machine's creators was a cybernetic conception of information in which its users would be able to influence and contribute knowledge to the network. Similarly, the NER Group (New Element of the Urban Environment / *Novye element rasseleniia*) – also active in the Soviet Union in the second half of the 1960s – conceived the future home not only as a networked one but also the engine for the production of a new kind of Soviet citizen.[5] In this setting, the householder would become something like an "operator" and so the differences between work and leisure or the factory and home could be diminished (thereby bringing the nirvana of communism ever closer).

A promise to get rid of drudgery was folded into the smooth casing of the console whether it was located in a Dutch School or a Soviet home … or, in fact, *everywhere* as Richard Brautigan's 1967 poem, "All Watched Over by Machines of Loving Grace" seems to suggest:

> I like to think (and
> the sooner the better!)
> of a cybernetic meadow
> where mammals and computers
> live together in mutually
> programming harmony
> like pure water
> touching clear sky.[6]

Echoing Marx's pastoral impression of Communism,[7] Brautigan augured a future utopia in which all toil, all want and perhaps even technology – as a distinct category – would wither away.

The pushing of the button

The idea that production in the future would involve progressively less human labor was found on both sides of the East/West divide during the 1960s. Automation would, according to its champions, eliminate drudgery

fig. 4 Cover of *Znanie Sila*, May 1964 designed by M. Zherebchevskii. Private collection.

and error. The role of the human in future manufacturing, agricultural and transport systems would be one of an *overseer*. This image of the fallible human being replaced by efficient machines was the subject of numerous fantasies in the 1960s, albeit ones which were often shot through with existential anxiety (fig. 4). One trope in science fiction of the period was that of the operator asleep at the console. In *Ikarie XB-1,* a Czechoslovak sci-fi film (dir. Jindřich Polak, 1963), for instance, the crew are rendered unconscious as an effect of passing through a radiation cloud. To ensure that the mission continues, the computer oversees an "unmanned shift," before the crew revive. This minor drama might well be read as an allegory for the future of man-machine relations. Many writers, including – famously – Norbert Wiener, Herbert Marcuse, Alvin Toffler and Stanisław Lem reflected on the twin threat and promise of automation. Each asked, in various ways, whether the console was the extension of humankind ("the humanism of control") or a step in the progressive marginalization of the human agent? In a 1960 essay "Some Moral and Technical Consequences of Automation" Wiener, for instance, reflected on the threat to humanity posed by cybernetic machines: "It is quite in the cards that learning machines will be used to program the pushing of the button in a new pushbutton war.[8] In this scenario, the thinking machine commands the console; in other words, it commands itself.

Similar questions were asked in Eastern Europe under communist rule in the late 1950s and 1960s too, albeit with different emphases. After Stalin's death, the matter of human control and agency was particularly pressing. Science was loudly proclaimed by post-Stalinist regimes as the harbinger of a new rationalism *after* the irrationalism and violence of Stalinism, as well as being the solution to the considerable economic failures of the command economy. As Slava Gerovitch outlines in his study of Soviet cybernetics, the computer was adopted as a "paragon of rationality."[9] A new rationalism guided by the *innate* logic of science and technology would revive the socialist project. In his attempt to harness science, Khrushchev was obliged to accommodate a degree of debate and even dispute about the effects of thinking machines that would not have been countenanced during the Stalin years. For instance, Academician A. Kolmogorov writing in *Izvestia* in 1962 suggested that thinking and feeling machines would "surpass man in his development" in the future. Evolution suggested that perfect machines would, one day, be able to build their own progeny without human aid. B. Byalik responded in *Literaturnaya Gazeta* in May 1962 in an article with a title which asked "Comrades, Is This Serious?" In turn, Academician Sobolev responded in the same journal: "Yes, it is very serious! […] In my view the cybernetic machines are people of the future. These people will probably be much more accomplished than we, the present people."[10]

Elsewhere in the Bloc, others – including some who had been vocal and brave critics of Stalinism during the turbulent period which followed Khrushchev's "Secret Speech" (1956) – were anxious that science and technology itself would deprive individuals of agency. These, for instance, are the words of Leszek Kołakowski, one of the critical voices in the People's Republic of Poland who came to the fore during the Thaw period of the late 1950s: "We observe […] the astonishing speed with which the new mythologies displace the old ones. In the intellectual life of a society in which the mechanism of traditional faith has become corroded, new myths proliferate with the greatest ease, even though they may originate in technical advances or scientific discoveries. Thousands of people fondly imagine that the friendly inhabitants of other planets will one day solve the problems from which humans cannot extricate themselves. For others the words 'cybernetics' embodies the hope of resolving all social conflicts."[11]

Designing the operator

After this brief survey of the settings in which the console was imagined and occasionally employed in the 1960s, let's look a little closer at the actions of its operator. How should the operator interact with the console? What was the script or notation for these kinds of interaction? It was clear to many commentators that the design of the console inferred the design of the operator: a new set of manual, metacarpal skills were required to operate it. As such, the console was the subject of considerable new research into man-machine inter-

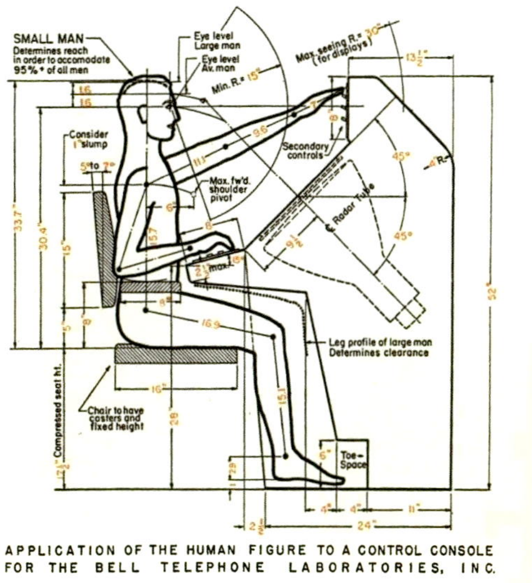

fig. 5 Illustration of a console operator from Henry Dreyfuss, *Designing for People*, 1955.

actions – not least that conducted within the sphere of ergonomics, then still a relatively young discipline which set out to measure the body and its capacities. This data could then be used to design more effective and efficient tools for the factory, the office, the kitchen or other sites of human action. Despite its peaceful applications, as a discipline, ergonomics owed much to military research. Henry Dreyfuss, the American industrial designer and pioneer of ergonomics, traced his engagement with the field back to a military commission:

> Shortly after the war, our office was working on the interior of a heavy tank for the Army. We had tacked a huge, life-size drawing of the tank driver's compartment on the wall. The driver's figure had been indicated with a thick black pencil line and we had been jotting odds and ends of dimensional data on him as we dug the data out of our files. Surrounded by arcs and rectangles, he looked something like one of the famous dimensional studies of Leonardo. Suddenly, it dawned on us that the drawing on the wall was more than a study of the tank driver's compartment; without being aware of it, we had been putting together a dimensional chart of the average adult American male.[12]

In his early text on ergonomics, *The Measure of Man* (1959), the American designer stressed the humanism of the endeavor: anthropometric data should be used to eliminate discomfort and mitigate against the fatigue of the operator (fig. 5). Nevertheless, in its attention to thresholds and limits, design was being used to contain and control behavior. In the ergonomic imaginary, the machine had to become more orientated to the human and, conversely, the human had to become more machine-like. Italian designer Ettore Sottsass admitted as much, when reflecting on his design of the Elea 9003 mainframe computer for Olivetti; "one ends up conditioning the man who is working, not only his direct physical relationship with the instrument, but also his very much more penetrating relationship with the whole act of work."[13]

Aiming to reduce distraction, error, friction, discomfort and noise, ergonomics was preoccupied with interfaces, the contact zone between man and machine, and above all, with the effectiveness of the interactions that took place there. This was not the efficiency of the fulcrum or the pulley converting muscle power into force, but that of speed and precision. Buttons, toggles, keys, switches, controls had to be designed to minimize human error; and screens, gauges, dials and signals should be transparent and easily read with a sweep of the eye. The ideal console should explain its operations via means of integrated design by employing simple text, pictograms, and symbols. For instance, in the case of the ELEA 9003 – the first computer produced by the Olivetti company from 1959 – designer Tomás Maldonado developed a new symbol system for the console (fig. 6). Maldonado's design did away with the Italian instructions which accompanied the design in favor of a sign system that could be easily assimilated by the operator, whatever his or her native tongue. Here the "noise" of linguistic difference was replaced by the smoothing and universalizing effects of the pictogram. The operator learned this machine language in order to better integrate his or her actions with those of the machine. Keying in instructions in response to data processed by the computer, the operator of the ELEA 9003 provided an image of cybernetic harmony. Similarly, a pioneer of ergonomics in the People's Republic of Poland, Andrzej Pawłowski, conceptualized his work not so much as the production of buttons and switches than as the design of gestures (fig. 7).[14] In his experiments conducted in Poland in the 1960s, he developed a language of man-machine encounters – a kind of notation system indicating direction of movement, the type of grip or depression and the force required. He too claimed the protection of the human operator as his purpose:

> Through creativity in the industrial field, we come to understand the most rational conditions for the protection of the biological and psychological existence of the human being, as well as the development of culture in industrial civilizations, the dynamics of which have become the cause of a dangerous loss of balance between civilization and the culture of its exploitation.[15]

This kind of design humanism notwithstanding, underlying such schemes was a kind of design linguisticism extrapolated from communication theory;

fig. 6 Elea 9003, 1959. Photograph by Michele Aquila / Flickr.

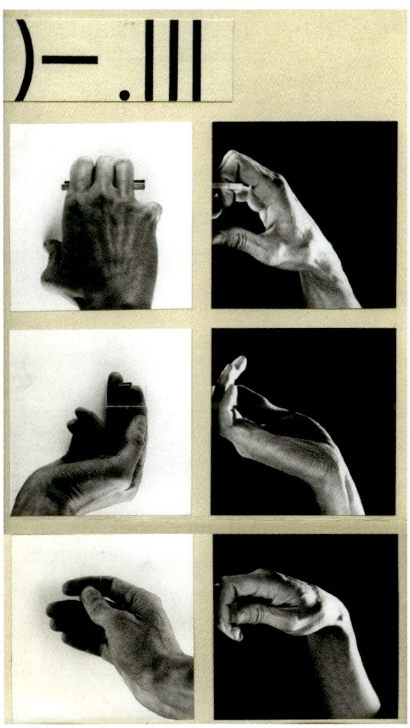

fig. 7 Andrzej Pawłowski, a study of "small manipulations" made at the Kraków Academy of Art, mid-1960s. This scheme features the action of pulling with three figures. Courtesy Maria Dziedzic / Kraków Academy of Art.

namely, that a universal language of operating gestures could be deduced and deployed in the service of progress. Perhaps this fantasy took (and still takes) its ultimate form in the illusion of *direct* manipulation of data. The light pen famously designed by Ivan Sutherland at MIT in 1966 was a precursor of the touch-screen developed in the mid-1970s. Its invention might well be taken as a kind of culmination of the ergonomic project, one in which the apparatus disappears and the body of the operator engages as directly and completely with the data as possible. The achievement of Sutherland and others was to suggest the means for a return to what had long been claimed as the origins of language in "natural" gestures.[16] Nicolas Negroponte suggested something similar when he speculated on the democratic effects of the assimilation of the computer in the studios of architects:

> With direct, fluid and natural man-machine discourse, two former barriers between architects and computing machines would be removed. First, the designers, using computer-aided design hardware, would not have to be specialists. With natural communication, the "this is what I want to do" and "can you do it" gap could be bridged. The design task would no longer be described to a "knobs and dials" person to be executed in his secret vernacular. Instead, with simple negotiations, the job would be formulated and executed in the designer's own idiom. As a result a vibrant stream of ideas could be directly channeled from the designer to the machine and back.[17]

Ergonomics also reproduced the modernist myth of the neutrality of technology. In such anthropometric schemes the worker never resists, never withdraws his or her labor. And in concentrating on the gesture, another kind of radical decontextualization occurred too. What, we might ask, were all these hands doing? What were the effects of these switches and buttons on the world? Here one might consider the first three-dimensional figure of a man drawn by a computer, William Allan Fetter's "Boeing Man" (1966–67). Often claimed as a landmark work in the history of computer art, Fetter created wireframe drawings of a seated figure reaching and stretching.[18] Supervisor of Advanced Design Graphics at the Wichita branch of the Military Aircraft Systems Division of Boeing, Fetter produced the line-figure to simulate the range of the pilot's upper-body movements in the cockpit of the company's civilian and military airplanes. The data was gathered to improve the layout of the instruments in the cockpit. Fetter's images were widely reproduced – often in versions which contained few or no impressions of the cockpit or its instruments (perhaps this explains their easy adoption as "computer art").[19] The humanistic rhetoric espoused by Dreyfuss and other champions of ergonomics tended to obscure the science's origins and present uses in military research. Few paid much attention to these characteristics, as Maldonado and Gui Bonsiepe pointed out in 1964:

> Without doubt the empirical data obtained from investigations of military equipment possess a prototype value for all fields, and even for such fields which are completely removed from military equipment. On the other hand, constant occupation with such issues has no doubt resulted

in a certain one-sidedness in the ergonomist – that particular tendency towards a too-abstract version of the human operator.[20]

Bone Generators

At a time when commentators – in the East and in the West – were imagining human redundancy brought about by intelligent and self-replicating machines, it is striking that *dance* formed a particularly rich and animated zone for imagining new human-machine interactions. Let me give some examples: for instance, American programmer Lee Harrison III was interested in how to animate dance on screen. In the early 1960s, he rigged up a body suit with potentiometers and created the first working motion capture rig animating movement in real-time on his CRT screen. He made several short animations with this system, called ANIMAC (or sometimes the "Bone Generator and Skin Scanner").[21] Harrison – whose work came to play an important role in computer animation – seemed to be investigating the ergonomics of dance. Similarly, A. Michael Noll, a computer programmer based at Bell Laboratories in the USA, developed a program to produce real-time notation for dance in 1967–8. Noll imagined that dancers could wear bright lights on their joints (much in the manner of the time-and-motion studies developed by figures like Frederick Winslow Taylor and Frank Gilbreth in the USA before the First World War, and Aleksei Gastev in the Soviet Union in the 1920s). Images of the motion of the dancers could be captured and analyzed by a computer, and then translated into accurate dance notation: "At the completion of the ballet," he claimed, "all the movements of the dancers are stored within the computer in digital form. These movements could then be automatically translated by the computer into any desired form of dance notation."[22] Noll also imagined that the choreographer could save the time and cost of working with a ballet company in preparation of a new performance by composing directly with the stick figures in his program. For Noll, ballet represented a fascinating set of programming challenges. Moreover, the difficulties of being able to program the movement of a number of interactive figures in space over time presented the kind of complex task that only computers could complete.

Noll and Harrison's experiments treated dance as data. Other experimental dance forms imagined interactive relations between human and machine. Nicolas Schöffer was the author of perhaps the most ambitious cybernetic dance works of the period, 'Kyldex 1' (Kybernetic Lumino Experiment 1), a ballet that he created with composer Pierre Henry and choreographer Alwin Nikolai for the Hamburg State Opera in 1973 (fig. 8). Five cybernetic sculptures were prepared by Schöffer to "dance" alongside members of the com-

fig. 8 Cover of the *Neue Zeitschrift für Musik* reporting the performance of "Kyldex 1" at Hamburg State Opera, 1973.

pany including the principal dancers, Carolyn Carlson and Emery Hermans. The sculptures featured sound sensors which reacted to Henry's music and the stage lighting. Revolving mirrors on the sculptures amplified the effect. The dancers were captured on close-circuit cameras, appearing simultaneously on the theater's 200 m^2 screen at the back of the stage. This mirror effect turned the dancer and her image into echoes of one another. One member of the audience was rigged to a heart monitor so that his pulse could provide a kind of rhythmic beat for the dancers.

Announced as a "Simultankonzert," the performance was an elaborate version of the kind of spectacular events Schöffer had orchestrated from the late 1950s in which dancers shared the stage with his cybernetic sculptures. Maurice Béjart choreographed dancers to perform with Schöffer's "CYSP 1" (Cybernetic Spatiodynamic 1), a mobile sculpture equipped with electric cells and a sound sensor which could respond to changing color, light intensity and sound, for the Festival D'Avant Garde in Marseille in 1956. In Hamburg, Schöffer updated his ideas by drawing the audience into the act of co-creation ("Create the Creation," announced the poster). By raising cultured paddles, each viewer seated in the *Staatsoper* could vote whether the scene should continue or not; whether to speed up or slow down a dance; or even to end the piece. Red circles signaled stop; green wedges indicated faster and blue diamonds, slower; yellow arrows meant repeat; and white squares were a request for explanation. Schöffer would periodically take to the stage to lead the audience in discussion. Here the logic of feedback was given a democratic gloss. Unsurprisingly, some of the fifteen evenings were very short, others long: all were chaotic and noisy affairs, much to Schöffer's apparent pleasure (he called it "eine gloriose Ungewißheit"[23]). In effect, the console from which all the electronic elements of the performance might otherwise have been controlled had been abandoned in favor of an illusion of participation. Its traces remained in the cultured signs, with forms echoing the graphic systems employed as the interface of consoles like that conceived by Maldonado for Olivetti. To maintain the illusion, Kyldex – with its voguish counter-cultural associations of participatory democracy – required that the controls for these electronic instruments remain backstage.

In this regard, parallels can be drawn to the environments created by the well-known Experiments in Art and Technology (EAT) group, the alliance of artists and engineers formed by Billy Klüver, a research scientist at the Bell Labs, engineer Fred Waldhauer and artists Robert Rauschenberg and Robert Whitman in 1966. Founded in order to provide artists with access to new technology and engineering expertise, by 1968 EAT had over six thousand members and chapters in many major American cities (Fetter, the author of the Boeing Man wireframes, was one of the founders of the NorthWest chapter). The high point of the association was its contribution to the Osaka World Fair in 1970. EAT artists and engineers were commissioned by the Pepsi company to create a pavilion which was full of immersive environments that ostensibly allowed for a kind of playful engagement with new, interactive artworks. Eschewing any kind of message (commercial or otherwise), the pavilion promised each visitor a unique individual experience: each person would direct himself or herself toward sounds, lights or whatever else might draw their attention. The pavilion was an environment in the sense used by artist Allan Kaprow a decade earlier; a space which entangled spectators in multisensory experiences.[24] Klüver recalled:

> The initial concern of the artists who designed the Pavilion was that the quality of the experience of the visitor should involve choice, responsibility, freedom and participation. The Pavilion would not tell a story or guide the visitor through a didactic, authoritarian experience. The visitor would be encouraged as an individual to explore the environment and compose his own experience. As a work of art, the Pavilion and its operation would be an open-ended situation, an experiment in the scientific sense of the word.'[25]

Accordingly, artist Robert Whitman – working in conjunction with engineer John Forkner – used mirrors and reflectors to produce three-dimensional "real" reflections, for instance. Visitors could play with their own image; a ludic form of feedback. Similarly, the floor was covered with different materials such as grass (perhaps suggesting Brautigan's cybernetic meadow) and gravel, yet the sounds in the headphones worn by visitors confounded the sensations underfoot.

Klüver's emphasis on the freedom of the individual to explore an open-ended artwork was sincere but somewhat exaggerated. The EAT artists and engineers sat behind a console in the pavilion monitoring and managing the experience of the visitor. In the basement, banks of tape decks supplying the underfoot sounds were controlled by programs on punched-paper tape. The team had built an environment over which they could exert extensive control. The console was rarely recorded in the streams of publicity produced for the Pepsi Pavilion. It was, of course, far less spectacular than any other part of the pavilion but it also disturbed the group's self-image as an anti-authoritarian force. EAT was accused of naivety by its politically-minded critics. Max Kozloff writing in *Artforum* in 1971 accused the group of making a fetish of technological progress and for being in "service" to the "violence industries" which were profiting from the manufacture of weapons being sold to the US military to prosecute the war in Vietnam.[26] His purpose was to stress the politics of actions and technologies which EAT artists liked to imagine as being neutral.

Dark Consoles

So where might we find a self-conscious politics of the console?[27] I'd like to suggest that we could look to Eastern Europe at around the same time. Just as in the West, there were a number of close alliances between art and science in the Eastern Bloc from the mid-1960s. Abstract artists and experimental film-makers could enjoy *relative* intellectual freedom and access to technology if they characterized their work as design or research. In the Soviet Union, for instance, the ARGO group (Russian abbreviation for Author Working Group) was formed in 1970 by Nonna Goriunova, Valerii Osipov, and Francisco Infante to create artificial immersive environments. It set out to realize the kinds of multimedia *Gesamtkunstwerk* which appealed to EAT's members. Infante recalled, "The combined forces of ARGO's engineers and artists were also utilized for the *Sound and Color* installation which I designed for the Chemistry '70 International Exhibition held at Sokolniki Park in Moscow in 1970. The group joined forces with the electronic music studio attached to the Skriabin Museum [...] Everything in *Sound and Color* was in motion: the constructions, the color, the sound, and even the smells."[28] And like EAT, ARGO's artists were largely indifferent to (or unwilling to reflect on) the ideological effects of their creations.

Others elsewhere in the Bloc were more critical. In 1970 *Warsztat Formy Filmowej* (Workshop of Film Form) was established as a section of a science club at the Łódź Television, Film and Theatre School in the People's Republic of Poland.[29] Critical of the teaching program of the School and, at the same time, drawing resources from it (including 35mm film stock, editing tables, video cameras and monitors), the Workshop belonged to the "experimental zone" which had been licensed by the scientism of the Khrushchev Thaw just over a decade earlier. The Workshop's members were, as one Paweł Kwiek recalls, "scientifically minded"; widely read in psychology and cybernetics.[30] Working with film, photography and – within a few years – video, they set out to explore the practices of the "operator" rather than the artist. Many of the films created by the Workshop's members have the procedural, though often improvised, character of a *test*: what will be the effect of *this* action in *these* conditions? Objectivity was set as an ideal: "A documentary film's aim is to provide the truth about man," wrote Kwiek in 1974 for instance, "both for the sake of Art as well as from a scientific point of view. *So far,* however, it has not been possible to prevent the distortion of the truth, which results from (the subjectivity of the creator)." Direct forms of image making like the camera could, he thought then, diminish such distortions: "We can conclude," he continued, "that the truth we receive from man is based on direct contact with him, regardless of what he would like to show himself or in what fashion he would like to be perceived [...]."[31] This was a statement which might have appeared on the pages of an ergonomic manual.

One approach to direct forms of image making was to combine medium and body (resulting in what member Józef Robakowski called "biological-mechanical records"). In an early "test" film, "Prostokąt dynamiczny" (Dynamic Rectangle, 1971), he recorded his attempts to match the insistent, mechanical rhythm of a piece of music created by Eugeniusz Rudnik in the Experimental Studio of Polish Radio. The on-screen image of a pulsing and mutating red rectangle was achieved by Robakowski opening and closing a diaphragm manually in front of the 35mm camera as he listened to the music. The piece is never quite in sync, as the image (created by the live movements of the artist) fails to accurately match the sound (pre-recorded music). Knowing that behind the image there is a body falling short of the measure of the machine lends poignancy to Robakowski's "test". Similarly, "Video C" (1975) by Paweł Kwiek, made when the members of the Workshop were given access to a television studio, records the hands of an operator (Kwiek himself)

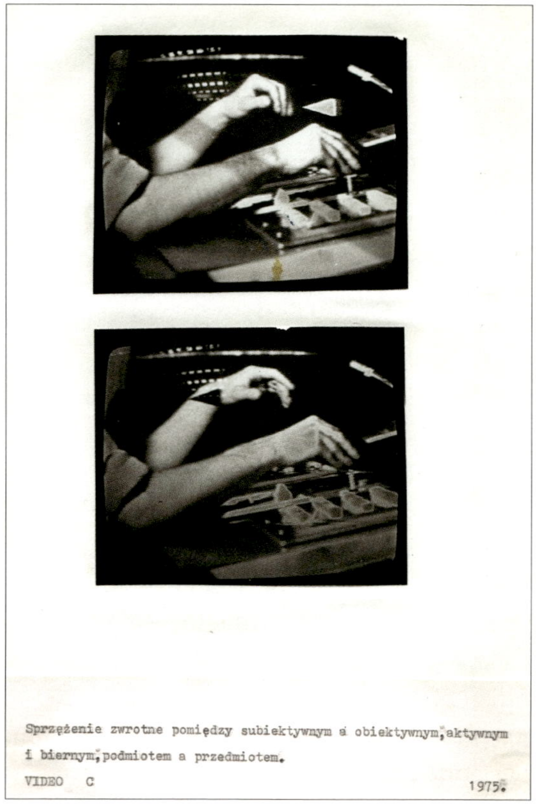

fig. 9 Still from "Video C" (1975) by Paweł Kwiek made in the studios of Polish TV. Image courtesy of the artist and Fundacja Arton.

manipulating the faders and buttons of a vision mixer, a device used to switch between video sources in a TV studio or to add graphic effects to the picture (fig. 9). The operator appears to be using his fingers to move a triangular cursor around the TV screen. Sometimes it seems to hover, as if trying to touch the on-screen hand or trace the line of the operator's arm in space: sometimes the on-screen hand responds, appearing to palm the cursor back or to map its three points with a pinch of the fingers. Kwiek explained his interest in this impossible union thus: "I construct such sets where the observed reality is the human being, for whom, in turn, the image of reality is his own constructed image."[32] In this *mise-en-abyme*, what distinguished a human being from his or her electronic image dissolved.

Parallels can be drawn between the Workshop of the Film Form and the output of the Béla Balázs Film Studio (BBS) in Hungary. Established in 1959 and enjoying official support from the early 1960s, BBS was relatively autonomous zone in which filmmakers could experiment with many different genres from social documentary to feature-length experimental films, with the benefit of professional crews and cameras. Censorship of the studio's output

fig. 10 Still from Gábor Bódy's "Négy Bagatell" ("Four Bagatelles"), Béla Balazs Film Studio, Hungary, 1975.

was rare (though the filmmakers could not affect the distribution of their ambitious films). At the end of the 1960s the BBS opened its doors to artists, musicians, theatre professionals, writers and sociologists. A young artist and writer Gábor Bódy – inspired by his readings of structuralism – was invited in 1973 to commission a series of films exploring the "Language of Film." Those commissioned included neo-avant-garde artists Tamás St. Auby – who made "Kentaur" ("Centaur") – and Miklós Erdély, who made "Partita." Bódy's own contribution to the series was "Négy bagatelle" ("Four Bagatelles"), a non-narrative film made by modifying or adapting existing films: archive footage of two peasants dancing is, for instance, augmented by a crosshair moving across the frame; while a sequence showing a ballet dancer is framed by an iris which opens and closes to capture her movements (fig. 10). In both cases, the naturalism of the documentary film is undermined by a set of technical operations which alert the viewer to the activities of an unseen operator. The fourth "bagatelle" in the quartet which forms the film puts the operator's hands (Bódy's own) before a screen which is being filmed by a video camera. The result is another *mise-en-abyme* in which both hand and screen repeat and recede into infinity.

Bódy's film – like those of the Workshop of Film Form – is usually discussed in terms of the hold of semiotics and structuralism on neo-avant-garde film in Eastern Europe. But, in pointing to the disappearance of the human actor under the pressure of the instrument, perhaps it is also possible to detect a critique of technology being made. There is little of the heady pleasure promised by EAT or Schöffer's illusions of participation. Here, the camera and the monitor infer surveillance, and the console suggests command and control of the individual who uses it. In other words, these films were self-experiments in which their makers were both performers and observers at the same time. In closed circuits such as this, self-portrayal becomes a form of self-observation. This is not the euphoric liberation of heighted sensation suggested in the Pepsi Pavilion Osaka, but a much darker conception of the cybernetic feedback. In the case of the films made by Workshop of the Film Form, one might also detect a kind of pathetic quality in human gestures too: Robakowski's body fails to fall in line with the rhythm of the machine; and Kwiek's "Video C" attempts an impossible act (one kind of immaterial pointer, a cursor, attempts and fails to *touch* another, a human finger).

One should be careful about distinguishing the works of these young artists/operators in Eastern Europe from those of others elsewhere in the world in the early 1970s. After all, one of the effects of the Cold War competition was that of a mirror: East and West came to look more and more alike (and the spread of consoles is one symptom of that fact). Moreover, many artists in the West – including, most famously, Joan Jonas, Vito Acconci and Bruce Nauman – also turned to the mirror effects afforded by video to split the subject. Rosalind Krauss has identified a degree of schizophrenia in their live gallery installations: "The medium of video art is the psychological condition of the self-split and doubled by the mirror reflection of synchronous feedback."[33] Nevertheless, in a setting where the state was increasingly using its security services to monitor the people, self-observation surely had different and distinct meanings.

Endnotes

1 This is Beatriz Colomina's phrase; see her "Enclosed by Images: The Eameses' Multimedia Architecture," *Grey Room*, no. 2 (Winter 2001): 6–29.
2 See Richard Fifield, "Audio-visual evolution or revolution," *New Scientist* (July 29, 1971), 277.
3 John Harwood, "The White Room: Eliot Noyes and the Logic of the Information Age Interior," *Grey Room* 12 (Summer 2003): 5–31.
4 A 1969 report written by G. Liubimova cited (and translated) by Tom Cubbin, *From Technocracy to Techno-Utopia: Futurology and the Soviet Home at VNIITE 1964–1974* (RCA/V&A History of Design MA Dissertation, 2012), 80–1.
5 Alexei Gutnov, et al., *The Ideal Communist City*, trans. Renee Neu Watkins (New York: George Braziller 1971).
6 Richard Brautigan, *All Watched Over by Machines of Living Grace* (San Francisco: Communication Company, 1967).
7 Karl Marx, *The German Ideology* (1845), available online, accessed May 1, 2015, https://www.marxists.org/archive/marx/works/1845/german-ideology/ch01a.htm.
8 Norbert Wiener writing in *Science*, vol. 131, no. 3410 (May 6, 1960), 1356.
9 Slava Gerovitch, *From Newspeak to Cyberspeak: A History of Soviet Cybernetics* (Boston, MA: MIT, 2004), 161.
10 This exchange is recorded by Willis H. Ware and Wade B. Holland in *Soviet Cybernetics Technology: I. Soviet Cybernetics, 1959–1962* (Rand Corporation Report, 1963), 11.

11 Leszek Kołakowski, "Kapłan i błazen" in *Twórczość*, 10 (1959) reprinted as "The Priest and the Jester" in Leszek Kołakowski, *Toward a Marxist Humanism: Essays on the Left Today* (New York, 1968), 57.
12 Henry Dreyfuss, *The Measure of Man* (New York: Whitney, 1959), 4.
13 Ettore Sottsass cited in Sparke, *Ettore Sotssas Jnr* (London: Design Council, 1982), 63.
14 Andrzej Pawłowski, *Inicjacje. O sztuce, projektowaniu i kształceniu projektantów* Biblioteka wzornictwa 6'87 (Warsaw: IWP, 1987).
15 A. Pawłowski. "Cel i założenia Wydziału Form Przemysłowych" [The aim and assumptions of the Industrial Design Department]. *Biuletyn 1965*, Industrial Design Department of the Academy of Fine Arts in Krakow, 1965.
16 On Vico's claims for the gesture, for instance, see Adam Kendon, *Gesture: Visible Action as Utterance* (Cambridge: CUP, 2004), 36.
17 Nicholas Negroponte, *The Architecture Machine* (Boston, MA: MIT 1970), 9.
18 See William Fetter, "Computer Graphics at Boeing," *Print Magazine*, XX:VI (November–December 1966), 32.
19 Gustav Metzger, "Automata in History," *Studio International* (1969): 107–9.
20 Tomás Maldonado and Gui Bonsiepe, "Wissenschaft und Gestaltung" in *Ulm*, 10/11 (1964): 10–29.
21 See Margaret Morse, *Virtualities: television, media art, and cyberculture* (Bloomington: Indiana University Press, 1998), 75.
22 A. Michael Noll, "Choreography and Computers," *Dance Magazine*, Vol. XXXXI, No. 1 (January 1967): 43–5.
23 "Kyldex: Dampf auf Zuschauer-Kommando," *Der Spiegel* (June 1973), 107.
24 Allan Kaprow, *Essays on the Blurring of Art and Life*, ed. Jeff Kelley (Berkeley, CA: University of California Press, 2003).
25 Billy Klüver, *Pavilion by Experiments in Art and Technology* (New York: EP Dutton, 1972), xi.
26 Max Kozloff, "The Multi-million Dollar Art Boondoggle," *Artforum* 10, no. 2 (October 1971): 72–6.
27 One answer to this question is to be found in the arguments made for the democratization of computers by figures like Ted Nelson in his book *Computer Lib* (self-published, 1974) or the magazine, *Radical Software* (est. 1970) in the USA.
28 Francisco Infante "Artificially Created Spaces: The Projects and Realizations of the ARGO Group" in *The Journal of Decorative and Propaganda Arts*, Vol. 5 (summer 1987), 116.
29 See Łukasz Ronduda, *Polish Art of the 1970s* (Jelenia Góra / Warsaw: Polski Western / CCA Ujazdowski Castle, 2009) 300–14.
30 Kwiek in conversation with the author, summer 2013.
31 Paweł Kwiek, "Dokument obiektywny o człowieku" [Objective Document About Man], 1976 unpublished mss, Center for Contemporary Art., Ujzadowskie Castle, CSW Archive.
32 Paweł Kwiek cited by Ryszard Kluszczyński, ed., *Warsztat Formy Filmowej* (Warsaw: Centrum Sztuki Współczesnej Zamek Ujazdowski, 2000) 71.
33 Rosalind Krauss, "The Post-medium Condition" in *Perpetual Inventory* (Boston MA: MIT Press, 2010), 10.

Torsten Lange

Rittel's Riddles: Design Education and "Democratic" Planning in the Age of Information

Published in the June 1973 issue of the journal *Policy Sciences*, "Dilemmas in a General Theory of Planning," co-authored by German mathematician and design theorist Horst Wilhelm Jakob Rittel (1930–1990) and American urban designer and theorist Melvin M. Webber (1920–2006), has become a seminal text in both planning and design theory.[1] In their article Rittel and Webber attested that modern Western models of planning based on the idea of "efficiency," rendering the former as a "process of designing problem-solutions that might be installed and operated cheaply," were in deep crisis. The flaws of "idealized" planning systems, they argued, had become widely visible. This was due to the peculiar nature of the problems that planning confronts. In contrast to the "tame" problems encountered by science, problems of planning and design were "inherently wicked," and as such characterized by complexity, contradictions, and unforeseeable consequences. The planning process thus ought to focus on open outcomes, accommodating indeterminacy and the role of argumentation. Rittel and Webber's article marked a shift from a positivist notion of science and technology within design and planning toward emphasizing their inherently social and political character.

Within architectural discourse, Rittel's extensive yet dispersed (due to its interdisciplinary nature) written work remained relatively marginal, however.[2] Not least, this may be the result of a dichotomy between techno-scientific approaches to planning and architecture's re-framing as an autonomous (even artistic) practice since the mid-1970s.[3] Despite his prominent position within design pedagogy and architectural education, Rittel remains a somewhat obscure figure. In recent years, design historians have turned to his ideas in an effort to historicize participatory design[4], while within architecture Rittel has slowly been rediscovered as part of a pre-history of computing and parametric design in architecture.[5]

This chapter revisits Rittel's theories in order to discuss, on the one hand, the intellectual context in which they formed, focusing in particular on his didactics and his involvement in the education of architects and designers in the foundation course at the *Hochschule für Gestaltung* (HfG) Ulm from 1958–1963 and during his tenure at UC Berkeley's College of Environmental Design since 1963. On the other hand, it will contemplate their legacy, situating Rittel's thinking within broader debates about cybernetics and the growing importance of communication and information technologies in design and planning, pointing also to Cold War theories of convergence between modern industrial societies in the East and West. I intend to show that the critique and revision of modern understandings of design and planning, highlighting above all their limits, was a reaction to the supposed omnipotence of individual actors and the withering faith in rational procedures, technical solutions and systems as much as it was linked to a growing recognition of the increasingly complex nature and vastly expanded scope of design in postwar modernity.

Changing the Game, or the Value of Tic-Tac-Toe for Design Education

The five years between 1958 and 1963 that Rittel spent at the HfG Ulm as a lecturer and – occasional – member of the *Rektoratskollegium* [governing board][6] were an incredibly tumultuous time in the design school's history (figs. 1, 2). Already in spring 1956, Argentinian painter and sculptor Tomás Maldonado, who had joined the faculty the previous year, had initiated a shift in the direction of the educational program from its grounding in art under Max Bill's leadership towards greater emphasis on the links between science, technology and design that would later become known as the "Ulm model."[7] Importantly, this change in pedagogy also involved the reorganization of the so-called *Grundlehre*, a one-year foundational program modeled on the Bauhaus *Vorkurs* that all students had to attend before pursuing their four-year studies in one of the four departments.[8] This remodeled foundation course, in addition to such "traditional" subjects as visual methods, workshop practice, presentation, and cultural history now also comprised methodology and the "scientific" disciplines sociology (taught by Hanno Kesting), perception theory (taught by Mervyn William Perrine from Princeton), and mathe-

fig. 1 Cover of the first issue of *ulm – The Quarterly Bulletin of the Hochschule für Gestaltung, Ulm*, no. 1 (October 1958). Source: Baubibliothek, ETH Zurich.

fig. 2 Portrait photo of Horst Rittel published in the first issue of *ulm – The Quarterly Bulletin of the Hochschule für Gestaltung, Ulm*, no. 1 (October 1958), 11. Source: Baubibliothek, ETH Zurich.

matics (taught by Rittel).[9] With its emphasis on methods and teamwork, and its aim to "adjust levels in previous education" while also acquainting students "with the most important questions of our technical civilization," the school had clearly expanded its scope toward becoming an *universitas*; much in line with its overarching goal of educating designers who have "the technological and scientific knowledge necessary for collaboration in industry" and who, at the same time, are able to understand and reflect "the cultural and social consequences of their work."[10] Because Maldonado and his colleagues had registered a fundamental shift in both the character and scope of design tasks from the interwar to the postwar period, they understood that the training of autonomous artists was no longer viable, and instead made the school's aim the education of "specialists" – responsible and reflective designers – fit for industry and media.[11]

It was against this background that the trained mathematician and physicist Rittel was recruited by the HfG,[12] presumably to fill the gap in "theoretical" subjects that was left after the departure of the philosopher Max Bense and his assistant Elizabeth Walther (following that of Bill in 1957), who taught semiotics and had introduced cybernetic thinking into the curriculum, and who had also developed the notion of information aesthetics.[13] Rittel was appointed to lecture operational research, a sub-field of mathematics aimed at improving decision-making processes. While its origins lay in WWII military planning, its application in industry (and society) became increasingly widespread after 1945.[14] There was a marked difference in approach between Bense and Rittel, however; the former having a "realist" outlook in contrast to the latter's "nominalism" – his fundamental skepticism of universalism and belief in the particular.[15] This impacted their teaching as well. While Bense, according to former HfG student Klaus Krippendorff, "had taught methodology as a philosophy of science, Rittel started with an empirical interpretation of methodology and talked about investigative techniques, statistical evidence and decision making."[16] Seeking to get to grips with design as a specific kind of activity, and fiercely opposing the strict separation between creative/intuitive and analytical/systematic aspects of designing, he used methods derived from mathematics alongside cybernetics and systems theory as well as planning and decision theory with a view towards improving conscious knowledge and understanding of that particular activity. Being critical, too, of dividing design education into the two sections "production" and "communication" (advocated by Maldonado), Rittel saw operational research as a methodology that was common to all departments, and that could be taught and practiced with the goal of integrating them. His view that problems of design have an organizational character while organizational problems are also problems of design is reflected in his aversion to the German term *"Gestaltung"* (because of its emphasis on objective qualities and form) and his preference for design and planning as substitutes – a sentiment that was shared by other colleagues such as the sociologist Kesting, with whom Rittel had formulated a proposal for the foundation of a "department for planning and organization" in 1958.[17]

This belief in the integrative potential of operational research and the capacity of its specific set of tools to cut across distinct and specialized design tasks, thus preparing the students for their later years of study, guided Rittel's lectures, seminars, and practical exercises in the foundational course, the latter usually done in collaboration with other teachers such as Vordemberge-Gildewart or the typographer Anthony Fröshaug. In particular, the tasks

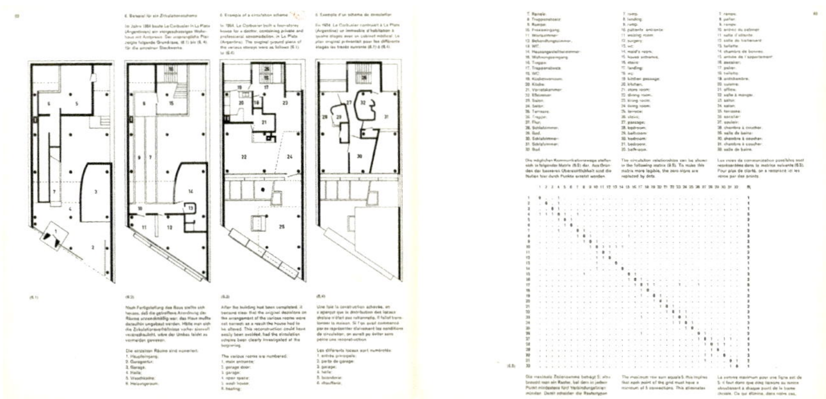

fig. 3 Exercises from Anthony Fröshaug's course in "visual methods" in the HfG's foundation course as published in *ulm – Quarterly bulletin of the Hochschule für Gestaltung, Ulm*, no. 4 (April 1959), 62–63. Source: Baubibliothek, ETH Zurich.

developed with Fröshaug combined mathematical logic with graphic representation (fig. 3). For instance, students were asked to visualize the principle of the Galton Box,[18] analyze the possible outcomes of a tic-tac-toe game, map the distribution of sizes in a given population of beans, develop diagrams in which different means of transport are logically grouped, represent spatial relations based on plan analysis, or develop abstract depictions of dance choreographies. A special task developed by Rittel was to picture a voting machine with its various circuits as well as its overall form and user interface.

Yet, what exactly did Rittel and Fröshaug believe could be achieved with such tasks? In the fourth issue of the school's bulletin *Ulm*, the latter wrote:

> The didactic function of the described tasks is obvious. It is important for students to learn from the start how to develop a work process methodically and systematically. Best suited to this end are complicated issues that cannot be grasped naively and intuitively, or with a good 'sense for form' alone. Instead of formalist drawing exercises, it seems sensible to study and train exact representational techniques on the basis of concrete problems.[19]

Thus, it appears as though the primary goal of these exercises had been to challenge the authority of the designer and debunk the myths of intuition and creative genius. In an article published in the Swiss journal *Werk* in 1961, Rittel characterized the HfG as a *Hochschule* in contradistinction to a "masters' school."[20] Again, refuting the ontological character of *Gestaltung* and instead emphasizing the epistemological dimension of design [*Entwerfen*], he stated that *Gestaltung* "appeals to that which must remain unspoken and can only be caught by emotion yet stands as absolute behind each thing," whereas design was "conscious behavior" aimed at "transforming given conditions while the consequences of this behavior can be assessed and calculated" – it is "planned action with the intent of transforming reality from an actual state to a desired state."[21] However, further below in the article Rittel reflects – if briefly – on the "tension between theory and practice" and the designer's agency in imagining this "desired state." Asked to provide solutions "within time constraints and limited means," designers had to "proceed analytically and deductively," while at the same time being "forced to imagine and realize something." Therefore, they could act neither like scientists "who are able to work on a given problem until it is solved without considering time constraints" nor like artists "who express their ideas and imagination with no restriction." Rather, designers were asked to develop individual images of the desired state, in which conflicting interests and functional aspects could only provide hints but no "solutions," making design an inherently political activity – and Rittel warned that attempts to cover this political dimension by foregrounding necessity meant turning design into a ploy.[22]

For Rittel, problem definition, analysis and the development of a solution as well as the capacity to reflect on this process were paramount; however, at that time he was still adhering to a strictly linear logic that would result in the production of a prototype and its evaluation. In other words, learning how to act as a designer in his view had primacy over being trained to come up with the perfect formal (and aesthetic) solution. Despite acknowledging that intuition was "always implicated in the choice and use of methods," Rittel insisted that "only communicable processes can be taught and only explicitly stated activities can be scrutinized critically, evaluated and improved upon."[23] Developing the ability to rationalize and articulate both design problems and decisions – understanding the role played by language and arguments in the design process – were therefore key. This pedagogy, though resonating strongly among students, was resented by designers who saw their competence undermined. Having pointed to design's inherently political character, Rittel and his other colleagues teaching "theory" soon found themselves in a position of open conflict with design practitioners in the school, who (mis-)construed the confrontation between science and design as a convenient "political scapegoat," eventually leading to the undoing of many of the institutional and educational reforms introduced under Maldonado.[24]

Encountering "Wicked" Problems: The Politics of Planning

With the start of the academic year 1963, Rittel left behind Ulm to further develop his ideas on the politics of design in the political hotbed of 1960s California.[25] He became lecturer, later Professor for Science of Design in the Department of Architecture at UC Berkeley's College of Environmental Design, founded in 1959 by William Wurster. The College integrated the disciplines landscape design, regional planning, architecture and design. Its conceptual roots stretched back to the group "Telesis," founded in the late 1930s by architects, landscape architects and planners as well as lawyers, artists, photographers, civic leaders and other engaged citizens, all of whom advocated a "comprehensive, planned approach to environmental development, the application of social criteria to solve social problems, and team efforts of all professions that have a bearing on the total environment."[26] Contacts between the College and Rittel were presumably established during a visit by Joseph Esherick – one of the architects behind the new college building that sought to spatially organize and give shape to this interdisciplinary cooperation – to Ulm in 1962. Esherick presented a paper on the education of architects, which also drew heavily on the importance of operations research.[27]

Rittel's first seminar on science and design at Berkeley built on, and expanded, his previous work; though a couple of important shifts demand our attention. First, theoretical reflection on the design process in the seminar became increasingly sophisticated and grew in complexity, as the field of design theory rapidly evolved on an international scale.[28] Second, a shift in scale can be recognized; from being concerned primarily with information, communication, industrial and building design at HfG Ulm to addressing questions of architecture, urban planning, and infrastructure at Berkeley.[29] The work of Christopher Alexander, whose *Notes on the Synthesis of Form* were published in 1964, and who worked alongside Rittel having been hired in the same year, 1963, specifically sought to apply new methods of design to architecture and planning.[30] Together with Alexander and fellow colleagues such as J. Christopher Jones, Rittel went to create the Design Methods Group and edited as well as contributed to their monthly newsletters. In 1970 he published across two special "Rittelthink" issues of this newsletter the paper "Some Principles for the Design of an Educational System for Design" (fig. 4).[31]

Assuming the position of an ethnographer among design professionals (i.e., architects at Berkeley), Rittel in the article attempts to discuss ways of providing the intellectual tools he thinks an architect should possess; however, acknowledging that his role as a methodologist – "aim[ing] at explicit, communicable, and plausible descriptions of the what, why, and how" of

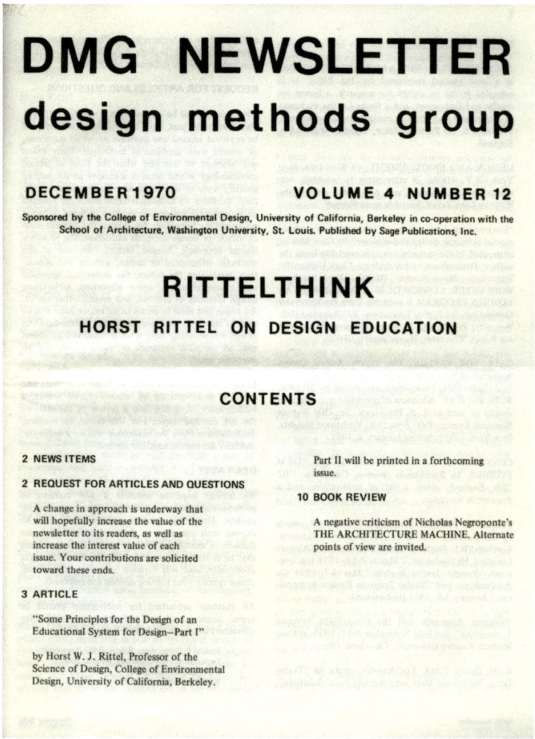

DMG NEWSLETTER
design methods group

DECEMBER 1970 VOLUME 4 NUMBER 12

Sponsored by the College of Environmental Design, University of California, Berkeley in co-operation with the School of Architecture, Washington University, St. Louis. Published by Sage Publications, Inc.

RITTELTHINK
HORST RITTEL ON DESIGN EDUCATION

CONTENTS

2 NEWS ITEMS

2 REQUEST FOR ARTICLES AND QUESTIONS

A change in approach is underway that will hopefully increase the value of the newsletter to its readers, as well as increase the interest value of each issue. Your contributions are solicited toward these ends.

3 ARTICLE

"Some Principles for the Design of an Educational System for Design–Part I"

by Horst W. J. Rittel, Professor of the Science of Design, College of Environmental Design, University of California, Berkeley.

Part II will be printed in a forthcoming issue.

10 BOOK REVIEW

A negative criticism of Nicholas Negroponte's THE ARCHITECTURE MACHINE. Alternate points of view are invited.

fig. 4 Cover of the first "Rittelthink" issue of *DMG Newsletter* 4, no. 12 (December 1970). Source: Baubibliothek, ETH Zurich.

design – might, in fact, "make things even more difficult than they already are." For, he continues, "raising the level of consciousness must be paid for with a loss of innocence and naivete – without at all guaranteeing better solutions."[32] Rittel sets out his argument by returning to the familiar notion of design not as an intuitive, but rather as a rational action, noting that "design is not an incessant stream of events; it is highly patternized and organized labor, only occasionally interrupted by sudden insights and ideas." He identifies four main "doctrines" and analyzes their implications for architectural education: first, skills such as hand drawing or model making, he argues, are best trained by conditioning; second, judgmental capacities are best transmitted by pointing at good and bad examples (note, not *right* and *wrong*!); third, factual knowledge about materials, construction and regulations are best taught by lectures, even by automated instruction. Only the fourth area "knowledge of problems and ways to go about them," requiring a "high level of consciousness and critical ability," is worthy of attention, he argues, for in contrast to the other more material forms of labor, it is this "intellectual" work that lies at the heart of architecture.[33] The second part of the article concludes by discussing a number of suggestions as to what principles his proposed "educational system for design" should follow. And while we find solutions ranging from taking an incremental approach to the use of "software" technologies, problem-oriented working, and understanding context (the mutual interrelationships between design and its "environmental" factors including culture, society, politics, and economy), it is this last area that takes center-stage. The central requirement for Rittel is thus that the designer "be fully aware of the inescapable dilemmas produced by his attempts to design responsibly. He must know that his results are 'political' by necessity because they are based on his and others' images of how the world is and how it ought to be."[34] Therefore, the larger the scale of a project, the greater its political dimension.

Political awareness was what Rittel missed among his practitioner colleagues, Alexander in particular, who in the early 1970s would also famously abandon on design methodology. Discussing the latter's work *Notes on the Synthesis of Form* in his seminars at Berkeley, Rittel seemed increasingly skeptical about Alexander's premise of "describing a way of representing design problems which makes them easier to solve."[35] Discussing the former's method of "decomposing" problems in "Seminar 8" and returning to Alexander's work in the concluding "Seminar 10," Rittel raises the question of agency and politics when arguing that in Alexander's purely axiomatic approach the designer was reduced to becoming a "need fulfiller," "a kind of 'reaction jar' into which the needs are poured as a kind of liquid and are crystallized into a design solution," thus turning him into a "neutral and disengaged kind of being."[36] The fulfillment of needs alone, Rittel believed, would not lead to innovation; instead, transcending needs demanded that the designer become aware of his own "political" being and interests; in other words, understand his situatedness:

> But if we assume that design beyond the manifest need exists, then it is required that the designer's objectives enter into the problem. He is no longer a "reaction jar" but a partner with his own interest, and if you want to express this rigorously he must behave politically, because his own preferences and values enter into the solution and this should be a deliberate process.

These criticisms signal Rittel's intellectual departure from the central premise of a "scientificity" of design and planning towards the developing of the notion of "wicked problems."[37] Had the former been theorized during the early 1960s as a kind of total science for the rational and optimal (i.e. planned) production of a total environment across all scales, towards the end of the decade this scientific paradigm was abandoned not least in the context of the "social/cultural climate of the late-1960s – the campus revolutions, the new liberal humanism and rejection of previous values" – but also because the application of scientific methods to design had few successes to show.[38] This revision had been engendered to large extent by the confrontation of systematic and rational design methods with the specificities and inherent complexity of architectural design and urban planning, where arguably not only the formulation of problems but also proposed solutions and implemented design decisions acquire different spatial, temporal, social, economic, and political dimensions than in industrial design. The result was a move "away from attempts to optimize and from the omnipotence of the designer (especially for 'wicked problems'), towards recognition of satisfactory or appropriate solution-types [...] and an 'argumentative', participatory process in which designers are partners with the problem 'owners' (clients, customers, users, the community)."[39] Writing in *Werk* 1967, Rittel noted that urban planning was not founded on data and statistics, but rather on individual values and perception; as data had meaning only against a "background of expectations," plans could not follow so-called facts with scientific necessity.[40] Instead, he advocated the use of models as argumentative tools for "negotiating conflicts." Rittel wrote: "Models demand that planners structure problems and do not make decisions that are based on vague statements. [...] Second, a model is a means of communication. Models are of great value in this regard, for representing opinions and problems, and to initiate discussions for negotiating conflicts. [...] It does not always come down to resolving conflicts but also to creating them."[41] Arriving at such conclusions wasn't merely an abstract thought exercise for Rittel, however, but was rather grounded in detailed participant observation of then popular advocacy and community planning approaches in the US, and of critical reflection of these processes and their outcomes as well as the roles of different stakeholders within them. For instance, one example discussed by Rittel is the San Francisco rapid transit planning, a project in the Bay Area that studied the impact of an infrastructural system on the development of residential neighborhoods.[42]

Regulating Nations: Information, Feedback and Planning Systems

Parallel to these urban and infrastructural planning projects in the US, Rittel also became involved in political advisory work in West Germany in the late 1960s and early 1970s, where a newly elected social-liberal government had been formed in 1969. This government was open to the implementation of innovative methods of planning while also advocating further democratization and public participation, and actively sought out the help of expert systems in doing so. Again, in this work we witness another jump in dimen-

fig. 5 Cover of the book *Die Computer-Demokratie* [*The Computer Democracy*] by Helmut Krauch, founder member of the Study Group for Systems Research, based in Heidelberg, Germany. Source: Author's archive.

sion – to "environmental" planning on a national scale. Since 1961, Rittel had been a member of the *Studiengruppe für Systemforschung* [study group for systems research] in Heidelberg, founded by systems thinker and artist Helmut Krauch in 1957, who in 1972 published a book in which he proposed greater democratic participation with the help of computer technology (fig. 5).[43]

To be sure, such utopian ideas about the possibilities of "democratic planning" and participation were by no means restricted to the West. They too enjoyed a brief phase of popularity in the East and in other socialist countries at the end of the 1960s, as cybernetics – after initially having been rejected for ideological reasons – quickly became an important meta-science with a (primarily theoretical) influence on other disciplines including economics, but also architecture and urban planning. A relatively well-known example is the project Cybersyn in Salvador Allende's Chile in the early 1970s, developed by Stafford Beer, whose interface was designed by a team led by Gui Bonsiepe, which included other HfG Ulm designers, too.[44] Its premise was to manage and control a centrally planned economy with the help of computers; a system of telex machines installed in the country's factories was connected to a central computer in the capital Santiago. In Soviet Russia Viktor Gluzhkov developed plans for a computing network[45] and designers at the All-Union Scientific Research Institute for Technical Aesthetics (VNIITE) spent the early 1970s developing a project for a so-called Domestic Information Machine[46], while in East Germany the logical philosopher and cyberneticist Georg Klaus proposed the implementation of an automated voting system for the East German population, fusing cybernetics with the Marxian promise of the withering away of the state.[47] This was an idea that may well have influenced the architectural theorist Bruno Flierl, who in the 1970s arrived, just as Rittel did, at a position where he became critical of the capabilities and non-democratic character of conventional authoritarian, top-down planning approaches.[48]

While experiments with inserting feedback mechanisms into the scientific management and control of political and economic relations within complex societies were a shared dream of the dawning age of information on both sides of the Iron Curtain as well as in the Global South, in socialist societies these experiments had a relatively short life (mainly on paper), if indeed they took off at all. They formed a part of broader attempts at social, economic and political reforms during the Krushchev-Thaw, as theories emerged about a shift from an industrial to a post-industrial (knowledge-producing) society. Following the materialist logic of historical development underpinning Marxist ideology, this process was referred to in the East as "scientific-technical revolution."[49] The latter, it was argued, would not only lead to the development of increasingly diversifying needs, but also result in the ability of society to regulate (and ultimately govern) itself. Thus, even though the control part of cybernetics seemed to chime well with the fundamental principles of a centrally, state planned economy, the communication part could be said to have been at odds with it; so that in the end it was presumably due to a combination of material (i.e., the lack of an information-processing infrastructure) and ideological factors that trials for the implementation of "democratic" information and feedback-based systems for planning and management remained limited to the West.

The work of the abovementioned West German *Studiengruppe*, which focused on futurology, the development of information systems, planning and operations research – and whose objective was to offer expert advice to the state leadership[50] – resulted in one such example. Alongside fellow group member Werner Kunz, Rittel developed what they called "Issues Based Information Systems" (IBIS), which were "meant to support coordination and planning of political decision processes" by guiding "the identification, structuring and settling of issues raised by problem-solving groups" as well as by "provid[ing] information pertinent to the discourse."[51] These IBIS were imagined as networked database systems that link existing documenting systems while also activating other, new sources. A practical application of this system was implemented with the foundation of the *Umweltbundesamt* [Federal Environmental Agency] in 1974, since the legislation surrounding the foundation of the Federal Environmental Agency also stipulated the development of an *Umweltplanungs- und Informationssystem* [Environmental Planning and Information System] (UMPLIS).[52] The aim of the system was to collect and analyze important data, measurements, and values as well as outcomes of scientific research for both government and industry, and to make this data available to everyone involved with environmental planning issues. The emphasis was on providing planners with instrumental knowledge to assist in decision-making processes. In designing the system, all the basic premises of Rittel's theory of planning as political, being based on conflict, argumentation etc. were considered, while the system was conceived as open to growth and constant fluctuation (fig. 6).

Conclusion: Rittel's Riddles

Rittel's revised understanding of the role played by scientific methods in planning and design from the first generation approach to that of the second generation of design theorists was part of a wider revision of modernity's promises from within these fields themselves – above all the decline of positivist beliefs in the determining (frequently interpreted as liberating) role of science and technology. This resonated strongly with popular doubts and the widespread perception of crisis between the mid-1960s and early 1970s. While initially adhering to, and promoting, the idea of a scientific basis for design – particularly during his tenure at the HfG Ulm – that would enable the designer to become a specialist in the planning and production of total environments across different scales and media, Rittel later abandoned this view. Instead, he argued that the "wicked" problems of design and planning remained inaccessible to the tools of science. No optimal – only better or worse – solutions could be found for problems whose very articulation depended on different values. Equally, designers, architects and planners (Rittel drew no sharp lines between these disciplines) could not maintain their position as "neutral" omnipotent experts. The familiar models of the "doctor planner," "egalitarian planner," "needs planner," and "decisions planner" in his view had all become problematic, as planners needed to acknowledge that their expertise lay not in knowing *what* there ought to be (only the multitude of affected stakeholders knew this); they were merely

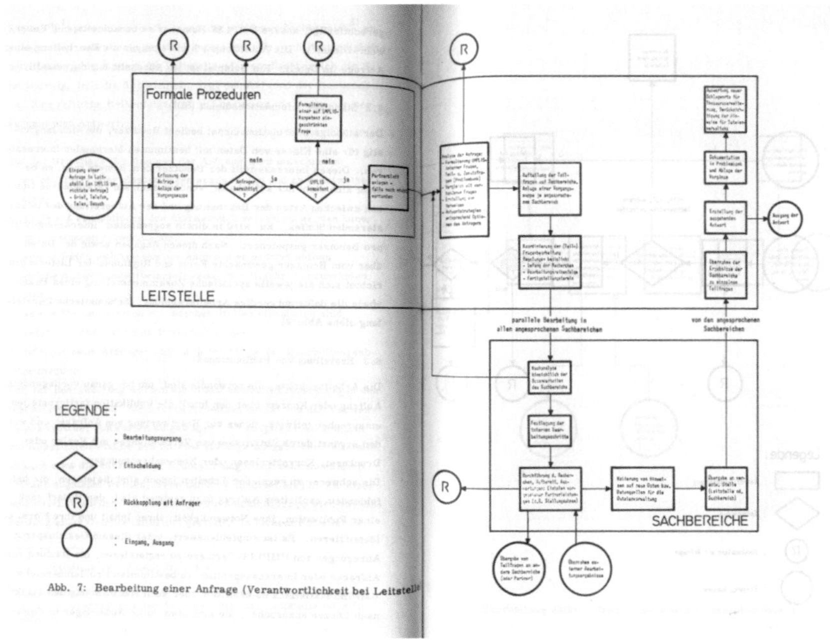

fig. 6 Functional diagram "processing of an enquiry" from the UMPLIS study by Werner Kunz, Wolf Reuter and Horst Rittel. Source: Baubibliothek, ETH Zurich.

able to contribute knowledge about *how* to implement a certain solution. Thus, rather than "mak[ing] plans for others, [planners should] tell people *how* to plan."[53] The most important "material" in this process became information. Access to, and the management of, the former was not only to maximize the number of proposals in response to a maximum diversity of views on a given design problem – as opposed to addressing a majority or "typical" user –, but should also help formulate arguments for or against satisfactory solutions. Hoping to make planning more "democratic" in this way, Rittel's ideas resonated with a growing interest in feedback systems within processes of management and planning that was common to states in both East and West, and also in the Third World as the impact of information science and technologies became noticeable – even if concrete experiments with such systems remained scarce.

But how do his ideas speak to our contemporary situation? While the social technologies anticipated in his thinking have meanwhile become commonplace, we surely need to take a soberer view on the status of information in light of the mechanisms of control and commodification that characterize contemporary information technologies than Rittel, who appears to have left this largely unproblematized (he did not witness the implementation of the technologies and systems he envisaged on a mass-scale). At the same time, computing technologies today seem a lot more suited to his imagined system of generating adaptable models and evolving variants as the basis of argumentative and participatory decision processes. Furthermore, his definition of planning as political action that is rooted in stakeholders' interests, and which doesn't avoid but rather cultivates conflict, seems highly relevant to current efforts of rethinking participation while avoiding the pitfalls of simplistic consensus-based models. It also speaks to contemporary work that seeks to "map[ping] controversies" in architecture with the use of specialized software to visualize and track the dynamics of agents involved in spatial production. Finally, the context of political structures upon (or against) which Rittel's ideas were formed has now completely changed. Can we imagine large planning tasks in the absence of agents that have the capacity to realize them? Rittel, I would like to suggest, thus leaves us with two major riddles: first, if the focus of design – at the intersection with information technology and data management systems – shifts to "curating" these data in argumentative processes, what, then, is the role of the production of form and images, traditional vestiges of architectural work? What is their status as particular kinds of information in these processes? Second, if – as Rittel has already noted – the reliance on data alone is a fallacy, and the designer, architect, and/or planner has a particular ethical and political responsibility in his role as facilitator of argumentative processes, how to account for the fact that neither information itself nor the algorithms for its collection or the parameters for its analysis are neutral?[54]

Endnotes

1 Their argument was initially presented as a paper to the American Association for the Advancement of Science in 1969. Horst W. J. Rittel and Melvin M. Webber, "Dilemmas in a General Theory of Planning," *Policy Sciences* 4, no. 2 (1973), 155–169.

2 See Horst W. J. Rittel and Wolf D. Reuter, *Thinking Design: Transdisziplinäre Konzepte für Planer und Entwerfer* (Basel: Birkhäuser, 2013), first published as *Planen – Entwerfen – Design: Ausgewählte Schriften Zu Theorie Und Methodik*, vol. 5, Facility Management (Stuttgart Kohlhammer, 1992).

3 Among Rittel's contemporary critics was the Italian Marxist architectural historian Manfredo, who in his book *Architecture and Utopia* attacked what he called the "ideology of the plan" on the basis of the theories of *Operaist* thinkers such as Mario Tronti. Tafuri mentions Rittel in the closing chapter of his book when turning to "the new phenomena and new participant forces" in planning techniques, arguing that the "ideology of equilibrium" (on the level of national economy and between city and

territory) was in deep crisis. While in the past planning had focused on restricted areas in order to eliminate disequilibrium, and in this process drew on static models, capitalist development now called for the creation of dynamic models in planning. Rittel is then cited on the importance of decision systems as guarantors for maintaining the flexibility in the face of future uncertainty. Tafuri took issue with the closed nature of the systems envisioned by Rittel in particular, who argued (in 1966) that "'what can be wanted depends on what can be made possible, and what must be made possible depends on what is wanted,'" since this meant that "[a]ll opposition between plan and 'value' falls away." Manfredo Tafuri, *Architecture and Utopia: Design and Capitalist Development* (Cambridge, MA; London: The MIT Press, 1976), 170–182, (pp. 172–175).

4 See Claudia Mareis, *Design als Wissenskultur: Interferenzen zwischen Design- und Wissensdiskursen seit 1960* (Bielefeld: transcript, 2011), 140–150. Claudia Mareis, Matthias Held, and Gesche Joost, eds., *Wer gestaltet die Gestaltung? Praxis, Theorie und Geschichte des partizipatorischen Designs* (Bielefeld: transcript, 2013). Jesko Fezer, *Deprofessionalisierungstendenzen: (Damals, in der Entwurfsmethodik)*, ed. Arno Brandlhuber and Silvan Linden, Disko (Nürnberg: AdBK 2011); Richard Buchanan, "Wicked Problems in Design Thinking," *Design Issues* 8, no. 2 (1992), 5–21.

5 See Manuela Irlwek, "Generating and Constraining Variants in Parametric Design: Possible Adoptions and Extensions of Horst Rittel's Design-Methodological Research in Computational Design" (ongoing doctoral project since 2010, Institute for Computational Design, Stuttgart); Isabel Clara Neves, "The contribution of Horst Rittel to the scientific approach to design in the beginning of the computational era," *PARC Research in Architecture and Building Construction* 6, no. 1 (March 2015), 39–55, accessed November 4, 2016, doi:http://dx.doi.org/10.20396/parc.v6i1.8635025.

6 The *Rektoratskollegium* [governing board] was constituted in March 1956 by a group of young faculty members – among them Otl Aicher, Tomás Maldonado, Hans Gugelot, and Friedrich Vordemberge-Gildewart – who sought to overcome the school's hierarchical structure under the "despotic" rectorship of Max Bill by creating a more democratic governing body, based on parity and a greater representation of the HfG's lecturers. A new set of bylaws guaranteed the transfer of power from Bill's hands, who would leave the school the following year, to this newly formed governing board as well as a council. See: René Spitz, *HfG Ulm: Der Blick hinter den Vordergrund: Die politische Geschichte der Hochschule für Gestaltung, 1953–1968* (Stuttgart; London: Edition Axel Menges, 2002), 192–193.

7 Ibid. The newly formed governing board implemented new study regulations with more or less immediate effect. On the curriculum and its ideology see also: Kenneth Frampton, "Apropos Ulm: Curriculum and Critical Theory," in *Labour, Work and Architecture: Collected Essays on Architecture and Design* (London: Phaidon, 2002), 44–63; first published in *Oppositions*, 3 (1974), 17–36.

8 Previously, under Max Bill's rectorship, there had been five departments. Maldonado had merged town planning with architecture into a building department, which, along with the department of industrial design, formed one section devoted to "the design of industrial products." The other section was devoted to "the design of visual and verbal means of

communication" and included the departments visual communication and information. *Ulm*, 1 (October 1958), 2.

9 Ibid., 3–5.

10 Ibid., 1.

11 Kai Buchholz, Justus Theinert, "Vom Handwerk zur industriellen Massenproduktion," in *Designlehren: Wege deutscher Gestaltungsausbildung* (Stuttgart: Arnoldsche, 2007), 152–153.

12 Rittel studied at Göttingen University, followed by a five-year employment at the *Maschinenfabrik Deutschland* in Dortmund (where, according to Jean-Pierre Protzen, he became accustomed with operational research as well as industrial design), and a brief appointment at the University of Münster. For a biography see: C. West Churchman et al., "In Memoriam: Horst W. J. Rittel," *Design Issues* 23, no. 1 (2007), 89; also: Clive Edwards, ed., *The Bloomsbury Encyclopedia of Design* (London: Bloomsbury Academic, 2015), Vol. 3, 163–164.

13 Klaus Krippendorff, "Designing in Ulm and off Ulm," in *HfG Ulm: die Abteilung Produktgestaltung: 39 Rückblicke*, ed. Karl-Achim Czemper (Dortmund: Verlag Dorothea Rohn, 2008), 55–72, (p. 64). On Bense see also: David Oswald, "Max Bense und die Informationsästhetik," in *Rückblicke: Die Abteilung Information an der hfg ulm*, ed. David Oswald, Christiane Wachsmann, and Petra Kellner (Lemgo: Dorothea Rohn Verlag, 2015), 116–122; Barbara Büscher, Hans-Christian von Herrmann, and Christoph Hoffmann, eds., *Ästhetik als Programm: Max Bense/Daten und Streuungen* (Berlin: Vice Versa, 2004).

14 "Lehrkörper 1958/59," *Ulm*, no. 1 (1958), 3.

15 Felicidad Romero-Tejedor, "Für eine Designwissenschaft," in *Positionen zur Designwissenschaft,* ed. Felicidad Romero-Tejedor and Wolfgang Jonas (Kassel: Kassel University Press, 2010), 105–109.

16 Krippendorff, "Designing in Ulm and off Ulm," 64.

17 Ibid., 67.

18 Also known as the bean machine, this instrument, into which balls are inserted at the top and collected in a row of narrow containers at the bottom after passing through a sequence of pins, was conceived by British scientist Sir Francis Galton to demonstrate what would later become known as the central limit theorem in statistics and probability theory – i.e. that the sum of independent random variables tends toward normal distribution.

19 Anthony Fröshaug, "Visuelle Methodik," *Ulm*, no. 4 (1959), 67–68.

20 Horst Rittel, "Zu den Arbeitshypothesen der Hochschule für Gestaltung in Ulm," *Werk* 48 (1961), 281–283.

21 Ibid, 281–282.

22 Ibid., 283.

23 Krippendorff, "Designing in Ulm and off Ulm," 64.

24 Ibid., 67–68. See also: Spitz, *HfG Ulm*, 239–241, 243–244, 258–262, 270–271, 277–279; "Auf dem Kuhberg," *Der Spiegel*, 12 (1963).

25 The so-called Berkeley Free Speech Movement, the first student protest, took place during the 1964–65 academic year.

26 Sally B. Woodbridge, "The College of Environmental Design in Wurster Hall," http://ced.berkeley.edu/frameworks/2010/ced-in-wurster-hall/.

27 Joseph Esherick, "Vorschlag zur Entwicklung eines Systems für die Arbeitsweise und Ausbildung des Architekten," *output*, no. 12 (1962).

28 The First Conference on Design Methods took place in London in 1962. Through this conference as well as a growing number of publications by its participants, including Alexander, Bruce Archer, and others, design methodology developed into a distinct field of enquiry during the 1960s, as new "scientific" methods such as operational research had entered the field of design in the previous decade. However, enthusiasm was short-lived and many proponents of the "first generation" – this generational model was proposed by Rittel – began to criticize or outright abandoned the field's underlying premises in the 1970s. J. Christopher Jones & D. G. Thornley, ed., *Conference on Design Methods: papers presented at the Conference on Systematic and Intuitive Methods in Engineering, Industrial Design, Architecture and Communications, London, Sept. 1962* (Oxford: Pergamon Press, 1963); For a history of design methods see Nigel Cross, "A History of Design Methodology," in *Design Methodology and Relationships with Science*, ed. M. J. de Vries et al. (Dordrecht: Kluwer Academic Publishers, 1993), 15–27.

29 See Jean-Pierre Protzen and David J. Harris, "Prologue," in *The Universe of Design: Horst Rittel's Theories of Design and Planning*, ed. Jean-Pierre Protzen and David J. Harris (London, New York: Routledge, 2010), 1–21.

30 Christopher Alexander, *Notes on the Synthesis of Form* (Cambridge, MA: Harvard University Press, 1964).

31 The paper was originally presented at the conference "Education for Architectural Technology" at Washington University in St. Louis in 1966, where Rittel also briefly served as a Visiting Associate Professor. Horst W.J. Rittel, "Some Principles for the Design of an Educational System for Design (Part One)," *DMG Newsletter* 4, no. 12, special issue "Rittelthink" (December 1970), 3–10; Horst W.J. Rittel, "Some Principles for the Design of an Educational System for Design (Part Two)," *DMG Newsletter* 5, no. 1, special issue "Rittelthink" (January 1971), 2–10.

32 Rittel, "Some Principles for the Design of an Educational System for Design (Part One)," 3.

33 Ibid.

34 Rittel, "Some Principles for the Design of an Educational System for Design (Part Two)," 9.

35 Alexander, *Notes on the Synthesis of Form*, 1, 6.

36 Horst W. J. Rittel, "Seminar 10: Conclusion" in *The Universe of Design*, ed. Protzen and Harris, 135–145 (p. 139).

37 In 1967, Rittel first introduced the term in an interdisciplinary seminar organized by systems scientist Charles West Churchman to describe complex issues that cannot be "definitively formulated." Horst W. J. Rittel, "On the Planning Crisis: Systems Analysis of the First and Second Generations," in *The Universe of* Design, ed. Protzen and Harris, 151–165.

38 Cross, "A History of Design Methodology," 16.

39 Ibid., 17.

40 Horst Rittel, "Systematik des Planens," *Werk* 54, no. 8 (1967), 505–508.

41 Ibid., 508.

42 Horst Rittel, "Democratic Decision Making," *AD: architectural design* 42, no. 4 (1972), 233–234.

43 Helmut Krauch, *Die Computer-Demokratie: Hilft uns die Technik entscheiden?* (München: Goldmann, [1973]).

44 See Eden Medina, *Cybernetic Revolutionaries: Technology and Politics in Allende's Chile* (Cambridge, MA; London: The MIT Press, 2011); Eden Medina, "Designing Freedom, Regulating a Nation: Socialist Cybernetics in Allende's China," *Journal of Latin American Studies* 38, no. 3 (2006), 571–606.

45 See Benjamin Peters, *How Not to Network a Nation: The Uneasy History of the Soviet Internet* (Cambridge, MA; London: The MIT Press, 2016).

46 Tom Cubbin, "The Domestic Information Machine: Futurological Experiments in the Soviet Interior, 1968–76," *Home Cultures* 11, no. 1 (2014); 5–32.

47 As early as 1961 Georg Klaus wrote, for example, "In gewisser Weise ist das Maß der Demokratie beziehungsweise Diktatur, die ein bestimmter Staat zulässt, der Gradmesser für das Überwiegen von Steuerungs- und Rückkoppelungsmechanismen." Georg Klaus, *Kybernetik in philosophischer Sicht* (Berlin: Dietz, 1961), 481. See also the article of Herbert Hörz, in which he recalls how Georg Klaus advocated feedback mechanisms and imagined "democracy at the push of a button" in the GDR. Herbert Hörz, "Kybernetik als Philosophieersatz? Kybernetik in der DDR zwischen Euphorie und Verurteilung," in *Kybernetik steckt den Osten an: Aufstieg und Schwierigkeiten einer interdisziplinären Wissenschaft*, ed. Frank Dittmann and Rudolf Seising (Berlin: trafo Verlag, 2007), 135–168 (p. 151). For a concise overview of the history of cybernetics in the GDR see Jérôme Segal, "Kybernetik in der DDR – dialektische Beziehungen," in *Cybernetics – Kybernetik: The Macy Conferences 1946–1953, Essays & Dokumente*, ed. Claus Pias (Zurich: Diaphanes, 2004), Vol. 2, 227–251. I am grateful to Detlef Borchers for his recommendations.

48 See, among others, Bruno Flierl, "Zur sozialistischen Architekturentwicklung in der DDR: 20 Thesen (1977)," in *Architektur und Kunst: Texte, 1964–1983* (Dresden: Verlag der Kunst, 1984), 130. On Flierl's understanding of *Komplexe Umweltgestaltung* [complex environmental design] in developed socialism as being "no longer [...] the reserve of experts in politics, economy and culture, who manage and plan social processes as a whole, including the process of complex environmental design, [... but as an increasingly] public concern of user-citizens, who demand and are able to participate in the process of designing their environment – singular areas or elements, or the environment as a whole," see: Torsten Lange, "Form as/and utopia of collective labour: typification and collaboration in East German industrialised construction," in *Industries of Architecture*, ed. Katie Lloyd Thomas, Tilo Amhoff and Nick Beech (London: Routledge, 2016). Flierl, KUG and the influence of cybernetics and systems thinking, Georg Klaus in particular, on architectural theory in the late 1960s and early 1970s see: Torsten Lange, "*Komplexe Umweltgestaltung* [complex environmental design]: architectural theory and the production of the built environment in the German Democratic Republic (GDR), 1960–1990" (unpublished PhD diss., University College London, 2015).

49 The term itself goes back to British scientist John Desmond Bernal, but was adopted and ideologically charged by socialist theorists. See Mikuláš Teich, "J.D. Bernal the historian and the Scientific-Technical Revolution," *Interdisciplinary Science Reviews* 33, no. 2 (2008), 135–139.

50 Reinhard Coenen and Karl-Heinz Simon, eds., *Systemforschung – Politikberatung und öffentliche Aufklärung: Beiträge von und im Umfeld*

von Helmut Krauch und der Studiengruppe Systemforschung (Kassel: Kassel University Press, 2011).

51 Werner Kunz and Horst W. J. Rittel, "Issues as Elements of Information Systems," in *The Universe of Design*, ed. Protzen and Harris, 181–185.

52 Werner Kunz, Wolf Reuter, and Horst W. J. Rittel, *Umplis: Entwicklung eines Umwelt-Planungs-Informationssystems: Fallstudie* (München, New York, London, Paris: K.G. Saur, 1980).

53 Rittel, "Democratic Decision Making," 233.

54 Kate Crawford, "The Hidden Biases in Big Data," *Harvard Business Review*, April 01, 2013.

Cornelia Escher

Nested Utopias: GEAM's Large-Scale Designs

The *Groupe d'études d'architecture mobile* or GEAM is known for its designs that have often been described as "utopian". This interpretation makes a valid point insofar as many of the group's most ambitious projects have never been realized, and their aim was, first and foremost, to scrutinize and criticize the contemporary conditions of architecture and planning. But though utopian, GEAM's projects had strong ties with the "real" world. They were embedded within national planning debates and loaded with assumptions about the society and technology emblematic of the times.

Even if the group's members were acting in different locations in both Eastern and Western Europe, they followed similar interests. They shared an interest in biological systems and cybernetic techniques, as well as in the models of humans, society, and space these techniques were associated with. In fact, the intermingling of social ideals with bio-scientific metaphors and models became a main feature of their architectural and utopian project. In "bio-technique", as the GEAM member Oskar Hansen called it, the idea of a mass society was questioned through more heterogeneous models, and conceptions of modernist space gave way to new images and imaginations of "environmental" design.

1. Individual Mobility

GEAM was founded in 1958 as a loose network of architects living in France, Germany, the Netherlands, Luxembourg and Poland. Its beginnings are to be found in the aftermath of CIAM 10 that took place in Dubrovnik in 1956, where some of its first members, Yona Friedman, Günther Kühne and Jerzy Sołtan had met. The members' professional ambitions and their interest in the theoretical basis of architecture had imbued them with the will to participate in international debates, but as CIAM had entered a crisis and the emerging Team 10 followed a restrictive line of membership, GEAM originated as a distinct group with a more technologically oriented profile and the intention to correct "rigidities" inherent in contemporary building practices through their concept of mobile architecture.[1]

In this essay I would like to focus on designs by Frei Otto, Oskar Hansen and Yona Friedman. These architects had lived in different European and non-European countries by the time they became members of GEAM. By then, they all had directly experienced the effects of National Socialism and Hansen also of Stalinism. Most of GEAM's members had also faced forced dislocation or detention in the war and the postwar period. In the 1950s, they were promoting a favorable idea of mobility, their professional practice was transnational, and they nourished high hopes for a new beginning.

Otto had served in the German air force during the Second World War and became a prisoner of war in Chartres (France). In 1950 he participated in a US-re-education program that permitted him to travel and study in the US for six months, and to subsequently publish his encounters with American modernism in German architecture magazines.[2] When he got in contact with the other members of GEAM in 1958, he had already realized some of the tent structures he would later become famous for. Since he had criticized the prestigious project for the Kongresshalle in Berlin in 1957, an American "present" to the Western part of the city, he felt that he could not get any commissions in Berlin and thus had a special interest to join in.

Friedman was a Hungarian jew and had faced discrimination and fascist repression during the war. After the war, he migrated to Israel and participated in the state-driven construction projects to house the arriving immigrants of the early 1950s. However, he became increasingly skeptical regarding the building practices that were employed to fulfill the demands of the rapidly growing population. His visit to Europe at the CIAM in Dubrovnik in 1956, and the several trips he undertook to West European metropolises in the following two years prepared the ground not only for GEAM, through a network of personal contacts, but also for his re-migration to Europe. In the late 1950s, he settled in France.

Hansen, who grew up in Poland, had studied in France between 1948 and 1950. When he returned to Poland afterwards, he had to face the alignment of architecture with the principles of socialist realism. His design for a temporary City hall in a former cinema in Warsaw was considered to contradict those principles and Hansen risked losing his license to work as an architect. It was not before the mid-1950s that the official building policies in Poland were shifting away from the paradigm of socialist realism, and

Polish participation in an international and modernist meeting such as CIAM was again becoming possible. His older colleague Jerzy Sołtan, who was of Polish origin and had worked with Le Corbusier in the late 1940s, then suggested Hansen to participate in CIAM Dubrovnik and in response Hansen prepared a presentation entitled "Biotechnika y człowiek" ("Biotechnics and man"); but in the end, only Sołtan attended the congress. Sołtan probably also arranged Hansen's contact with GEAM that did not commence before 1960. Hansen communicated with the other GEAM-architects through letters and the exchange of publications, and his work was shown in the group's touring exhibition for which he organized the presentation in Warsaw, though he never participated in any of the group's meetings.

The experiences of war and migration, and the confrontation with totalitarian regimes violating the rights of individuals and restricting their personal frames of action for the sake of a homogeneous and malleable mass society have to be kept in mind to understand the idea of a "mobile" architecture, as it was articulated by the group. GEAM's idea of mobile architecture fundamentally opposed contemporary building practices that originated from the need to compensate for the damages of the Second World War and to satisfy the growing demand for housing. GEAM criticized the redundant forms and layouts, which they saw as resulting from a standardized understanding of the human being and society and the application of rigid planning schemes. This critique also addressed the idea of mass society, and criticized normalizing tendencies within modern architecture. Architecture, according to GEAM's members, should become more adaptable to the actual changes of society, notably to individual needs.

Part of this claim may be connected to a "new humanism" in architecture emerging in the 1950s. This new humanism is often attributed to Team 10, as some of its members discovered the anthropological component of buildings and showed a growing interest in the phenomenological philosophy of Martin Heidegger, or in Martin Buber's philosophy of dialogue. However, Otto's, Hansen's and Friedman's "humanism" rather followed Karl Popper's theories of an "open" society and the prospect of a humanization of technology and the sciences, as it was promoted in the writings of Lewis Mumford. Accordingly, they directly addressed the technological side of architecture, redefining it as bio-technique, meaning a technique that should both resemble and serve the human (or, as they rephrased it: biological) world in a new way.

It is thus not surprising that the idea of mobility was articulated in technical terms and biophysical metaphors: They seemed to aptly illustrate the core ideas of mobile architecture: as for example in the case of Hansen's Pavilion

"Biotechnica" that was designed for a fair in Rio de Janeiro in 1957 and finally assembled at Sao Paolo in 1959. The pavilion consisted of a thin membrane that protected the visitors and the objects exposed from tropical rain and sun. The membrane directed the wind along its surface, but it was also permeable and reactive. Moving with the currents of the wind, it staged an amorphous breathing and seemed to be imbued with life (fig. 1).

Other examples are Otto's early designs for individual houses in which he studied how the building could be inscribed into its natural surroundings, how heat could be gained from the sunlight falling in through the windows and how heat would slowly pass back outside through the architectural envelope.[3] In his writings, Otto highlighted the connection between the individual and nature and the role of architecture as an active membrane in between. He illustrated his idea by using images of bubbles that enclosed individuals or groups, thus circumscribing the human environment. As his drawing suggests, these bubbles would react to growing spatial needs (fig. 2).[4]

These metaphors of natural growth also influenced the perception and description of socio-spatial processes inside housing units. In 1957, Jan Trapman, a Dutch member of the group, published his project Kristallbouw, in which inhabitants were to have been able to "crystallize" freely, i.e. choose their own place and their personalized layouts inside a pre-established building structure (fig. 3). These ideas circulated among the members, and Otto and Friedman designed their own versions of "adaptable" architectures. Their main features were a fixed structure or grid, in which flexible elements – walls, windows and flexible furniture – could be inserted at will, and were able to remain continuously exchangeable and "mobile".[5]

2. Large Scale Design and "International" Planning Euphoria

From the early 1960s onwards, GEAM architects addressed new scales and redirected their interest from housing towards urbanism and territorial planning. Their designs bore utopian features as they were projected into a near but radically different future. However, they were rooted in their contexts of origin and bound up with contemporary tendencies in architectural debate. The field of planning, at the time when GEAM members began to envisage it, was undergoing rapid expansion: New alliances between political and technocratic planning experts became possible, as institutions of territorial planning and large-scale projects were integrated into governmental practice – a phenomenon that could be observed in European countries on both sides of the iron curtain.

Referring to the 1960s as the point of culmination of modern planning initiatives, historians such as Dirk van Laak have argued that these years were

fig. 1 Oskar Hansen, Zofia Hansen and Lech Tomaszewski, Pavilion *Wachlarz*, Sao Paolo, 1959. Zofia & Oskar Hansen Foundation.

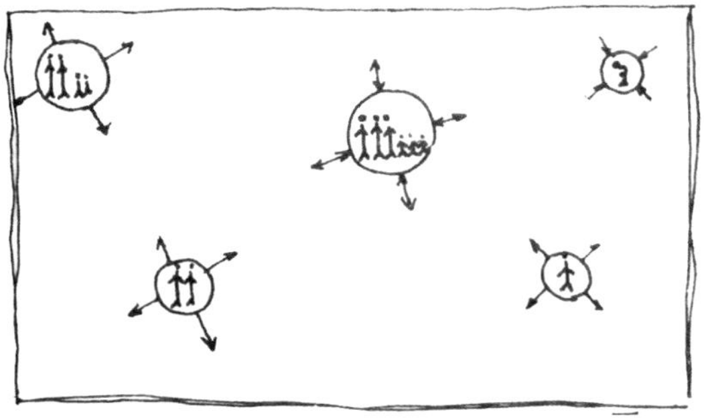

fig. 2 Frei Otto, Growing Cells for Living, c. 1959. Frei Otto, Das Wachsen der Wohnzellen, in: *Mitteilung – Entwicklungsstätte für den Leichtbau* 6 (1959), p. 53.

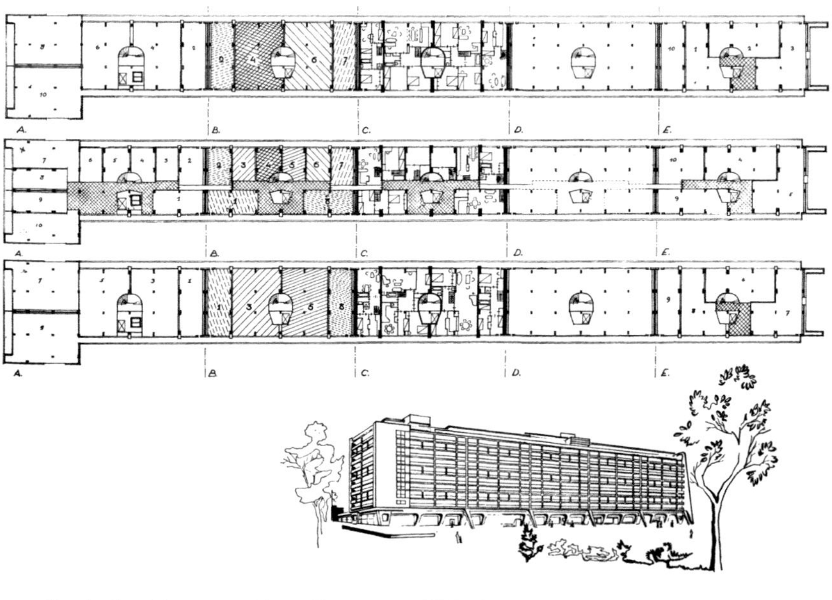

fig. 3 Jan Trapman, *Kristallbouw*, c. 1957. Jan Trapman, "Principiële mogelijkheden van de flexibiliteit in de woningbouw, nieuwe lettertekens voor de taal van de stedebouw/ Essential Possibilities of Flexibility in Housing, New Characters in the Town-Planning Language," *Forum* 18, no. 4 (1964), p. 15.

a decade of international planning euphoria.[6] However this argument needs to be refined for the particular cases we are looking at: While this new interest in planning can be considered as an international phenomenon, its implementation was articulated by national planning laws and planning policies that were specific to national contexts. In some aspects, French planning policy of the 1960s seems closer to Eastern European models than it was to West German practice. In Poland as in France, centralized physical planning institutions were founded; they were integrated into or harmonized with economic planning in the 1950s and early 1960s.[7] In the Federal Republic of Germany, the legal framework for physical planning was reformulated in the 1960s, but there was no central institution that would have been responsible for the design or drafting of national plans; the implementation of planning legislation remained in the hands of regional institutions.[8]

It is against this backdrop that we have to read the large-scale designs by Hansen, Friedman and Otto. They were shaped by (and also partly addressed to) an international experts' discussion in architecture magazines, in which they manifested the integration of planning discourses into architecture in a somewhat lofty and "utopian" fashion. But since national or regional institutions were the main actors in charge of implementing these kinds of projects, planning law and planning practices originating from these sources were perhaps the more graspable frames of reference for the GEAM architects.

Furthermore, the role of technology and science within society should be taken into account in order to identify the architects' individual agenda, and to elucidate their utopian divergence from the present situation of their fields of action.[9] If today's theories in the field of Science and Technology Studies tend to describe politics and science as entangled with each other and as co-productive, in the 1960s there was a strong belief in the independence and neutrality of technology. This presumed neutrality endowed the individual designer (if he assumed the role of a technocratic expert) with a certain authority that could be used somewhat paradoxically to argue from a seemingly "neutral" position within a politicized debate.

In the late 1950s and 1960s, Hansen designed housing estates for the cities of Warsaw and Lublin in cooperation with his wife Zofia Hansen. They were a first step towards the larger scale of urban and territorial planning. In 1966, he began to work on his idea of a Linear Continuous System (LCS). This large-scale organizational scheme, which he was to develop well into the 1970s, encompassed the entirety of the Polish territory. It consisted of four urban strips complemented by transportation infrastructure and by industrialized strips, traversing the country from north to south. Large strips of greenery, in

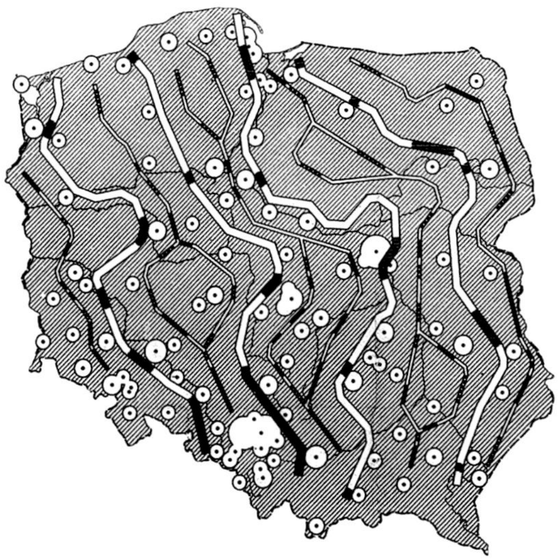

fig. 4 Oskar Hansen, Linear Continuous System, c. 1972. Zofia & Oskar Hansen Foundation.

which the sites of historical cities were to remain untouched, would be separating the living space from industry (fig. 4).

Hansen's argumentation for a more homogeneous distribution of the population is characteristic of the planning experts of the time; it was used in a similar way in France, where projects of linear cities were developed for the congested Paris region from the early 1960s onward. At the time, Hansen was in contact not only with GEAM, but also with Team 10 and other Western European architects and urban planners. Hansen himself inscribed his design for the Linear Continuous System in the tradition of plans for a linear city that were the common heritage of an international community.[10]

However, the proposal focused on Poland, where economic planning predominated physical and urban planning. Hansen approached the spatial layout from the position of a designing architect. His proposal aimed to modify the consequences of the subordination of spatial layouts to the logic of industrialized production which had led to the concentration of the population around the economic centers. Hansen underlined the specific power of the socialist state to realize his proposal. He described his system as model for a socialist method of planning, which was at the same time permeated with Polish nationalism: From the sea in the north to the mountains in the south, it should constitute a sense of belonging.[11] His design can thus be considered as an opposition against the dissolution of Poland into the Eastern Bloc – or a cure against recent history. His strips seem to oppose concentric planning schemes that were projected onto the Polish territory during the Second World War, when Poland was partly occupied by the German army.

When Frei Otto first addressed the subject of physical planning in the 1950s, positions stemming from the German planning practice of the 1940s were still graspable. Otto's early interest in physical planning can best be explained through the education he received. He had studied at Berlin Technical University with Gerhard Jobst who had been employed during the Nazi Regime and, at the time, stood for traditionalist positions in planning.[12] In Otto's writings we can find features that point towards these influences such as a certain hostility against the city and a tendency to idealize the village. We are also confronted with an unquestioned use of the ideas of Walter Christaller, whose Central Place Theory had been an important element in the German "Generalplan Ost" (a secret large-scale design for the German colonization of Central and Eastern Europe) during the war.[13] Indeed, a kind of technocratic amnesia had permitted the political implications of Christaller's schemes to be neutralized and "forgotten" and his model to be used as a neutral instrument of planning.[14]

In an essay published in 1956, Otto described the principles of an adaptable building practice that was to reach from the individual house to the patterns of urban growth.[15] Compared to Christaller's idealized schemes, Otto's layouts look distinctly less ordered, more complex, and more adapted to local topographies (fig. 5). However, the most outstanding feature of Otto's layouts is not so much the presence of topography but the absence of territory – that of any regional or national point of reference. Otto does not refer to a specific territory; maybe partly due to the lack of an institutional framework that addressed planning on a national scale. But it can be supposed that he also refrained from the political implications that the mapping of a "German" space would have encountered – with regard to both the "Raumpolitik" of the recent past and to the political division of Germany, split between East and West.

Though Otto claims a seemingly neutral, imaginary terrain, his description suggests a distribution of the population that would contribute to a pluralistic society. Otto explained the process of urbanization as the result of attraction and distraction between human actors. He harmonized his proposal with contemporary sociological theories on German society: For him, distraction – meaning the individual's desire to determine his or her own place – resulted from a resistance against the normalizing force of the masses. The subtext of his argument was the opposition to "Gleichschaltung" (totalitarian control) of German society with the principles of Nazi ideology;[16] the right to determine one's own space was thus essential for an anti-totalitarian design.

Compared to Hansen's and Otto's designs, Yona Friedman's proposals were more international in scale and more utopian in character. From the

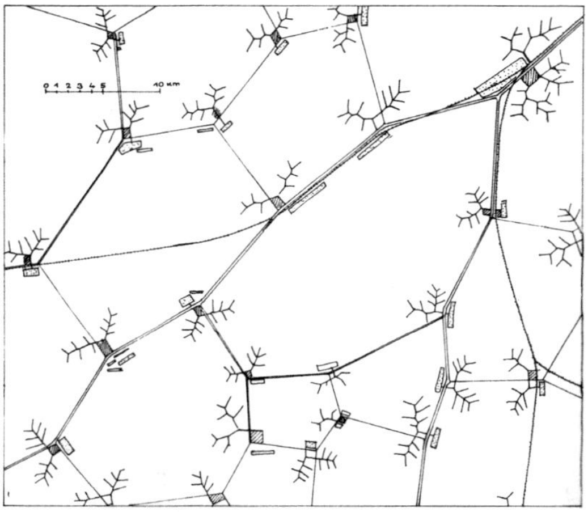

fig. 5 Frei Otto, Dispersion of towns in a highly industrialized region, c. 1956. Frei Otto, "Die Stadt von morgen und das Einfamilienhaus," *Baukunst und Werkform* 9, no. 12 (1956), p. 644.

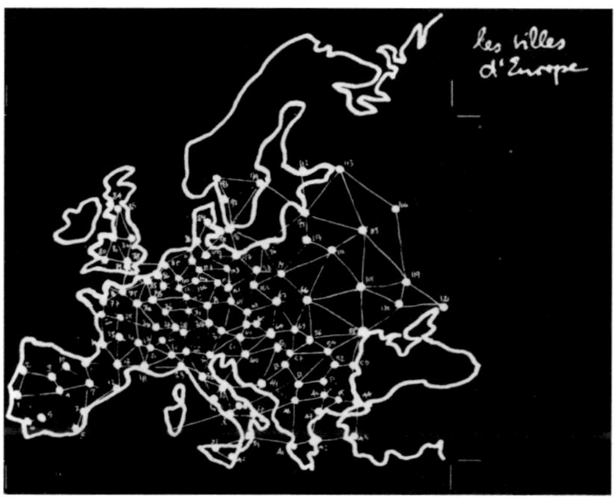

fig. 6 Yona Friedman, *Villes d'Europe*, 1963. © VG Bild-Kunst, Bonn 2016.

end of the 1950s to the early 1960s, Friedman's interest shifted from the design of the modular unit, passing designs for *Paris spatial*, an urban agglomeration above the city of Paris, and for several *Villes ponts*, large mixed-use infrastructure conglomerates, towards the a design for the Cities of Europe. In this design Friedman drew a network connecting 120 existing European metropoles, bound together by traffic infrastructure (fig. 6).

Similar ideas can be found in international publication networks of the times, where architects and designers such as Richard Buckminster Fuller and Constantinos Doxiadis promoted "world planning" on a global scale. However, Friedman was well aware of the French debates. His designs for *Paris spatial* were a contribution to the debate on Parisian urbanism, for *Villes ponts* coincided with the French "grands projets" in port areas. Friedman's *Villes d'Europe* projects have to be read as a statement regarding the aims of contemporary French territorial planning: While the official plans intended to decentralize existing agglomerations, and to build nine *Villes nouvelles* in their proximity, Friedman proposed the densification of existing cities and their connection along new and more efficient axes of traffic and infrastructure.[17]

But on a more abstract level, his design was an outright refusal to think in the categories of French institutionalized planning. With his design, Friedman deliberately ignored both the limits of political agency of the national planning institutions – the French territory – and existing political borders: notably the political division of the European continent in the Cold War. He drew an alternative – utopian – map, binding together East, West and Central Europe, drafting a system through which individuals could circulate freely. Friedman's position at the time was close to a technocratic anarchism (and he occasionally came to question politics by means of neutral technology in a radical way): In a 1962 paper prepared for a conference in Amsterdam, Friedman criticized the state's monopoly on violence and suggested a strategy to subvert its power. His idea was to introduce automated systems of administration and distribution of goods in the city which should tacitly undermine the *raison d'être* of the state apparatus and thus initiate its erosion.[18]

Forecasting Change – the Individual and the System

David Harvey has described the end of "Fordist modernity" as the starting point for a new organization of space, which tends towards its dissection into places and the absorption of space into time.[19] GEAM's designs and descriptions shift from a functional space-bound logic to spatial orders that tend to dissolve into a flexible network of forces. However, the spatial concepts in GEAM's designs differ from the spatial refractions that Harvey describes. Instead, they developed a more nested, "environmental" conception of space. In this respect, cybernetic metaphors and terms were an important reference. Indeed, cybernetics brought up a new understanding of modeling techniques and the idea of self-regulating systems, which tied in with biotechnological ideas.

In the 1960s, societies both in Eastern and Western Europe became economically more homogeneous than ever before. At the same time, the utopias of the mass-movements of the interwar years were already unraveling,[20] and a tendency towards individualization and a more pluralistic conception of society was articulated among sociologists and in politics. Cybernetic accounts were attractive to the architects, as they permitted the harmonization of planning with pluralism. They allowed the ideas of bio-technique to be transferred into the domain of large-scale planning. If Hansen's team did not allude to cybernetic accounts in its large scale projects, the idea of housing individual agency and human interaction with space within the a large scale design was central to the Linear Continuous System. The relation of the inhabitant with the environment that the LCS suggested was twofold: Firstly, the inhabitant should be able to participate in shaping her or his own place as proposed in GEAM's concept of adaptable architecture. The inhabitant – on the basis of a homogeneous parceling of terrain – should choose how to build her or his own home. Individuals should choose how to build their own homes on the basis of a homogeneous parceling of terrain. Secondly, Hansen also underlined the close connections that inhabitants should have to nature as the linear layout of the LCS ought to guarantee the proximity of recreational space. Moreover, in the studies of the early 1970s, he adapted the layout to specific regional landscapes by including geographical data – topography and wind directions were considered important and measurable factors.[21]

For Otto and Friedman, the most promising way of harmonizing large-scale planning models with individual agency was to replace spatial layouts with mathematical or experimental tools. Departing from a set of assumptions on spatial processes and human behavior, they served to model social systems with many individual actors. In 1963, Friedman published his ideas on Comprehensive Systems, an axiomatic that (co-)related different factors of the urban environment (the group structure of society, the physical structure of the built environment and the distribution of goods) (fig. 7). What is interesting about this project is not so much the results it produced but the role it occupied in the design process. According to Friedman, it could serve as a tool for architects and urbanists to analyze and model different urban "types", corresponding to specific social orders and their spatial behavior. Otto's earlier ideas on physical planning were re-actualized in a similar way. From 1964 Otto directed a research lab for lightweight construction at Stuttgart Technical University, the Institut für Leichte Flächentragwerke, where Gernot Minke and Günther Schöfl developed a modeling technique, or rather a tool for optimizing connections between human settlements with the help of soap films. The technique used the nonlinear, self-regulating properties of the soap film and can be described as a simulation practice that worked on the basis of a physical analogy. It served to develop "optimized" path systems, between specific topographical landmarks (cities, houses …) that minimized the distances for people walking along those paths.[22]

The Comprehensive systems and the soap film experiments both have to be considered as prognostic tools for the emergence of spatial orders. They are simulations of bottom-up processes that connect material configurations to human movements rather than finished large-scale designs projected onto a territory. Especially the studies that originate from Otto's laboratory simu-

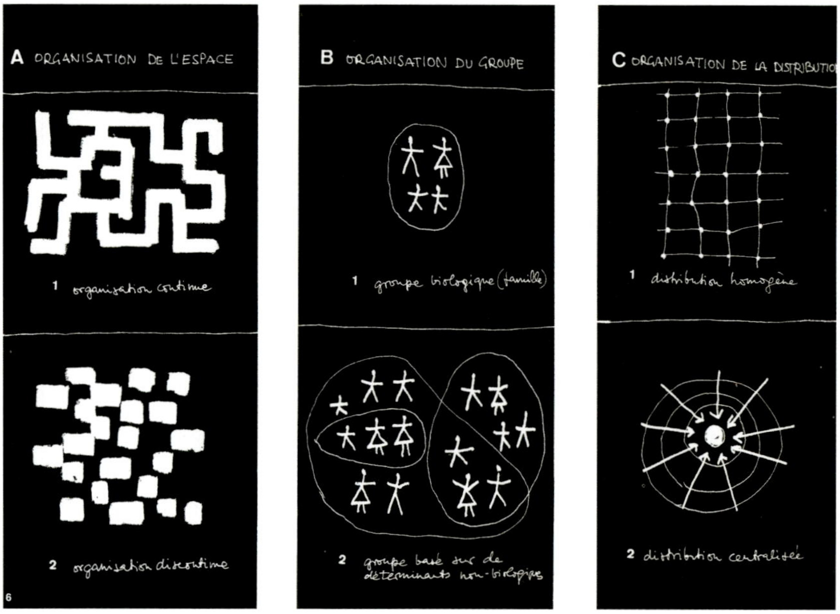

fig. 7 Yona Friedman, *Comprehensive Systems*, 1963. © VG Bild-Kunst, Bonn 2016.

fig. 8 Frei Otto, German Pavilion for the *Universal and International Exhibition Montreal*, Model for wind tunnel experiments, c. 1966. saai | Südwestdeutsches Archiv für Architektur und Ingenieurbau, Karlsruher Institut für Technologie, Werkarchiv Frei Otto. Foto: Atelier Frei Otto Warmbronn, FO_KB-P_1966-01_01-01.

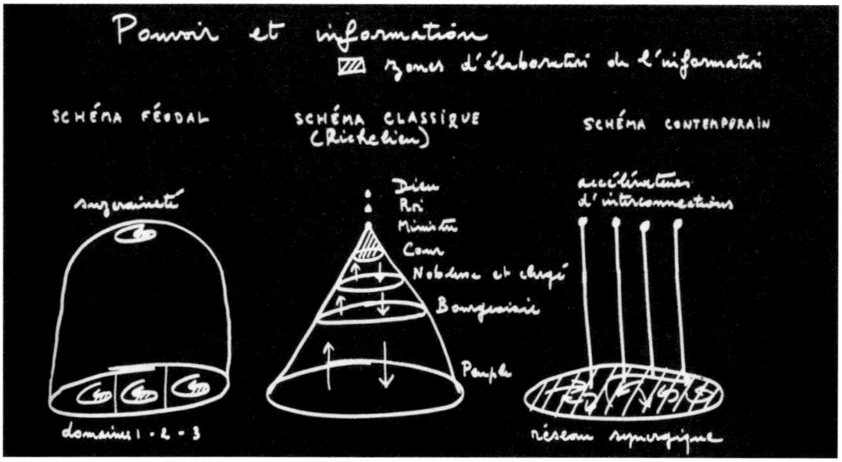

fig. 9 Henri van Lier, Power and information, 1968. Henri van Lier, *Architecture synergique*, Cahiers du centre d'études architecturales 4 (Brussels: Mignot, 1968).

late an interaction of human and material forces and the emergence of spatial orders through this interaction. These designs respond to descriptions of space present in GEAM's writings, where it can be noted how the idea of a flexible system of forces replaced the idea of function as the driving force behind form.[23] Physical forces were used to describe the formation of human agglomeration and the built environment.

Following this imagery, Otto's designs of the times offered the most appropriate symbolic forms for a society that no longer conceived of itself as an indistinct mass. Parallel to the experiments with path systems, Otto designed the German Pavilion for the world exhibition in Montreal 1967 together with Rolf Gutbrod. Its complex shape had been developed with the help of soap film experiments (fig. 8). Indeed, for the Belgian philosopher Henri van Lier, its spatial layout represented a contemporary society that was structured according to the principles of communication. In this society, van Lier claimed, power could not be organized hierarchically, but would follow the complex layering and the polycentric arrangements created by the interactions between individuals (fig. 9).[24]

Comparing the projects by Hansen and Otto, one may conclude that Hansen's designs were influenced by a more pronounced institutional context, whereas the idea of the "self-regulation" of society appeared more prominently in Otto's proposals. Friedman in turn had an equally strong interest in the latter, but his projects also answered directly to the framework of French institutional planning. Despite these differences, GEAM's ideas originated from a shared type of environmental thinking. Their approach was not exclusively technological, it rather used a technical imagery that overlapped with a participatory view of architecture. GEAM's environmental designs demonstrate how the scales in which architects thought had widened. But their main contribution was the refinement of planning on the micro-level, the idea of a bottom-up approach that went hand in hand with cybernetic accounts. The designs were environmental not only in dimension, but also in the way they bear proof of a post-Fordist thinking in networks, in which the scale of individual environments was nested into and reconnected with a social and geographical landscape.

Endnotes

1 On GEAM, see Cornelia Escher, *Den Zufall behausen: Architekturentwürfe der Studiengruppe für mobiles Bauen (GEAM)*, (Zurich: gta Verlag, forthcoming).

2 See for example Frei Otto, "Ein Besuch bei Frank Lloyd Wright," in *Neue Bauwelt* 7 (1952): 24–6.

3 Frei Otto, "Vom ungeheizt schon warmen Haus und neuen Fenstern," in *Deutsche Bauzeitschrift* 3, no. 3 (1955): 228–30.

4 Frei Otto, "Das Wachsen der Wohnzellen," in *Mitteilung – Entwicklungsstätte für den Leichtbau* 2, no. 6 (1959): 51–3 (p. 53).

5 Jan Trapman, "Kristalbouw. Een bijdrage tot de woningbouw," in *Bouw* 12, no. 11 (1957): 230–40; see also Frei Otto, "Anpassungsfähig bauen," in *Bauwelt* 49, no. 21 (1958): 496–7 and the GEAM-issue on adaptable building from Otto's publication series *Mitteilung – Entwicklungsstätte für den Leichtbau* 6 (1959).

6 Dirk van Laak, "Planung, Planbarkeit und Planungseuphorie," accessed August 1, 2012, http://docupedia.de/zg/Planung.

7 Joseph Zikmund, "Administrative Aspects of Urban and Regional Planning in Poland 1944–1977," in *East European Quarterly* 16, no. 2 (1982): 217–29; Olivier Coppin, "Les trois temps de l'aménagement du territoire en France," accessed February 17, 2016, http://riifr.univ-littoral.fr/wp-content/uploads/2007/04/doc44.pdf.

8 Karl R. Kegler, *Zentrale Orte* (PhD diss., Technische Hochschule Aachen, 2011), 486–87.

9 For the critical dimension of utopia see Frederick Jameson, *Archaeologies of the Future: The Desire Called Utopia* (London: Verso, 2005).

10 Jola Gola, ed., Oskar Hansen. Towards Open Form/ Ku Formie Otwartej (Frankfurt a. M.: Revolver, 2005), 28.

11 Lukasz Stanek, "Oskar and Zofia Hansen: Me, You, Us and the State," in *Team 10 East: Revisionist architecture in real existing modernism*, ed. Lukasz Stanek (Warsaw: Museum of Modern Art in Warsaw/ University of Chicago Press, 2014).

12 On Otto's education see Cornelia Escher and Kim Förster, "Ich war Dr. Zelt. Frei Otto über Ökologie, Ökonomie und Anpassungsfähigkeit im Bauen: Interview mit Frei Otto am 22.10.2012 in Warmbronn," in *Arch+*, 211/12 (2013): 72– 80 (p. 72–3).

13 Kegler, *Zentrale Orte*, 230–78.
14 On the role of technology in German postwar society see Gabriele Metzler, *Konzeptionen politischen Handelns von Adenauer bis Brandt: Politische Planung in der pluralistischen Gesellschaft* (Paderborn: F. Schöningh, 2005), 64–69; on the reception of Christaller see Kegler, *Zentrale Orte*, 443–500.
15 Frei Otto, "Die Stadt von morgen und das Einfamilienhaus," in *Baukunst und Werkform* 9, no. 12 (1956): 642–52.
16 "Masse, in der er [der Mensch] nur gleichgerichtet werden kann," Otto, "Stadt," 644.
17 Towards the middle of the 1960s, plans for the construction of nine *Villes nouvelles* were formulated by DATAR, with the aim of relieving the pressure on urban centers such as Paris, Grenoble/Lyon and Marseille, but they had been circulating well before: see for example Pierre Randet, "L'urbanisme de notre temps: Un example: Toulouse – Le Mirail," in *Techniques et architecture* 22, no. 5 (1962): 83–4.
18 Yona Friedman, La société et l'urbanisme mobile, [05. 1962], RKD (Netherlands Institute for Art History), archief Constant, 2.7.334.
19 David Harvey, *The Condition of Postmodernity: An Enquiry to the Conditions of Cultural Change* (Oxford: Blackwell, 1990), 293–307.
20 Susan Buck-Morss, *Dreamworld and Catastrophe: The Passing of Mass Utopia in East and West* (Cambridge: The MIT Press, 2002), X–XIV.
21 Gola, Hansen, Towards Open Form, 41.
22 Klaus Bach, "Minimalwegegerät," in *Seifenblasen/Forming Bubbles*, ed. Klaus Bach, Berthold Burkhardt and Frei Otto, in *Mitteilungen des Instituts für leichte Flächentragwerke* 18 (Stuttgart: Krämer, 1988): 320–5.
23 See David Georges Emmerich, *Cours de géométrie constructive. Morphologie*, (Paris: Centre de diffusion de la grande masse [1967]), 15–7.
24 Henri van Lier, *Architecture synergique. Cahiers du centre d'études architecturales* 4 (Brussels: Mignot, 1968), 22.

Mirko Baum

On Bees and Bolts: Školka SIAL – An Architects' Commune in Czechoslovakia

The beginning of our studies was marked by a "strictly secret" explosion. Officially it never took place. It was forbidden to photograph it and anyone who did risked a long prison sentence. What blew up on the Letná plateau above Prague city center in November 1962 was the last and also the largest memorial ever dedicated by the vassal states of the Soviet Union to the great dictator and mass murderer Iossif Wissarionowitsch Stalin. The cautious liberalization that led up to this inconceivable event took place very slowly: however, it had become tangible and was of great importance for the intellectual and professional development of my generation. Although the flat file cabinets in the Department of Architecture in Prague were overflowing with optimistic watercolors and columns in the style of real-socialist classicism, we were spared this nonsense. After the mandatory break, some of our professors searched their memories for the Czech functionalist architecture, making it a theme of their lectures. The more elderly among them even remembered their apprenticeship years with Adolf Loos, Le Corbusier and Frank Lloyd Wright. The hydra of totalitarianism was not yet completely defeated, however the climate still grew "warmer" and for us it was a big stroke of luck that we studied during this political thaw.

It was quite a sensation and certainly no coincidence that the UIA congress was held in Prague in 1967. It was accompanied by an international student competition, in which some of us participated with great enthusiasm. Initially, the entries were viewed by an internal panel of experts. The selection of best entries was then to be passed on to the international panel. The overall theme of the competition was urban and landscape planning, however

fig. 1 Mirko Baum: Housing development Starý Hrozňatov, UIA student competition, 1967.

the participants were able to choose their own individual tasks. I chose Starý Hrozňatov, a small village in the Jizera Mountains, which still very much bore the traces of the displacement of the Sudeten Germans. I added a large, symmetrical building with atrium flats and terrace apartments to the picturesque setting of the depopulated countryside, which included the ruin of a medieval castle and a destroyed baroque Loreto chapel. A completely automated dairy farm hovered above the approach road, which ended in a small administration center. The cows, held in an air-conditioned space, had an artificially accelerated day-and-night rhythm. They were fed with pills to the perpetual background music of Mozart, and their milk – extracted in a fully automated process – hurtled each morning, cleanly packaged, through pneumatic tubes into the apartments (fig. 1).

The forward-looking content of my message was not recognized. The university jury denied my taking part in the international round. The stated reason was "copying of Western role models." If the jury was thinking of Hans Hollein and his "Aircraft Carrier City in Landscape," then they were absolutely right. However, I still doubt that they knew Hans Hollein at all, not to mention his visionary project. Yet the wind still always came from the West and the real-socialist conventions blew strongly in the other direction.

For me, my friendship with John Eisler was a cultural quantum leap. The son of an English aristocrat and a Czech/Jewish soldier of the British army, he was born in London and was allowed to travel to the West due to his British passport. For his circle of friends that meant access to rare literature and to equally rare drawing material, which was not available in acceptable quality in Czechoslovakia at that time. From that moment on, English lettering stencils, Letraset and colored adhesive foil infinitely enhanced the graphic quality of our drafts.

The discourse we had with one another was as if a window had suddenly been opened for me. In the "swinging sixties," London was not only the capital of pop music but also of architecture and hence I also became familiar with the work of James Stirling, and above all with Archigram, a group of London architects still very young at that time. My personal contribution to the bilateral cultural exchange was my technical knowledge, which was quite well-developed for that period, as well as my fondness for technological products – above all from the arms industry, as it is a well-known fact that the devil is the best designer.

In these debates, the foundation stone was possibly laid for an architectural movement that was later disparagingly labeled as "Machine Style" by our adversaries. One of these critics even maintained that in spring I would rather see bolts flying over the meadows than bees. At any rate, our discourse had an influence on my final study designs and with regard to my diploma thesis, one could certainly speak of Stirling plagiarism. The term "Machine Style" architecture has survived until today, gradually losing its originally negative connotations.

My years of study ended just as they began – with an explosion, or more precisely, with a whole series of explosions. Through the whole night, from August 20 to 21, 1968, huge Antonow transport aircrafts landed at Prague-Ruzyně airport, not far from the university campus. The next day at dawn, endless lines of Russian T–55 tanks with white invasion stripes rolled into the streets of Prague. The soldiers cowering on them, most of them very young, looked dirty, exhausted, nervous and dangerous. Thankfully, the Czechoslovakian army, for which I was a reserve officer, was ordered to stay in the barracks and hence only the civilian population put up a senseless resistance, which, despite its touching qualities, resulted in numerous injuries and deaths.

The period that followed could be divided into two different chapters. First of all there was the passive resistance, which partly had some very creative traits. What followed was paralysis and pure lethargy. While the first short phase with its inventive spirit was by all means amusing and inspiring, the period of graveyard peace was not only unbearable but also showed every sign of lasting indefinitely.

During this desolate time, John and I decided to leave Prague to work in the North-Bohemian city of Liberec for the architect Karel Hubáček (1924–2011). Hubáček was head of the engineering office SIAL, which, thanks also to the brief liberalization period of the "Prague Spring," was not state owned. At that time, he and his engineers were in the process of building the hotel and television tower on the 1012m-high Ještěd mountain, not far from the city. The building project, which was the result of a devastating fire and subsequent public competition, combined several functions. At the base of the building there was a cable car station; above it a restaurant and two hotel stories, as well as a section for antennas made up of several stories and encased in fiberglass, which was positioned at the tip of the spire. Later, a cylindrical fixture was added which had been produced using a wet filament winding process. With its shape based on a hyperboloid of revolution, the building is still both a harmonious continuation of the mountain peak and also very interesting from a technological point of view (fig. 2). Having been built by the most advanced production technique at the beginning of the seventies, today it still seems almost avant-garde. Other new elements were the industrially manufactured cladding of the hotel stories, the fiberglass casing for the antennas and the self-supporting antenna fixture. In particular, the wet filament winding technique from the field of tank and container construction still represents the current state of technology and is also used in state-of-the-art aerospace construction.

In order to dampen the oscillation caused by the Magnus effect, Hubáček's friend Zdeněk Patrman (1927–2001) developed an innovative vibration absorber, at that time the first of its kind in the whole Eastern Bloc. His installation came at the same time as the discovery of the cracks in the tower construction of the Ostankino tower in Moscow, caused by vibration. With a height of 537m, the tower was at that time the highest building in the world. Hence when a top Russian delegation announced their attendance at the test run of the vibration absorber, all efforts were made not to disappoint them. The day of their arrival was known, however the anticipated weather conditions on this day were not. In order to avoid potential disgrace, rockets provided by the army were installed on the last gallery of the tower spire and ignited at a specified moment. Their abrupt cut-off provided the necessary momentum for the vibration.

For us, with our passion for technology, this building had a huge appeal.

fig. 2 Karel Hubáček (Architect) and Zdeněk Patrman (Engineer): Antenna tower with hotel and cable car on Ještěd Mountain near Liberec.

The presence of the charismatic personage of Karel Hubáček also promised to be an ideal environment for gaining extraordinary experience.

After some time, several like-minded friends joined John and me in Liberec. Hence Hubáček's employee Miroslav Masák had the idea of setting up a postgraduate study program for select graduates. Although it was a good idea which he pursued for some time, it failed due to the intellectual homogeneity of the group members, who wanted to stay together and didn't for one moment consider parting on finishing their "postgraduate studies." It goes without saying that this was only possible with a big financial disadvantage as nobody of the team earned a standard salary, and it speaks for the idealism of the group that they were willing to take such restrictions into account. A disused restaurant for day trippers near Liberec was purchased at a low price and converted for living and working using the most primitive means. The restaurant was used as a drawing studio. Small rooms were grouped around it, each of which accommodated a desk, a drafting machine, a bookshelf and a raised platform for sleeping (fig. 3). In addition there was a kitchen, a small dining area (which we called the refectory), a photo and model-making workshop, as

fig. 3 Former countryside restaurant "Na Jedlové," Školka's living and working rooms.

well as a WC and showers. Usually, it was the most faint-hearted or hungriest person that went shopping to the next village and cooked. We ate together. This war of nerves meant that the first warm meal was often late at night and little by little, the rhythm of night and day merged to become a homogenous continuum.

In the beginning we didn't really have much to do. Hence Miroslav Masák, who still hadn't given up on the idea of the postgraduate studies, gave us fictive design tasks, which we worked on in the form of an in-house competition. The first was the design of a chapel for a Catholic summer school on the banks of the Oslo Fjord in Norway. My design was a tetrahedron made of steel plate, situated close to the riverbank on three floats. It could be entered via a short pier and the emergency exit route (for the priest after a bad sermon) was a lifeboat. My idea was to have the chapel manufactured in a shipyard in Oslo and for it to be towed to its place of operation. If one looks at John's design, an intense exchange of ideas is evident. His chapel was also a tetrahedron and was also situated in the water by the riverbank. However, it was firmly anchored in the ground and lit by waterproof, underwater windows, which

fig. 4 John Eisler: Chapel on the banks of Oslo Fjord, one of Školka's "exercises."

fig. 5 Hubáček with his circle of "followers." From left to right: Emil Přikryl, Jiří Suchomel, Zdeněk Zavřel, Karel Hubáček, Dalibor Vokáč and (with his back to the camera) John Eisler.

projected light onto the walls of the chapel via tilted strips of mirror (fig. 4). While my design conveyed a certain childish naivety, John's design was more professional and architecturally more mature.

It was probably these kinds of toys that gave our group the name Školka (Kindergarten). I no longer know who came up with this name but it stuck, right up until today, initially as a self-ironic understatement and later as a regular term.

After a relatively short time, we grew out of our infancy and dedicated ourselves to real projects and building tasks, which we received either from competitions or through the support of the "old boys' club" of our charismatic *Übervater* Karel Hubáček (fig. 5). During its "heroic" period, between approximately 1969 and 1974, the Školka comprised of eleven male and two female architects.

Although females were rather unrepresented on the purely professional front, *de facto* this was by no means the case. The appeal of our way of life, as well as some of us in person, ensured that our community never had to exercise celibate asceticism, despite its secluded location in the countryside. As an example for all, one should remember Květa V., who was not only very attractive but also worked for the post office and was hence able to backdate the stamp of competition entries submitted too late.

In the first five years following the Russian invasion, at the time of the so-called "normalization," Školka soon became an insider's tip among opponents of the regime and a meeting place for politically undesired artists, including the at-that-time dissident and (after 1989) first post-communist president of the country, Václav Havel. It seems strange and almost unbelievable that, especially during this period of increasing oppression of all oppositional forces, Školka experienced its brief heyday. Of course, the community was also under observation by the state security forces; however aside from some interrogations and threats (which were then often followed by orgiastic "farewell celebrations"), no more serious action was ever taken against it. It was a time in which the forces of the "Prague Spring" had not yet been completely quashed and those of "Neo-Stalinism" were not yet consolidated enough; a time in which both everything and nothing was possible.

Particularly at this time of unstable interregnum, Školka worked on its big commissions; the department store *02* (later *Máj*) in Prague by Miroslav Masák (fig. 6), Martin Rajniš and John Eisler, the department store *Uran* (later *Banco*) in Česká Lípa by Emil Přikryl and the cable car station on the Sněžka Mountain by Zdeněk Zavřel and Dalibor Vokáč. These three projects were of emancipatory importance for the group and brought it a high level of professional recognition.

Whereas the two department stores could be constructed, the cable car station remained only on paper, despite its high level of design detail. It was technologically the most challenging project by the group and was to replace a building destroyed by fire on the highest mountain of Bohemia, the 1,600m high Sněžka Mountain. The harsh climate at the mountaintop meant that the potential building time was very limited and only cable cars or helicopters were considered as means of transport. For this reason alone, the building

fig. 6 Miroslav Masák, John Eisler and Martin Rajniš: Department store "Máj" in Prague.

fig. 7 Zdeněk Zavřel und Dalibor Vokáč: cable car station on top of the Ještěd mountain, model.

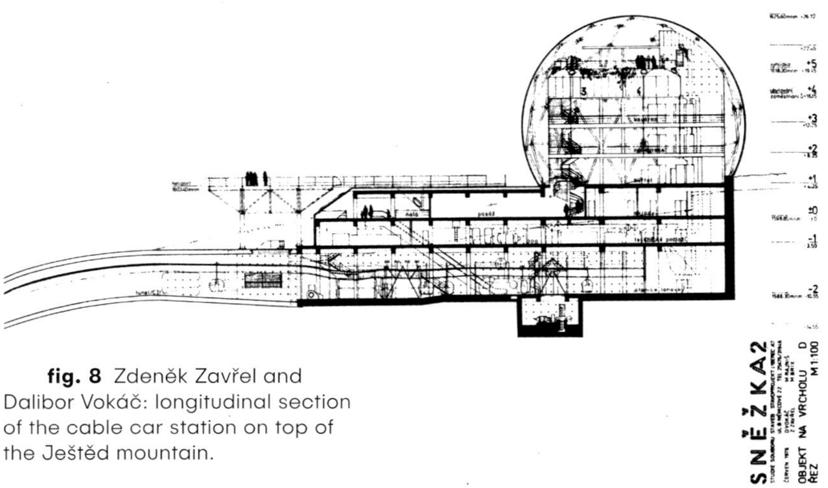

fig. 8 Zdeněk Zavřel and Dalibor Vokáč: longitudinal section of the cable car station on top of the Ještěd mountain.

had to be divided into two technologically separate sections. The first section – the cable car station itself – was designed using conventional in-situ concrete technology, while the second section was to be assembled using lightweight, completely prefabricated parts that could be transported by helicopter. A landing pad for the transport of material was to be incorporated into the first section, which after building completion was to be used for the mountain rescue helicopters (fig. 7).

The geodetic dome, which was to be assembled from parts flown in by helicopter, was selected for several reasons. As the shape with the greatest capacity and the smallest surface area, it promised the lowest thermal losses as well as good aerodynamic and structural qualities. The three-quarter sphere, framed by a horizontal section on the lower level of the base icosahedron was divided into 15 spherical triangles, which also corresponded to the geometry of the main supporting structure below. This was to consist of seamless steel pipes of 400 mm diameter and three pentagonal levels, of which the first and the last were to be connected at five adjustable points to the dome-shaped outer skin. These levels were designed as triangulated grilles (fig. 8). The triangular sections of the grilles were to be sealed with profiled steel plates and filled with reinforced concrete. This single, water-bound construction process was to be carried out beneath a protective envelope, hence independent of weather conditions. All the works to be carried out on the second section were to serve the technical infrastructure of the first section completed in the previous year, including the cable car.

The spherical envelope was also divided into a primary and secondary construction. The primary construction was to be produced using steel tubes with a diameter of 240 mm and the structure was to correspond to the basic icosahedron, while the secondary structure made of rectangular steel profiles of 120/100 mm was a reference to the division of the spherical casing. The plan was to connect all these rectangular profiles with one another using two-part clamp connections. This relatively complicated supporting structure bore the traces of an uncertainty caused by entering unchartered waters. A self-supporting construction for the dome seemed too risky in view of the anticipated wind forces and for a long time, no clear decision could be made regarding the material for the production of the outer skin. A solution was finally found by a company near to Plzeň, which specialized in the production of polyurethane seats for buses and trams. These self-supporting sandwich products precisely fulfilled the criteria required for the mantle. The integral panels developed by this company were made of a lightweight, insulating core, which was surrounded on all sides by a load-bearing skin of the same material. Some of these panels were to be covered with glazing that could not be opened. The plan was to situate a restaurant, a café, some emergency accommodation for the mountain rescue service and a panorama terrace inside the sphere.

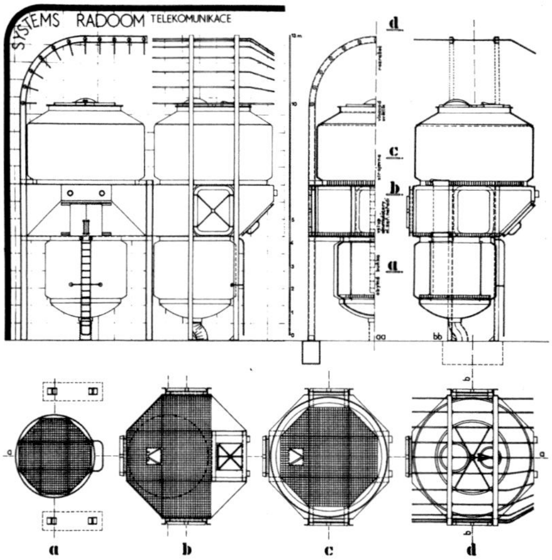

fig. 9 John Eisler: Design for the retransmitter RADOOM, plan of the first draft.

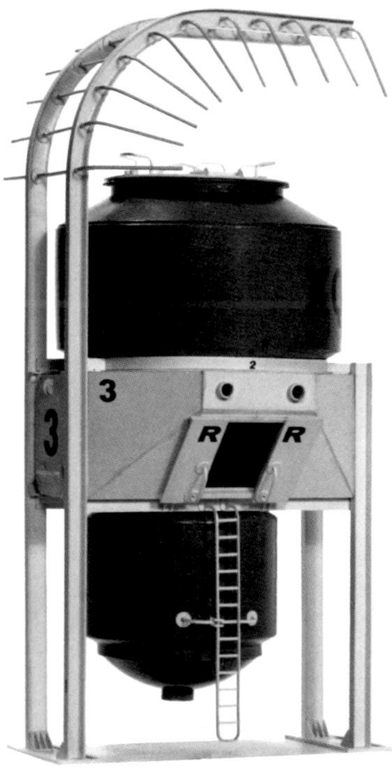

fig. 10 John Eisler: Design for retransmitter RADOOM, model of the first draft.

Both the inside and outside of the building was to speak the uncompromising language of technology and highlight the sense of being in an extreme location. All the subjective criteria were left aside and only the objectivity of the technology at the highest achievable level was the declared goal. With its

fig. 11 John Eisler: Design for the retransmitter RADOOM, model of the final draft.

technological approach, this project was the first work by Školka with which the group departed from the forms of infantile "Machine Style" and came closest to the ideal of uncompromising, technological determinism. In the words of Hannes Meyer, the radical propagandist of "scientific functionalism," it was a building that was "neither beautiful nor ugly but should only be evaluated as a constructive invention."

Despite the elaborate planning, the building was not realized. Even the posters, which had already been printed and which showed the building on top of the mountain as a photo montage, were withdrawn because Školka received a publishing ban. Just like the existence of the group itself, this restriction was also a typical product of the interregnum, the product of a time in which everything and nothing was possible. The group never really recovered from this blow and the growing sense of hopelessness was also a reason for the increasing erosion of the group, which in its most drastic form involved the emigration of the members. The two responsible project managers Dalibor Vokáč and Zdeněk Zavřel also ultimately chose this route.

It may be telling for this narration to follow the ways and fates of the Školka group members after the end of their time in Liberec, and to have a look at their important works from the years 1969 to 1974. *John Eisler* (b. 1946) worked, among other things, on the development of a modular antennae system for Czech telecommunication (figs. 9–11). After the building project was stopped, he emigrated to the US and worked for Richard Meier in New

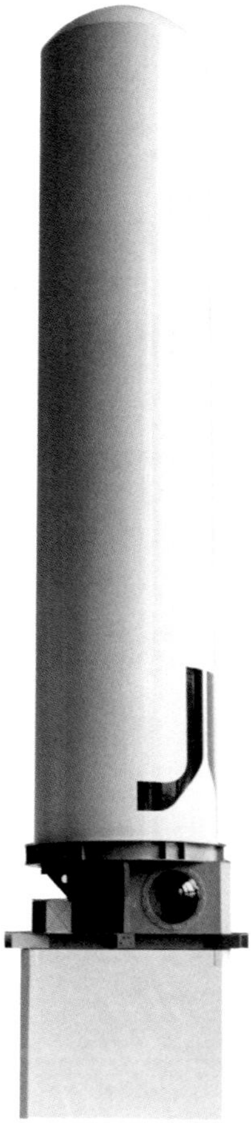

fig. 12 Mirko Baum: Model of the pneumatic advertising medium for the department store "Ještěd" in Liberec.

York. He returned after 1989 and now works as a freelancer in Prague. *Helena Jiskrová* (b. 1943) worked on the designs of different recreational facilities and collaborated with Zdeněk on the design of a telephone exchange for Prague. Their two children Jakub and Háta soon confronted the group with completely new tasks and challenges. With her husband Zdeněk and her family, Helena emigrated to the Netherlands where she still lives in Amsterdam today. *Václav Králíček* (b. 1945) had from the very beginning his main interest in urban development. His preferred "playground" was Žižkov, a working class district of Prague. After the political turnaround he held a leading position in the Prague Department of Urban Development. Today he carries out scientific work in the field of cultural heritage preservation.

Miroslav (Mirek) Masák (b. 1932) was the only one among us who had practical construction experience from the very beginning. Ten years older than us, he enjoyed the natural authority of a *primus inter pares*. When we

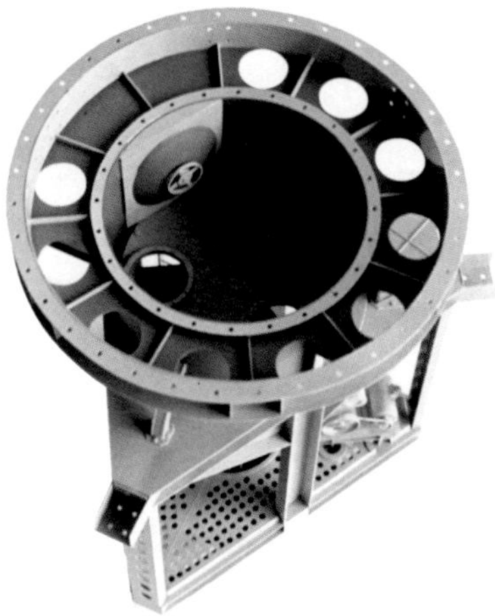

fig. 13 Mirko Baum: Pneumatic advertising medium for the department store "Ještěd," model of the machine room.

met, he was working on the realization of a department store in the center of Liberec. In this building, several of us (including myself) received our first building tasks in the form of store fittings (figs. 12, 13). After 1989 Mirek belonged to the close circle of senior staff around Václav Havel and became professor in the Faculty of Architecture at the TU Brno. *Emil Přikryl* (b. 1945) was the first of us to receive a "real" commission: a villa for the *Grande Dame* of Czech film, the film director Věra Chytilová. Today he works as a freelancer and is head of the class of architecture at the Academy of Fine Arts in Prague. *Martin Rajniš* (b. 1944) was the first to become commercially successful. His pneumatic luminaire, which he submitted for the design competition of the Italian company *Artemide*, won first prize and was mass-produced. Since the political turnaround he has worked as a freelancer and has above all achieved high levels of recognition with his innovative wood constructions.

Jiří Špikla (b. 1943) lived a little apart from the general group dynamic. He lived with his wife in Liberec and came to us each day to work and was for the most part spared the long evenings and sleepless nights. With strict working discipline, he designed spectacular buildings for winter sports, some of which were realized. After the political turnaround in 1989, he continued his work in Liberec. He still lives and works there today. *Jiří (Suchta) Suchomel* (b. 1944) was a fan of alternative energy sources from the very beginning. He developed, among other things, an experimental passive house, in which several energy systems were combined. Furthermore, he was the first one of us to grapple with computer-aided design. Following the political turnaround, he founded a faculty of architecture at the TU Liberec, which was dominated by mechanical engineering, and became its founding dean. *Petr Vaďura* (1945–1974), the theorist of the group, was articulate and educated in many different

fig. 14 The author

fig. 15 Mirko Baum: Extension of the Baťa department store by Vladimír Karfík in Liberec.

fields; he worked on numerous writings and translations. He died at the age of 29.

Dalibor Vokáč (b. 1943) was one of the two persons responsible for our flagship design, the cable car railway station on top of the Sněžka Mountain. After the building project was stopped he very decidedly turned his back on the "Old World." He now lives and works in Vancouver. *Dana Zámečníková* (b. 1945) turned her back on architecture very early on and dedicated herself to fine art. She was very successful and had many exhibitions throughout the world, including The Metropolitan Museum of Art in New York. Today she lives and works in Prague. *Zdeněk Zavřel* (b. 1943), together with Dalibor Vokáč, was commissioned with the project management for the cable car railway station on the Sněžka Mountain. When the building project was stopped, he emigrated to The Netherlands and worked for Van den Broek and Bakema in Rotterdam, where he later also had his own office. After 1989 he returned to the Czech Republic and became dean of the Department of Architecture at the TU Prague.

The story of Školka has long since emerged from its forced seclusion. Today, it is well known as having been, for a decade at least, an active hub for technological determinism on Czech soil. However, looking back, I believe that its significance was less due to its influence on one architectural style or another and more based on the realization of a social utopia, which could only really be realized under the conditions prevalent before the political turnaround in 1989.

One day I left too. On a Norton ES 2 motorbike – the same model that the young Che Guevara used for his trip through South America –, which I purchased from the master butcher Čeněk Černý in Kladno, with my toothbrush in one pocket and my emigration papers in the other I very reluctantly left this utopia (fig. 14). However, that is the beginning of a very different story.

***

The author (b. 1944) worked, among other things, on the extension of the "Ypsilon" theater in Liberec and the annex of the 1934 Baťa department store by Vladimír Karfík (fig. 15). After moving to the Federal Republic of Germany, he was an employee of Josef Paul Kleihues for 20 years, and in 1993 he was appointed Professor for Constructive Design at Aachen University (RWTH Aachen). He lives and works in Roetgen near Aachen.

II
Planning, Design and Territory

Hashim Sarkis

Le Corbusier's "Geo-Architecture" and the Emergence of Territorial Aesthetics

In 1960, when the French journal *L'Architecture d'Aujourd'hui* published its decadal state of the field issue, it dedicated a hagiographic space to Le Corbusier. Following his wishes, the editors chose excerpts from *The Three Human Establishments* and his entry to the International Planning Competition for Berlin for this volume.[1]

The Berlin proposal had been completed in 1958, but *The Three Human Establishments,* which the Berlin project was meant to illustrate, was to be republished in 1959 with the group ASCORAL from an original version written in 1945. *The Three Human Establishments* is one of the more elusive and least known of Le Corbusier's treatises, even if he considered it to be one of his seminal books. If read closely, it shows a clear departure from the urban principles that he had been developing with the CIAM group since the 1920s, but it nevertheless enfolds CIAM into its conceptual and geographic breadth. Importantly, the book also places geography, specifically human geography, at the forefront of architectural and urban thinking.

In this paper, I will focus on how human geography was interpreted by Le Corbusier in his writings and projects. I will also look at the impact of human geography on the urban theories of architects from the 1950s to the 1970s like Constantinos Doxiadis, Kevin Lynch, Vittorio Gregotti, and Aldo Rossi. Concentrating primarily on the French and Italian schools in human geography, the paper will examine how architecture evolved in the following two decades and revolved around three key themes; namely the world, territory, and typology.

During this period, architects made several incursions into geography and brought back ideas about how to address human settlements beyond the urban confines. These incursions were primarily a result of dissatisfaction with prevalent schools of thought about the future of cities. These incursions also straddled national boundaries in as far as that they included transregional and transnational organizational schemes. They also worked through the strong ideological East-West-divide either by combining ideas of collectivity from both sides or by proposing models that met the social and economic conditions of both. They transcended the urban towards the regional and the oekoumenal. Even if human geographers sought to essentialize nascent nationalist identities in the permanence of the land, the geographic often prevailed over the political. They introduced a discourse of possibilism (as opposed to causality) and permanence (as opposed to functionalism), and a long-term historical and environmental awareness (the *longue durée*).

By the 1980s however, human geography's influence would give way to political geography. Within architecture, the regionalist aspirations it brought into the field would be eclipsed by a more traditionalist view of the city. However, a current resurgence of interest in geography among architects has inadvertently revived some of the models and themes initiated by the post-WWII contacts between architecture and geography. As such, this paper aims to reconstruct the genealogy of the present relationship back to this important but somehow forgotten historical link. The two fields had surely been in contact with each other before the Second World War, but the specific engagement with the concept of territory and the aesthetic possibilities of it may have found its most provocative, if not best articulated, link in the concept of geo-architecture.

"Geo-Architecture"

The term "geo-architecture" is only used once in Le Corbusier's *Town-Planning of the Three Human Establishments*:

> With three explicit terms, the Three Human Establishments of our machinist civilization shall be determined. It is useful to know the key of this biology, capable of achieving the functions, of taking on the tasks. The study of these three sorts of establishments will enable us to move towards certainty. Land use may be revised, which means: putting space to order, practicing human geography and geo-architecture, terms that have appeared gradually in those days, in serious essays, reports and studies. We were demanding a morphology capable of securing rankings and hierarchies, driving initiatives, and situating actions.[2]

According to this quote, the term was coined somewhere else by someone else, but it resonated with many of Le Corbusier's neologisms. Even if Le Corbusier himself was the forger of this new word, he did not make much use of it. Neither did scholars of his urbanism. Unlike his other famed assemblies that have been integrated into the modern architecture's vocabulary, like "Modulor" or *citrohan* to name a couple, geo-architecture maintains a hyphen and, curiously, the integrity of one of its halves, "architecture."

Somehow, since its appearance at the end of WWII in this rather hurriedly-assembled text and a rather rough and much-delayed English translation of the second French edition, the term geo-architecture was subsequently repeated in some lectures, including one in Switzerland in 1957 and another in Brussels in 1958. There is very little mention of it in scholarship except in a notable review of the book by Patrice Noviant.[3] Curiously, the name survives in the "Center for Géo-architecture" at the University of Western Brittany in Brest, a research center that combines regional planning, urbanism, and architecture and that attributes the origins of the word to Le Corbusier's *Three Human Establishments*.

Tracing the possible origins of the term reveals how indelible geography had already become with urban planning. The term may have been entered into Le Corbusier's atelier at Rue de Sèvres through one of the interdisciplinary doors opened by members of ASCORAL. The correspondence between Le Corbusier and economist François Perroux, director of the newly founded *Insitut de Science Economique Appliquée*, suggest that the geographer François Gravier may have been a possible conduit.[4] The geographer Jean-Francois Gravier would become a key figure in the postwar reconstruction planning under Charles de Gaulle and his 1972 book on Paris and the French Desert, a highly influential condemnation of centralization politics. The reference to the urbanization desert in the second edition of *Les Trois Etablissements* may be read as a cameo nod to François Gravier.

According to Daniel Le Couédic, director of the Center for Géo-architecture in Brest, the term originated in American geomorphology and was then used to describe the large New Deal projects such as the planning work of Tennessee Valley Authority (TVA) which combined engineering with architecture and planning. The American historian of architecture, Carl W. Condit used it in this context as well in 1947. Le Couédic infers that it is most probably in this context that Le Corbusier also heard the term and appropriated it.[5]

The term encapsulates the territorially based principles developed during WWII, namely the four routes and the three human establishments, but they were somehow eclipsed by the four land uses and the seven roads ratified earlier by CIAM and by Le Corbusier's own Charter of Athens.[6] The "func-

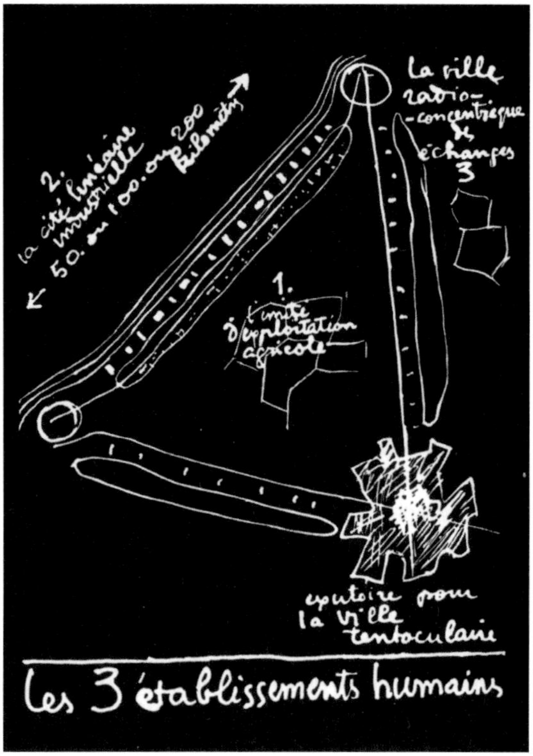

fig. 1 Le Corbusier. Diagram of the Three Human Establishments, 1945.

tional city" prevailed no matter how much Le Corbusier tried to distance himself from it.[7] Le Corbusier himself may be partly to blame. He continued to endorse the metropolitan model of CIAM while his urban proposals for such cities like Algiers, St Dié, and La Rochelle, challenged its singularity as an approach. Even in *The Three Human Establishments* where the first part of the book takes on territorial form, the second part brings back prose from previous metropolitan treatises as if they were consistent with his new ideas about extra-urban order.

Putting aside these peculiarities and inconsistencies, geo-architecture could provide a much-needed grounding to the renewed interest in the concept of territory; namely an aesthetic dimension. Operating beyond the performative and systemic approaches that govern and overwhelm much of the thinking about the role of architecture at the urban scale today, the concept suggests yet another moment when Le Corbusier was complementing the functional with the expressive. Integrating an aesthetic into the functional city had already been interpreted as a regressive move for which he got reprimanded by the likes of hardcore functionalist Karel Teige. An aesthetic at the scale of territory would almost seem unattainable from a dis-

fig. 2 Le Corbusier. Section through Firminy Youth Center, Stadium, and Chapel. Firminy, France, 1964.

ciplinary perspective, let alone from an experiential and expressive one. Yet, in this brief but open exchange between human geography and architecture, Le Corbusier shows how to achieve territorial form and to extend beyond the urban.

If the term was first used by Le Corbusier in 1945, his interest in establishing a connection between geography and architecture could be traced several years further back. In *The Four Routes,* the treatise on transportation written during the first years of World War II, Le Corbusier recalls:

> At Buenos Aires, in 1929, as I was trying to tell the public where best to place the *four routes,* I began to think in terms of *geography* and *world,* and finally arrived by means of that and the lines which expressed it at a prophetic point of convergence where the lines would best achieve their end.[8]

Dating his discovery of geography back to 1929 implies that the City of Three Million Inhabitants, the Charter of Athens, and the whole Algiers sequence of plans came after this revelation. Le Corbusier had often linked his architectural forms to territorial attributes that expanded beyond the confines of the city. The towers in the Plan Macia for Barcelona could be re-evoked here. The Latin American city plans were bound to either mountain chains or to horizons. The highways of the *Plan Obus* provided a whole new interregional scale to the city by emulating topography and merging it with the road and inhabitation. The clearing around and under Villa Savoye connected the building to a landscape that far exceeded in perception the immediate confines of a private estate.[9]

Even in the seemingly anti-contextual projects like *Plan Voisin* and Stockholm, there is a sense of evolutionary understanding of cities that anchors them in a Brunhesian geomorphic causality which would become explicit only much later in such designs as the plan of the Venice Hospital and in the town center of Firminy (fig. 2).

This explicitness is shared with his earlier historically based writings, like the *Voyage, The Construction of Cities,* and *The City of Tomorrow*, where the growth of cities and the persistence of historical form are analyzed and embraced as constitutive dimensions of urban form.

If in 1929 Le Corbusier had skipped over the city to discover geography and the world, in the 1930s, he experimented with how architecture can connect to the territory without the mediation of the city. Through the concept of *equipment,* for example, the viaduct and the *villes aredents,* the road and the housing, merge into new typologies that anchor the city in the larger territory. Through this approach, the key urban tropes of the new metropolis scale up. Liberated from the blind repetition of old urban typologies, this new equipment derives its validity from a renewed connection with geography, but with new geographies of the industrial territory that are expressions of new forms of life.

Even his most architectural of equipment acquires a geographic connection. In an essay on the aesthetic dimension of Le Corbusier's urban planning, Francesco Passanti conjures the skyscraper from the *Plan Macia* as an extruded element from the rational grid of the functional city that expresses the city's rationality but that also links to the mountains beyond the city. Inadvertently, the skyscraper – in its architectural specificity – expresses but also transcends the urban towards the territorial.

Conversations with Geography

Slowly then, through the evolution of Le Corbusier's writings and projects, and despite some misleading anachronisms, the metropolitan context of architecture retreats in his work. It does not disappear but rather moves aside, allowing the architecture to converse directly with geography. This conversation takes place at three levels: 1) between the domains of architecture and human geography, 2) between Le Corbusier and a geographer, and 3) between the form of the building and the form of the territory.

Conversation 1: Forms of Life

The first edition of *The Three Human Establishments* (fig. 1) was co-authored by the group ASCORAL that Le Corbusier had established in 1943 upon his return to Paris from his contentious stay in Vichy. The *Assemblée des Constructeurs pour une Révolution Architecturale*, then renamed *Assemblée des Constructeurs pour une Rénovation Architecturale*, acted as a mini-CIAM during the war. It authored many a postwar reconstruction scheme like the never-executed plans for St Dié and La Rochelle. The group's members included several architects among them *Beaux Arts* students who had finally been allowed to study with him as part of an arrangement during the war. Two syndicalists namely Hyacinthe Dubreuil (a former industrial worker) and Norbert Bézard (a former agricultural worker) were the only two members of the ASCORAL team whose names would be associated with individual chapters in the book on work and agriculture respectively.

The opening pages define the charge of the book as a search for a way out of the urban morass, namely out of the chaotic spread of factories and suburbs that industrialization has brought about. The book acknowledges the failure of the concentric model of settlements to absorb these two phenomena. The challenge of overhauling the historic centers of cities that dominated the discourse around the *Plan Voisin* and *La Ville Radieuse* is now displaced by challenges beyond the metropolitan.

The solutions presented are rather direct: The revision of the suburban dwelling unit, so that it becomes concentrated high-rises, and the integration of factories and roads into linear industrial cities. This coupling of the dwelling with the road comes straight out of Jean Brunhes' *Human Geography*. Brunhes describes them as the main building blocks of inhabitation; as the elements of non-productive land use (or occupations of the ground).[10] The cities and towns that have gone out of control will once again find their bearings in geography:

> Geography has preceded, subsists and will endure whilst our civilizations are transitory. Geography speaks, proclaiming certain fundamental truths. Its discourse spreads its effect in proportion to man's improvement of his means of contact, of information, of penetration.[11]

Geography provides a spatial and temporal constant. For an architect in constant pursuit of constants – permanent grounds for architecture and urbanism, be they for color, proportion, or form – the emerging field of human geography provided the much-needed grounding for the rapidly transforming cities. During his first stays in Paris, Le Corbusier had attended the lectures of Jean Brunhes and Charles Gide at the *Collège de France*.[12] Brunhes, who was a disciple of famous geographer Paul Vidal de la Blache, the founder of French human geography, was the first holder of a human geography chair at the *Collège de France*. Brunhes defined human geography as the interaction between the physical and the human. Roads, housing typologies, and settlement forms were explained in terms of their relationship to their geographic setting even if mediated.

The Three Human Establishments resonates with the content and structure of human geography but in more projective terms, aiming to put order to the morass that industrialization has generated and to redress (if not restore) the geographically deterministic logic that linked settlement with place. Each of the three productive land uses, namely agriculture, industry and commerce, projects its specific form onto the territory. Agriculture takes the form of a mesh, inspired by the patterns of agricultural settlements studied by Walter Christaller. Industry follows the form of linear cities that extend from sites of material extraction to factories to shipping harbors along highways and canals. These, according to Jean-Louis Cohen, were inspired by the projects of Nikolai Miliutin for Stalingrad and Magnitogorsk.[13] Commerce is associated with the concentric metropolitan model whose cures would come from CIAM's principles.

Beyond its attempt at describing differences in the territory based on climate, geology, and land-use, human geography is also invested in describing the methods humans use to adapt to their environments. This interaction is achieved through recurring patterns or ways of life. To paraphrase from Maximilien Sorre, another disciple of Paul Vidal de la Blache, architecture engages geography by expressing how people's "forms of life" or *"genres de vie"* interact with their environment.[14] Through persistent patterns of intervention, Vidal proposes – and after him Brunhes and Sorre elaborate – that human beings have managed to shape their environment through recurring types of engagement and with the application of similar tools that persist over generations. The collective and spatial dimensions of this process of adaptation have been further developed by Sorre, bringing them closer to the concept of architectural typology. Importantly, a form of life incorporates agency at different scales. Le Corbusier spoke in different voices fluctuating between advocating a collective project such as a national plan to a syndicalist model in his definition of the agricultural grid, to a more discreet collectivity in the social housing projects.

Conversation 2: The Unnamed Geographer

After identifying these three land uses, and in a section titled "Realities," the book leaps out of the scale of the urban towards the territorial and out of the national into the interregional in a manner that warrants a change of tools as well. In one of the chapters of this section, titled "From the Ocean to the Urals" (a latitude of Europe), the architect turns to an unnamed geographer for help in shifting scales.

The chapter is written in the form of a dialogue between Le Corbusier and this geographer. The geographer may very well have been François Gravier who had critically reviewed parts of the manuscript of *The Three Human Establishments,* which would probably explain why Le Corbusier keeps him nameless and is at the same time critical and deferential towards him. Another possibility suggested by Mary McLeod is André Siegfried, a geographer and political scientist with whose work Le Corbusier was familiar.[15] It may also have been someone from the vast network of ASCORAL. It is very intriguing that he remains unnamed in print.

The geographer is initially asked to delineate the industrial city, and he draws lines that connect mines and material sources in the French – then European – hinterland to factories of production and then harbors of exchange. The linear city is initially organized over the mines map of France, a map very similar to the ones found in Jean Brunhes' *Human Geography*.

Geography speaks. Here is a first discourse, a map for the distribution of industries on French territory, legacy of a society which in the last century, opened up the book of industry. Industry is here distributed as the men themselves were fixed, punctuating the territory at distances dictated and motivated by the play "contact-information-penetration" itself regulated by the available speeds (the pace of the horse) and thus fixing normal centers of administration.[16]

Geography speaks but its discourse seems to be outdated. Le Corbusier's geographer is invited back to reconsider the nationally bounded map. Industry and transportation cannot be confined to national boundaries. "France is only a fragment of production, passage and exchange. The two Americas bear on the Atlantic estuaries and the East acts with all the fullness of its immense territories, its quarries, mines and its industrial forces."[17] In response the geographer proposes "a parallel line across the planisphere" that crosses national boundaries and oceans. It does not follow the artifice of political boundaries but relies on geography in order to effectively operate at this larger scale. This idea of geographic continuity over time is central to the work of Gaston Roupnel, a historian and ethnographer who was highly influential on the agricultural ideas in the book. Roupnel's work was also cited by Fernand Braudel in his formulation of the *longue durée*.[18]

Following Brunhes, Le Corbusier looks for the persistence of certain forms (like roads) that have endured longer than political boundaries, but he also looks to internationalize the concept of linear industrial cities, a topic "most essential for the future statute of the world."[19] The Europe of industrial codependency is conjured again in his plans for *Vallée de la Meuse* and in Berlin. In a lecture delivered in Brussels on June 26, 1958, Le Corbusier suggests that it was the geographer, not him, who expanded the map towards Europe.[20] If that is the case, it was Le Corbusier and his geographer that released geography from its nationalist confines. The geonomic potential of geography is reactivated to assist the architect in outlining new territorial forms.

The industrial linear city transcends the national, but it is still bound by geography. The routes are drawn over historic trade routes and they meander through terrains delineated by topography parallel to waterways, even if canalized in certain sections. However, the second "reality" in *The Three Human Establishment* – the airplane – provides a new mode of transport that detaches itself from the surface of the earth only to redraw this surface as an aerial view, as a two-dimensional image which Le Corbusier celebrates by proposing a "two-dimensional architecture" to express this new reality. The two-dimensional architecture gives a *Gestalt* to the territory by being understood and composed within the aerial view as the new context, while the lived experience of geo-architecture on the ground adds the third dimension.

Conversation 3: A Formal Exchange

The uses of geography in the book extend beyond borrowing the structure of the argument and the book from human geography. They include recasting context in a more comparative and less culturally specific manner, bringing the physical and social together and confronting the temporally oriented accounts of history and causality. Many levels of complicity are uncovered between architecture and human geography in writing the surface of the earth.

The three types of territorial organization associated with the three land uses produce three distinct architectural forms: the linear for industry, the radial for commerce, and the grid for agriculture.

These patterns overlap with different intensities producing architectural ensembles. Patrice Noviant has referred to geo-architecture as the open plan of urbanism. The compositional order of the ensemble transforms the city into an assembly of self-contained urban formations with an open field of territorial connections between them. This is evident in projects like St Dié, La Rochelle, and Firminy. From the discrete confines of the project, architecture gives the territory a visible shape. Even to a certain extent in Chandigarh, new formal strategies emerge that reactivate the *Grands Travaux* of the pre-WWII years and redeploy them as orchestrators of larger settings. In this sense, a new scale of formal types emerges between architecture and city in parallel to a new engagement of landscape in the urban composition.

Importantly, geo-architecture skips over the city, to stretch from the Ocean to the Ural to imbue these formations with a sense of legibility and a sense of beauty. Beauty is both possible and necessary at this scale.[21] Therefore, through geo-architecture, the relationship between territory and architecture is inverted. It is architecture's new role to give the territory its visible shape and it does so from the discrete confines of the project.

A last level of formal exchange occurs again around the concept of forms of life. In the projects of Izmir, St Die and later Marseilles, new types of dwelling imagine as much as they express new forms of life. Within each land use, a new rhythm and ethic of work and living are expressed in new territorial patterns, in the dispersal of the farms and the concentrations of commerce, all the way down to types of dwellings that Le Corbusier invents for each establishment. For example, into the radiant farm a new typology of dwelling and working is thrust to stand alone as testimony to a new form of life ahead of the land uses that will support it. A new architecture is capable of radiating a new form of life.

Geography is therefore presented as an abstract organization of territory but also as *landscape*, as the visual expanse and evidence of a formation beyond the urban artifice. Placed somewhere between the constants of urbanism and "the objects with poetic potential," mountains, rivers, and urban skylines are employed as constants of urbanism to inform Le Corbusier's visual strategies at different scales. They are able to impact the territory from the scale of the architectural object. By locking a skyscraper's height to that of a distant mountain, by rotating Villa Savoye's silhouette to mimic the profile of its meadow, by springing the Sao Paolo viaduct from its aerial two-dimensionality to relate to the Brazilian hinterland, by unfolding and radiating possible worlds, architecture becomes geo-architecture.

Towards an Aesthetic of Territory

Since the publication of *The Three Human Establishments,* several architects have taken on the challenge of defining the form of the territory through planning and analysis up to the 1980s. Surely, Le Corbusier's treatise was not the first to evoke the regional scale and its potential in guiding architecture. Since Patrick Geddes, this connection has been established very strongly among modern architects and town planners in the United Kingdom and the United States, including the regionalists Clarence Stein and Henry Wright as well as the adversarial Team 10 group. Indeed, and as has been observed by several historians, there are many overlaps between Le Corbusier's approach and that of Geddes, especially at the territorial scale. However, what distinguishes Le Corbusier's approach is that it foregrounds the agency of architectural form in redressing the territorial scale.

Since WWII, and with the increasing encroachment of metropolitan expanses on regional territories, it was not surprising to see the domains of geography and urbanism converge on several fronts. Beyond Le Corbusier and his approach, which assumed a strong role of agency for the nation state and the public sector, in other contexts this entailed defining the means by which the agency of the architect could give a sense of order to the territory that resonates with some hidden order; whether coming from human geography, from the historical landscape, from urban and transportation planning, or from cognitive capacities to connect the immediately visible with the invisible. A few examples from this period can help illustrate the way in which architecture's aesthetic impact on the territory was being explored.

Kevin Lynch

Articulating the aesthetic dimension of the post-WWII American city, Kevin Lynch introduced a visual and cognitive order to the different scales that mediated between the frictionless and scaleless, networks produced by the transportation engineers inside and outside cities and the resultant disorienting environment of everyday commuters. The tools needed to redress this disorientation varied from one scale to the next. The visual was no longer sufficient and had to be complemented by other perceptual aids. Revealingly, Lynch applied the term "form" to the historic city scale in his book *Good City Form,* "image" to the metropolitan scale in his notion of *imageability* and the book *Image of the City,* and the equally tenuous term "sense" to the regional scale when he used the book title *Managing the Sense of a Region* (fig. 3). Here again, human geography played an equally important role in the generation of the cognitive approach extracted from another – even if mnemonic – form of life; that of collective memory as developed by French sociologist Maurice Halbwachs.[22]

Vittorio Gregotti

Since the 1960s and the publication of his *Territorial Form* essay, Vittorio Gregotti has been one of the most vocal, if more ethereal, advocates of a new aesthetic of territory. In this discussion, he has further contributed to elevating historic form to urban consciousness by folding the historic into the geographic through the phenomenon of phylogeny. Gregotti has also insisted that the tools of the architect could still be useful at the territorial scale; but importantly, he has also expanded architecture to include landscape as the medium and venue for the overlap between the different factors that define post-WII settlement.

Gregotti applied a duality of typo-morphologies, the *field* and the *ensemble*, to organize and relate across scales from the architectural to the territorial. There is no shortage of influences from human geography in his work, starting with the geographers Max Sorre and Lucio Gambi, who introduced the human geographers to Italy. The direct collaboration with Gambi, particularly on such projects as the 1973 Calabria University (fig. 4), led to a repertoire of large horizontal and abstract forms applied against the topography of Italian hills and delineating and activating different forms of life identified

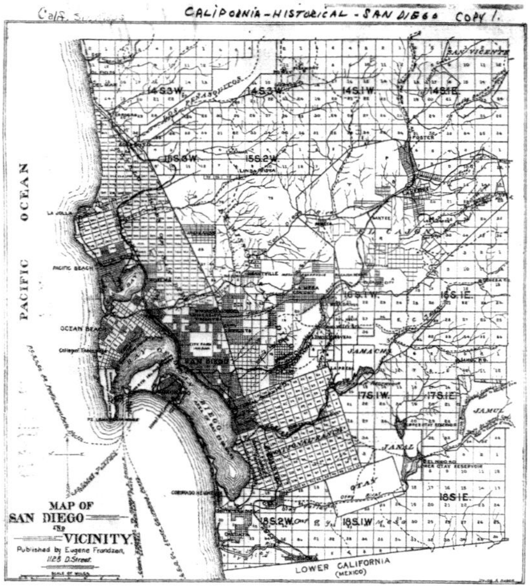

fig. 3 Kevin Lynch and Donald Appleyard's report *Temporary Paradise? A Look at the Special Landscape of the San Diego Region* draws attention to the urban sprawl problem. 1974. Image Source: San Diego, circa 1895. Published by Eugene Fraudzen. Reproduced from the historical collection, Morgan Local History Room, National Public Library.

fig. 4 Vittorio Gregotti, Università della Calabria, "Territory and Architecture," 1985.

by Gambi. Reciprocally, these collaborations helped Gambi develop an active definition of geographic agency, close to what Jean Labasse called volitional geography.

Aldo Rossi

Gregotti shared this fascination with human geography and abstracted historical forms with Aldo Rossi, but while he brought landscape in to hold together the fragments and residues of the extra-urban condition, Rossi historicized and aestheticized its fragmentation.[23]

In his canonical *The Architecture of the City*, Rossi translates the recurring patterns of environmental adaptation he found in human geographers like Sorre into architectural typologies, and the oekoumenal setting of these different patterns into the city. In its structuralist interpretations, typology gives architecture deeper, longer-term patterns through which it can mark and express its relationship with society and place. Rossi applied this reading of forms of life as typology, particularly in housing projects such as the one in Gallaratese (fig. 5).

What is perplexing about Rossi is the equation between the oekoumene and the city, especially considering that Sorre wanted to transcend the city and comprise the rural environments as *genres de vie* worth examining and included in the *oekoumene*. Instead of "the architecture of the *oekoumene*," Rossi proposed "the architecture of the city." This skipping over the region and the reduction of the world to city is also surprising considering that Rossi had maintained a strong fascination with territory – especially agriculture – since as far back as a 1954 Milan conference on underdeveloped areas, when together with his fellow architect and later professor at the Politecnico Silvano Tintori he had criticized an attending Le Corbusier and his *Les Trois Etablissements Humains* for being too theoretical in his conception of territory and for not considering the historical, cadastral, and cultural dimensions of territory.

Constantinos Doxiadis

The strategy of casting the net very wide toward the *oekoumene* was actually adopted by Greek town planner Constantinos Doxiadis, who projected what in 1974 he called *Ecumenopolis: the Inevitable City of the Future.*[24] This city, according to Doxiadis, would evolve out of the existing and growing phenomenon of what geographer Jean Gottman called megalopolises, metropolitan areas stretched along communication corridors creating a necklace of cities. Doxiadis' earlier work on *ekistics*, his science of human settlements, was indebted to another geographer, Walter Christaller, whose Central Place Theory and his study of spatial distribution of agricultural towns had influenced Le Corbusier's agricultural settlement pattern in the *Les Trois Etablissements Humains*. Throughout his career, Doxiadis had extensive conversations with geographers, especially during the famous Delos symposia of the 1960s and 1970s in which he hosted both Christaller and Gottman. The evolution of his urban models from the *polis* to the *ecumenopolis* clearly illustrates how Doxiadis absorbed different models from different schools of geography and translated them into urban models (fig. 6). However, and even if he worked in highly specific regional settings like Islamabad and Athens, he always fell short of developing a geographic aesthetic.

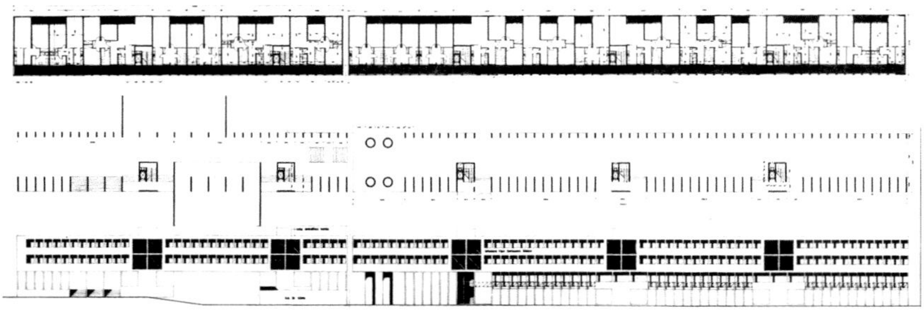

fig. 5 Aldo Rossi. Case a Gallaratese, Milano, 1970. Source: Aldo Rossi, *Architecture of the City* (Cambridge (Mass.): MIT Press, 1982).

fig. 6 Constantinos Apostolou Doxiadis. Islamabad, Pakistan 1960. Photograph: Constantinos and Emma Doxiadis Foundation.

Towards a New Aesthetic of Territory

In the wake of what critic David Gissen has called the "geographic turn"[25] in architecture, the term geo-architecture has recently resurfaced as a neo-neologism, with no lineage back to Le Corbusier's concoction. Instead, it has been used to describe a range of architectural tendencies from Paolo Portoghesi's fascination with cultural expression to Dominique Perrault's burrowed building and passing by way of sustainable design.

As ambiguous and technocratic as it sounds, the term geo-architecture could provide a prehistory of this fascination but also its projection. Kenneth Frampton's megaform, Stan Allen's landform building and the search for new territorial tropes among several architects like Design Earth (fig. 7) and Terreform One, all aim to rectify the territorial disorder through formal means. These three approaches concur in their appeal with a deeper affinity between architecture and geography than the prevalent geo-mimicry, whether

fig. 7 Design Earth. Pacific Aquarium. Illustration for Oslo Architecture Triennale, After Belonging, 2016.

via geo-morphology, horizontality, or through an interplay between historical and geographic forms. Such positions, along with the scaled-up monumentalities of Alexander d'Hooghe (fig. 8) and Pier Vittorio Aureli, also concur that form could turn the process of territorial differentiation from a process of aggressive appropriation through imposed inequalities into an aesthetic.

In contrast, the work of Bernardo Secchi and Paola Vigano, echoing the work of Ignasi de Sola Morales,[26] takes the diffused condition of the territory in an opposite direction by accepting it. Echoing the attack by Jean-Francois Gravier on the unevenness of development between Paris and the "French Desert," Secchi and Vigano propose a more "isotropic" form of development. Through their designs for Paris and Antwerp, they have proposed a variety of provocatively tentative forms and open clearings in the porous city.

In parallel, contemporary urban discourse may very well have once again become fascinated with human, or social, geography; especially because social geography has rediscovered space as one of the means by which capitalism prevails and persists. Henri Lefebvre's long shadow, the work of the cultural philosopher and historian Michel de Certeau, or of the geographers David Harvey and Edward Soja come to mind in this respect. Architecture has also become fascinated with physical geography independently. This can be detected in a number of theoretical inquiries[27] and in the historical revival of the work of Bruno Taut, Superstudio, Yona Friedman, (and certain opaque terms like "geo-architecture").

This reengagement of architecture with geography in its human and physical dimensions does not necessarily mean a rapprochement between these

fig. 8 Alexander d'Hooghe. Organization for Permanent Modernity, 2013. Masterplan "Abatan 2020" for Abattoir nv, Brussels, Belgium.

two dimensions. However, an increasing overlap between them in architecture suggests yet another potential role for geo-architecture. But could we still speak of a geo-architecture in the way that Le Corbusier used the term to project an aesthetic of the territory, to express the forms of life that represent the interaction between the physical and the human? After numerous and tenuous trials, could an aesthetic exist beyond the visible or the sensible? Could the increasingly unrecognizable forms of settlement that have been described as everything from archipelagoes to cosmopolises to global city regions, allow for effective intervention? Have the systemic approaches through networks and infrastructures not yet failed their self-defined performative criteria? Have the neo-organicist adulations of informality not yet elevated this logic of illogic to the level of disbelief? Is it not time to reconsider the potential of form as a means of intervention at the scale of territory?

Faced with another wave of regional urbanizations but with the persistent weakness of planning beyond the urban scale, we can infer that the agencies imagined by Le Corbusier and the reconstruction machine did not survive long enough to validate their own terms of practice. Furthermore, the strong association between single land-uses and specific forms of living has also been diffused by a chaotic, if sometimes deliberate, mixing of uses. Above all, the exploitative attitude towards the land has since been tempered by a stronger environmental consciousness whose parameters often include a skepticism towards the finality of form, especially at the larger end of the scale.

We may also have to re-examine the concept of territory. Recent investigations into the history of the term by scholars like Antoine Picon and Stuart

Elden have clarified but also broadened the spectrum of its uses between its natural, political and representational attributes.[28] It is important to note however that the currency of the term during WWII, at the time of *The Three Human Establishments*, had to do with the sudden dissociation of the physical dimension of territory from its administrative and political determinants. As such, a more fluid definition of space was made possible. This is not dissimilar to the fluidity confronted today beyond the parameters of what we consider urban or even national space where the spread of an as-of-yet unclassified and unnamed variety of territorial formations is facilitated by the absence of effective agency at this scale.

In this context, the aesthetic may need redefinition as well. By aesthetic here, I mean a fulfilling experience of the beautiful, but I also mean what Jacques Rancière has proposed as a new regime in the arts that promotes autonomy of the forms of art from the forms of life in order for art to impact life. As such, if the form of the territory, proposed through architectural means, does not abide by the cultural and geographic terms of territory then the displacement could help in imagining other possibilities of social association, of living together.

Territory proposed through architectural means should not fully correspond to that produced by political boundaries or geomorphological ones. Geo-architecture is able to create geography through architecture precisely by displacing given territorial formations. New forms of architecture imagine new forms of life.

Let me conclude by illustrating this possibility and by returning to Le Corbusier and to the reconstruction of the urban center of Firminy to show how an ensemble of disparate elements placed at the center of the city pulls the different land uses into a composition that then radiates out a new geographic setting. Among the pieces of the ensemble, the youth center, placed on the ridge of the hill, projects a new but untested optimism for the city's youth. Set against the intensified social life of the *Unités d'Habitation* hovering in the distance, the arch of the center and the canopy of the seating area stretch the natural bowl of the stadium into the skyline without mimicking it. The chapel's frustum foregrounds the hillscape into the architectural ensemble. The chapel, the stadium, the *Unité*, and the youth center are all unified by a ground section and by a skyline held in suspense over the shape of the land and against the silhouette of the historic city. This displacement preserves the integrity of architecture in the same way the word architecture is preserved in the neologism "geo-architecture." Unlike geo-mimicry, geo-architecture maintains its tectonic integrity against the land; its distinctly concrete forms inscribe new forms of life on the surface of the earth.

Endnotes

1 An earlier and abridged version of this paper appeared in *Harvard Design Magazine* 37 (2014) under the title "Geo-Architecture: A Prehistory of an Emerging Aesthetic." The paper comes out of past research work I have been conducting through the New Geographies Lab at the Harvard Graduate School of Design and the course Geo-Architecture that I taught in the fall of 2012, and subsequently through research I have been conducting at the Massachusetts Institute of Technology. I am indebted to the students who took part in these endeavors, I am also grateful to the generous and swift minds of Jean-Louis Cohen, Mary McLeod, Christine Boyer, Ines Zalduendo, Nikos Katsikis, Roi Salgueiro, and Jarrad Morgan. Thanks go to Rania Ghosn for her insightful comments on an earlier draft. I am also grateful to the Fondation Le Corbusier, to Antoine Picon for several discussions over the years on territory and on Le Corbusier, and to Delphine Studer and Arnaud Dercelles for all their help in the detective work and paper chase.

2 Author's translation. Le Corbusier, *The Three Human Establishments,* ([Chandigarh:] Punjab Government, Department of Town & Country Planning, 1979).
In French, it reads: *"En trois termes explicites, seraient fixés les établissements humains de notre civilisation machiniste. Il est utile de connaitre la clef de cette biologie apte à réaliser les fonctions, apte à assumer les tâches. L'étude de ces trois sortes d'établissement nous permettra d'avancer vers des certitudes. L'occupation du sol pourra être reconsidérée, ce qui signifie proprement: ordonner l'espace, faire de la géographie humaine et de la géo-architecture, termes qui sont apparus petit à petit en ces temps, dans de graves mémoires, dans des rapports et des études. On réclamait une morphologie capable d'assurer les classements et des hiérarchies, de conduire les initiatives, de situer les actes."* ASCORAL, *Les Trois Etablissements Humains,* (Paris: Denoël, 1945). The French edition of 1959 (*L'Urbanisme des trois établissements humains*, ed. Jean Petit (Paris: Édition de Minuit, 1959)) and the published English translation of it is slightly different: "Here then is the outline of the task: To acknowledge the number and form of the human establishments of machinist civilization for the needs of today. To give a statute to these three establishments, to confer on them a biology taking into account the nature of the ground which receives them and the nature of men who will animate them, this is the plan that one feels right in following. The study of these three types of establishments will permit us to advance towards certitudes. The utilization of the ground can be reconsidered, that which signifies particularly: to organize space, to make human geography and geo-architecture."

3 See Patrice Noviant, "Les Trois Etablissements Humains," in *Le Corbusier, une encyclopédie*, ed. Jacques Lucan, (Paris: Centre Georges Pompidou, 1987).

4 Letter from Francois Perroux to Le Corbusier, June 9, 1944, Fondation Le Corbusier, Archive (B2-630-001). In a lecture delivered in Brussels in 1958, Le Corbusier gives the geographer, not himself, credit for enlarging the map of the mines from France to Europe. However, he refers to the map as ASCORAL 1943, which predates his first encounter with Gravier. See Fondation Le Corbusier, Lectures, U3(8)307 p14.

5 Correspondence with author. Carl W. Condit used the term to describe the TVA work in 1947 two years after its appearance in *The Three Human Establishments.*
6 Le Corbusier, *The Athens Charter* (New York: Grossman Publishers, 1973).
7 On this issue of suppressing the aesthetic in favor of the functional, see Francesco Passanti, "The Aesthetic Dimension of Le Corbusier's Urbanism," in *Josep Lluis Sert: The Architect of Urban Design,* ed. Eric Mumford and Hashim Sarkis, (New Haven and London: Yale University Press, 2008), 24–37.
8 Le Corbusier, *The Four Routes* (London: D. Dobson, 1947).
9 Passanti, "The Aesthetic Dimension."
10 See Jean Brunhes, *Géographie Humaine* (Paris: Alcan, 1925).
11 Le Corbusier, *The Three Human Establishments,* 148.
12 Pierre Saddy, "The Riches of Nature," in *Casabella* January–February, 1987, 118.
13 Jean-Louis Cohen, "Moscow: Asian Village to Metropolis," in *Le Corbusier, An Atlas of Modern Nature,* ed. Jean-Louis Cohen (New York: The Museum of Modern Art, 2013), 150–155.
14 Jean Brunhes, *Human Geography: An Attempt at a Positive Classification, Principles, and Examples* (Chicago: Rand, McNally and Co., 1920).
15 Mary McLeod, correspondence with author.
16 Le Corbusier, *The Three Human Establishments,* 149.
17 Ibid.
18 Ibid.
19 Ibid. 152.
20 Fondation Le Corbusier, Correspondence, (U3-8-307) 14.
21 Le Corbusier, *The Three Human Establishments*, 152.
22 See Hashim Sarkis, "Disoriented," in *A Second Modernism,* ed. Arindam Dutta, (Cambridge, Mass.: The MIT Press, 2014).
23 Vittorio Gregotti, "Territorial Form," in *L'Architecture d'Aujourd'hui,* 1966.
24 Constantinos A. Doxiadis and Ioannis G. Papaioannou, *Ecumenopolis: the inevitable city of the future* (Athens: Athens Center of Ekistics, 1974).
25 David Gissen, "Architecture's Geographic Turn," in *Log* 12 (2008): 59–67.
26 De Sola Morales explains: "Empty, abandoned space in which a series of occurrences have taken place seems to subjugate the eye of the urban photographer. Such urban space, which I will denote by the French expression *terrain vague*, assumes the status of fascination, the most solvent sign with which to indicate what cities are and what our experience of them is." Ignasi de Sola Morales, "Terrain Vague," in: *Anyplace*, ed. Cynthia C. Davidson (Cambridge, Mass.: MIT Press, 1995), 109.
27 To name, among others, the works of Stan Allen, Vincente Guaillart, Inaki Abalos, Rania Ghosn and El Hadi Jazairy, and Michael Jakob.
28 See Antoine Picon, "What Has Happened to Territory?" in *Territory: Architecture Beyond Environment, Architectural Design* 80, no 3 (2010), ed. David Gissen, 94–99. See also Stuart Elden, *The Birth of Territory,* (Chicago and London: The University of Chicago Press, 2013).

Kenny Cupers, Igor Demchenko

Projective Geographies Between East and West

In his 1947 book *U.R.S.S.: Haute Asie, Iran*, the French geographer Pierre George surveyed Soviet mass housing construction and regional planning with admiration.[1] George was certainly not the only leftist academic in France at this time who looked east in search of solutions to French problems. One particularly acute challenge was housing. France had come out of the Second World War with an extreme housing shortage, and the chaotic suburbanization of the interwar decades – in the form of small allotments of often self-built cottages without infrastructure or public services – was the antithesis of the orderly industrial and housing schemes that George had witnessed being built in the Soviet Union during his visits in the early 1930s.[2]

With its gargantuan projects of heavy industrialization and its pervasive planning apparatus, the Soviet Union seems to have been engaged in an exceptional experiment, testing whether the geography of the union's vast landmass could be remade in the image of a well-oiled production machine. Here, the discipline of geography was no longer just the description of natural features or human activities on the surface of the earth; it actively contributed to comprehensive planning at a new regional and even continental scale. Nevertheless, such projective geography – a design approach as opposed to descriptive science – was developed not only in the Soviet Union. From the 1940s to the 1970s, planners, architects, and a range of new kinds of experts in the so-called First World as well as the Second World expanded their ambitions from designing housing, neighborhoods, and cities to reshaping the national geography at large. This explicitly geographic register of design, in which nature was first and foremost a resource to exploit, can be considered a paradigmatic product of the Cold War world order: a consequence of the global proliferation and institutionalization of modernism and a tool of economic development and international competition.

French planning experts, even if they were not able to put territorial design fully into practice, articulated this geographic register most explicitly, using the term *géographie volontaire*. According to the geographer Jean Labasse, *géographie volontaire* was a scientific approach born out of the growing realization, from the 1930s onward, that the "geography of laissez-faire capitalism had failed." The ultimate goal of *géographie volontaire* then was to organize private enterprise geographically, through the "controlled evolution of landscapes."[3] But where did French geographers stand in relation to their Soviet colleagues who restructured territory for the state-run economy? How was projective geography – as theory and as practice – shaped by the intertwined political realities of East and West? And what did the massive projects of territorial design do to the architectural expertise essential for turning the chimera of development into facts on the ground under both democratic and authoritarian regimes?[4]

Gestations

Projective geography offers a particular mode of understanding and making territory, one in which the state assumes an unquestionable centrality. How did this approach develop? In the second half of the nineteenth century, a new regime of empire building emerged through territorial expansion and consolidation, but only after the Second World War did that internal territorial development, under the influence of modernist precepts, become the quantifiable measure of state-led modernization. In the 1920s, modernist architecture and planning had begun to promote the use of objective parameters for design. From the 1920s until the 1950s, state planners gradually harnessed this approach to present territorial development as the vehicle of economic and social progress.

In the Soviet Union, projective geography was initially both implicit and central to the new communist state. Regional planning informed by descriptive geography and aiming at the reconstruction of the Soviet Union into a uniformly developed industrialized nation was born out of the GOELRO plan.[5] This was an ambitious scheme for the electrification of Russia drafted under the personal supervision of Vladimir Lenin in the early 1920s. The plan was both a technocratic modernization project and a blueprint for regional planning masterminded by Ivan Aleksandrov (1881–1954) and Nikolai Kolosovskii (1891–1954). These geographers, with a background in railroad engineering, proposed a projective and proactive approach to regions as an

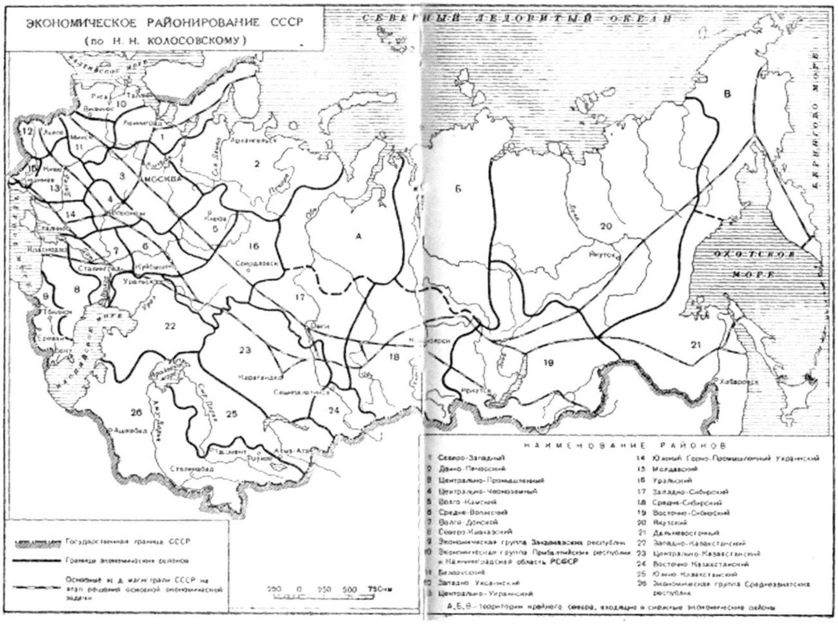

fig. 1 Economic regions of the USSR according to N. N. Kolosovskii (#19 is the East-Siberian Region). Source: Kolosovskii, N. N., *Osnovy ekonomicheskogo raionirovaniia* (Moscow: Gospolitizdat, 1958), 120–1.

instrument of scientifically informed territorial development.[6] However, not until the 1950s did the Soviet state acquire enough economic stamina and expertise to realize its vision (fig. 1).

The science of economic regionalization, associated since the 1960s with the name of Nikolai Kolosovskii, whose *Foundations of Economic Regionalization* (1958) and *Theory of Economic Regionalization* (1969) defined and framed the discipline, is hardly mentioned in the context of post-Stalinist urban planning and prefab construction – and for good reason.[7] First, Kolosovskii passed away in 1954 just a year after Joseph Stalin and therefore could not envision the role of modernist design in the realization of his schemes for the economic development of Siberia, northern Kazakhstan, and the Russian Far East that he had advocated since the 1920s. Second, and more important, even though his students and other proponents of economic regionalization played a decisive role within Gosplan, the central planning agency of the Soviet Union, unlike Stalin's government they never dictated to architects and urban planners the exact formal parameters of urban settlements (beyond the most basic demographic requirements) – needed to house the workforce that was transported to regions east of the Urals.

At the same time, several important axiomatic moves and pragmatic procedures within the discipline of economic regionalization allowed for the reshaping of functionalist design and planning principles to such an extent that by the 1980s Soviet planning had almost lost its connection with the original ideas of the *Congrès Internationaux d'Architecture Moderne* (CIAM; International Congresses of Modern Architecture) or even Nikolai Miliutin's Sotsgorod (1930) – an earlier attempt at merging architectural modernism with Soviet industrial planning. Above all, the goal of economic regionalization was to locate alternative sources of raw materials and energy for Soviet industry, thus securing the Soviet economy from an overdependence upon its industrially developed western regions, which bordered the 'imperialist', capitalist, and inevitably hostile Western Europe. (The Donbass in eastern Ukraine had already twice been occupied by the Germans – first in 1918 and again during World War II.)[8] This goal necessitated the introduction of mining, hydroelectric construction, and heavy industry into sparsely populated territories gridded by Kolosovskii into regions (raiony) – economic rather than administrative units – based on the available natural resources (primarily metal ores, but also timber, arable soils, phosphates, etc.) and types of energy (coal, oil, or hydroelectric power).

Siberia, northern Kazakhstan, and the Far East suffered from a deficit of demographic resources – that is, a workforce – which, therefore, had to be imported from the western regions of the Soviet Union. But whereas before Stalin's death the workforce was transferred East mostly as forced labor (urban settlements attached to new industries thus constituted an ugly combination of "high style" palaces for the administrative elite and slums – barracks and dugouts – for workers), the Khrushchev and Brezhnev governments hired free labor and stimulated its move across the Urals by offering simple apartments in functionalist microrayons (clusters for residential neighborhoods with separate service facilities) designed and planned by the new post-Stalinist generation of Soviet modernists. Yet in their designs they had to take into account the climate of the newly developed regions, the hectic pace of construction, and the numerous limitations of the Soviet planned economy.

In France, the idea of projective geography can be traced to the early 1930s. In the wake of the 1929 economic crisis, political elites marshaled older technocratic ideas as a way of overcoming the failures of capitalism. They were guided by a particular tradition of political thought, rooted in Saint-Simonianism, which advocated resolute leadership in the form of neutral expertise. Cast in direct opposition to the ideology of economic liberalism and nourished by the crisis of parliamentary politics during the 1930s, *planisme*, or expert planning, found enthusiastic supporters – including modern architects such as Le Corbusier – but could not be put into practice until wartime, when the authoritarian, conservative, and anti-Semitic government of Vichy took it on. One of that regime's most urgent concerns – especially after the bombardments of the Renault factories in the suburbs of Paris in 1942 and 1943 – was what experts called "industrial congestion." The concentration of key industries and infrastructure around the capital was a danger to national military and economic interests and required a comprehensive relocation of industry at the scale of the French hexagon. Furthermore, this industrial and military strategy could be linked to the modernization of rural France, another key point in the Vichy government's agenda. To this end, the government commissioned a team of experts, led by engineer and businessman Gabriel Dessus and including Pierre George. Their work was published in 1949 as *Matériaux pour une géographie volontaire* (Materials for a Volitional Geography).[9] The book, firmly establishing the notion of *géographie volontaire* in French political culture, expounded a theory for the geographic localization of French industry that was intricately linked to mass housing construction. Partially inspired by Le Corbusier, the authors left little doubt as to who would bear this rationality and its executive power: the centralized state.

After Liberation, the French government distanced itself from Vichy but continued to rely on the idea of expert planning for postwar reconstruction and economic development. France became a "planning state" in which national pride and economic modernization went hand in hand. Under the influence of Jean Monnet, the economist and diplomat who would later become one of the main architects of the European Union, planning became the product of enlightened bureaucracy, crafted behind the scenes of public politics. In 1946, the Commissariat général du Plan (CGP, or Plan Commission), a governmental think tank established by Monnet, was charged with the creation of a detailed five-year plan for industrial modernization.

This state apparatus brought the disciplines of geography, planning, and architecture unparalleled opportunity. Even though experts' political leanings diverged widely – from Communist to far right – the postwar state offered a key platform of exchange between these different forms of expertise. Eugène Claudius-Petit, minister of reconstruction and urbanism from 1948 until 1953, further promoted *géographie volontaire* with his *Plan national d'aménagement du territoire* (National Plan for Territorial Planning). Advocating for a harmonious distribution of people and activities over the national territory, his plan proposed a radical decentralization of industry away from the Paris region. National economic development could be achieved only through such geographic volition, Claudius-Petit and his experts argued. Their plan was inspired not only by decentralist geography but by the ideas of CIAM and Le Corbusier in particular. In 1945, Claudius-Petit and Le Corbusier visited the projects of the Tennessee Valley Authority together, and both were deeply influenced by the experience. *Géographie volontaire* required not only geographic knowledge but architectural vision, even if the relationship between international modernism and French state-led planning remained indirect until the 1950s, when projective geography finally came to shape large-scale realizations in both East and West.

The Territorial Production Complex

After Stalin, projective geography in the Soviet Union took the form of the territorial production complex. This concept, propagated by Gosplan, was first introduced by Kolosovskii, although he himself preferred the term "combinate" ("kombinat" in Russian).[10] The territorial production complex was intended to streamline the flow of raw materials, energy, and labor within a geographically limited area usually defined by a locally specific type of mineral resource. In many ways the territorial production complex replaced the idea of a city in the mind of Soviet urban planners, much in line with Le Corbusier's dismissal of a city in favor of a geographically defined region, as expressed in the Athens Charter. However, if for Le Corbusier a region was a product of natural topography's ability to contain population, Soviet planners perceived it through the prism of production cycles planned and often constructed before the arrival of the workforce. Thus, for example, Kolosovskii pointed to hydroelectricity in the East Siberian Region as a core natural resource that would generate several combinates; that is, the combination of electric power generation with the production of timber and aluminum (fig. 2). The cascade of hydroelectric power plants built on Angara River and its tributaries primarily in the 1960s and the 1970s after his death supplied a general scheme for the distribution of urban settlements within the region.

The parameters of the new urban settlements built or radically expanded one after another east of the Urals in the last three decades of the Soviet era were defined by central and local institutes of planning. In every specific case those institutes used the plans for prospective industrial development outlined by Gosplan as a point of departure and combined them with the data on local climate, soils, and available and projected population. Generally, the institutes of planning did not publicize their work, and actual design and planning procedures were presented to the public as an outcome of scientifically defined algorithms. One exceptional case was Tselinograd (currently Astana) in northern Kazakhstan, for which in 1964 the Moscow-based Central Scientific-Research Institute of Urban Planning (TsNIIP Gradostroitelstva) published a detailed survey of its planned radical expansion. In 1961 the small colonial town of Akmolinsk was renamed the City of

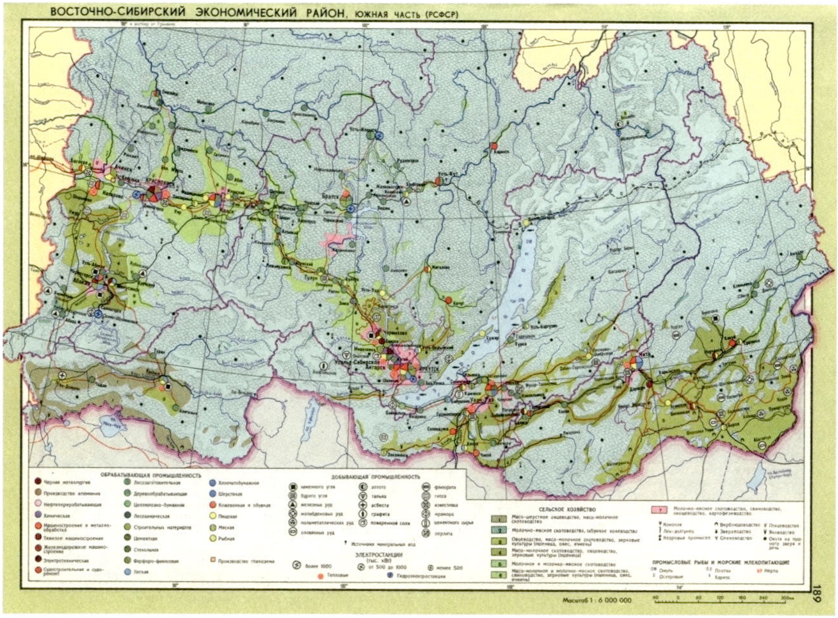

fig. 2 East-Siberian economic region. Southern part (RSFSR). Source: *Atlas SSSR* (Moscow, 1983), 189.

Virgin Lands (Tselinograd) and made a capital of the new region patronized by Nikita Khrushchev, who hoped that northern Kazakhstan would become a new center of wheat production; its population was expected to increase from 115,000 in 1961 to half a million in the next two decades.[11] The elevated status of the new regional center stimulated the publication of its planning documentation[12] (fig. 3).

Soviet planners expected that the industrial profile of Tselininograd would be defined by its central location within a newly projected wheat-growing region that would rely on the heavy mechanization of agricultural production. Hence the city was to house the factories and workshops that either repaired agricultural machinery or produced the replacement parts for them. Besides, Tselinograd served as a center for the initial processing of agricultural goods and had two textile factories. The planners made every effort to structure both industrial and residential zones along two parallel lines separated by a narrow green belt. Here they were apparently inspired by the Athens Charter and Miliutin's ideas of a linear city – without quoting either. What made their approach to planning radically different from that of Le Corbusier was the pragmatic distinction between the residential and the recreating zones, with the latter placed along the river that defined the linear expansion of the urbanized area. A point of significant concern was the

fig. 3 The future of Tselinograd as imagined in the early 1960s. Source: *Tselinograd (opyt proektirovshchika)* (Moscow: Stroiizdat, 1964), 60.

minimization of public transportation usage. Every segment of the residential zone had to have pedestrian access both to corresponding production area and to the recreation zone.

The increased density of residential areas organized in microrayons with local schools, kindergartens, policlinics, food stores, and service centers provided protection from the strong winds of the northern steppes and created pockets in which trees and shrubs could grow. Due to the intentional suppression and thus lack of private initiative that was characteristic in the Khrushchev years, the planners had to go into the smallest details when calculating the number of facilities – shops, restaurants, and so on – per inhabitant based on the estimated number of active workers and dependents expected to flow into the new center. The same procedure applied to public transportation. Private car ownership was expected to be restricted – not exceeding one car per 20 people by 1980. Leisure facilities were not limited to the immediate recreation zone but extended into the region forming a network of camps, tourist centers, and sanatoria intended at improving the hygienic and health conditions of industrial workers stuck between fairly densely populated residential quarters and the industrial zone. The population density of historic Akmolinsk would be increased as existing one- and two-story houses were demolished and new five-story apartment blocks were constructed in their place, essentially turning the old part of the city into another microrayon with some additional administrative and cultural functions. By increasing the density, the planners of Tselinograd hoped to save on costs when building the new infrastructure (fig. 4).

The reality of Soviet planning for the new urban settlements in the prospective regions was equally far from the utopia of Ebenezer Howard's garden city and the modernist vision of the Athens Charter. Returning to the East Siberian Region advocated by Kolosovskii and moving forward in time to the

fig. 4 Tselinograd (Astana) in 2009. Photo: Igor Demchenko.

fig. 5 Residential quarters of Ust-Ilimsk in 1977. Source: Günter Mosler, *Sibirien 1977–1978. Ein DDR-Auslandskader erzählt* (Engelsdorfer Verlag, 2013), 39.

mid-1970s, we see a microrayon in Ust-Ilimsk provisionally constructed for the pulp combinate powered by Angara River[13] (fig. 5). Ust-Ilimsk was built from scratch in the middle of taiga. The town was photographed by the East German engineer Günter Mosler, who was contracted by the Soviet Union to supervise a brigade of German youth willing to contribute their labor to the development of Siberia. Its apartment blocks are distinctively uniform, which is explained by the absence of a housing market in the Soviet Union. Design is reduced to pure function, while the role of an architect is limited to the climatically sensitive arrangement of the blocks. Thus, by the 1970s the mass production of urban settlements became an aspect of economic regionalization.

Projective geography, institutionalized as the science of economic regionalization (raionirovanie) at the Geography Department of Moscow State University, provided opportunities for urban planners and architects and simultaneously constrained them. The giant machinery of territorial production complexes necessitated functional solutions for housing the workforce imported to the newly developed regions. Modernist functionalism, initially

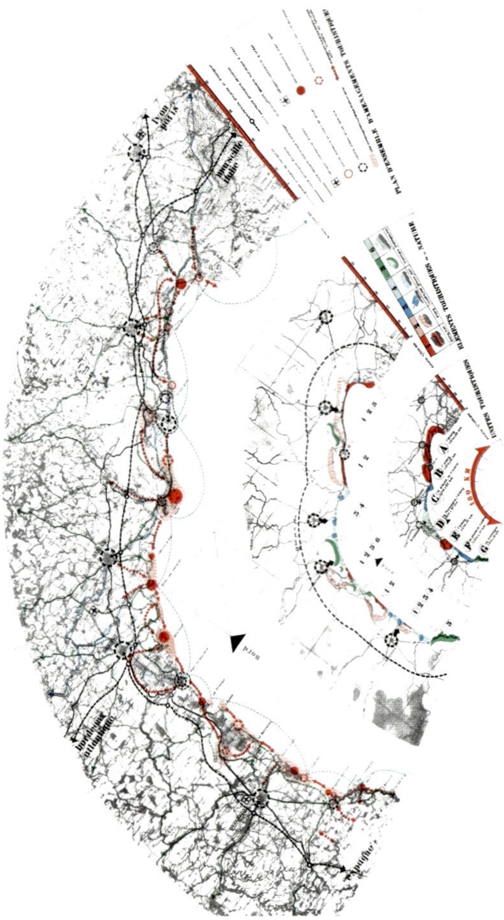

fig. 6 The overall plan for the development of the Languedoc-Roussillon into a mass tourism region (Source: *Urbanisme* 86 (1965): 30).

intended to improve dwelling conditions, was processed and utilized by the Soviet system of projective planning, resulting in the complete evaporation of its original messianic spirit embodied in the figure of an architect-creator. Overtaken by anonymous planning institutes, the design of new residential neighborhoods was reduced to algorithms, genetically related to the ideas of CIAM and the dreams of the Russian avant-garde, but simplified, serialized, and trivialized to ensure reproducibility.

Géographie volontaire

In France, one of the first large-scale realizations of *géographie volontaire* was the work of the *Délégation à l'aménagement du territoire et à l'action regional* or DATAR (Delegation for Territorial Planning and Regional Action). Created in 1963 and populated by the country's powerful corps of engineers, it became France's centralized body for regional planning in the following decades. One

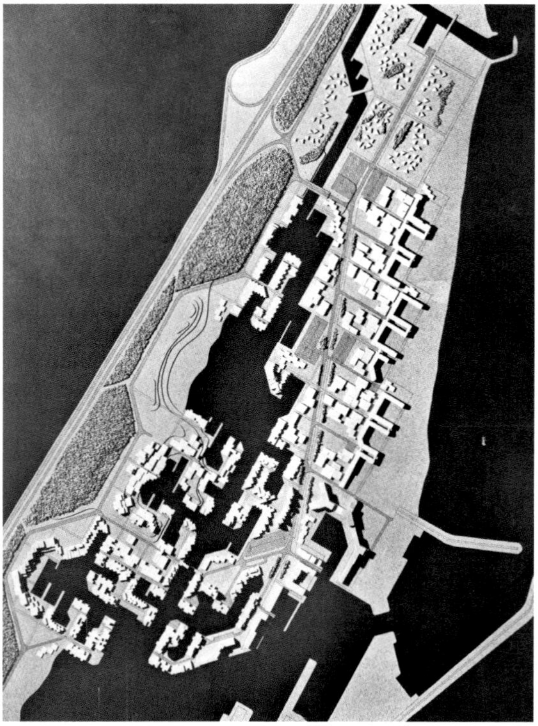

fig. 7 Leucate-Le Barcarès by Georges Candilis (Source: *Techniques et Architecture* 31, 2 (1969): 94).

of its first projects was the development of the Languedoc-Roussillon into a tourist region. Compared to the wealthy and densely populated Côte d'Azur, the western side of the French Mediterranean coast was a relatively unpopulated swampy area suffering from depopulation and economic decline. DATAR understood this region to be a potential for the state-led development of mass tourism (fig. 6). The modernist architecture of new tourist resorts, such as Jean Balladur's La Grande Motte or Georges Candilis' Leucate–Le Barcarès (fig. 7), represented the ambition to design comprehensive regional territories, inclusive of highways, artificial pleasure ports, camping grounds, and mosquito removal measures. In order to realize such enormous and complex projects, planners had to stave off land speculation by secretly buying up vast amounts of land through intermediaries. This was exactly the type of situation for which *géographie volontaire* could offer a particular logic for managing private development territorially; it was a geography that viewed territory as a function of both state intervention and the dynamics of a market economy. That meant accepting both the omnipresence of the state and surplus value as the basic motor of territorial development. While regional balance could never be permanently achieved because of the inherent dynamics of capitalist development, it needed to be continually pursued through state intervention.

This idea of soft guidance corresponded to the ideology of state planning, which went back to the mid-1940s when the national Monnet Plan had set the basic parameters for postwar reconstruction.

In parallel with these projects for regional development, the French government focused its efforts on the decentralization of Paris, following earlier proposals such as Claudius-Petit's. To this end, Charles de Gaulle launched the *villes nouvelles* project in 1965. Building on the precedent of the British and Scandinavian New Towns, which French planners studied carefully, the *villes nouvelles* project aimed to decentralize Paris and to promote regional development by creating a series of new, independent cities in the countryside. Five were eventually constructed in the Paris region and four in the provinces (fig. 8). In contrast to the Soviet Union, transportation and mobility was at the forefront of planners' concerns. By the mid-1960s, modern housing estates built in the suburbs of Paris were criticized for their lack of public facilities and, in particular, the lack of public transportation. The *villes nouvelles* were planned in conjunction with a new regional express network, the RER, but would also be connected to the new highway network that was being built at that time. Another concern for planners was mono-functional zoning. To avoid building bedroom suburbs, they aimed to integrate housing with commercial and other functions. In contrast to Soviet planners, however, they focused on tertiary economic development rather than heavy industry. Their concern was ultimately with the territorial organization of consumption rather than production: *géographie volontaire* differed from projective geography in the Soviet Union in that the geographic exploitation of natural resources was focused on the creation of new landscapes of dwelling, mobility, and leisure rather than on mineral or other forms of industrial extraction.

The resulting concepts and methods of *villes nouvelles* planning were "softer" than their Soviet counterparts and at the same time more expansive than the conventional master plans that had continued to shape urban development in France. This is perhaps not surprising since planning by the late 1960s had become a multi-disciplinary field, fundamentally reshaped by the social sciences. While such planning was still to be geographically volitional, it also needed to be realistic, meaning it had to take as its basis the dynamics of the market, and thus consumer choice in the urbanization process. Consequently, planning could no longer revolve around a static master plan. Designers faced the complexity of an actual geography rather than an imagined one. Even though projects were no longer generated in a tabula rasa, they were inflated to the scale of ever-larger swaths of territory. Instead of the imposition of a set of functional zones allocated to specific human activities on empty land, the existing territory was reinterpreted as a field

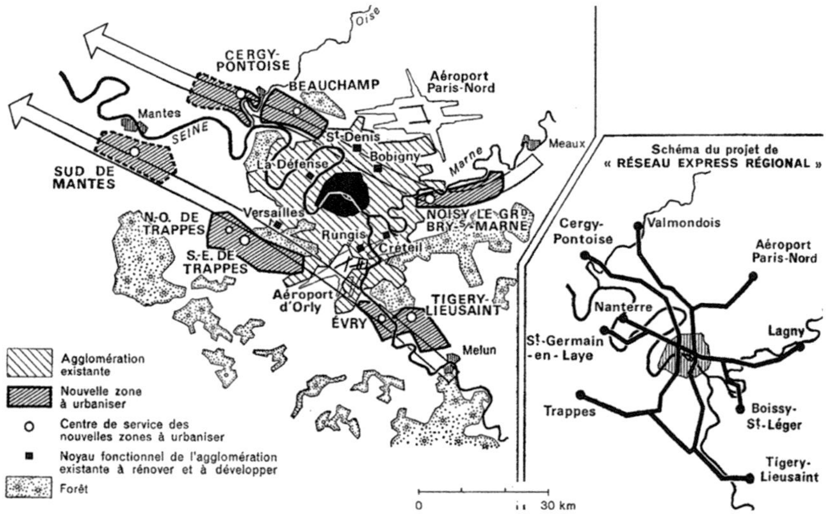

fig. 8 The *villes nouvelles* for the Paris region, integrated with the new RER public transportation network (Source: Jean Vaujour, Le plus grand Paris, Paris, PUF, 1970).

of relations and connections, force lines and attraction poles. Only such an approach would be able to efficiently reorganize very large areas of suburban or exurban land while inserting entirely new forms of urbanity that could compete with the center of Paris.

For the New Town of Evry in the exurban outskirts of Paris, this approach amounted to the large-scale and flexible programming of new development zones distributed in the midst of existing suburban developments. For the New Town of Cergy-Pontoise, it meant drawing up an *armature urbaine* (urban armature) for the existing territory, which included the old village of Pontoise, nearby forests, and an old river bend turned into a lake. A similar approach characterized the New Town of Trappes, later renamed Saint-Quentin-en-Yvelines (fig. 9). Planners reinterpreted existing landscape features as new recreational facilities that became central elements in the New Town's projected identity.

When these New Towns were built half a decade later during the 1970s, the look of some of the proposals had changed dramatically, even if their conceptual underpinnings were the same. The urban centers of New Towns like Cergy, for instance, were still megastructures, but they downplayed that fact in various ways. During the 1970s, experts and the general public alike fundamentally criticized the kinds of large-scale urbanism sponsored by the centralized state in collaboration with large private developers. They saw the New Towns as the last gasp of such unwarranted megalomania. Where they

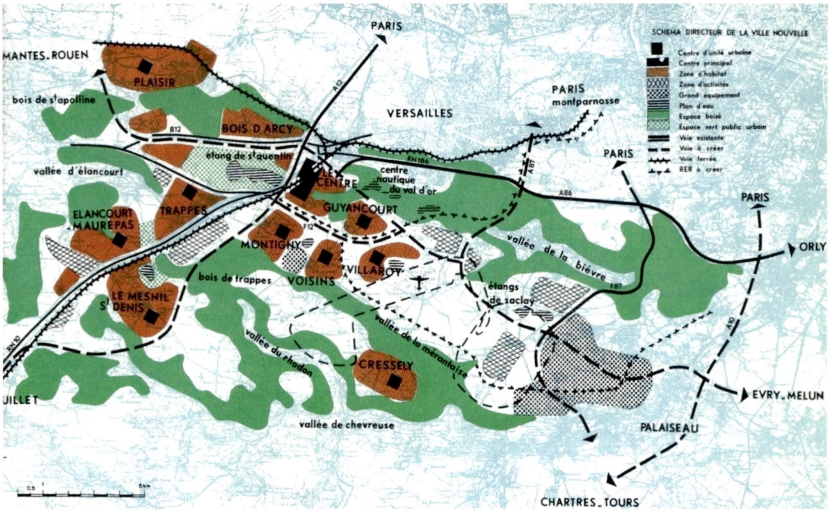

fig. 9 Structural plan of 1970 for the New Town of Trappes (Saint-Quentin-en-Yvelines) (Source: *Techniques et Architecture* 32, 5 (1970): 46).

could, planners thus cloaked their projects – many of which were already underway – in a new aesthetic, informed by a desire for more intimate environments and for more attention to the site and the historic urban fabric of the city. Based on architectural-modernist concepts such as the vertical separation of vehicular and pedestrian traffic, the center of Cergy-Préfecture was still a single architectural environment united by a plinth – an artificial territory dedicated only to pedestrians, two stories above the existing ground. But with a fine-grained articulation of diverse programs distributed on top of its artificial topography, designers meant to give the new center an intimate scale and the characteristics of "Latin" inner-city neighborhoods like those of central Paris (fig. 10). Despite these transformations, the *villes nouvelles* and the regional planning and development policies of DATAR constitute the belated actualization of *géographie volontaire* in France, even if fundamental gaps separated planners' ambitions from their real impact on urban and regional change.

Conclusion

Soviet geographers seem to have remained generally unaware of *géographie volontaire*. They tended to look farther west than France, at American planning, even if planners there remained far more skeptical about the civilizing powers of the centralized state than their French colleagues. American liberalism and perceived "opportunism" provoked strong reactions among Soviet planners. For instance, in 1966, Abram Probst (1903–1976), a leading

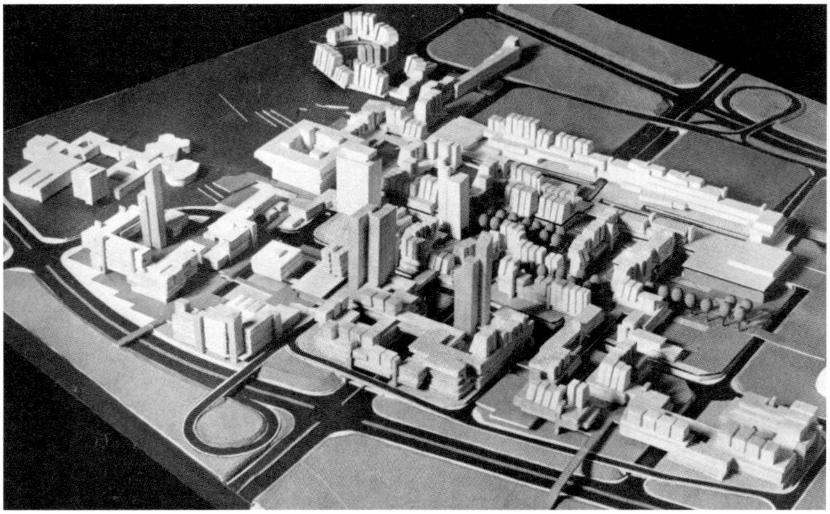

fig. 10 Model of the urban center of Cergy-Préfecture in 1970 (Source: *Techniques et Architecture* 32, 5 (1970): 54).

Soviet economic geographer and Gosplan bureaucrat, in an introduction to the Russian translation of Walter Isard's *Methods of Regional Analysis* (1960), wrote: "[Isard] proceeds from the supremacy of the demand (sales) over the production even though it is completely obvious that consumption is defined by the production, since people can only consume what has already been produced [...] Therefore it is incorrect to point exclusively at the dynamics and location of the demand for the objects of personal consumption as the direct first cause of the dynamics of development and particularly the territorial placement of the production."[14] Thus, Probst – echoing the French geographers – insisted on the volitional and non-descriptive nature of regional planning; and yet he highly valued the mathematical statistics of inner- and inter-regional exchange developed by the American economist and explicitly advised Soviet planners to learn from him. Regional planning clearly spanned the Cold War ideological divide; at least in its technocratic modes.

Considering the Soviet Union's continued reliance on heavy industrialization and France's shift towards a postindustrial society in the 1960s and 1970s, it is not surprising that one of the key differences in Eastern versus Western projective geographies was the attitude towards production and consumption. While French planners in the 1940s still dreamt of reorganizing industrial production on a national territorial scale, the next generation of planners in the 1960s focused almost entirely on consumption and mobility. Their neglect of issues of production and employment was arguably also one of the factors in the gradual downfall of the *villes nouvelles*, some of which suffered the same social problems as the modern housing estates that preceded them. France's combination of liberal capitalism with centralized planning shaped *géographie volontaire* as an attempt to marry state volition with individual freedom and consumption, a tension that came to characterize French New Town designs as they were gradually being conceived, revised, and ultimately built. Soviet projective geography, by contrast, remained production-oriented until the dissolution of the Soviet Union in 1991.

In contrast to French planners' increasing focus on consumption, Soviet territorial design remained elevated above the "petty" needs of citizens, an approach that tended to trivialize architectural modernism. The experimental modernism of French architects and urban planners reflected a much more nuanced culture of design, never completely dissociated from an older, bourgeois respect for the customer – even when the figure of an individual commissioner was replaced by the state. Despite such differences, however, projective geography was fundamentally the product of transnational exchange – as when Le Corbusier and Claudius-Petit visited the built projects of the Tennessee Valley Authority, Pierre George studied Soviet planning, and Soviet planners themselves looked west, adopting both the modernist approaches of CIAM and the American methods of industrial and regional development.

Endnotes

1 Pierre George, *U.R.S.S.: Haute Asie, Iran* (Paris, Presses universitaires de France, 1947).

2 See: Frédéric Dufaux, "La naissance de 'grandioses ensembles': Le regard distancié des géographes français sur la métamorphose urbaine des années 1950–1960," in: *Le monde des grands ensembles*, eds. Frédéric Dufaux and Annie Fourcaut (Paris: Créaphis, 2004): 63–73; 68.

3 Jean Labasse, *L'organisation de l'espace: Éléments de géographie volontaire* (Paris: Hermann, 1966): 15, 13.

4 Our analysis of the French material relies on: Kenny Cupers, (2016) "Géographie Volontaire and the Territorial Logic of Architecture," in *Architectural Histories* 4 (1): 1–13 (p. 3), DOI: http://dx.doi.org/10.5334/ah.209. The Soviet material was researched by Igor Demchenko.

5 For the early history of geographers' involvement in regional planning see N. N. Kolosovskii, "Razmeshchenie proizvoditelnykh sil SSSR i zadachi Akademii nauk" (The distribution of production forces of the USSR and the goals of the Academy of Sciences) in idem, *Osnovy ekonomicheskogo raionirovaniia* (Foundations of economic zoning) (Moscow: Gospolitizdat, 1958), 49–59.

6 See N. N. Kazanskii, "N. N. Kolosovskii v nauke i zhizni" (N. N. Kolosovskii in life and work) in N. N. Kolosovskii, *Izbranannye trudy* (Selected works) (Smolensk: Oikumena, 2006), 10–25.

7 With Diana Kurkovsky-West's doctoral dissertation *CyberSovietica: Planning, Design, and the Cybernetics of Soviet Space, 1954–1986* (Princeton University, 2013) being the only notable exception.

8 Kolosovskii, *Teoriia ekonomicheskogo raionirovaniia* (1969), 88.

9 Gabriel Dessus, Pierre George, and Jacques Weulersse, *Matériaux pour une géographie volontaire de l'industrie française* (Paris: Armand Colin, 1949).

10 See N. N. Kolosovskii, "Budushchee Uralo-Kuznetskogo kombinata" (The future of Urals-Kuznetsk industrial complex), first published in 1932; selected chapters. *Prostranstvennaia ekonomika*, 4 (2009): 125–141 and idem, *Osnovy ekonomicheskogo raionirovaniia* (1958), 133–175.

11 A. F. Dubitskii, *Gorod na Ishime* (The city upon Ishim) (Alma-Ata: Kazakhstan, 1986), 100.

12 V. A. Shkvarikov et al. eds., *Tselinograd (opyt proektirovshchika)* (Tselinograd (planner's experience)) (Moscow: Stroiizdat, 1964).

13 Günter Mosler, *Sibirien 1977–1978. Ein DDR-Auslandskader erzählt* (Engelsdorfer Verlag, 2013).

14 Walter Isard, *Metody regionalnogo analiza: vvedenie v nauku o regionakh* (Russian translation of Walter Isard, *Methods of Regional Analysis: An Introduction to Regional Science* (New York: Press of the Massachusetts Institute of Technology 1960)); with an introduction of Abram E. Probst (Moscow: Progress, 1966), 8–9.

Karl R. Kegler

Towards the Functional Society: Paradigm Shifts in the Regional Planning of West and East Germany

Large-scale planning is a phenomenon of modern, knowledge-based industrial societies. Historically, institutionalized regional (and economical) planning evolved in Europe, the United States and the Soviet Union during the interwar period.[1] Based on earlier experience and their respective political orientations after the Second World War, the European nations took different paths into the politics of planning. The countries under Soviet influence set up a system of comprehensive state-directed programming of the economy.[2] In Western Europe, countries like France and the United Kingdom adopted a number of large-scale government planning programs in the first decades after the war, while for a longer period the governments of the democratic Federal Republic of Germany (FRG, or West Germany) and Italy regarded economic planning as an oppressive socialist strategy virtually incompatible with a free market and a democratic society. Nevertheless, in West Germany a number of large-scale planning schemes also came into being, but interestingly most of these programs evolved more than two decades after the war in the context of changed economic, social and political conditions.

Strategies of planning are based on hypotheses about key factors and driving powers within modern societies; as a consequence, regional planning may be understood as a system of basic ideas about economic and social demands, and about the effects and the adequate spacial expression of such powers in the development of the territory. Seen in this way, development programs for housing, industry and infrastructure are not mere projects of architecture but designs for life within complex systems of production, consumption, mobility, technology and the interrelation between these factors as it appeared to planners and experts in a certain historical situation. Changes in planning programs are indicators, accordingly, of changes in ideas about the nature of society, economy and development. This gives special interest to the study of the shifts in government planning systems as they took place in East and West Germany in the decades after 1960.

For West Germany, 1965 marks an important turning point for regional planning on a legal and institutional level. In this year, the Federal Regional Planning Act (*Raumordnungsgesetz*) was passed by parliament after fifteen years of political debate, and triggered more than a decade of intensive regional-planning activities in the federal states of West Germany, and on the federal level itself. Four years later, the new social-liberal government of chancellor Willi Brandt that assumed power in 1969 embraced the idea of a politics of planning and programming for social and economic change on a scientific basis.[3] This development reached a certain climax with the Federal Regional Planning Program (*Bundesraumordnungsprogramm*) of 1975[4] – a unique program of this kind in West Germany. Looking back, a number of historians have described the late 1960s and 1970s as a period of "planning euphoria" in the Federal Republic.[5] However, the Federal Regional Planning Program never reached its highly touted objectives and was therefore not continued.[6]

This changed attitude toward planning in West Germany had been preceded by changes in the politics of planning in the eastern German state. A few years earlier, between 1963 and 1970, the established model of centralized economic planning in the socialist German Democratic Republic (GDR, or East Germany) had experienced a period of reform with the so-called New Economic System (*Neues Ökonomisches System*, or NES). This new system allowed certain branches of the economy a broader space for local decision-making with respect to reaching their production targets; the economic units were even allowed to gain profit for the financing of future investments and innovations within the larger framework of the planned economy. The lack of substantial economic success with this experiment of reform, the critique of supporters of centralized economic programming and, ultimately, the implications of Soviet and Warsaw Pact intervention in Czechoslovakia in 1968 brought this idea of a more open form of planned economy to an end and forced the East German leader and Chairman of the GDR State Council Walter Ulbricht to retire in 1971, which resulted in Erich Honecker taking power as Ulbricht's successor.[7]

Regional Planning in the Federal Republic of Germany

Regional planning as a scientific discipline emerged in the first half of the twentieth century as a response to repeated crises. A leading generation of planners, which would later hold important positions in East and West Germany, witnessed the economic and social collapse of their country in 1919 and then again in 1945, and had experienced the global depression of the 1930s. Important principles of spatial planning in the German Empire, then later in West Germany – the critique of agglomeration, decentralization politics, the promotion of self-sufficiency and local economic units – have their roots in this historical background. Territorial planning in Germany first became successful as a new academic discipline, and then was institutionalized in the interwar period as a means of national autarky to cope with unpredictable ups and downs of global economy and global crisis.[8]

The professional community of regional planners in West Germany adhered for a very long time to principles and ideas developed in the interwar period.[9] Though industrialized and urbanized concentrations were the economic backbone of West Germany, the negative effects of imbalanced industrialization dominated planning discourses into the 1960s. In 1961, the so-called Expert Commission's Report on Regional Planning (*Sachverständigenausschuss für Raumordnung*) became one of the important stepping stones that led to the Federal Regional Planning Act of 1965. The text of the commission's report stressed that although urban and industrial agglomerations had their value in the overall system of settlements, "the limitation of concentration and the promotion of decentralization [was] still urgently needed."[10] It argued that agglomerations as "unilateral spatial positions of power must be rejected"[11] in the same way that economic monopolies had to be avoided in a market economy. Antagonism between strongly industrialized areas and the rest of the country, especially, was seen as a major reason for the active role of the state in regional planning. As a kind of visual translation of this thesis, a suggestive map of the commission's report showed agglomerated centers of production in Germany as malignant black proliferations virtually emitting a damaging radiation on the countryside, while dispersed industries covered the country like soot or filth (fig. 1).[12]

Such a critique of industrialized agglomerations – a more or less common point of view among planning experts of the time – had evolved out of earlier statements. In the initial postwar years, many professional planners in West Germany had argued that decentralization of industry was the best strategy to answer the challenges of the future. This position could claim a number of important supporting reasons: bad living conditions and pollution in the centers of agglomeration, and the threat of the kind of industrial crisis

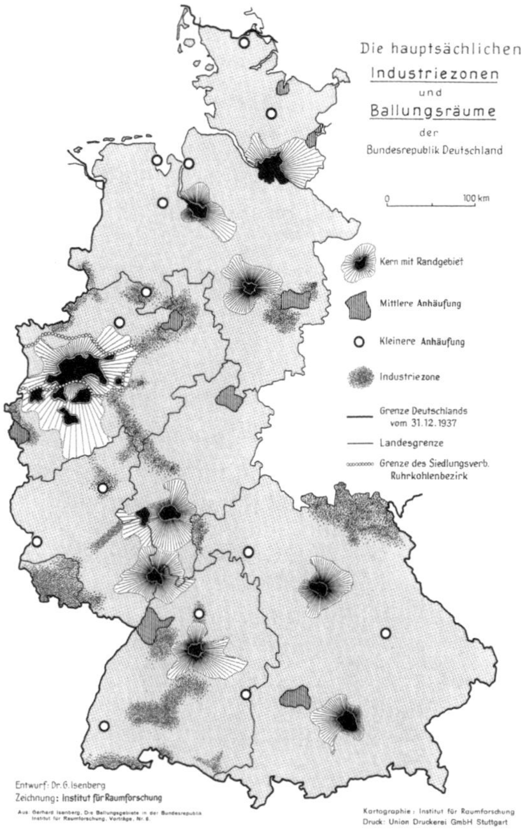

fig. 1 Gerhard Isenberg, The Main Industrial Districts and Agglomerations of the Federal Republic of Germany, 1961. "Sachverständigenausschuss für Raumordnung," *Die Raumordnung in der Bundesrepublik Deutschland*, map 2.

that most of these planners had witnessed in their own lives when industrial centers had suffered the highest rates of unemployment in the worldwide depression of the 1930s, and had then suffered inadequate food supplies again in the initial period after the war.

The dominant approach in regional-planning politics for meeting such problems was the idea of restructuring seemingly unordered relations in the gravitation field of large industrial agglomerations into an ordered hierarchy of settlements aligned to local or regional centers that should be independent economic units (fig. 2). In this way unordered, unclear and "inefficient" interrelations between settlements of different types and sizes would also be redefined in a clear and supposedly efficient way. An exponent of this school of thought was Hans Staubach (1894–1968), who had been the leading regional planner of the district of Hesse-Nassau in the early 1940s and then in West Germany had become a high-ranking official in the planning administration of the state of Baden-Württemberg. During the reconstruction period, Staubach proposed a number of strategies for decentralization in order to use

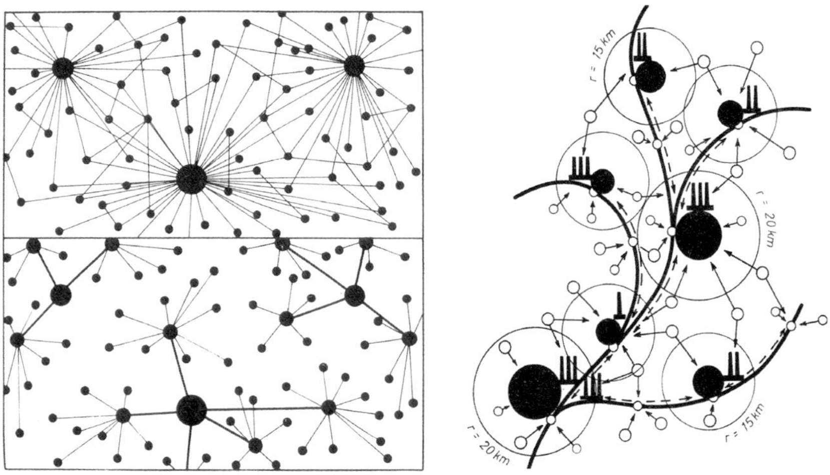

fig. 2 Left: Unordered and Ordered Settlement Patterns. Heinz Baumann, "Gezielte Entwicklung ländlicher Gemeinden in Schleswig-Holstein," in *Das Unternehmen Landentwicklung. Programm Nord. Eiderraum*, ed. Claus Bielfeldt (Kiel: Agrarsoziale Gesellschaft, 1967), 272–280 (p. 272).

Right: Organic Distribution of Places of Work and Residence, Catchment Areas and Commuter Routes. Hermann Staubach, *Siedlungslenkung und Raumordnung* (Hanover: Jänecke, 1963), ill. 9. Staubach at that time advocated for a strategy of decentralization along lines of individual traffic.

the devastation of German cities as an opportunity for a new distribution of the population.[13] In 1963, he argued that the progress and achievements of modern traffic would help establish such a pattern of settlements focused on decentralized centers of work and industry.[14]

One of the earliest examples of a comprehensive regional-development plan within a federal German state, the state development program of North Rhine-Westphalia, followed precisely this approach when it was passed in 1964 (fig. 3).[15] The program showed a complex network of linear infrastructures for transport, energy and supply, but the centers for future development named in the program were all situated outside the existing agglomerations of the Rhine and Ruhr regions. Neither Cologne nor Düsseldorf, Duisburg, Essen or Dortmund were listed as centers to receive further government aid. When in the late 1960s the first signals of the upcoming crisis of the steel and mining industries became obvious, the conservative Christian Democratic state government in Düsseldorf initially welcomed this development as an opportunity for a "passive reconstruction" (and depopulation) of the Ruhr agglomeration[16] – a political strategy that changed profoundly just few years later when a new Social Democratic state government tried to attract new industries to replace the old ones in the Ruhr region.

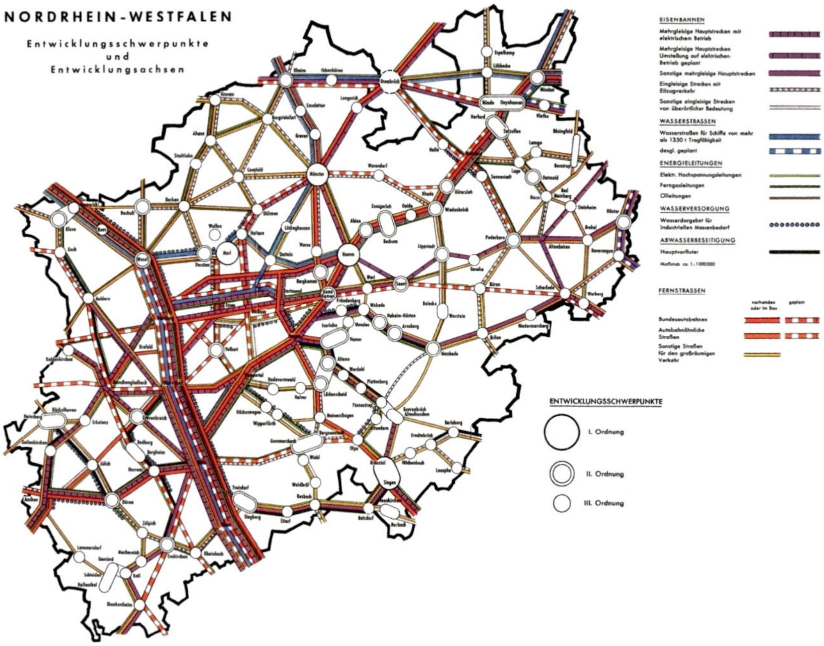

fig. 3 State Development Program of North Rhine-Westphalia. Axes and Centers of Development, 1964. The schematic map shows linear infrastructures and centers to receive further development aid from the federal state. None of the existing large cities of the Rhine or Ruhr region are listed. The program is an expression of anti-agglomeration politics then pursued by the state government.

Gerhard Isbary and the "Functional Society" Concept

In the context of such approaches toward planning that were critical of urban and industrial concentration, the work of Gerhard Isbary (1909–1968)[17] marks a thoroughly new interpretation of the basic mechanisms of a modern, wealthy, open and industrialized society. In Isbary's theoretical and programmatic work, he replaced the antagonism between agglomeration and decentralization with an awareness of the driving forces of opportunity and accessibility offered by new means of transport and communication resulting in a broader scale of activities in daily life. One of Isbary's basic insights was that West Germany was on its way to becoming a "functional society." In contrast to the "old agricultural society that was based on land and local economies," the approaching way of life, according to Isbary, was characterized by the fact that various functions may come to be related to very different places in a region. "The place of work may be situated at a totally different location than the place of residence, while school, university, theater, church, hospital, recreation may be situated at a third or fourth location, distant in terms of geography, but in close correlation in terms of function."[18] This "diversification of being" produces and demands a new organization of space on the ruins of the older structures that were shaped by forces of the past. Isbary pointed out that the forces and demands of efficient modern systems of supply and traffic caused a general increase in scale, and this larger scale of life could no longer be organized in the outdated heritage of past patterns of infrastructure, land use and settlement. "These structural remnants of past ages dam the stream of development."[19] The logic of development asks for "concentration in living structures with a certain minimum of inhabitants."[20] Settlements not in close proximity to such concentrations, will – such was Isbary's expectation – sooner or later be abandoned by their populations, underprivileged in terms of central opportunities:

> Life in a society that is based on the division of labor demands presence in close distances. Proximity is constituted by rapid accessibility by means and infrastructures of traffic and not by topographic distances. The basis for such life is a highly diverse market for labor and residence, and a large variation of opportunities for transport, education, culture, recreation and wellness. For this reason structures of concentration do not demand patterns of settlement reduced to single cores but patterns that cover a larger area, which are, in a hierarchic way, related to and across each other. The nature of their centrality marks the zones of their influence […] Concentration of being in the scale of space and time means: condensation of population in a pattern of settlements of different centrality.[21]

Arteries of Accessibility

In one of his last studies – he died in 1969 – Isbary tried to prove that the new pattern of functional living was not a mere abstract idea but could already be seen in the structure and development of space and settlements (fig. 4). Using statistical material, maps, aerial photos and aggregating the information of thousands of bus timetables, Isbary and his team drew a map of concentration, accessibility and opportunity for West Germany. His map illustrated that the territorial logic of spatial development was something very different from what conservative regional planners had long believed was right with respect to their concept of decentralized concentration. Isbary's map showed a new structure in which the hierarchical pattern of central places was embedded in linear zones of concentration and accessibility. It marked highly integrated bands of concentration in contrast to areas with an insufficient number of qualified non-agrarian jobs with a travel distance to other professional opportunities of more than thirty-five minutes.

The fundamental difference of this interpretation of state and territory becomes obvious if Isbary's map is compared with the map of the Experts'

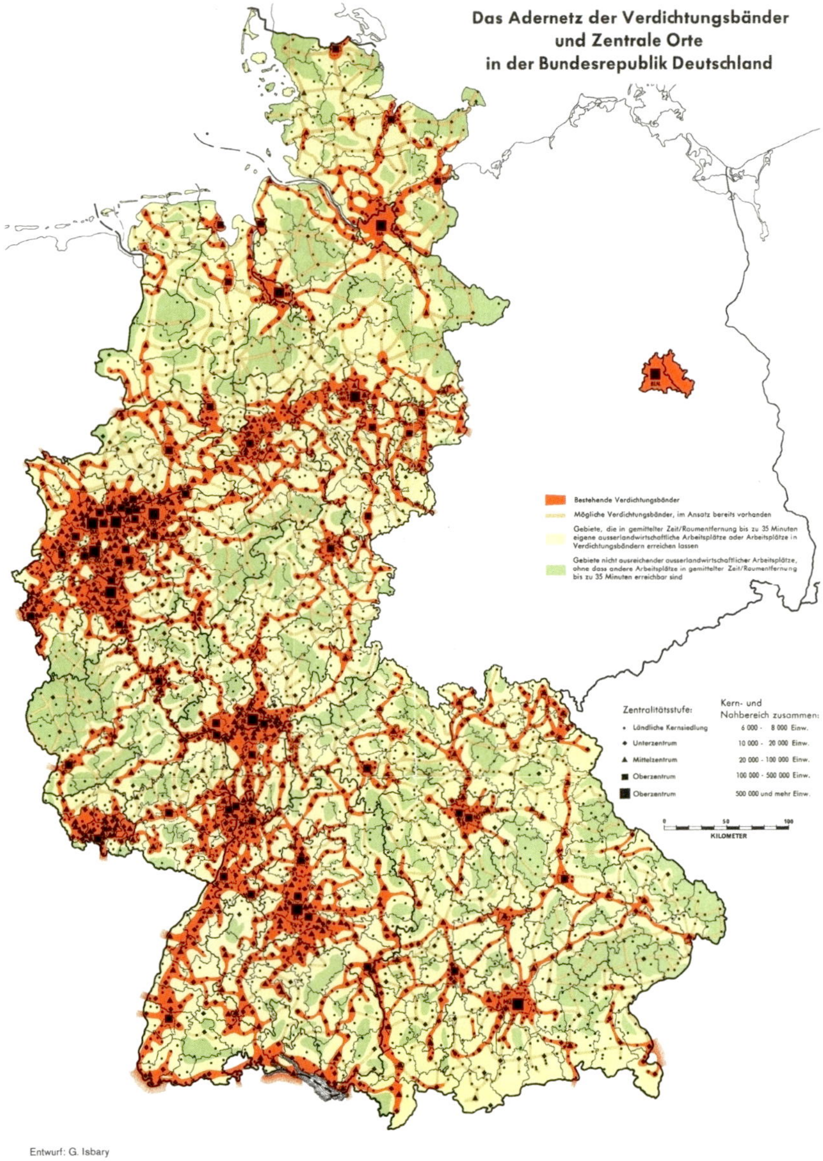

fig. 4 Gerhard Isbary, The Arterial Network of Densification Ribbons and Central Places in the Federal Republic of Germany, 1969. Isbary, von der Heide, Müller, *Gebiete mit gesunden Strukturen*, map 9.

Commission of Regional Planning of 1961. Now rural areas and not-urbanized agglomerations would be seen as problematic – an interpretation that could also be stressed by unemployment statistics that, at that time, marked a much higher number of unemployed in rural districts than in agglomerations. Isbary, in contrast to the experts' commission that had published its

fig. 5 Ruhrtangente near Hagen, early 1960s. *Deutsche Autobahnen im Luftbild*, 40.

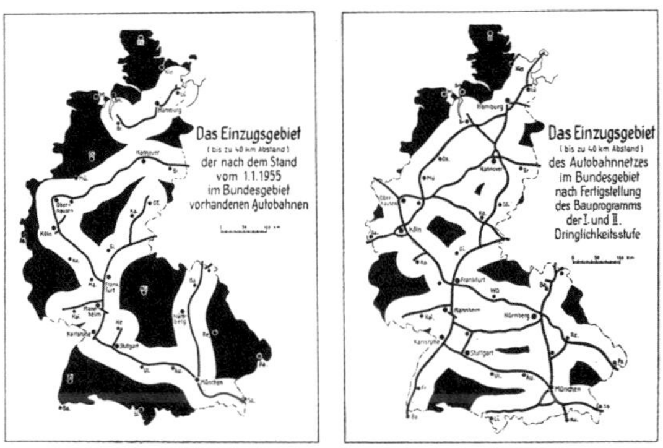

fig. 6 Forty-kilometer catchment areas of existing and planned highways on the federal territory. Source: Rudolf Hoffmann, "Autobahn und Raumordnung," 190–191.

results eight years before, characterized the arterial network of urban concentrations as "one of the most positive features in the distribution of population and spatial development in Germany. Regional planning should develop this network following the logic of the social economic evolution and not work against it."[22]

The logic of territorial networks and accessibility may be traced exemplarily in West Germany in the large-scale project of expanding the autobahn system (established in the 1930s) over the course of the 1960s and 1970s (fig. 5). In the view of traffic experts, access to the next planned autobahn became as important as Isbary considered access to a diverse market for labor, residence, service and other opportunities to be (fig. 6).[23] Infrastructures of traffic and especially the network of autobahns and suburban trains were interpreted as a basic grid that would no longer distinguish between urbanized and non-urbanized areas; the network of traffic would develop a region as a whole and not just in relation to existing urban nodes or centers (fig. 7). Traffic infrastruc-

fig. 7 Schematic pattern for an individual-traffic network in an urbanized region. The highway grid generates zones of accessibility and opportunity outside the urban centers. Illustration in Alfred Brüll, "Schnellbahnsystem im Ruhrgebiet," *Stadt Region Land* 21 (1971), 8.

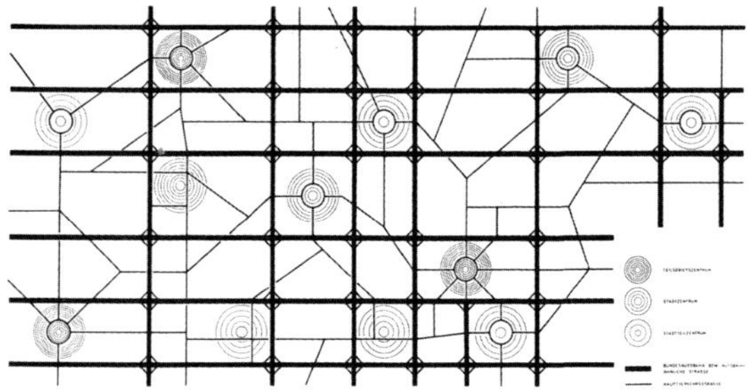

tures and accessibility would also indicate areas of future concentration, following the logic of "structures with a certain minimum of inhabitants." In this way, for example, a group of planners of the Technical University of Aachen explored different patterns for high-speed traffic in the Ruhr region. To back their investigation team, the traffic experts quoted the urban-concentration strategy (*Siedlungsschwerpunktkonzept*) for the Planning Association of the Ruhr Coal District (*Siedlungsverband Ruhrkohlebezirk*):

> A greater concentration of people, jobs and public facilities in appropriate areas in a planning region like the Ruhr region requires a powerful regional rapid-transit system as an answer to the various problems of transport; correspondingly, the development of a means of high-speed rail transport in this area must necessarily lead to urban concentration and densification.[24]

This example illustrates the close connection between the development of transport networks and a renewed interest in the concentration of housing in the late 1960s and early 1970s that corresponded in many ways to Isbary's concepts of the larger scale of life within a functional society. New satellite towns were developed in close connection to networks of transport, and designed to meet the needs of a mobile population both in respect to accessibility and in terms of public facilities and leisure.

Such contemporary patterns of concentration may be studied for example in the (unrealized) plan for the new Duisburg Angerbogen quarter, a satellite town within the Ruhr region designed for twenty thousand inhabitants and almost eight thousand cars, as every apartment should have its own parking lot in the basement or at the first level of a concrete megastructure. Plans for this project by the architectural firm Bähr, Dückert & Spengelin based in Hanover were presented in 1971 by the Institute of Urban Planning of Aachen University (RWTH Aachen) in its journal as a model example of compact housing developments, with the comment that planned concentration was something basically positive in comparison to unplanned agglomer-

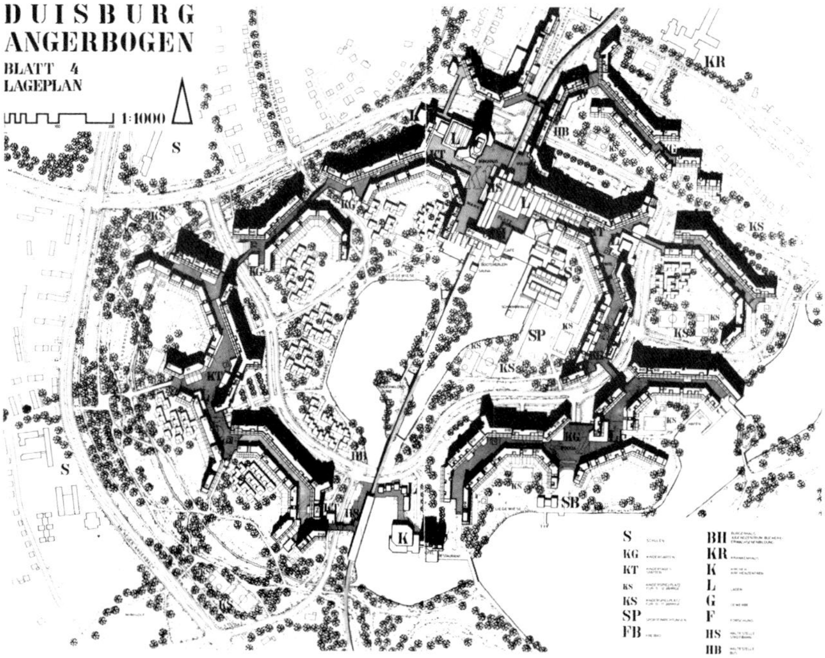

fig. 8 Plan for the new Duisburg Angerbogen quarter, 1969. A suburban railway runs through the central green zone of the complex. The project was not realized; stations for the railway were the only structures of the design that were built. Design by R. Bähr, D. Dückert, F. Spengelin, H. Stumpf. Source: *Stadt Region Land* 22 (1971), 28.

ation (fig. 8): "The strong migration into large urbanized regions dictates the efficient use of infrastructure – especially regarding the investments in public transport – and demands the protection of landscape from destruction by urban sprawl."[25] This interpretation of functional concentration was at once technocratic and capitalistic, as it allowed a high return on investment in relation to the land acquired for construction.

A Technocratic Vision

Isbary believed that in a functional society, the local roots of the citizen were just one of the remnants of past eras that "dam the stream of development." The evolution of modern functional society included the metamorphosis of "the citizen" into "the inhabitant." "It is for certain that the inhabitant wants service first of all [...] if this service is offered by city A or by city B will matter only as far as the local authorities offer services of different quality."[26] Therefore the city dweller would only be interested in his home community as far as his personal well-being was involved with regards to schools, recreation, waste disposal or parking lots; he would not be interested in the communal democracy that organized all these things. "This is a problem for those 'up there,' namely the local government."[27] Seen in such terms, the state would be a technocratic agency doing nothing more than a trade group or oil company that covered an area with stores or gas stations to supply all its clients in the most efficient way (fig. 9). For this reason, local communities and their municipal boundaries should be shaped in relation to the optimal dimensions for efficiency of public service and administration, without any regard for outdated local patriotism:

> The advance of central places in local service areas are at first of all an economic and financial problem for public investment that can be solved in an almost arithmetical way. This is no greater difficulty than the supply of water, energy, schools, post offices or other institutions.[28]

Planning and efficiency schemes of a similar nature had a significant influence on the project of municipal reform and regional reorganization in West Germany, during which the number of local political entities was substantially reduced in the 1970s by campaigns to incorporate and consolidate smaller municipalities.[29] Related considerations were also programmatic for the design of the typical large residential estates (*Großsiedlungen*) that followed the then widely accepted model of "urbanity by densification" (*Urbanität durch Dichte*).[30] Interestingly, the Angerbogen project in Duisburg tells a slightly different story: it shows that the realization of the centrality imagined by Isbary was anything but easy to foresee or program by planning institutions. In the mid 1970s, the Mannesmann steel and trading company that had planned to build the Angerbogen satellite town together with the city of Duisburg dropped the project and the development was canceled altogether. The only part of the scheme that was realized by 1974 was a suburban railway station, which was never used for its purpose and is today a *Geisterbahnhof* along the suburban line at which trains never stop. The episode illustrates the difficulties with large-scale projections and prognostics.

Limited Mobility and the Promise of Consumption

When compared with (published) outlooks on the future by planning and traffic experts, Isbary's reflections on mobility and concentration in a functional society are not fundamentally different from discourses raised in East Germany at the same time. In 1970, Wolfram Paetzold, collaborating at Central Department Planning in the GDR Ministry of Traffic,[31] published an article which diagnosed the rising transport needs in East Germany. According to Paetzold, the mobility of the population was going to increase predominantly in the area of individual-vehicle traffic.[32] As one of the experts then working

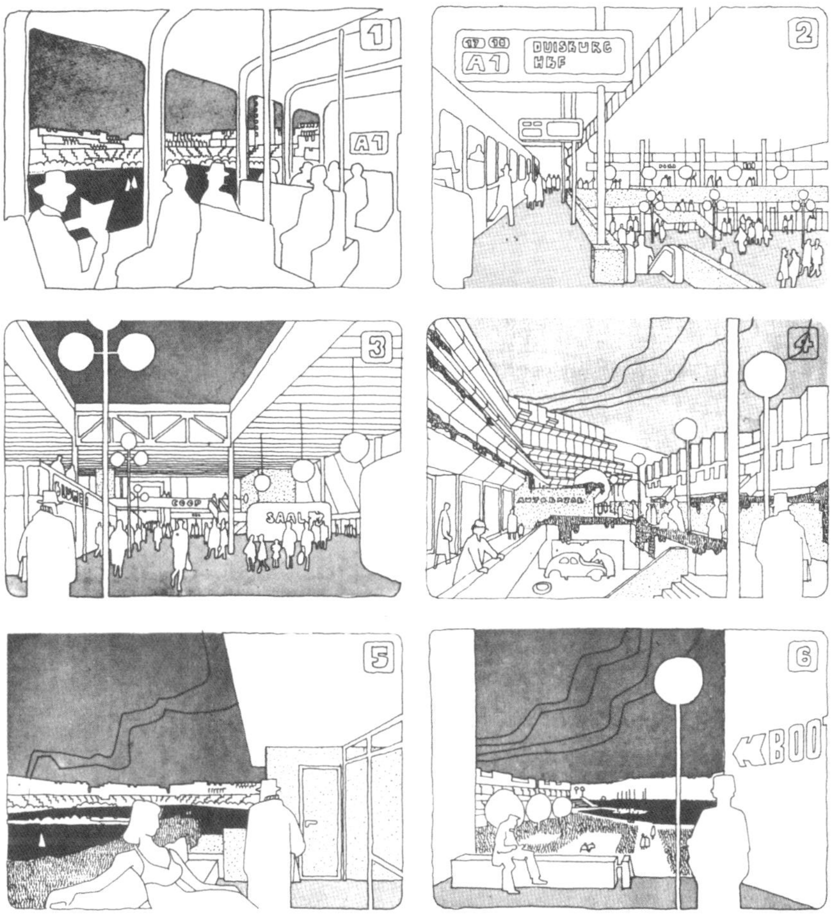

fig. 9 Transport, supply and leisure in the Duisburg Angerbogen satellite town, envisioned by its planners. In an indirect way, the sketches illustrate the metamorphosis of the citizen into "the inhabitant" predicted by Gerhard Isbary. Illustrations: *Stadt Region Land* 22 (1971), 30.

on the GDR General Traffic Plan (*Generalverkehrsschema*), Paetzold also concluded that the changes in the territorial, settlement and economic structure of East Germany would lead to an increasing concentration of population and economy. Such agglomerations would produce significant new traffic relations and needs of mobility: "The overall tendency is to concentrate and channel traffic on a few high-performance transport routes. The idea is therefore to enhance especially the motorway network and improve significantly the quality railway network."[33]

However, while in West Germany a large-scale program of motorway construction had been being realized since 1957[34] and the autobahn network would quadruple from roughly 2,200 kilometers in 1955 to 8,800 kilometers in 1990, in East Germany there were few additions to the existing motorway network from the National Socialist era during its whole existence. Those few larger projects that were built were basically a line from Berlin to Rostock, a connection between Leipzig and Dresden and, finally, a link from the Berlin-Rostock autobahn to Hamburg that answered West German requests for a better connection to Berlin and was mainly financed by Western money. These additions increased the total length of the GDR motorway system by a modest 37 percent, from to 1,378 kilometers in 1949 to 1,888 kilometers in 1989.[35] Against this background, Paetzold's speculations about the future shape and extent of individual traffic, or about concentration tendencies in East Germany, may appear as mere interpolations. However, profound changes in the planned economy took place only shortly after the publication of Paetzold's article. In 1971, the planning directives of the NES (New Economic System) were abandoned and replaced by a system of renewed centralized economic planning and controls.[36] With the fall of the NES, an ambitious (though impracticable) program of enforced motorway construction, which had been passed in 1967 and aimed to catch up with West Germany by producing a hundred kilometers of autobahn every year from 1970 on, was also given up.[37] Characteristically, in later publications Paetzold did not come back to his idea of concentrated traffic lines, settlements and the rise of individual mobility but stressed "the pushing through of socialist rationalization in traffic."[38] He declared that "So for example it has to be decided in every city to what extent, where and when restrictions in the use of [individual] motorcars are necessary!"[39] and maintained that:

> A "traffic chaos," as we observe it in capitalist countries, will not take place for us because of appropriate, scientific transport research and additional phases of coordinated practical implementation of management and control of private transport, in connection with the further development of public transport.[40]

Mobility should now become a resource to be directed just like other sectors of a centrally planned economy. However, Paetzold still expected a future tendency of "intense interdependence of cities and their hinterlands, with the result that commuter traffic will continue to increase beyond city limits."[41]

Paetzold's turn, which immediately followed the programmatic change in GDR economic policy in 1971, should not be overestimated in terms of its effect for later development. According to Siegfried Grundmann, regional planning had little influence on the orientation or location of investments in East Germany's planned economy – the decisions of the central government in favor of certain branches of production were always more relevant

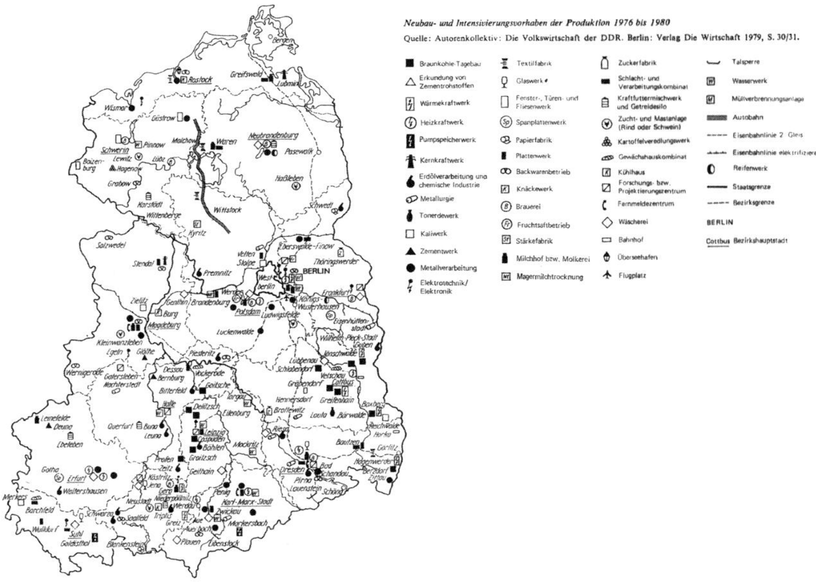

fig. 10 Projects for new and intensified production in East Germany, 1976–1980.The single highway project in the northern part between Wittstock and Rostock illustrates the rather marginal position of traffic development compared to other branches within the centrally programmed GDR economy. Source: Rolf Bönisch, Gerhard Mohs and Werner Ostwald, *Territorialplanung* (Berlin: Die Wirtschaft, 1982), 46.

than the influence of experts or regional entities.[42] Regarding the development of traffic and infrastructures, Uwe Müller has pointed out that, due to such mechanisms of political decision-making, large-scale investments in industry or other focus investments were usually preferred over less visible infrastructure or maintenance projects (fig. 10).[43] Accordingly, investments in traffic infrastructure played a more marginal role in the economic plans of the government and the central-planning committee. In addition, after 1971, East German economic policy was focused on the political idea that the population should visually profit from an increase in socialist productivity. Thus the GDR's planned economy then focused on an ambitious public-housing program and, in addition, spent significant parts of the national income subsidizing food and consumer goods that had to be bought in part with hard foreign currency on the global market, becoming one reason for East Germany's international debt problems.[44]

Even with these basic differences conceded, the economic and political strategy that was followed in East Germany in the late 1970s in the way of a technocratic mirror image echoes the economic and political idea that Isbary developed in his speculation about the citizen turning into a mere inhabitant.

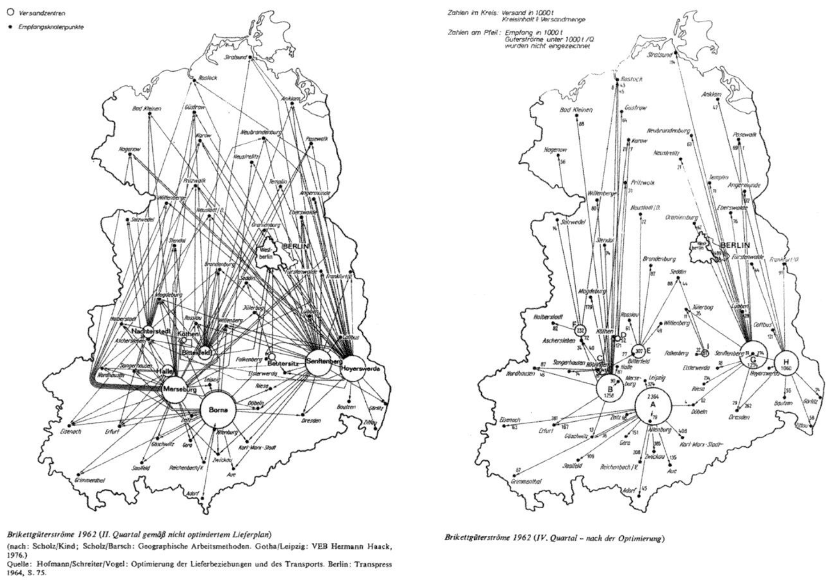

fig. 11 Supply relations for soft coal briquettes before and after their optimization, 1962 – a textbook example of traffic-efficiency planning in East Germany based on railway transport. The logic of disentangling complex economic relations recalls contemporaneous ideas about "ordered" settlement patterns in West Germany (see fig. 2). Source: Bönisch, Mohs, Ostwald, *Territorialplanung*, 254–255.

Isbary believed that, in the long run, political participation and local commitment would be replaced by the mere organization of patterns of efficient supply, consumption and administration in the larger scale of a functional society of the future. The socialist regime in East Germany, in a related logic, tried to generate acceptance by offering supply to its inhabitants – meaning housing, consumer goods and services – without granting the population the full spectrum of democratic citizenship. Both strategies relate to a technocratic logic of needs, supply and scale based on specific ideas of efficiency. But while East Germany's planned economy stuck to the Fordist logic of economy of scale, in West Germany a thorough change toward much more integrated and flexible methods of production and innovation was taking place that heavily relied on powerful infrastructures of mobility. Fixed on the ideal of centrally directed efficiency, the East German economy became less and less competitive with the increasingly automobile-oriented and versatile society of the West. Unable to reproduce the economic possibilities and implications of individual mass mobility, GDR planning professionals at the end of the 1970s tried to identify the remaining reserves of efficiency in existing networks of traffic based mainly on railway transport (fig. 11).

The well-known failure of this strategy – at the end of its existence, most

GDR networks of transport infrastructure were obsolete and in urgent need of repair[45] – says something about the limits of planning concepts. But this statement is also true for West Germany, for there it took more than twenty years of regional-planning discourses before Isbary had voiced the idea that mobility and accessibility rather than anti-agglomeration politics and decentralization were the keys to a modern functional society. Fortunately, one can say, regional planners in the Federal Republic had much less to decide on than their counterparts in the economic planning agencies of East Germany.

Endnotes

1 There are as yet no comprehensive comparative studies about the history of regional planning and of national planning strategies in the twentieth century. For the roots of regional planning in Great Britain and the US see the older studies of Daniel Ritschel and Walter Creese: Daniel Ritschel, *The Politics of Planning: The Debate on Economic Planning in Britain in the 1930s* (Oxford: Clarendon, 1997); Walter Littlefield Creese, *TVA's Public Planning: The Vision, the Reality* (Knoxville, Tenn.: University of Tennessee Press, 1990). A comparative approach for the 1930s is worked out in Wolfgang Schivelbusch, *Three New Deals: Reflections on Roosevelt's America, Mussolini's Italy, and Hitler's Germany, 1933–1939* (New York: Picador, 2007). For Germany, see Mechtild Rössler, "'Area research' and 'spatial planning' from the Weimar Republic to the German Federal Republic: Creating a Society with a Spatial Order under National Socialism," in *Science, Technology and National Socialism,* eds. Monika Renneberg and Mark Walker (Cambridge: Cambridge University Press, 1994), 126–138; Ariane Leendertz, *Ordnung schaffen. Deutsche Raumplanung im 20. Jahrhundert* (Tübingen: Wallstein, 2008); Karl R. Kegler, *Deutsche Raumplanung. Das Modell der "Zentralen Orte" zwischen NS-Staat und Bundesrepublik* (Paderborn: Schöningh, 2015). For France, see Gilles Massardier, *Expertise et aménagement du territoire. L'État savant* (Paris: L'Harmattan, 1996); Matthew Wendeln, *Contested Territory: Regional Development in France, 1934–1968* (Lille: Atelier national de reproduction des thèses, 2014).

2 For a general presentation, see Barry J. Eichengreen, *The European Economy since 1945: Coordinated Capitalism and Beyond* (Princeton: Princeton University Press, 2007), 131–62.

3 Gabriele Metzler, *Konzeptionen politischen Handelns von Adenauer bis Brandt* (Paderborn: Schöningh, 2005), 232–259; Michael Ruck, "Ein kurzer Sommer der konkreten Utopie – Zur westdeutschen Planungsgeschichte der langen 60er Jahre," in *Dynamische Zeiten. Die 60er Jahre in beiden deutschen Gesellschaften*, eds. Axel Schildt, Detlef Siegfried and Karl Christian Lammers (Hamburg: Christians, 2000), 363–401.

4 *Raumordnungsprogramm für die großräumige Entwicklung des Bundesgebietes.* (*Bundesraumordnungsprogramm*) (Bonn: Ministerium für Raumordnung, Bauwesen und Städtebau, 1975).

5 See Heinz Gerhard Haupt and Jörg Requate, eds., *Aufbruch in die Zukunft. Die 1960er Jahre zwischen Planungseuphorie und kulturellem Wandel. DDR, ČSSR und Bundesrepublik Deutschland im Vergleich* (Weilerswist: Velbrück,

2004); Michael Ruck, "Planung als Utopie. Gesellschaftsutopien der 68er und gesellschaftliche Planungseuphorie in den sechziger Jahren," in *Vorgänge, Zeitschrift für Bürgerrechte und Gesellschaftspolitik* 47/1 (2008), 13–22.

6 Heinrich Mäding, "Raumordnungspolitik auf dem Prüfstand 1977: Die Kommission für wirtschaftlichen und sozialen Wandel im Kontext der Fachdiskussion," in *Raumplanung nach 1945. Kontinuitäten und Neuanfänge in der Bundesrepublik Deutschland*, eds. Wendelin Strubelt and Detlef Briesen (Frankfurt, New York: Campus, 2015), 225–254.

7 For this topic, see André Steiner, *Die DDR-Wirtschaftsreform der sechziger Jahre. Konflikt zwischen Effizienz- und Machtkalkül* (Berlin: Akademie Verlag, 1999); André Steiner, *Von Plan zu Plan. Eine Wirtschaftsgeschichte der DDR* (München: DVA, 2004), 123–164; Jörg Roesler, *Aufeinander zu reformiert? Zur Charakteristik der Wirtschaftsreform in der DDR und der BRD und die Entscheidungen des Jahres 1966* (Berlin: Helle Panke, 2006).

8 Hans Wilhelm Hoffacker, *Entstehung der Raumplanung, konservative Gesellschaftsreform und das Ruhrgebiet 1918–1933* (Essen: Hobbing 1989).

9 See Karl R. Kegler, "Krisenangst und Krisendiagnose. Deutsche Raumplanung nach 1945," in *Raumplanung nach 1945*, 69–91.

10 Sachverständigenausschuss für Raumordnung, *Die Raumordnung in der Bundesrepublik Deutschland* (Stuttgart: Kohlhammer, 1961), 56

11 Ibid, 59.

12 Ibid, map 2. The map was designed by Gerhard Isenberg (1902–1982), one of the most influential regional-planning experts in the early years of the Federal Republic. Isenberg's long career in regional planning started in Nazi Germany; after the war, he appealed for a redistribution of the refugee population in West Germany on the basis of a pattern of regional economic capacity. See Kegler, *Deutsche Raumplanung*, 360–367, 229 (footnote 9). Gerhard Isenberg was also a member of the expert commission.

13 Hans Staubach, "Möglichkeiten und Grenzen der Großstadtauflockerung," in *Raumforschung und Raumordnung* 8 (1948), 138–141; Hans Staubach, "Die Ordnung des deutschen Raumes als Grundlage unserer sozialen und wirtschaftlichen Gesundung," in *Volk Raum Landschaft. Die Neuordnung der Verhältnisse von Stadt und Land im deutschen Aufbau*, ed. Deutscher Landkreistag (Heidelberg: Jedermann, 1949), 9–56.

14 Hans Staubach, *Siedlungslenkung und Raumordnung* (Hannover: Jänecke, 1963).

15 "Landesentwicklungsprogramm Nordrhein-Westfalen," in *Ministerialblatt für das Land Nordrhein-Westfalen* 17/107 (1964).

16 Joseph Paul Franken, "Regionale Strukturverbesserung im Rahmen des Landesentwicklungsprogramms," in Joseph Paul Franken, *Landesplanung und Strukturverbesserung. Begriffe – Aufgaben – Probleme* (Essen: Wingen, 1965), 5–16 (p. 13). Franken was Minister for Regional Planning, Housing and Public Works in the federal state of North Rhine-Westphalia from June 1963 to July 1966. For the connections between state politics of deglomeration and the crisis of Ruhr industries, see Karl Lauschke, "Von der Krisenbewältigung zur Planungseuphorie. Regionale Strukturpolitik und Landesplanung in Nordrhein-Westfalen," in *Demokratisierung und gesellschaftlicher Aufbruch: Die sechziger Jahre als Wendezeit der Bundesrepublik*, eds. Matthias Frese, Julia Paulus and Karl Tebbe (Paderborn: Schöningh, 2003), 451–471.

17 Gerhard Isbary was of the founding generation for regional planning as an academic discipline in Germany; then he worked in subordinate positions in this field during the Nazi dictatorship. In 1952, Isbary fled from East Germany to the Federal Republic, and from 1959 to 1963 was head of the research department at the Federal Institute for Regional Research in Bonn. See Kegler, *Deutsche Raumplanung*, 574 (footnote 12).

18 Gerhard Isbary, "Ziele einer deutschen Raumplanung," in *Deutschland ohne Konzeption? Am Beginn einer neuen Epoche. Zwanzig Beiträge internationaler Wissenschaftler, Schriftsteller und Publizisten*, eds. Robert Jungk and Hans Josef Mundt (Munich, Vienna, Basel: Desch, 1964), 97–140 (p. 105). This translation and all subsequent translations by the author.

19 Ibid, 106.

20 Ibid, 134.

21 Ibid, 130–131.

22 Gerhard Isbary, Hans-Jürgen von der Heide and Gottfried Müller, *Gebiete mit gesunden Strukturen und Lebensbedingungen. Merkmale und Abgrenzung* (Hanover: Gebrüder Jänecke, 1969), 31.

23 A government publication from 1968 envisioned that upon completion of the autobahn network "Nearly the whole federal territory is then passed by highways so that the distance to a motorway junction even in sparsely populated areas will be 40 km away at most, or in densely populated areas not more than just 15 km." *Deutsche Autobahnen im Luftbild*, ed. Bundesminister für Verkehr (Konstanz: Stadler, 1968), 11–12. This was similar to earlier ideas for the comprehensive development of the network envisioned during the Nazi dictatorship, with motorways not more than forty kilometers away from any part of the territory; see Rudolf Hoffmann, "Autobahn und Raumordnung," in *Raum und Verkehr I*, ed. Akademie für Raumforschung und Landesplanung (Bremen-Horn: Dorn, 1956), 171–195 (p. 173).

24 Alfred Brüll, "Schnellbahnsystem im Ruhrgebiet. Grundlage der Ausbildung von Siedlungsschwerpunkten," *Stadt Region Land* 21 (1971), 1–22 (p. 2).

25 Dieter Dückert, "Verdichtete Wohnformen. Voraussetzungen und Konsequenzen," *Stadt Region Land* 22 (1971), 1–30 (p. 2).

26 Isbary, "Ziele einer deutschen Raumplanung," 120.

27 Gerhard Isbary, "Verlust der Funktionseinheit der Gemeinde," in *Polis und Regio. Von der Stadt- zur Regionalplanung. Frankfurter Gespräch der List Gesellschaft 8.–10. Mai 1967*, eds. Edgar Salin, Niels Bruhn and Michel Marti (Basel/ Tübingen: Kyklos/ Mohr, 1967), 86–91 (p. 90).

28 Gerhard Isbary, *Zentrale Orte und Versorgungsnahbereiche. Zur Quantifizierung der zentralen Orte in der Bundesrepublik Deutschland*, (Bad Godesberg: Bundesanstalt für Landeskunde und Raumforschung, 1965), 35.

29 Every federal state organized the process of territorial and municipal reform based on specific schemes; North Rhine-Westphalia, for example had more than 2,300 independent municipalities and 57 counties in 1968, then after the completion of territorial reform in 1974, the federal state counted within its borders no more than 419 greater communities and 31 counties. See Wolfgang Gärtner, "Der Landtag NRW und die kommunale Neugliederung in den sechziger und siebziger Jahren des 20. Jahrhunderts," in *Der Kraftakt. Kommunale Gebietsreform in Nordrhein-Westfalen,* ed. Regina van Dinther (Duisburg: Landtag Nordrhein-Westfalen, 2005), 15–53 (p. 16).

30 See Jörn Düwel, Niels Gutschow, *Städtebau in Deutschland im 20. Jahrhundert. Ideen – Projekte – Akteure* (Stuttgart: Teubner, 2001), 197–202.
31 Peter Christian Ludz, *Parteielite im Wandel. Funktionsaufbau, Sozialstruktur und Ideologie der SED-Führung; eine empirisch-systematische Untersuchung* (Cologne: Westdeutscher Verlag, 1970), 118.
32 Wolfram Paetzold, "Das Generalverkehrsschema der DDR und die Bedeutung der Anschlußbahnen," *DDR Verkehr. Zeitschrift für komplexe Fragen der Planung und Leitung des Verkehrswesens* 3 (1970), 93–97 (p. 93).
33 Ibid, 94.
34 *Ausbauplan für die Bundesfernstraßen*. The program passed the parliament on July 27, 1957; for the program and its history, see Klaus Kuhm, *Moderne und Asphalt. Die Automobilisierung als Prozeß technologischer Integration und sozialer Vernetzung* (Pfaffenweiler: Centaurus, 1997), 59–64.
35 Figures after Günter Weise, "Straßenverkehrs- und Straßenplanung," in *Das Straßenwesen der DDR 1949–1989* eds. Erich Fiedler, et al (Bonn: Kirschbaum, 2002), 18–61 (pp. 27, 29).
36 Steiner, *Von Plan zu Plan*, 165–196.
37 Uwe Müller, "Autobahnbau in der DDR. Die Wandlung eines verkehrspolitischen Großprojektes vom Prestigeträger zur Devisenquelle," in *Die DDR in Deutschland. Ein Rückblick auf 50 Jahre*, ed. Heiner Timmermann (Berlin: Duncker & Humblot, 2001), 381–404 (pp. 390–396); Axel Doßmann, *Begrenzte Mobilität. Eine Kulturgeschichte der Autobahnen in der DDR* (Essen: Klartext, 2003), 304–313.
38 Wolfram Paetzold, "Die Entwicklung des Verkehrs in den Städten der DDR. Aufgaben für Forschung und Generalverkehrsplanung," in *DDR-Verkehr* 9 (1975), 357–60 (p. 357).
39 Ibid, 360.
40 Ibid. In another article, Paetzold stressed in 1972 the necessity of minimizing traffic needs via a favorable choice of sites, in order to reduce commuter traffic as much as possible. See Wolfram Paetzold, "Die Entwicklung des Personenverkehrs in den Großstädten und Ballungsgebieten der DDR," in *DDR-Verkehr* 5 (1972), 184–191 (190), quoted after Kuhm, *Moderne und Asphalt*, 125.
41 Paetzold, "Die Entwicklung des Verkehrs," 358.
42 Siegfried Grundmann, "Territorialplanung in der DDR. Indikatoren zur Analyse regionaler Disparitäten," in *Regionale Strukturen im Wandel*, ed. Annette Becker (Opladen: Leske & Budrich, 1997), 105–146 (pp. 105–7, 128–29).
43 Müller, "Autobahnbau in der DDR," 381, 402.
44 Steiner, *Von Plan zu Plan*, 187–191; Stephan Merl, "Staat und Konsum in der Zentralverwaltungswirtschaft. Rußland und die ostmitteleuropäischen Länder," in *Europäische Konsumgeschichte. Zur Gesellschafts- und Kulturgeschichte des Konsums (18. bis 20. Jahrhundert)*, eds. Hannes Siegrist, Hartmut Kaelble and Jürgen Kocka (Franfurt, New York: Campus, 1997), 205–241.
45 For the decay of the GDR state-railway system, see Ralph Kaschka, *Auf dem falschen Gleis. Infrastrukturpolitik und -entwicklung der DDR am Beispiel der Deutschen Reichsbahn 1949–1989* (Frankfurt, New York: Campus, 2011).

Daniela Spiegel

Vacationing within the Walls. The Design and Development of Holiday Resorts in the GDR

Mass tourism is an international phenomenon that developed after the Second World War when everyone's right to a vacation was laid down by law in more and more countries. In this process of deprivileging vacations, the socialist states took a leading role in Europe. This article considers the environmental, urbanistic and architectural aspects of vacation planning in the former GDR in the period between the 1960s and 1980s. The key question in the underlying research project – which concerns East German holiday architecture in an European context – is how vacationing and its architectural framework were organized in a State where, because of restrictive policies on travelling, more than three-quarters of the population spent their holidays in their own country.[1]

Historical Context

The origins of German mass tourism date back to the labor movement when, at the turn of the twentieth century, trade unions began to fight for the workers' right to holidays. In addition, unions and also some firms erected special holiday homes as an affordable alternative to the expensive accommodation in hotels.[2] These homes, rather simple in number and size, were situated mainly in central, low mountain areas, while the touristically developed coastal regions remained reserved for the middle and upper classes.

An important step in the architectural development of such districts can clearly be seen in the seaside resort Prora on the island of Rügen; the resort was one of the most well-known megalomaniac projects of National Socialism. With this "Sea Bath for 20,000," the organization *Strength through Joy* (KdF) tackled the conquest of the German coast by mass tourism, and – as the name suggests – for the first time projects involving large-scale holiday resorts of urban dimensions were planned. As is well known, the ambitious Prora project remained unfinished. After the Second World War, the GDR refused to finish work on it as a tourist resort. Later on, however, a holiday home for military personnel was provided in the part of the complex that had been used by the army.[3]

The Organization of Holidays in the GDR

The right of every worker to a vacation was a key concern in the GDR; this right had already been constitutionally recognized when the State was founded in 1949.[4] Holidays were an important pillar of the social policies. It was an instrument "for enhancing the worker's pleasure of working and his ability to work, and capacity, and such to make an active impact on the increase of productivity."[5] In addition to being a rejuvenation service provided for the workforce, holidays played an important role in the propaganda model for a new socialist society. Vacationing in the GDR should thus be understood not as getting away from everyday life and work but, on the contrary, as complementing them.[6] Therefore, vacationists were accommodated primarily in vacation homes and holiday camps built to facilitate collective activities.

Intended to demonstrate the welfare and superiority of socialism, state-organized holidays were mainly subsidized: on average, each vacationist had to bear less than one third of the actual costs.[7] As a result, a thoroughly organized, state-ordered form of mass tourism arose in the GDR in the 1950s. The most important provider – besides the individual recreational facilities of single companies – was the *Freie Deutsche Gewerkschaftsbund* FDGB (Free German Trade Union Federation).

Because of the rapid growth at the beginning of the 1950s, the FDGB's holiday service started to build new holiday homes in traditional vacation regions such as on the Baltic coast as well as in the mountainous areas of the Harz, in the Elbe Sandstone Highlands (the so-called "Saxon Switzerland"), the Ore Mountains as well as in the Thuringian Forest. New buildings were erected in those villages where tourism infrastructure had already existed.

Two important aspects should be emphasized regarding the architecture of these early buildings: first, there is a typological similarity to the European hospital and sanatorium architecture of the early twentieth century, which can be recognized by the slightly curved form of the accommodation blocks,

fig. 1 FDGB-holiday homes of the early 1950's: a. Gernrode, "Fritz Heckert," b. Friedrichroda, "Walter Ulbricht," c. Dierhagen, "Ernst-Moritz Arndt," d. Tabarz, "Theo Neubauer." Contemporary postcards.

by the semicircular wing buildings and also by the cantilevered balconies (fig. 1).

Secondly, regarding the architectural form, there was a wide range of building styles which is typical for this early phase of GDR architecture ranging from influences of the Modern Movement up to the representative socialist classicism and the so-called national traditions.[8]

Strategic Expansion

The strategic planning for developing recreational holiday resorts began at the end of the 1950s; i.e., before the erection of the wall, when special commissions were created at district levels. In addition, the German Architecture Academy (*Deutsche Bauakademie*) began scientific research on the planning of recreational holiday resorts. The Academy commissioned landscape architect Frank Erich Carl to do a study on *Planning of Holiday Recreation in the GDR* – this was published in 1960 (fig. 2).[9]

Carl found that it would be insufficient just to expand the existing, traditional recreation areas. He carried out extensive investigations and drew up maps in order to find other suitable sites for touristic development. His postulate is very interesting: modern tourists would prefer man-made cultural landscapes rather than unspoiled nature. In support of his statement, which might result from a certain pride at that time in cultural and industrial devel-

fig. 2 Frank Erich Carl, *Erholungswesen und Landschaft*, Berlin 1960, front cover.

opment but also from a lack of unspoiled landscapes in the GDR, he quotes from a text named *Landscapes of the Poets* of 1959 by the writer Annemarie Auer:

> Bathing in the lake is refreshing even if the lake has been created by human hand. A walk through meadows and fields is delightful, because we know that they are part of a planned, useful landscape, interspersed with roads, with pipelines or even whole mines below. Next to our path behind the shrubbery there is a motorway with its hum of traffic. The train steaming around the edge of the forest, the electric lines swinging over woods and meadows, the old fields and pastures, they all belong to it. They have become landscape themselves.[10]

However, while looking for possible recreational regions, Carl surveyed not only population density and the topographic distribution of forests and lakes, but also the location of industrial sites and the resulting pollution of air and water, so that certain regions were then excluded. The data basis for these maps was collected in the framework of a so-called "Landscape diagnosis" of the GDR.[11]

fig. 3 Klink, FDGB-holiday resort *Völkerfreundschaft*. Source: *Architektur und Städtebau der DDR*, ed. Dt. Bauakademie (Leipzig: Buch- und Kunstverlag 1969), 62.

Regarding the future development of recreational holiday areas, Carl recommended first of all the Mecklenburg Lake District for intensive touristic development. It would be particularly suitable because of its mild climate and abundance of water and would relieve the touristically overloaded Baltic coast.[12]

Already in May 1962, the first holiday resort named *Völkerfreundschaft* (People's Friendship) was opened at Klink by Lake Müritz. Instead of one big holiday home, 50 multi-family bungalows with flat roofs and 4 small, two-storied accommodation buildings (each with 10 double rooms) were erected directly at the lakeside (fig. 3). The urban design utilized the curved form of the shore and the slightly rising terrain. The bungalows were not equipped with kitchens or lavatories. These were outsourced into the central building, which underlined the collective aspect of the trade-union holiday spent together. In addition to the central clubhouse building, a bowling alley, a tennis court, and childcare facilities were provided.[13]

Because of the low financial and structural costs involved, bungalow resorts became popular in the holiday sector. Starting from Klink, eleven bungalow resorts with a total capacity of 2,000 beds had been erected by 1964, not at the lakes but on the Baltic coast. They were built with the help of firms and collective combines in so-called "communities of interests." This means the FDGB bought the ground, the firms erected the bungalows with their own resources and manpower and, in return, they had circa 50 % of the holiday places at their disposal.[14]

With these FDGB-controlled communities of interests the fragmented, unstructured building of individual holiday resorts should be prevented. This financially and logistically well-functioning system came to an abrupt end, when Walter Ulbricht, Chairman of the State Council of the GDR, in his speech on the occasion of the fifteenth anniversary of the GDR in October 1964, criticized the bungalow resorts as being too fragmented. Instead, he demanded the construction of "modern, standardized five-storied buildings."[15] Consequently, the FDGB had to give up the construction of bungalow resorts, defining them at that time as a stopgap solution for the difficult initial period. The firms and collective combines, nevertheless, continued building bungalow resorts on their own.

Cross-functional Recreation Planning

Coming back to the question of possible sites for new recreation areas, apart from the Mecklenburg Lake District, further potential for touristic development was seen in the mining areas for lignite. The fact that these areas that would lose their natural appearance as a result of open-cut mining provided favorable conditions for the creation of new vacation sites.

The transformation of a disused, open-cut brown-coal pit into a recreational landscape was realized in the Niederlausitz (Lower Lusatia).[16] Otto Rindt, again a landscape architect who specialized in the field of the renaturation of disused mining areas, was responsible for the planning that started at the beginning of the 1960s; i.e., years before the coal extracting work was finished. Between 1967 and 1972 the coal pit was flooded to form the Senftenberg Lake. By 1985 the holiday capacity at the beach there had increased to 6,000 people.

Another important part in this field of cross-functional interests in industrial and recreational planning was the construction of dams (fig. 4). By 1972, sixty-six dam lakes and reservoirs had been constructed to provide the increasing demand for water in the GDR.[17] When looking for appropriate sites, recreational areas were also taken into consideration. When the Pöhl dam in Saxony was built from 1958–64, a corresponding recreational area was integrated into the planning right from the start. To keep most of the natural environment free, especially the beach zone, the recreational buildings were concentrated at certain sites.[18] Sometimes the overlapping of interests extended to architecture as well. At the Rauschenbach dam (1963–67) as well as at the Eibenstock dam (1974–84), both situated in the Ore Mountains, the FDGB erected their holiday homes even before the dams were built so that the homes could also be initially used to accommodate the workers.

According to Ulbricht's requirements, the FDGB now concentrated on

fig. 4 Rauschenbach dam, FDGB-holiday home "Paul Gruner." Source: *Das neue Ferien- und Bäderbuch* (Berlin: Tribüne 1985), 239.

fig. 5 Mamaia in Bulgaria, "complex of the 1,000 beds." Source: *Deutsche Architektur* 11 (1962), 307.

the development of suitable, architectural types with prefabricated constructions. The first prototype, erected in Feldberg at the Mecklenburg Lake district,[19] did not go into serial production but remained a single case, mainly because the counties were not able to provide adequate financial and building capacities. Regarding all of these problems, the experts from the Bauakademie defined the holiday planning of the GDR as backward and trifling compared to other socialist countries that had made immense progress in the field of vacation planning: Bulgaria and Romania were regarded as model examples by Carl as well as by many other experts.[20]

To learn from the socialist sister states, GDR architects went on excursions to the Black Sea coast. For example, in 1962 two architects reported their experiences and findings in the journal *Deutsche Architektur*.[21] Though the famous "Golden Sands" resort in Varna, Bulgaria was criticized for lacking a clear, conceptual design because its buildings were too widely spaced and too differentiated architecturally, the authors were very impressed with the holiday complex at Mamaia in Romania (fig. 5). The alternating sequence of high-rise accommodation buildings and flat gastronomical or social buildings was characteristic for the complex. At Mamaia, they noted, the development towards industrial construction was the most advanced – only a small number of different types, good use of varying construction heights, and an elegant, simple design without having abandoned historical architectural motifs.[22]

A few years later, in the same journal Johannes Bauch promoted Bulgaria as a model.[23] Although the country would face the same challenges as the GDR in the housing and industrial sector, Bulgaria could afford to have its own Ministry for Tourism, the author stated. This was due to the important fact that Bulgaria (and other socialist countries) saw tourism as an important economic factor.

This is in fact the most unique feature of the GDR's recreation planning: in contrast to other socialist countries, tourism from abroad was very rare and happened mostly within the framework of exchange programs between firms or trade unions. Of course, the varying and uncertain weather conditions either on the Baltic coast in summer or in the mountain areas in winter also played an important role. However, it should be noted that the State did not invest in touristic development that was able to meet the requirements of foreign tourists with western currencies: the focus lay on its own population. Serving as legitimacy for the State system, highly subsidized holidays proved to be a huge loss financially.

Therefore, Bauch suggested thinking about whether the complex planning of entirely new and well-equipped holiday resorts that could bear comparison on an international level would be necessary as well as economically profitable.[24]

In fact, a few years later the FDGB started two large projects that should resolve or at least relieve the immense capacity constraints: one at the seaside and one in the mountains. The first project was an entirely newly-planned resort on the island of Rügen. On the so-called Schaabe, a narrow, flat and wooded spit of land between the Baltic sea and the Jasmund Bodden, the "first socialist sea resort" was planned to have 20,000 beds when completed (i.e., about the same size as the famous National Socialist Resort of Prora and nearby and twice as big as Mamaia). After comprehensive preliminary examinations of the anticipated structural changes in 1969, a closed urban design competition was held.[25] The winning project, proposed by the Rostock Office for Urban Planning, was afterwards adapted to the recommendations made by various responsible authorities (Office for Territorial Planning Rostock, County Council Rostock, FDGB Holiday Service, Experimental Workshop of the Deutsche Bauakademie, etc.). The final project[26] proposed two resorts: one complex in the north with 7,200 beds for all-year-round use and with the possibility of being extended by another 4,500 beds. The other big com-

fig. 6 Model of the planned seaside resort "Schaabe North" (left) and "Schaabe South" (right) on the Island of Rügen. Source: *Deutsche Architektur* 1 (1973), 42–43.

plex in the south was provided with 4,500 beds that were to be used mainly in the summer, especially by large families. Two children's camps, each for 1,600 kids, campsites and youth hostels completed the complex (fig. 6).

Regarding the urban design, North Schaabe showed certain similarities to the Romanian and Bulgarian resorts on the Black Sea coast: typical high-rise accommodation tower blocks that were always grouped in pairs, alternating with low, flat-roofed buildings for social functions and other curve-shaped buildings up to five stories high. By comparison, the holiday homes at South Schaabe were intended to have four stories and were to be constructed as prefabricated concrete slabs. To produce the curved forms, special wedge-shaped sections were to be developed. If it had been built, this "first socialist sea resort" of the GDR could surely have matched Mamaia or other sea resorts of the 1960s. In the end, however, the Schaabe project was not only too ambitious but also too expensive to be realized.

"Complex reconstruction" of Oberhof

The second flagship project of the FDGB was situated diametrically opposite in the Thuringian forest. It involved the so-called "complex reconstruction" of Oberhof. Since the end of the nineteenth century this little village had been a popular and sophisticated health resort and winter sports center. Furthermore, it was the favorite holiday destination of Walter Ulbricht, Chairman of the State Council of the GDR. In 1967 Ulbricht decided to transform Oberhof

fig. 7 Model of the "complex reconstruction" of Oberhof. Source: *Deutsche Architektur* 5 (1972), 288.

into a modern winter sports and recreation center for the working class, but with an international flair.

In "socialist teamwork"[27] together with the Office for Urban Planning Suhl, the Experimental Workshop of the *Deutsche Bauakademie* (led by Hermann Henselmann) worked out a comprehensive urban redesign that was then only partly executed. The aim of this "complex reconstruction" (as urban modernizations or restructurings used to be called in the official lan-

fig. 8 Oberhof, Interhotel Panorama. Source: *Deutsche Architektur* 5 (1972), 288.

guage of that time) was to "create a souvenir picture of the highest memorability" that would "offer charming new views from hilltops and mountain trails over and over again."[28] The new design of the village was characterized by a combination of high-rise buildings together with flat, warehouse-like, low-rise constructions, but having spectacular and unique architecture (fig. 7). Consequently, architects from Yugoslavia were commissioned to design the main buildings. This surely did not happen by chance, but was probably requested because of the strong wish to catch up with international development – indeed, Yugoslavian architecture was part of the international avant-garde in the 1960s when symbolic architecture was considered modern and *en vogue*.[29]

The start and highlight of the reshaped village was Hotel *Panorama*, built in 1967–69 at the north end above the new ski jumps (fig. 8). *Panorama* was a so-called "Interhotel" with a comparable standard of luxury, because it was meant to accommodate exclusively foreigners with western currencies. Consequently, not only the views of the surrounding landscape from the building were highly important but also the view on the building itself as it was placed in the landscape. The Yugoslavian collective from Belgrade, led by Kresimir Martincović, created the figurative shape of two elevated, triangular accommodation wings that were interpreted as a mountain-top motif as well as two ski jumps facing each other.

The Trade Union's holiday home "Rennsteig", another example of symbolic architecture in the "reconstructed" village, was also made by Yugoslavian

fig. 9 Oberhof, FDGB-holiday home "Rennsteig." Source: *Deutsche Architektur* 10 (1974), 630.

architects (fig. 9). For this building they chose the characteristic shape of the boundary stones of the historic hiking trail "Rennsteig." Emphasizing the symbolism, a huge "R" was attached to the north gable wall. Already recognizable from afar, the two vacation buildings indicated the village's main tourist attractions: winter sports and hiking.

As already mentioned, the elaborate design for Oberhof's "reconstruction" was only partly implemented. Like the Schaabe project, it fell victim to the resolutions passed by the eighth Congress of the Socialist Unity Party (SED), held in June 1971. Erich Honecker, the new leader, propagated socialism as no longer an objective to reach in the distant future but as "really existing" now.[30] Consequently, the living standards of the people had to be improved immediately. Of course, the first priority was given to the famous comprehensive housing program, though the nationwide provision of vacation places was also an important target to be achieved.

Consequently, after 1971 the construction of new vacation homes or resorts had to be quick and economic. The majority of these homes were multi-storied, slab-type buildings, often directly taken from standardized housing construction; they were quick and easy to erect. It is interesting to note that instead of creating big vacation complexes such as those planned for Schaabe, these kinds of single holiday homes were decentralized, especially in the Thuringian Forest. You can often find them there in small villages dominating the place and the landscape with their out-of-scale dimensions (fig. 10).[31]

fig. 10 Finsterbergen, FDGB-holiday home "Wilhelm Pieck". Contemporary postcard.

Conceptually, these buildings were more like hotels than holiday homes; they were well-equipped with swimming pools, theme restaurants, nightclubs and various other facilities that were meant to satisfy people's vacation dreams.

Nevertheless, it would be wrong to allege that the planners did not care about the surrounding cultural landscape. Of course, there was the intention to hallmark the site, but very often attempts to integrate the buildings into the landscape are recognizable, for instance by using local wood or stones for the paneling. This was based on the demand for maintaining the local character of the places: sightseeing, apart from sporting activities, was one of the main objectives of the vacationists.[32]

However, despite all the efforts made, the GDR did not succeed in satisfying the population. This was not only due to a lack of capacity, but mostly to the overall "homemade" problem of the restrictions placed on foreign travel. Only one quarter of the tourist trips went abroad, most of them to Czechoslovakia, Hungary, Poland and Bulgaria. The really lucky ones grabbed a place at "Golden Sands" or "Sunny Beach" on Bulgaria's Black Sea coast.

Finally, the severely restricted freedom to travel contributed to the fall of the GDR: "visa-free to Hawaii" was one of the main slogans shouted out again and again at the demonstrations of 1989.

As one might imagine, after the political change the recreation system collapsed like a house of cards. Former GDR citizens wanted to travel elsewhere and for interested vacationists from the west the standard of the holiday homes was far too low. Now, after a quarter of a century, the tourist situation has stabilized. Of course, a lot of holiday homes in the former GDR have been demolished or are now disused; some of them have been given other functions, but a surprisingly high number of them are still in touristic use. Contrary to common belief, it does not seem to be a question of size nor of architectural design as to which of the former GDR's vacation buildings have managed to survive. The key to success is the location of the place, its regional attractions, and, above all, the concept behind it.

Endnotes

1 Hasso Spode and Kristiane Klemm, "Zur Geschichte der Ferienarchitektur," in *Tourismusarchitektur: Baukultur als Erfolgsfaktor*, ed. Felizitas Romeiß-Stracke (Berlin: E. Schmidt, 2008), 103–105.

2 See Wolfgang Bagger, "Arbeiterkultur und Arbeitertourismus im Kaiserreich," and Hans Krumbholz, "Zur Geschichte des Sozialtourismus: Die Anfänge der gewerkschaftlichen Ferieneinrichtungen," in *Zur Sonne, zur Freiheit! Beiträge zur Tourismusgeschichte*, ed. Hasso Spode (Berlin: Verlag für Universitäre Kommunikation, 1991), 33–46; 61–70.

3 For Prora see Bernfried Lichtnau, *Prora auf Rügen: Das unvollendete Projekt des 1. KdF-Seebades in Deutschland: zur Geschichte und Baugestaltung* (Peenemünde: Dietrich, 1995); Jürgen Rostock and Franz Zadniček, *Paradiesruinen. Das KdF-Seebad der Zwanzigtausend auf Rügen* (Berlin: Links, 2006); Heidi Pinkepank, "Prora between Enlightenment & Commercialization: Dealing with Dictatorship Heritage in Germany," in *A Reader in Uncomfortable Heritage and Dark Tourism*, ed. Sam Merrill and Leo Schmidt (2009), 232–248, https://www-docs.tu-cottbus.de/denkmalpflege/public/downloads/UHDT_Reader.pdf (accessed January 21, 2016).

4 For the history of holidays in the GDR see Christopher Görlich, *Urlaub vom Staat: Tourismus in der DDR* (Köln: Böhlau, 2012); Heike Wolter, *"Ich harre aus im Land und geh, ihm fremd": Die Geschichte des Tourismus in der DDR* (Frankfurt a.M.: Campus Verlag, 2009); Hasso Spode, "Tourismus in der Gesellschaft der DDR: Eine vergleichende Einführung," in *Goldstrand und Teutonengrill: Kultur- und Sozialgeschichte des Tourismus in Deutschland 1945 bis 1989*, ed. Hasso Spode (Berlin: Moser, 1996), 11–34.

5 Erhard Sonntag, "Damit der Urlaub immer schöner wird," in *Das Ferien- und Bäderbuch* (Berlin: Tribüne, 1970), 10.

6 Görlich, *Urlaub vom Staat*, 48. See also Görlich's comments about Hans Magnus Enzensberger's Theory of Tourism, 17–18.

7 Gundel Fuhrmann, "Der Urlaub der DDR-Bürger in den späten Sechziger Jahren," in *Goldstrand und Teutonengrill. Kultur- und Sozialgeschichte des Tourismus in Deutschland 1945 bis 1989*, ed. Hasso Spode (Berlin: Moser, 1996), 39–40; Görlich *Urlaub vom Staat* (see note 4), 36–37. Instead of travel agencies, trips were sold directly by the company unions in the form of so-called "travelers checks". These checks were applicable for a fixed period of thirteen days and for a particular holiday home.

8 Described in detail by Daniela Spiegel, "Ferienarchitektur der DDR – Ein unbeachtetes Erbe," *In Situ* 1 (2013): 101–116.

9 Frank Erich Carl, *Erholungswesen und Landschaft. Ein Beitrag zur Planung der Ferienerholung in der Deutschen Demokratischen Republik* (Berlin: Deutsche Bauakademie, 1960).

10 *"Ein Bad im See erquickt, mag er immerhin von Menschenhand angelegt sein. Der Gang durch Wiesen und Felder beglückt uns, und doch wissen wir ja, dass sie Teil einer planvoll nützlichen Landschaft sind, von Fahrstraßen durchzogen, von Rohrleitungen unterhöhlt, vielleicht von ganzen Bergwerken. Neben unserem Pfad läuft hinter Gebüschen die Autobahn hin mit den summenden Wagen. Der Eisenbahnzug, der um den Waldhang dampft, die elektrischen Leitungen, die sich über Gehölze und Wiesen hinschwingen, die Äcker und Weiden von altersher, sie alle gehören mit dazu. Sie sind selber Landschaft geworden."* Carl, *Erholungswesen und Landschaft*, 15. English translation by the author.

11 For landscape diagnosis see Olaf Hiller, ed., *Die Landschaftsdiagnose der DDR: Zeitgeschichte und Wirkung eines Forschungsprojekts aus der Gründungsphase der DDR* (Berlin: TU Universitätsbibliothek, Abt. Publikation, 2002). The Landscape Diagnosis was a research project in the early 1950s carried out by Carl and his colleague Reinhold Lingner, one of the most famous landscape architects of the GDR. The aim of this project that was commissioned by the Ministry for Planning was to examine the interventions in the productive potentialities of the landscape caused by the former "capitalist robber economy." Therefore, the survey was meant to be the data basis for future economic landscape interventions on a large scale.

12 Carl, *Erholungswesen und Landschaft*, 25.

13 Although bigger in its dimensions, the Klink resort was reminiscent of a project carried out by Carl's colleague Reinhold Lingner in 1958, which Carl had published in his study. Lingner's project was meant to be a prototype for "a small holiday-resort in the landscape of the Mecklenburg Lake District." See Spiegel, *Ferienarchitektur der DDR*, 106.

14 FDGB-Bundesvorstand, *Zum Bau von Bungalows*, undated (probably 1965), SAPMO-BArch, DY 34/5952, 1.

15 Walter Ulbricht, "Festrede des Genossen Walter Ulbricht zum 15. Jahrestag der DDR," in *Sozialistische Demokratie, Organ des Staatsrates und des Ministerrates der DDR* 41 (1964), 25.

16 For the renaturation of the Senftenberg lake see Torsten Meyer, "Der Senftenberger See oder das Ende der 'Mondlandschaft,'" in *Jahrbuch für Regionalgeschichte*, ed. Rainer S. Elkar (Stuttgart: Steiner, 2005), 113–142.

17 Osmar Münzner, "Erholungsgebiet Talsperre Pöhl," *Deutsche Architektur* 5 (1972), 302.

18 Ibid., 302–305. The recreation area included one newly built holiday house with approx. 220 beds, 13 camping sites for 2,500 caravan and tent sites; three specific locations were reserved for bungalows and summer cabins. For gastronomic needs a large restaurant was provided at the dam.

19 Carl, *Erholungswesen und Landschaft* (see note 9), 40.

20 Ibid., 37.

21 Ambros G. Gross and Dietrich Wellner, "Ferien, Schwarzes Meer und Architektur. Reiseeindrücke und Anmerkungen zur Architektur in den Erholungszentren der Volksrepublik Bulgarien und der Rumänischen

Volksrepublik am Schwarzen Meer," *Deutsche Architektur* 6 (1962): 295–298.

22 Ibid., 297.

23 Johannes Bauch, "Volksrepublik Bulgarien. Erholungsplanung," *Deutsche Architektur* 3 (1965): 158–161.

24 Ibid., 161.

25 SAPMO-BArch, DY 34/24942: Ausschreibung für einen städtebaulichen Ideenwettbewerb zur Gestaltung des sozialistischen Erholungskomplexes Schaabe auf der Insel Rügen, April 1969.

26 Hartmut Colden, "Schaabe – städtebauliche Studie für einen sozialistischen Erholungskomplex an der Ostsee," *Deutsche Architektur* 1 (1973): 40–43.

27 Klaus Angermüller, "Der Thüringer Wald – ein Zentrum der Erholung der Werktätigen," *Deutsche Architektur* 5 (1972): 288.

28 Ibid., 289.

29 See Michael Zinganel, Elke Beyer and Anke Hagemann, ed., *Holidays after the Fall. Seaside architecture and urbanism in Bulgaria and Croatia* (Berlin: Jovis 2013).

30 See Görlich, *Urlaub vom Staat*, 100–103.

31 Described extensively in Daniela Spiegel, "Orts-typisch-typisiert? Adaption regionaler Bautraditionen in der DDR-zeitlichen Ferienarchitektur," in *Bericht über die 48. Tagung für Ausgrabungswissenschaft und Bauforschung vom 28. Mai bis 1. Juni 2014 in Erfurt* (Dresden: Thelem, 2015), 313–320.

32 Ibid., 316–319.

Tamás Meggyesi

Urbanism and Academia: Teaching Urban Design in the East

From Socialist Realism to Modernism

Town planning education at the Budapest Technical University underwent spectacular transformations from the late 1950s until the turn of the millennium. The first stage of this transformation, which took place in the 1960s and 1970s, can be described in three phases. They did not always succeed one another, but represented typical patterns of mental images reflecting the spirit of the time. The first phase began with the end of so-called socialist realism already from the mid-1950s. The crushing of the revolution in 1956 reinforced the political commitment of the old leadership in the town-planning department, but the younger generation of teachers slowly broke through the barriers of professional conservatism. This phase may be described as a release from the heritage of the early 1950s with a timid and cautious but enthusiastic reception of West European trends – namely, modernism and functionalism. Slowly, the most important professional periodicals and books from the West became available. As I remember, the publications *AD* and *L'Architecture d'Aujourd'hui* exerted an especially deep influence on teachers as well as students. The academic and static formalism of the former block system was replaced by freestanding sets of slabs and towers on green-field sites. At the same time, new forms of building groups and semi-enclosures came into fashion as compositional patterns. Mechanical repetition of units prevailed, as a simplified means of order – which, when it did not reflect mere personal preference, can be said to represent the examples of the professional environment, the society and the spirit of the age. It is not only about a "re-scaling of the environment," but about a radical re-forming of the image of the city. The first phase from the mid-1960s is deeply rooted in the idea of a rationalized chaos (fig. 1).

In academia, the first small exercises had to correspond to the topic of the official lectures. They included a remarkable ensemble from the history of town planning: a roundabout traffic junction and its environment, the layout of a single block, and (later) the structure and layout of a smaller neighborhood unit with its primary public institutions. I would not say that from then on Western and Eastern urban design proceeded on parallel tracks, but it is clear that Western tendencies and fashions deeply influenced design patterns in Eastern academia. My diploma work, for instance, was one of the planned dormitory towns around Budapest in 1960, which also demonstrated the popularity of the English new town movement.

Team 10 and Structuralism

The method and spirit of design was soon reformed by the principle of traffic segregation. This led to the new formalism of linear sorting – despite the fact that car ownership actually lagged behind that of West European countries. That was the decade of Team 10 and structuralism in architecture and urban design. Since it represented a basically new and different design approach, it may be regarded as the second phase of transformation. It coincided with the ten-year boom in the state-owned building industry (or mass housing) both in the East and in the West. It was the period of "the architecture of great numbers," as Charles Polonyi described it in the late 1960s. It was also characterized by an unshakable belief in the future of modern technology, not to mention the systems view of planning, which promised to answer all economic and social problems. This belief and dogma was so common that the 1968 revolution in Paris exerted practically no impact on the way people were thinking – at least, inside academia. Design programs and exercises were determined mainly by new housing estates around the city or at the site of obsolete quarters. At the end of the 1960s, "low rise – high density" programs were catching on in design exercises, in spite of the fact that very few ensemble of this type were realized (fig. 2). The old ideology of the "socialist city" had not fully disappeared; it was transmuted, however, into research topics like "the impact of lifestyle changes on the living environment." Mass housing was a political issue, so building and construction remained a central aim of the ministerial administration. Old ideas and models still survived at the same time, so we had course programs like "a new dormitory town," "a new campus town," "a new industrial city," or even "a new agricultural town." The latter example was a reflection of the new large-scale agricultural state farms program, seen as the possible future for the outmoded village

fig. 1 A new dormitory town near Budapest, 1960. Tamás Meggyesi archive.

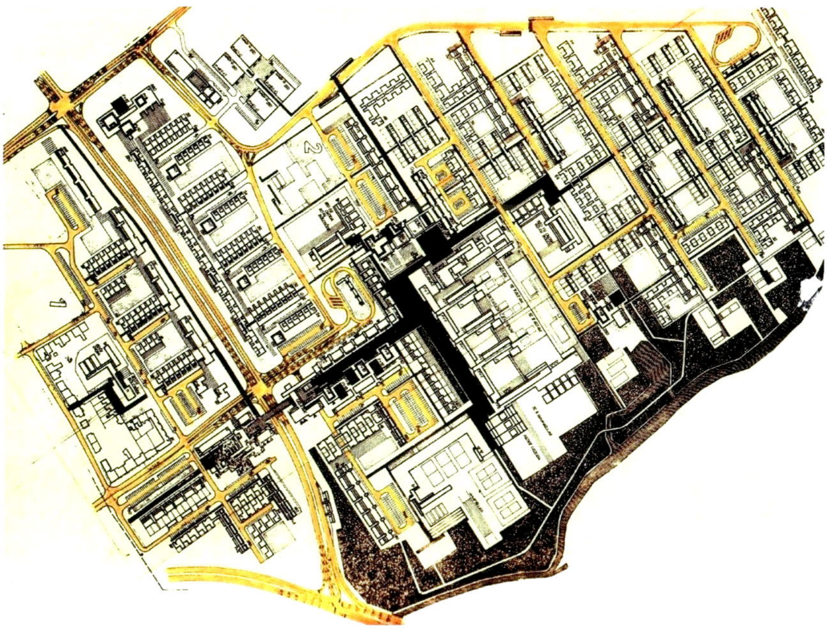

fig. 2 A new housing area near Sopron, 1970. Tamás Meggyesi archive.

system. Interest was focused on structural and compositional questions, and students could indulge their creative imaginations mainly in new housing estates and new towns. Design formalism of development plans on the map played the most important role, as if they were abstract three-dimensional canvasses by Piet Mondrian. They represented a kind of autotelic art in their own right – belonging more to monumental plasticism, or realizing a kind of new arts-and-craft movement on the urban scale. Simply on account of its curious genre, this phenomenon may arouse our interest as a special self-expression of the spirit of the time. These design compositions represent the contemporary version of the ideal city in the shadow of the "architecture of great numbers" and can be seen as the late descendants of their Renaissance ancestors. Mega-structures played a less important role in education, as the housing estates of the 1960s were designed in order to be realized. It was the first time in history when projects of this scale were surrendered to subjective invention. The student could experience the dangerous temptation to play the role of a demiurge. In this context, contemporary design may be seen as a psychological test revealing not only the spirit of the age, but at the same time the personality of the designer, too. It will be worthwhile to return to this aspect at the end of this paper.

To come back to the real processes, we can say that urban design in academia represented the different scale and attitude of urbanism on the one hand, but it was more urban planning than architecture on the other. This contradiction later became an important factor in the alienation of the department from the "designer" departments of the faculty. As I know, the situation was very similar in other communist countries, but I have no information about the relation of urban planning to architecture in different academies. It was a sign of change in Budapest when, independent from the official courses, I could organize liberal, popular and successful semi-private seminars on urbanism from 1972 (that was the so-called R Club in Budapest). These represented the interdisciplinary dimensions of the profession. We were enthusiastic followers and interpreters of the ideas of Patrick Geddes as the father of urbanism. We admired the booklet *Team 10 Primer*. We shared the ideas of the *The City is Not a Tree* and *A Pattern Language* by Christopher Alexander. Also we admired the urban planning culture of the English new towns generation from Hook to Milton Keynes. That was the time when sociologists like Iván Szelényi published their critical research about the anti-urban attitude of the official development policy. He used to be the guest of the R Club. It caused a sensation when he had to leave the country as he refused to withdraw or at least to correct his theses. The leaders of the department put a stop to our liberal initiative to invite professionals from different disciplines, and they decided to take over control of the lecturers. As a result, interest suddenly decreased, and the club finally ceased altogether.

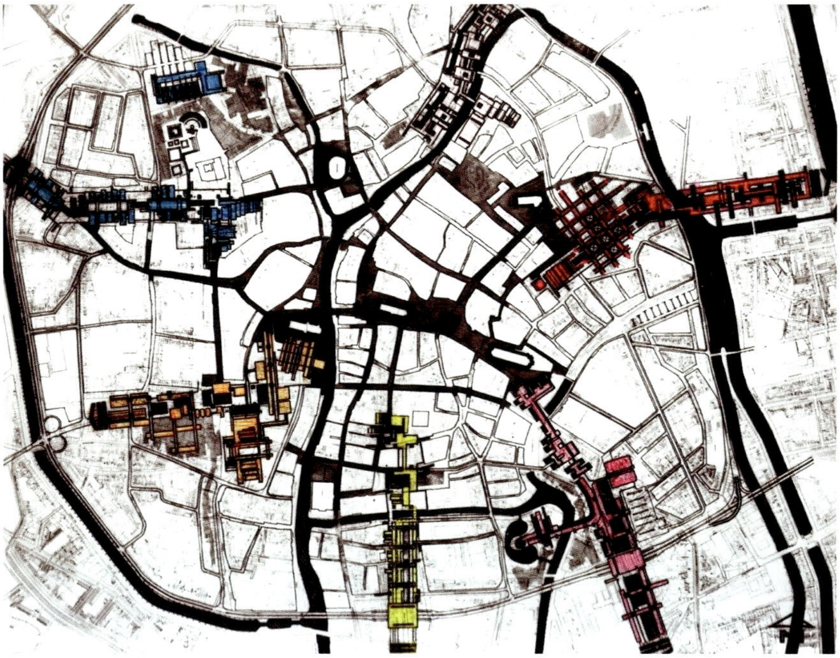

fig. 3 International competition 'Gent morgen' in 1976. Tamás Meggyesi archive.

Development of Existing Towns

The third phase of transformation in the work and programs of the department may be reckoned from the late 1960s and the 1970s. It can be characterized by a shift of interest from housing estates and new towns to the future of existing ones (fig. 3). This centered, in part, on the actual development of the core areas of old Hungarian cities, but with the preference for new housing that had to be fitted into the existing structure. Only the historical buildings remained untouched, practically demonstrating little interest in local identity. Sometimes valuable old but neglected areas were sacrificed to ensure space for new development. In spite of this insensibility – mostly determined by state-financed dwelling development programs welcomed by the local governments – the dialogue on urban geography, organic growth patterns, natural environment and social phenomena slowly manifested itself as a kind of critical thinking – not only in official detailed development plans, but in design exercises and programs as well. It required a new professional attitude to make the shift from a top-down to a bottom-up design philosophy. Even patterns of structuralism were gradually imbued with features alluding to topographical or other local conditions. This was in spite of the fact that in the official course book (by Mr. Imre Perényi, head of the department) "town planning in class-based societies" was discussed separately from "town planning in emerging socialism." In addition, problems of the rehabilitation of existing cities were tackled briefly, only as "special planning items" at the end of the book. Later, he himself changed his earlier views, but never relinquished the academic standpoint – based on political premises – that urbanism is first and foremost a technical science. It was opposed by a minority in the Hungarian Academy of Science, who claimed that urbanism belongs more to the social sciences. However, in professional practice it was clear that the future of our cities could only be derived from real environmental, economic, social and cultural conditions, not the other way round. In spite of this evidence, the majority of the staff was inclined toward the primacy of design-oriented statutory planning, and the dialogue with disciplines beyond architecture could not take deeper root.

Educational Structure

Lectures and training in town planning operated within the framework of the general five-year architectural education by the Architectural Faculty. The curriculum covered two theoretical and two design subjects in three succeeding semesters. The town-planning department was one of the five independent design departments, which included dwellings, public buildings, and industrial buildings departments, as well as the department of architectural history and monument preservation. From the second half of the 1970s, a slight specialization was introduced. This evoked a natural rivalry, reflected in the share of student interest. The department of urban design could never attract more than ten to fifteen percent of the total number of students of a year.

In the 1970s, demand emerged on the part of the faculty for the creation of an integrated design exercise covering two semesters that would address all the problems and represent the different tasks of real architecture practice – from urban design to construction details of a selected building in different scales. This was the so-called complex design which exists to this day. The town-planning department placed stress upon the urban scale, of course – with special emphasis given to investigations and evaluation of the wider urban context. As a consequence, relatively less time and energy remained to focus in depth on a selected building as it was expected by other chairs. Other departments neglected this and concentrated on a single building. The same shift in proportions manifested itself in the students' theses and diploma work. The faculty tolerated the "special nature" of the department for a while, but the stress intensified. In the end, we had to meet the unitary requirement. It was stated that the architecture diploma should reflect the same discipline and skill across the board. Consequently, the town-planning department retreated greatly from its original professional profile, and now it is one – albeit one of the best – of the faculty's general architectural design workshops. However, this brings us into the 90s and could possibly be regarded as the fourth phase of development.

Postgraduate Courses

From 1962 to the present day, the special nature of urbanism has been represented by a specialized Urban Planning postgraduate course. This is a two-year education program for those who have earned a diploma in architecture, and who are already engaged in planning firms, thus representing the up-and-coming professional generation. Most leading planners and chief architects have graduated from this course. The curriculum covered the most important related fields, but represented a more Prussian style of education with separate and controlled lectures. It concluded with a state examination. Yet, as a token of political liberalization, Mr. Ferenc Vidor (a former lecturer of an early, specialized professional branch, later abolished) launched a postgraduate course independent of the university within the framework of the Hungarian Society of Urbanism. It was based on open-ended dialogues and an interdisciplinary approach. At the time, we can say that the rather peaceful co-existence of professional ideas, courses and workshops (which were either formalized and official or informal and liberal) was a very typical feature of Hungarian education. It ensured healthy competition – not only in scientific life, but in cultural and social life as well. This is one of the reasons Hungary was considered the most liberal and cheerful country in the Communist Bloc at that time.

Pedagogy

As promised, I return to education at the end of this paper. I have spent more than 50 years in it, and I have evolved an idea and practice relating design with students. I feel that we have pedagogical experiences surely rooted in our common European culture. Let me try to sum up its philosophy as a credo of teaching. It is based on the fact that the personality of the designer is always projected in his project. He cannot help but reveal his hidden aspirations, his cultural background and his taste – whether he is aware of it or not. He is not able to lie; a skilled viewer can read his design – just as the graphologist reads a person's handwriting. This recognition is of pedagogical importance. It is possible to confront the young designer candidate with his own drawing that reflects his ego and his unconscious being from the very beginning. We have found it important to make him aware of what he really did, what kind of blind signifiers and unconscious models are working in him. His design work is a means for making him conscious of his inner nature, but it is also a kind of a medium for self-transformation. It is a means, because – supposing he has the courage to face it – he may use it as a mirror. Yet, it is also a medium insofar as he is able to correct, to reform, and to develop his own personality with its help. He has to regard his design work as his own image; if he makes changes to it, he changes himself. The correction made on one hand appears on the other as well. There is a magical correspondence between the plan as an *imago* and his personality – just as Dorian Grey had to face his hidden portrait in the novel by *Oscar Wilde*. Nonetheless this process only occurs when the teacher does not restrict his activities to "correction," but hints upon the hidden, unconscious defects, unresolved conflicts, immaturity, infantilism, defects of family background, and educational deficiencies of such that he must confront. This "therapy" may be painful, so it is not all the same who undertakes the role of the "guru." The process may involve some kind of "labor pains," too. The planner has to bring himself into the world. The role of the guru is similar to that of an obstetrician. However, when the candidate – or, as we can say now: the *adeptus* – accepts himself and the inevitable misery of his own transformation, he may experience the same process that took place during evolution, only accelerated. It is just like the medieval alchemist who actually enacted a sort of accelerated evolution in his mental efforts to bring about the mystical transformation of the dross of his present life into the gold of his future enlightened being. This experience may be dangerous, but can also unleash liberating and cathartic power. Creation in design is a kind of therapy, and as such, it is akin to the traditional initiation mysteries. This era was probably not so suitable for an objective scientific approach to reality, but it could be used as a school for self-knowledge and as a path to creativity. The time has not yet come to change the static object-attitude of design into a thinking process, but we could model it mentally, and maybe it will help us to remain free and open to any kind of transformation. When we speak about research by design today, we have to keep in mind that it is also related to internal research and to the development of the designer's personality as well.

III
Practices and Agencies

Ljiljana Blagojević

Architectural Intelligence and Scarcity-Driven Design in the 1960s Yugoslavia

Introduction: Notes on Architectural Intelligence

In 1965, the architects Alison and Peter Smithson predicted that in some forty years – that is, in 2005 – architectural records would contain documents not on "buildings" but on "built-places," and that the documents themselves "will be mostly air views, sequential photographs and system explanations."[1] What the Smithsons predicted, clearly, was not the future of today, with its archipelago of singular built-objects floating in the ocean of informal built-places of the world city. Rather, they reflected ideas about the built environment and the nature of the architectural knowledge of their own era that was brought about by the major upscaling of spatial production. The design practice of which they spoke has been retooling itself since, from analog to system and, closer to our own time, to digital modes. In this way, the correlation of architecture to production and productivity of work has been an underlying feature throughout the modern era. In parallel, the means of documentation geared up to record the rescaling process from static to dynamic explanation and imaging. As it were, the camera had been taken off the tripod and onto the moving crane then further to satellite imaging devices, and the drawing pen has given way to the keyboard and an algorithmic set of procedures.

In this text, I explore a particular case of architectural method and practice which is argued to have been advanced in response to rising demands for the industrialization of construction in conditions of relative economic and technological underdevelopment in 1960s Yugoslavia.[2] In the current age of digital design and fabrication, it may seem outdated to look back at changes in analog design methodology toward the industrialization of construction. Thus, rather than exploring the well-rehearsed narrative of a technological shift or its outcomes, I will focus on the shift in what I propose to call architectural intelligence. The multiple meanings of "intelligence" apply for architectural intelligence also: the capacity for understanding, the action or fact of mentally apprehending knowledge of something, information, the mutual conveyance of information, the obtaining of information and the like.[3] Critical for both analog and digital design and fabrication – that is, for both high-end and scarcity-driven low-technology construction – architectural intelligence is becoming increasingly relevant for contemporary practices operating in a world polarized by the uneven development of global capitalism.

As with any intelligence operation, architectural intelligence relies on gathering information and evidence, deciphering documents and codes, and deploying acquired knowledge cleverly in the right moment. Its sources are both internal to the design discipline and interdisciplinary. Its use, likewise, may be either internal or mediatory between disciplines or circumstances, access to knowledge, technology, power and such. My aim is to find points of intersection where architectural intelligence makes possible shifts between disparate worlds, even opposite ones: developed or developing, central or peripheral and mainstream or marginal, first or second or third worlds, North-South, West-East, and so forth. In this, I propose to look specifically into operational, political and design intelligence deployed in finding an innovative method and the practice of carrying out state-of-the-art system design for efficient low-budget and low-technology construction on sites located in what were among the most peripheral and underdeveloped municipalities in socialist Yugoslavia in the 1960s, namely the towns of Prizren and Ulcinj.

Operational Intelligence: Collaborative Troika

The question of operational intelligence concerns findings about working models that are effective, valid or operative in a given situation. It is commonly considered that the shift of architectural focus on productivity and standardization that gave rise to mass construction in the second world had been spearheaded by mainstream state actors; that is to say, ideologues of the socialist economy and politicians, along with executives in major state-planning offices and construction enterprises. Across the socialist landscape, a series of nationally enacted five-year plans attested to this, as did speeches and pronouncements by politically engaged party leaders and building-sector ministers, captains of the state construction sector, chief planners or architects. I would propose that the advancement in this sector toward system-

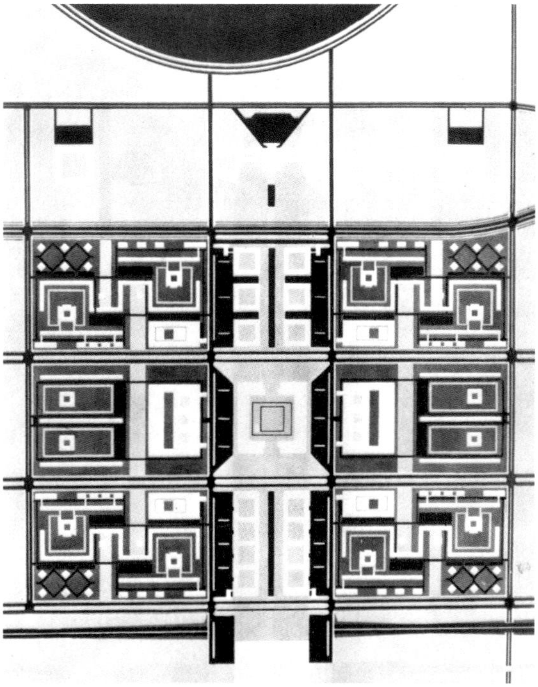

fig. 1 Uroš Martinović, Milutin Glavički, Leonid Lenarčič, Milosav Mitić and Dušan Milenković, plan of the New Belgrade Central Zone, 1960, in Aleksandar Đorđević, "Urbanističko rešenje centralnog dela Novog Beograda," *Arhitektura urbanizam*, I:2 (1960), 4.

design knowledge and production was due to a key catalyst which came from the sourcing of specialist knowledge of alternative collectives of practitioners, researchers, academics and individual expert architects. More to the point, I would propose that these alternative practices provided key intelligence, as it were, of postwar architecture. Marginalized and operating without the system of state planning and design offices or construction companies, they ran sideshow setups – at home, in research institutes or in university labs – which resulted in their lateral impacts being analogous to those of the historical avant-gardes.[4]

In postwar socialist Yugoslavia, one of the central projects of sociopolitical and spatial rescaling had been the planning and construction of New Belgrade (fig. 1), which showcased not only the overall concept of socialist urbanization, mass-housing design and construction, but the conservatism and inertia intrinsic to large undertakings of that kind.[5] It does not come as a total surprise, then, that we would find vigorous and innovative planning, design and construction methods elsewhere; that is to say, tested in places far from the centers of political power and finance, out of sight but not out of designers' minds. To corroborate this proposition, I will later discuss two low-tech, low-cost, fast-track projects realized at the beginning of the 1960s in Ulcinj and Prizren, small cities situated in the liminal multiethnic zones along the state border between the former Yugoslavia and Albania.[6] I will focus on three crucial operational points in these two projects, unique for their time and place and introduced by their architect Milan Zloković in co-authorship with his son Đorđe Zloković, architect and structural engineer, and his daughter, architect Milica Mojović (*née* Zloković).[7] The projects discussed are the Teachers' School (1959–1960) and Pedagogical College (design 1965, 1968–1969; construction 1969–1970) in Prizren (fig. 2),[8] and the tourist colony Hotel Mediterranean in Ulcinj (design 1959–1961; construction 1962–1963 (fig. 3), first phase, and 1963–1964).[9]

First, operative methodology in both projects is shifted from object to system design and from site to landscape/townscape planning. Second, both projects introduce consistent dimensional modular coordination throughout, as well as prefabricated, assembled types of construction. The Prizren project plans, for instance, are annotated solely with grid numbers and letters indicating modular positions and relations, with no dimensions annotated anywhere on the drawings. This innovation not only made design documentation more efficient to produce but decreased error margins and enabled direct communication on multilingual (Serbo-Croat and Albanian) construction sites. The Ulcinj project, on the other hand, combined local stonemason handicraft with efficient use of a very limited number of simple prefabricated elements; to great cost-cutting effect, needless to say. Third, I would point to the "elastic typification" as an effective method of socio-spatial and aesthetic differentiation, invented through typology studies of accommodation units for the Ulcinj project.[10]

The decisive moment that triggered this particular path to innovation, I would argue, was the change of operational mode; that is, the restructuring of a sole-practitioner prewar type of private architectural-design practice of Zloković toward an effective collaborative teamwork with his son and daughter in the organizational *troika* mode, and the subsequent operationalization of detail design and research stages through the Institute of Architecture and Urban Planning of Serbia (IAUS). I would contend that the chosen mode of practice relates closely to Zloković's advanced research of modular coordination and his role in the federal bodies for standardization that led to meetings and intersections with colleagues through his participation as a delegate in international organizations and networks including the International Organization for Standardization (ISO), the European Productivity Agency (EPA), the Congress of the *Conseil International du Bâtiment* (CIB) and the International Modular Group (IMG).

For the purposes of the present study, I would single out relations between Zloković, Guiuseppe Ciribini[11] and Konrad Wachsmann[12] that are argued to

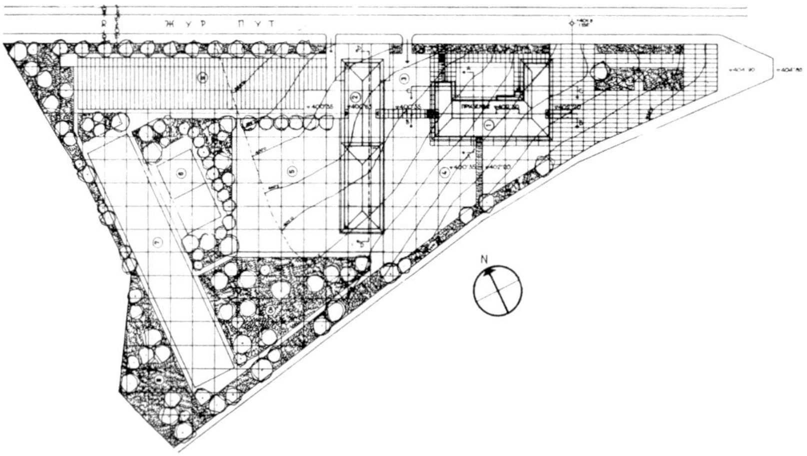

fig. 2 Milan Zloković, Đorđe Zloković and Milica Mojović, Teachers College in Prizren, 1959–1960. Site plan, in Zloković, Mojović and Zloković, "Nova učiteljska škola u Prizrenu: studijska primena modularne koordinacije mera na projektat zgrade montažnog tipa," *Zbornik radova IAUS*, 1 (1961), 16.

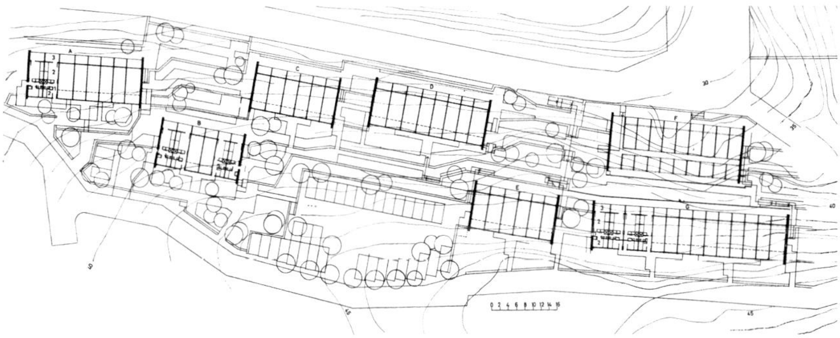

fig. 3 Zloković, Zloković and Mojović, Tourist Colony Hotel Mediterranean in Ulcinj, 1959–1961, 1961–1964. Site plan of phase 1 showing structure of accommodation pavilions superimposed on the topography, in Milan Zloković, "Novo turističko naselje u Ulcinju," *Arhitektura urbanizam*, IV: 22–23 (1963), 49.

have been decisive for procuring operational intelligence in the Prizren and Ulcinj projects. The direct intersections of the three experts are recorded in several instances, outlined here: as members of IMG and CIB, Ciribini and Zloković met at regular intervals in international forums in the mid-1950s and mid-1960s; along with Wachsmann, all three crossed paths as authors of research articles in the thematic issue of the journal *La Casa* published in 1957 by the Italian National Institute for the State Employees (Istituto nazionale per le case degli impiegati dello Stato, INCIS).[13] As guest lecturers, all three took part in the course on current culture of industrialized construction at the University of Bari Faculty of Engineering in 1963–1964; and as authors they contributed three consecutive chapters in the book on industrialization of construction, resulting from that same course and published in 1965.[14] Comparative analysis of Zloković's research in modular design, Ciribini's application of industrial-process programing in building construction, and Wachsmann's model of collaborative teamwork, lead me to the conclusion of an operational interrelation of three theories that led to their direct application in the Prizren and Ulcinj projects.

The adaptation of the model of the industrial-process programing applied in building, as advocated by Ciribini, is seen as the key to efficient construction, especially in the case of Ulcinj. Programing was central for achieving the goal of having buildings constructed in record time in peripheral locations with no rail connection and very poor road-traffic connectivity, such as Ulcinj in the 1960s. Consequent to building works' programing based on that used in industrial production, in Ulcinj the construction and fitting out of seven three-story accommodation pavilions of almost five-hundred beds in hotel category "B" were finalized in six months, from the end of the tourist season in October 1962 to the beginning of the next in May 1963. This timescale owed much to the tight design and supervision operation devised by Zloković's team, which is comparable to the teamwork model concurrently proposed by Wachsmann (fig. 4).

The proposal by Wachsmann envisages a collaborative team of twenty-one participants gathered around one general problem, organized in seven subgroups formed by three members – "team leader," "specialist," "assistant" – each working consecutively on seven separate, specific problems with discussion and coordination between the subgroups at seven interregnum points.[15] In the schematic diagram presented in the lecture held in Bari, Wachsmann lists the following particular problems: communications, material and method, construction, modules, elements, installations, and designs in the sense of *delineamento*, with a timescale allowing for discussion and coordination between topics and subgroups on a third day after each of seven serial two-day work phases, followed by final discussion, subsequent elaboration and critical presentation of results which involves the whole team.[16]

Zloković's model is downsized to a given situation of a three-member family team, a troika working from home. Comparative insights demonstrate that the troika addressed seven particular themes, effectively switching decision-making roles as fitting to the design topics at hand. According to conversations I had with Đorđe Zloković in 2013 and 2014, Milan Zloković is likely to have been the team leader in charge of topic 1, typology and modular coordination; of topic 2, method and materials; and of topic 3, socio-cultural,

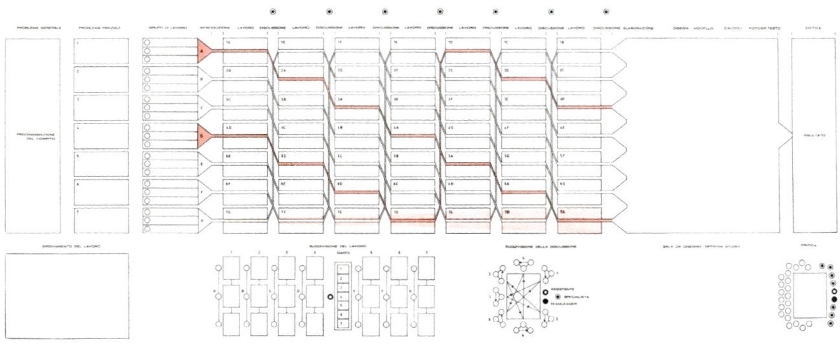

fig. 4 Konrad Wachsmann, "Schema del piano di lavoro collegiale di un 'team' anonimo," *La Casa*, 4 (1957), n.p.

climatic and environmental factors. Đorđe Zloković, team specialist in structural engineering, was team leader in charge of topic 4, structure and seismic; topic 5, construction, bill of quantities and site supervision; and topic 6, interior and furniture design. Milica Mojović, an architect specializing in descriptive geometry and a team assistant, was principal team leader in issues of topic 7, drawing production. The integration of teaching and research figures into both models.

Wachsmann had developed a method of study and research in collegial groups of three that correlates to the troika members, who were simultaneously carrying out research and design at home and detail design in IAUS and were teaching and/or subspecializing at the University of Belgrade: Milan Zloković as full professor of architectural design at the Faculty of Architecture, Đorđe – having graduated in architecture (1951) and civil engineering (1955), and having defended his doctorate in structural engineering in architecture (1961), and as assistant professor in Structural Systems at the Faculty of Architecture; and Milica Mojović as teaching assistant at the Faculty of Mechanical Engineering and postgraduate in Descriptive Geometry at the Faculty of Architecture. To summarize, operational intelligence of industrial-process programing and complex decision-making were correlated to the practical experience of carrying out state-of-the-art programs in Prizren and Ulcinj by Zloković's team, not by reduction of theory but through its rigorous rationalization.

Political Intelligence: Self-Management

The operational innovation outlined above, as my investigation of the political context indicates, was consequent to constitutional, legislative and governance changes introduced in Yugoslavia in the mid-1950s. Correlative to that, I would propose that in Prizren and Ulcinj, political intelligence engendered certain design intelligence while innovative design engendered new forms of territorial governance. Most notably, the Constitutional Law of Yugoslavia, enacted in 1953, introduced local authorities' right to communal self-management. Subsequently, the new legislation on municipal authority over communal urban-planning issues was passed in 1957, bestowing decision-making power to the municipalities – independent of state and federal levels – over questions of priority development planning and financing, and economic, communal, social and cultural matters of common interest.[17] Thus, in planning matters, the initiative, financing and executive decisions were effectively transferred from the level of republic or federal state to the communal level, through institutes of self-management supported by the local economy, enterprises, citizens and associations of citizens. Consequently, local communities gained the authority to pass general master plans for areas, places and towns within the municipal boundaries and to establish municipal-planning councils and town-planning departments, and for related matters.

The municipalities of Prizren and Ulcinj exercised this new legislative right of territorial self-management by a municipal development initiated and funded locally in the common interest: the development of middle and higher education in Prizren, and of tourism in Ulcinj. This explains how in 1959 local authorities could decide independently to invite an architect of their own choice to draw proposals, then could subsequently commission the architect directly to carry out the projects that were approved locally (fig. 5). As noted by the architects Zloković, Zloković and Mojović,[18] in Prizren, the decision by local community authorities was made on the basis of the rationality of projects, the speed of construction and the lowest construction-cost proposals, making the project a pioneering one across Yugoslavia for a consistent modularly coordinated, prefabricated assembly construction. This also explains the kind of political intelligence needed to procure employment of this particular co-authorial team as independent architects in charge.

Milan Zloković had been one of the most prominent modern architects in Serbia and the former Kingdom of Yugoslavia since the late 1920s.[19] Despite his extensive design and construction experience in the interwar period, during which he realized more than forty buildings, some of outstanding significance, he was completely ignored in the postwar period by the system of state design offices and construction enterprises, and was not involved in projects for wide-scale urbanization of the country. In fact, after 1945, even though more than twenty of his competition entries were awarded, commissioned or honorably mentioned, he only realized the projects in Prizren and Ulcinj. This exclusion from the process of mass construction in the postwar period

fig. 5 Zloković, Zloković and Mojović, Teachers College in Prizren. Panorama from the period, the college building in the mid-ground. Courtesy of Foundation Milan Zloković, Belgrade.

was partly a consequence of his interwar practice, as he had been seen as a representative of a deposed system. This was partly due to the architect's own reluctance to forfeit individual authorial practice during the period of the dominant state sector and collectivistic organization models.

The political decision for territorial self-management then opened the possibility of independent architectural agency and of direct work for a local community. The early 1950s also brought about a liberalization of professions in Yugoslavia, including that of architecture.[20] A number of prominent architects across the country set up individual design offices, societally owned but organizationally run as a master/team leader type of practice that could enter into the (socialist) market competition. Thus, direct contracts between client-municipality and expert architect enabled both parties to act independently, free from top-down directives from the state or federal levels. In addition, a growing segment comprising individually authored or specialist design and academia on one side and the mass-construction sector on the other was gradually taken over by a number of interdisciplinary offices that combined research and design. The architects Zloković, Zloković and Mojović took advantage of this change by contracting detail-design commissions with IAUS, the first such institution in Belgrade, established by the University of Belgrade Faculty of Architecture in 1954. To sum up, a clever setup of political intelligence and self-management in the right moment was decisive for the successful acquisition of the projects in Prizren and Ulcinj.

Design Intelligence: Architectural Theory

Finally, I would propose that the principal source of design intelligence or method lay in an architectural theory that should be comprehended across the horizon of the discipline's history. Over the postwar period, when his private practice had ceased, Milan Zloković dedicated himself to academic and research work and gradually built up original research that was published in some twenty articles. In sum, this work led to something that I would call a fully elaborated aesthetic theory of architecture, synthesized under the title Modular Coordination; it was published in Italian in 1965 as a chapter in the book *Industrializzazione dell'edilizia* (fig. 6).[21] As has been discussed in more detail in previous research, the theory argues for relating the proportional systems of the past with the contemporary notion of modular coordination; its aim is to prove the elasticity of the rational compositional method and its capacity for varied architectural interpretation.[22] Zloković tests his hypothesis through a series of geometric, numerical and diagrammatic analyses of the proportional systems of historical case studies and their translation into the *lingua franca* of the International Standards Organization. Indicative in this respect is his article published in 1960, testing a method of integrating Le Corbusier's "Modulor" as foot-and-inch proportional system with the metric-based international modular system. This is derived by a series of recurrent numbers as means of translation, through comparative analysis of cases ranging from the Vitruvian-man interpretations by Leonardo da Vinci and Gio. Antonio Rusconi to contemporary proposals by Ernst Neufert, Frederick Kiesler and himself.[23] In the 1950s, Zloković's research and analytical drawings were correlative to the method and content of the exhibition *Studi sulle proporzioni* by Carla Marzoli and architect Francesco Gnecchi Ruscone at the ninth Milan Triennale, in 1951.[24] It corresponded with a consensus – all too brief – of architects, art historians and artists of the period who gathered as participants at the First International Congress on Proportion in the Arts, held concurrently in Milan,[25] and who shared the view that some kind of controlling or regulative system of proportion was desirable. By reading the unpublished papers from the congress that Zloković got hold of through contacts with Ms. Marzoli in Milan,[26] he felt confident to continue analogous research of compositional methods despite criticism and opposition from his peers in Yugoslavia.

Design intelligence in both of the projects discussed in this article drew directly from such research into rational compositional methods. Due to

fig. 6 *Industrializzazione dell'edilizia* (Bari: Dedalo, 1965), dust-jacket drawing by Milan Zloković. Courtesy of Foundation Milan Zloković, Belgrade.

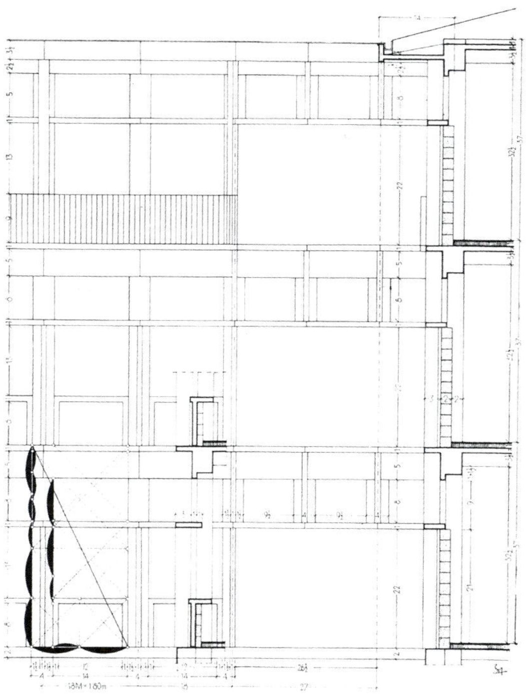

fig. 7 Zloković, Zloković and Mojović, Teachers' College in Prizren. Study of facade proportions, drawing by Milan Zloković, in Zloković, Mojović, and Zloković, "Nova učiteljska škola u Prizrenu," 21.

extreme budget constraints, the architectural articulation of an otherwise basic volume of the Prizren school relays on what the architects called "final surface facture,"[27] that is, the contour modulation of prefabricated facade elements, assembled with no finishing work needed. The proportional relations of the basic facade unit were tested by a proportional diagram (*tracé régulateur*) of the elements and their relations, and were taken as a basis for com-

fig. 8 Zloković, Zloković and Mojović, Tourist Colony Hotel Mediterranean in Ulcinj. Panorama from the period, the colony in the mid-ground (Hotel Co-op, penultimate building on the right). Courtesy of Foundation Milan Zloković, Belgrade.

positional and structural elaboration of the overall external appearance of the building. It is interesting to note that the ratios 9:5 and 8:5 in the Prizren project were derived from Zloković's study of the Roman compass as a proportioning tool (fig. 7). The Ulcinj project, on the other hand, consists of ten separate buildings arranged on a rather topographically complex site[28] (fig. 8). The design intelligence there originated from the typology study of accommodation units that was to be carried out prior to the design stage by Milan and Đorđe Zloković who were commissioned with this research by the local communities of Budva and Ulcinj in Montenegro.[29] The resulting elements' "typification" in the Ulcinj colony combined criteria of "compositional efficiency" (modular coordination), and "maximum economy" (minimum expenditure to maximum effect).[30]

Concluding Notes

The two respective projects discussed in this chapter – that is, the higher education school in Prizren and the tourist colony in Ulcinj – are directly related to the debates on construction which took place in and around the international framework of European productivity and standards organizations at the end of the 1950s and the beginning of the 1960s. The resonances of this debate gave rise to a worldwide organizational restructuring of the construction industry as a whole and of the professions of architecture and engineering specifically; mass construction then became a global phenomenon. In other words, the change in scale of spatial production as a consequence of postwar societal changes was instituted worldwide by an effective agenda to position architectural, engineering and construction management practices in respect to system design, programing and multidisciplinary team work – an agenda that arose from growing demands of productivity, standardization and industrialization of construction. In parallel, the tremendous changes that were brought about by societal transformations after the Second World War caused a significant increase in social mobility and an empowerment of local actors on both sides of the polarized Cold War world. This chapter has aimed to explore alternative design-practice modes and innovative design strategies that emerged in 1960s Yugoslavia under the political, ideological, economic and social constraints of the socialist period. The projects discussed demonstrate alternatives regarding the design itself, and regarding the diversity of professional practice. In sum, it can be argued that the two cases demonstrate the full spectrum of architectural intelligence as its key agencies established through dialectical relations of operational intelligence, political intelligence and design intelligence. They also illustrate, I would propose, connections between public and private sectors that may be worth considering in the transitional contexts of today.

Endnotes

1 Alison Smithson and Peter Smithson, "The Heroic Period of Modern Architecture," *Architectural Design*, XXXV-12 (1965), 587–637 (p. 590).

2 The chapter ensues from the present author's introductory lecture titled "Modular Design: Architect Milan Zloković and Discourse of Industrialised Construction," held on November 29, 2014, at the international symposium "East West Central 02. Re-Scaling the Environment: New Landscapes of Design, 1960–1980" at ETH Zurich, Department of Architecture, Institute for the History and Theory of Architecture, Chair for the Theory of Architecture: Prof. Dr. Ákos Moravánszky. The lecture and the chapter expand on, re-examine and elaborate on the modular design thematic initially presented in a lecture by the same author at the international symposium "Modular Design: Prefabricating the Post-war Landscape," at the *Politecnico di Milano, Dipartimento di Architettura e Studi Urbani* on October 22, 2013, and in the article pending publication: Ljiljana Blagojević, "Modernism of Scarcity: Architect Milan Zloković and Debates on Industrialization of Construction in the 1950s and 1960s," *Le culture della tecnica* 27 (2016): forthcoming.

3 Based on *The Shorter Oxford English Dictionary on Historical Principles*, 1973.

4 See Ljiljana Blagojević, "Collectives: Notes on Alternative Design Practices of the Second World," in *Lifting the Curtain*, eds. Samu Szemerey, Igor Kovacevic and Piotr Bujas (Liège: Fourre-Tout Editions, forthcoming in 2016).

5 Initially envisaged as the new administrative capital of the Yugoslav Federation – with the seats of the Presidency of Federal Government and the Central Committee of the Communist Party of Yugoslavia located at its center – New Belgrade was planned as a modern, functional city for some quarter-million inhabitants. See related research by the author: Ljiljana Blagojević, "The Residence as a Decisive Factor: Modern Housing in the Central Zone of New Belgrade," *Architektúra & Urbanizmus: Journal of Architectural and Town-Planning Theory*, 46: 3–4, 228–249; Ljiljana Blagojević, "Novi Beograd: Reinventing Utopia," in *Urban Revolution Now: Henri Lefebvre in Social Research and Architecture*, eds. Łukasz Stanek, Christian Schmid and Ákos Moravánszky (Farnham, London: Ashgate, 2014), 301–318. See also Ljiljana Blagojević, *Novi Beograd: osporeni modernizam* (Belgrade: Zavod za udzbenike, 2007).

6 Prizren, ancient Theranda, is located on the north side of the Albanian border along the Prokletije Mountains and Ulcinj, the ancient Olcinium is on its south side, near the confluence of the river Bojana into the Adriatic Sea.

7 Prof. Milan Zloković, architect (1898–1965), academician Đorđe Zloković of the Serbian Academy of Sciences and Arts (b. 1927), architect and civil engineer, and Prof. Dr. Milica Mojović, architect (b. 1932).

8 Milan Zloković, Milica Mojović and Đorđe Zloković, "Nova učiteljska škola u Prizrenu: studijska primena modularne koordinacije mera na projektat zgrade montažnog tipa," *Zbornik radova IAUS*, 1 (1961), 15–22; "Viša pedagoška škola u Prizrenu," *Zbornik radova IAUS*, 6 (1972), 38–39.

9 "Turističko naselje u Ulcinju," *Zbornik radova IAUS*, 5 (1970), 216–223.

10 For a detailed analysis, see Ljiljana Blagojević and Marija Milinković, "The Beauty of Production: Module and Its Social Significance," *arq: Architectural Research Quarterly*, 17:3–4 (2013), 253–268.

11 Prof. Dr. Giuseppe Ciribini (1913–1990), engineer; see Daniela Bosia, ed., *L'opera di Giuseppe Ciribini* (Milano: Francoangeli, 2013).

12 Prof. Konrad Wachsmann (1901–1980), architect.

13 Giuseppe Ciribini, "Introduzione all'applicazione di metodologie industriali nella construzione"; Konrad Wachsmann, "Per una indistrializzazione della produzione"; Milan Zloković, "Interpretazione modulare degli ordini del Vignola," in *La casa. Quaderni di architettura e di critica*, III:4 (1957), 81–87, 120–137, 162–169.

14 Ciribini, "Il processo dell'industrializzazione edilizia: problemi e sviluppi"; Wachsmann, "La complessità delle decisioni in architettura"; Zloković, "La coordinazione modulare," in AA.VV. *Industrializzazione dell'edilizia* (Bari: Dedalo, 1965), 117–127, 129–138, 139–196. For a more detailed account of the contacts between the three experts, see: Ljiljana Blagojević, *Itinereri: Moderna i Mediteran. Tragovima arhitekata Nikole Dobrovića i Milana Zlokovića* (Belgrade: Službeni glasnik and Arhitektonski fakultet, 2015), 146–155.

15 Wachsmann, "Per una indistrializzazione della produzione," 123–125.

16 Wachsmann, "La complessità delle decisioni in architettura," 135.

17 Vladimir Bjelikov, "Komuna kao predmet prostornog planiranja," *Zbornik Arhitektonskog fakulteta Univerziteta u Beogradu*, 5 (1962), 3.
18 Zloković, Mojović and Zloković, "Nova učiteljska škola u Prizrenu," 15.
19 On Zloković's interwar architecture, see Ljiljana Blagojević, *Modernism in Serbia: The Elusive Margins of Belgrade Architecture, 1919–1941* (Cambridge, Mass.: MIT Press in association with the Harvard University Graduate School of Design, 2003), passim. Also, by the same author, see Blagojević, *Itinereri: Moderna i Mediteran.* …, passim.
20 For an account of the changing forms of practice in the postwar period, see the case of APZ in Zagreb, a hundred-employee central-design office in Croatia, formed in 1947 and dissolved in 1954 by splitting into fourteen design offices led by prominent individuals; see Darko Venturini, *Arhitektonski projektni zavod – APZ: prilog poslijeratnoj hrvatskoj arhitekturi* (Zagreb: APZ, 1982).
21 Zloković, "La coordinazione modulare."
22 Blagojević and Milinković, "The Beauty of Production," passim.
23 Zloković, "Integrisanje 'Modulor'-a u internacionalni modularni sistem," *Arhitektura urbanizam*, 6 (1960), 28–31.
24 See Maria Netter, "Panorama des Formexperiments an der 9. Triennale von Mailand," *Werk*, 38:9 (1951), 257–262; Alfred Roth, "Das Wohnquartier QT8 und die Triennale von Mailand," *Werk*, 38:9 (1951), 263–265; and Alfred Roth, "Erster internationaler Kongress über die Proportionen in der Kunst (in Mailand am 27., 28. und 29. September 1951)," *Werk* 38:11 (1951), 154–155. See also Franceseco Gnecchi Ruscone, *Storie di Architettura* (Milano: Francesco Brioschi Editore, 2015), 47–48, 93–96, tables 12, 13.
25 Rudolf Wittkower, "The Changing Concept of Proportion," *Daedalus* 89:1 (1960), 199–215 (p. 210).
26 Milan Zloković, "Antropomorfni sistemi mera u arhitekturi: njihovo integrisanje u kompoziciske metode prošlosti, posebno objašnjeno na nekoliko karakterističnih primera drugostepene kamene plastike Boke Kotorske, Korčule i Dubrovnika," *Zbornik zaštite spomenika kulture*, IV–V (1955), 181–216.
27 Zloković, Mojović, and Zloković, "Nova učiteljska škola u Prizrenu," 20.
28 The colony continues along the natural amphitheater rising above the beach, lined along roughly the same isohypsis with the Hotel Co-op (a modernist hotel from the interwar period, that was demolished in the 2000s), that offered communal and restaurant services to pavilions of the first phase. On the exceptional project of the hotel, see: Ljiljana Blagojević and Borislav Vukićević, "Hotel Ko-op u Ulcinju arhitekata Hinka Bauera i Marijana Haberlea," *Prostor* 21:1 [45], 14–25.
29 Milan Zloković and Georges Zloković, *Coordination modulaire appliquée en architecture. Types touristiques en Yougoslavie, Côte Adriatique – Littoral Monténégrin* (Belgrade: Institut Yougoslave pour la Productivité du Travail, 1961), four pp. separate extract.
30 *Tipizzazione, efficienza compositiva, massima economia*; see: Zloković, "La coordinazione modulare," 190–192.

Erik Sigge

From New Empiricism to Structuralism. The Swedish National Board of Public Building (KBS)[1]

In an essay published in 1972, architectural historian Henry A. Millon of MIT examined the legacy of Rudolf Wittkower's seminal book *Architectural Principles in the Age of Humanism* from 1949 and its specific influence on the development and interpretation of Modern architecture.[2] Millon's essay offers insight into the (1970s) comprehension of Wittkower's importance specifically in regards to "(a) modular construction, (b) views on proportion and composition, (c) reassessments of aims and achievements of the 1920s and '30s." Millon saw *Architectural Principles* as having the greatest and longest impact on the latter (c); with its precedent as historical research and its methodology primarily represented by Wittkower's pupils, such as Colin Rowe.

Particularly interesting and thought-provoking is the link Millon made between Wittkower and the modernist standardization research, with American architect Ezra Ehrenkrantz as an example. Ehrenkrantz referenced a number of theories and studies on proportion and modules from Alberti to Wittkower, and perhaps, as Millon asserted, the reason for giving the practice of using modules a historical tradition was that Ehrenkrantz wanted to "legitimize and promote his new expanded modular system."[3] Reyner Banham also acknowledged the principal influence Wittkower's research had on postwar architecture. In his seminal essay "The New Brutalism," Banham claimed that *Architectural Principles* was "by far the most important contribution – for evil as well as good – by any historian of English architecture since [Pevsner's] *Pioneers of the Modern Movement*."[4]

From a Swedish perspective, the discussion in the U.K. is particularly interesting as it contained several links to Sweden and because the British expressed an open and sincere interest in Swedish architecture and planning after the war. The British interest was in fact directed toward Swedish projects that were directly influenced by the English New Town movement's theory and practice.

By this time, the interest in Swedish planning also curiously took a more specific turn, as the *Architectural Review* reiterated the somewhat vague story of the coining of the term "New Brutalism" as it referred to the designation of the Villa Göth (1950) in Uppsala by Bengt Edman and Lennart Holm as a "brutalist" building during a site visit with British architects in 1951.[5] Banham stated further on, when contextualizing the phrase New Brutalism: "The history of the phrase itself is revealing. Its form is clearly derived from *The Architectural Review*'s postwar *trouvaille* 'The New Empiricism,' a term which was intended to describe visible tendencies in Scandinavian architecture to diverge from another historical concept 'The International Style.'"[6] Whatever the origin of the phrase Brutalism, or for that matter, the New Brutalism, Banham asserted that the latter was first a derogatory term of architecture that deviated from The New Humanism, which in turn meant "brickwork, segmental arches, pitched roofs, small windows (or small panes at any rate) – picturesque detailing without picturesque planning."

New Empiricism was clearly a Swedish (or perhaps Scandinavian) variation of The New Humanism and indeed displayed building features of bare brickwork, pitched roof, etc. However, what Banham called "picturesque detailing" was fading by the mid-1950s and gave way to more uniform buildings. An example of this shift was the new suburb of Vällingby, which opened in 1955 and immediately became the new destination for architects, planners and politicians from abroad as an exemplary "best practice."

The National Board of Public Building (KBS)

It is at this time that the Swedish National Board of Public Building (KBS) started a programmatic approach towards processes of architectural production that stressed structural rationalization and efficiency instead of social and humanist ambitions. KBS's role as builder had evolved substantially since its founding in 1918, and at the same time it was, even in the 1960s, an institution that in the end was tied to the same main tasks of building management and building construction. The regulatory and investigative duties increased during the first half of the twentieth century, and as the Government grew bigger, the building sector's importance grew stronger and KBS's importance increased. From 1940 to 1980 the staff of KBS grew by almost tenfold, from

fig. 1 KBS's buildings for the National Telecommunication Board in Farsta outside of Stockholm, completed in 1969 and designed by Bengt Hidemark and Gösta Danilesson. Photo Holger Ellgaard, CC, 2012.

344 to 2151.[7] Part of the reason for this big increase of employees was the fact that KBS had expanded its work duties with permanent management staff in offices facilities and in the main administration of the agency, but the main reason was the growth of the Government and with it, the increased need for premises[8] (fig. 1).

During the 1960s, KBS intensified its efforts in finding efficient working methods in order to complete building projects within budgets. The agency had been forced to focus on these matters after a major miscalculation of costs for the renovation of the Stockholm Opera House in 1955–1961.[9] KBS also acquired insight into and knowledge of contemporary trends and developments abroad; and as we will see, they were making direct contacts through study-trips, for instance to the United Kingdom, West Germany and the Netherlands.

If we were to characterize KBS's development work during the 1960s, it could roughly be divided into ways of working (process), ways of making (technology), and naturally, a combination of the two. KBS specific development projects were usually aimed at producing a report or some kind of document, and there were many reports initiated and published during the 1960s. Three larger projects stand out both because of their size and the scope of undertaking, and for their subsequent importance for the development of the theoretical and practical framework of KBS's new thinking: *Byggprocess och verksplanering* (1966), *Office Building Investigation 1966* (1967) and *Om byggnader för högre utbildning* (1967).[10]

The first report focused on building processes and organization, and was largely a result of KBS's longstanding efforts to find efficient working methods in order to make building projects with a high degree of predictability and control. The work with the office buildings report was an investigation to find rational systems for constructing new office buildings. The last of the three reports dealt with university buildings and was primarily a continuation of the office building report and developed those concepts and methods further and in relation to the work with educational facilities. The majority of the report consisted of technical analyses and studies of how to implement best the recent findings of flexibility and adaptability.

In the early 1960s, KBS conducted a number of study trips abroad to look at other countries' state or regional civil building programs. In the Netherlands, KBS visited the technical universities in Eindhoven and Delft. In West Germany the delegates visited the technical universities of Stuttgart and Karlsruhe and the universities of Freiburg and Tubingen, all in the state of Baden-Württemberg. The trip to the United Kingdom was made specifically to visit institutions working with maintenance and the new construction of state buildings. One of these was the Ministry of Health. KBS's delegation carefully noted the detailed working methodologies that were presented to them. The Ministry of Health's building process when constructing new hospitals was divided into six phases: 1, 2 and 3 were brief, program writing and costs estimates; 4 was design; 5 was construction; and phase 6 was post-inspection.[11] This "working methodology" sprung out of a notion that: a building is an organism and not a pile of building material; the planning has to be governed by the cost; the projected users of the building must participate in the planning; and the division of responsibilities changes throughout the different phases. In regards to responsibilities, phases 1 and 2 were dominated by the users whereas 3, 4, and 5 were by architects, technicians, and contractors. And finally, phase 6, the users again. This display of a foreign state institution's experiences with construction – and their thoughts about the process of building – must have been of the highest interest for KBS, which in the fall of 1964 had most likely started the work of the above-mentioned report *Byggprocess och verksplanering*, an investigation of building processes.[12]

Hospital planning, in the United Kingdom and elsewhere, gradually adopted the concept of flexibility during the 1960s.[13] British architect John Weeks was perhaps the clearest proponent of structuralist ideas in hospital planning. In his article *Planning for Growth and Change* from 1960 he discussed ideas of how to accommodate for change and expansion in new hospital buildings. He stated that "in a growing, changing hospital, it is the communication pattern which can tie the whole together maintaining its pattern in spite of extension and shifting of the parts within the whole."[14]

Weeks later developed his ideas into something he called "indeterminate architecture," in which buildings were divided into three categories: 1) where growth occurs through additions; 2) growth occurs through new construction; 3) growth does not occur.[15] We do not know if KBS's meeting with the

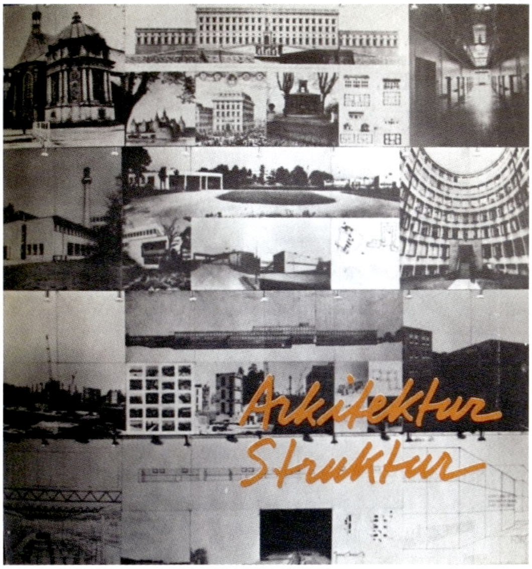

fig. 2 Cover of catalogue for the 1968 exhibition *Arkitektur – Struktur* (Architecture – Structure) published in 1969. Catalogue is in the holdings of the Swedish Center for Architecture and Design, Stockholm. Photo of catalogue by the author.

Ministry of Health included presentations of John Weeks' ideas or if they discussed building examples of recent hospital design. In any case, it is clear that English hospital architecture of 1964 comprised many of the issues that became significant in KBS's own developments during the latter half of the 1960s.

As a more general comment, the travelers remarked on England's use of modular systems as being at the forefront when it came to light systems, and on the contrary – England had "a lot to learn from abroad" in regards to heavier and large-scale building systems.[16] The group especially noted highly rational, efficient and sophisticated methods and results in the construction of educational facilities, and most notably through the so-called CLASP program. KBS later looked more carefully into CLASP and other British and American building systems as they prepared the report on systems construction published in 1973.[17]

KBS's "Structure Philosophy"

In 1968 the National Board of Public Building (KBS) officially adopted a structuralist philosophy of architecture, and in order to publicly introduce the new ideas, KBS organized an exhibition in 1968 titled *Architecture-Structure*.[18] It presented the work of KBS and introduced a new approach to building, which came to be known as KBS's "structure philosophy." The exhibition introduced KBS's current and future ideas of architecture; more specifically of the design, construction and management of buildings, and in particular the processes of building (fig. 2).

The exhibition's promise of "a new set of concepts for building that recognizes the plurality and mutability of reality and the potential of technology"[19] echoes various renowned architecture ideas such as Oskar Hansen's theory of Open Form and the theories of the Dutch structuralists. KBS's ideas were also similar to the work of other nations' federal and regional institutions, such as those working with the building of educational facilities in the Netherlands, West Germany and the United Kingdom. Their approaches were similar, primarily, in their emphasis on structure over function, and in incorporating the aspects of time and change in planning. However, they were also parallel and comparable for focusing on building processes and organization, developing working methodologies that could ensure ideas were transferred into built form.

A considerable part of *Architecture – Structure* was devoted to the Swedish functionalism of 1930–1968. Statements from the seminal manifesto *acceptera* from 1931 were quoted in the exhibition as to represent the key ideas of Swedish functionalist thinking.[20] Phrases such as "accept the present reality," denoted that the modernization had made both architecture and the building process obsolete in meeting the needs of society, and that there were new architecture and means for production available that were more pertinent if Sweden should become a modern country. The extracted declarations that were quoted in *Architecture – Structure* were selected to fit the arguments leading to KBS's new structuralist theory.

At large, KBS embraced the modernist developments in Sweden, especially with the increased interest in "social justice" and "public responsibility" and the benefits of investigative work, although this mainly applied to housing. Also positively regarded was the functionalists' work with the standardization of building components and the progression that was made in building technology with the use new materials, systems and methods. However, KBS stated that the main problem with functionalist architecture and its design process was the strong emphasis on functional analysis.

Specifically problematic was the "certainty that the function of a building could be finitely determined" and that "each functional part (= room) was designed to fulfill a specific purpose." In *Architecture – Structure*, KBS's critique against this perspective was pronounced: "Respect for functional requirements has hindered the evolution of methods whereby economy, adaptability, etc., could be taken into account. The aim has been to achieve a product that is perfectly matched to function at a given instant in time."[21] It is true that adaptability was not a premiered attribute in buildings before 1960 – and was still sparse during the 1960s – although experiments and proposals for adaptable systems could be found much earlier in such diverse works as Le

Corbusier's "Dom-ino" structure and Rudolph Schindler's "Schindler Frame," to mention just a few. The prevailing attitude towards function during this period was still close to "form follows function" which, despite its ambiguous nature, was more than just a set phrase.

The second part of *Architecture – Structure* dwelled further on the problems with modernism's insistence on functional analysis and how that caused not only problems in adapting buildings to a new function, but flaws in the organization of the building industry and the process of building. KBS did not settle with giving such criticism. The majority of the second half of the exhibition presented KBS's own research work of finding principles and methods for building, and introduced structuralist thinking in relation to KBS's mission of "premises production." The main problem with the building process since 1930 was, according to KBS, that the design phase was in an initial stage of the building process and thus the design choices of the architect decided the outcome of cost and technical requirements. The new proposed building process should instead, in the first stage, put emphasis on technical requirements and costs, and make decisions based on them. The actual design phase should not start until all decisions were made and then be a so-called "controlled design."

Nils Ahrbom (1905–1997), one of KBS's leading programmatic architects, argued that these structuralist concepts and methods were developed within KBS from 1965 until 1968, without direct influences from similar international theories.[22] Ahrbom claimed that the KBS managers probably were unaware of the international developments and that KBS's structuralist methodology was a result of other aspirations and not a goal within itself.[23] It is not surprising that architects at KBS did not see their own investigative work as leading to an "architecture philosophy," neither is it unexpected that they did not see the study-trips and international contacts as directly influencing their own work. Still it is obvious that many of KBS's official international contacts during the 1960s were occupied with similar problems and developments, and, arguably, we could describe KBS's development work as following a few steps behind.

Ahrbom claimed *Office Building Investigation 1966* to be the earliest signs of KBS's structure philosophy. The KBS report is reprinted in the exhibition, stating that "a building should be designed so as to facilitate the replacement of its component parts as indicated by their functional and technical life. Parts should be arranged in distinct groups so that changes in one group do not involve interference with another group that may have a longer life."[24] From this paragraph we can follow the logic of the new thinking, and two important concepts could emerge from the ideas: interchangeability – the building's components could be replaced by others; and life-span separation – parts are grouped according to life expectancy. In spite of the strong rejection of the functional analysis of Swedish modernism, KBS proposed "[i]ntegration of functional studies, in a form which takes the time factor into account and finally departs from the static concept of functionalism."[25]

The discussion of the "time factor" was at the core of structuralist debates from the early 1950s onwards. It was also discussed in the meetings of the organization *Congrès Internationaux d'Architecture Moderne*, CIAM (1928–1959). Nils Ahrbom wrote regarding the interim CIAM meeting in Sigtuna in 1952, which was one of his first as a new member. The report from the meeting emphasized the importance of "adaptability" (*föränderbarhet*), the interplay between human being and environment, and the city's "inner context" and "integration."[26] The CIAM meeting in Sigtuna was announced in preparation for the ninth meeting in Aix-en-Provence 1953, and the Swedish host, Sven Markelius wrote the report in question. Ahrbom speculated on Markelius' own influence on the content as he worked with similar issues as chairman of the committee of building standardization and director of city planning in Stockholm. Nevertheless, the "time factor," or "time aspect," was indeed central to the discussions in Sigtuna and Dutch architect Wim van Bodegraven has been credited with bringing up the ideas on the meeting agenda.[27] Van Bodegraven thought architecture needed a "structure of forms" that could be altered with time but still keep its "coherence" and "meaning."[28]

Ahrbom himself was also interested in the aspects of time in building and had already in 1934 written a text on flexible room divisions in apartments,[29] which could be seen as the embryo of this thought in his own work. In 1945 he wrote an article title "Spatial Design: Philosophy or Architecture?" in which he stated: "Flexible plans become dynamic over the years as the room divisions can be changed from time to time. This kind of mechanical mobility in the planning had nothing to do with the nature of the spaces that are altered."[30] Ten years later, Ahrbom brought his reasoning around flexible space further in a lecture in Helsinki, stressing that "mobility, changeability, adaptability, and generality" should be favored in new buildings.[31] These ideas became central in KBS's development of its "structure philosophy."

Returning to CIAM. The ninth meeting caused a major split between the older and the younger members. The younger ones got the mandate to organize the next meeting, the tenth, which they did under the name of Team 10. The reasons for the conflict were many but the unifying voice of the younger essentially sprung out of the ideas of the Sigtuna meeting.[32] However, it was not until their eleventh meeting in Otterlo 1959 that the theories of Team 10 were crystallized into something more cohesive.

One interesting but little known event in Otterlo was Norwegian-Polish architect Oskar Hansen's presentation of Open Form.[33] Hansen's theory could be described as a principle allowing for the user's active participation. The aim was to resolve architecture's problematic relationship between the individual and the collective. The two are, in Hansen's theory, represented by subjective components (individual engagements) and objective components (societal and social commitments) in building and planning. The division of components was thus also done according to scale, from the individual space up to city planning. During the 1960s, Hansen developed the Open Form ideas into something he called "linear continuous system," which could also be seen as related to Le Corbusier's proposed plans for Algiers or Rio de Janerio, with a long, continuous meta system of housing. Le Corbusier's design for Algiers was planned for a sort of in-fill units. A similar idea was realized the same year as Otterlo in Swedish architect Erik Friberger's experimental building in Kallebäck.[34] Friberger built a three-story structure of concrete decks on columns, for which the floors were divided into lots for individual houses – a multi-story parking garage for dwellings. Previously, Friberger had made numerous experiments and designs for flexible systems of standardized modular units. In 1937 he had written an article[35] that Nils Ahrbom argued had almost identical objectives as Hansen's Open Form, some twenty years later.[36]

Nonetheless, Hansen's vision of a total, continuous environment as the platform for changing activities, or "the art of events," was the theoretical foundation for many structuralist ideas during the 1960s. KBS's distinction between components according to duration of use or lifespan was another structuralist approach, and it became a very important perspective for KBS.

The Division of Parts

Nils Ahrbom had predicted in his 1955 Helsinki lecture that the concepts "mobility, changeability, adaptability and generality" should be premiered in building and not be hindered by "rigidity" and "narrow-mindedness" in production.[37] Although he presented the concepts in relation to the theme "modular construction," the historical significance of Ahrbom's statements is evident, and arguably, the lecture is the historical origin of KBS's "structure philosophy." In the late 1960s, KBS then adopted a categorization system with three levels, which was described in the *Architecture – Structure* exhibition as:

– function or activity-related parts (*funktions- or verksamhetsknutna delar*) that are short-lived, can be replaced or removed, can be adapted to changing activities

– building-related parts (*byggnadsknutna delar*) that are long-lived, static, and cannot easily be moved

– environment-related parts (*samhällsknutna delar*) that together with other parts, constitute the total environment[38] (fig. 3).

The organization of building parts according to this categorization was the feature of KBS's structuralist philosophy that had the most significant practical implementation in daily work.

The conceptualization of parts, small or big, as being interrelated and connected across the scale corresponds directly, as well as the link to Hansen, to John Habraken's "support structures." Habraken stated that "a support structure is a construction which allows the provisions of dwellings which can be built, altered and taken down independently of the others."[39] In other words, the "support structure" could be outfitted with an "in-fill." In a comment on the difference between the support and in-fill, Habraken said that "the distinction is primarily one of control and design responsibility and only secondarily technical. It is intended to restore, what is called the 'natural relation' between environmental form and inhabitant as it was found for millennia before our times."[40]

The supports and in-fills correspond to Hansen's "objective" and "subjective" components and his wish to reconcile the interests of society with those of the individual citizen. Both Hansen and Habraken's theories were grounded in an aspiration towards individual freedom and personal identification in architecture, where an individual's present and future needs and wishes should be taken into account when planning for a new building or structure. Both were primarily considering housing. KBS's structure philosophy also considered the freedom of the individual, although this was not stressed as the primary reason for making buildings "flexible" and their parts "interchangeable."

The outcome of KBS's approach with "the separation of parts" was that it created a methodology from which KBS could work. It was made easy adaptable, I argue, primarily because the recognition of groups according to characteristics corresponded to a logical division in scale. The anticipated results of using the new "methodology" were: "the abandonment of the static concept of functionalism, the simplification and systematization of work processes, industrial attitudes in building, improved opportunities to limit the number of variants, the reduction of costs (partly due to the simplification of maintenance and conversion)."[41] To KBS, the benefits of adopting the new ideas were clear. Yet, the approach needed further refinement in clarifying how and what KBS actually should build.

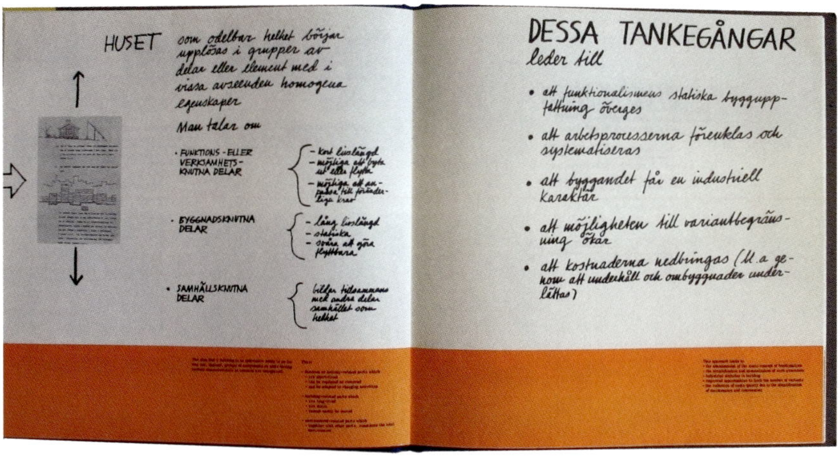

fig. 3 Spread from the catalogue *Arkitektur – Struktur* that explains the division into "function or activity-related parts, building-related parts, environment-related parts." Photo of catalogue by the author.

In this regard, KBS were influenced by a report from the Danish National Building Institute (Statens Bygge forskningsinstitut) on standardization and rationalization of building, titled *Måltypisering 1966*.[42] KBS referred to this report in the *Architecture – Structure* exhibition as they launched four new concepts: "Generality; Dimensional co-ordination; Classification according to component life, and Adaptability."[43]

1) "*Generality*" meant that a building should be "versatile" and "adaptable to different types of activity." Further, the frame of the building should be consistent with a "general dimensional system." This referred to both smaller parts of a building and to whole buildings, which together formed a larger context and related to "a universal grid."

2) "*Dimensional co-ordination*" was a concept that naturally sprung out of the efforts of standardization research, which was conducted by several institutions and since 1942 legally implemented in Sweden through *Byggstandardiseringen*. For KBS, the concept meant "rational production" and "industrial manufacturing" of units that could be combined with other units and grouped in "sufficient large number of combinations" – a strategy that would enable a rational choice between what components and manufacturers, and simplify planning, design and the work on site (fig. 4).

3) The concept "*Classification by life*" was a comprehension of buildings as being made of essentially different parts with "different life expectations," rejecting the view of buildings as "indivisible entities." In the exhibition KBS stated that "throughout its existence, the frame of the building is a construction site on which parts will be moved, modified or torn down. These changes

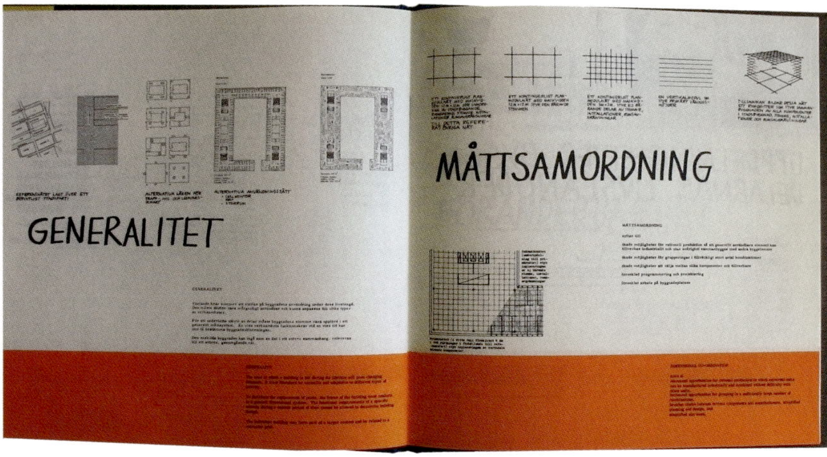

fig. 4 Spread from the catalogue *Arkitektur – Struktur* illustrating "generality" and "dimensional co-ordination." Photo of catalogue by the author.

will be designed to improve the return on the investment of the building, through better performance." Thus, in the planning process of a building, the parts should be "classified according to life." Through this statement, the impetus for a separation of parts seemed to have been purely economical and for the benefit of the builder (compare to Hansen and Habraken). And certainly, KBS were interested in cost-efficient and predictable systems for building, and most of their research was primarily concerned with the issues of control and predictability. On the other hand, KBS had also worked with quality control under the label of "performance," and this was further developed in various reports during the late 1960s and throughout the 1970s, such as *Incitamentsavtal*, *Systembyggande*, etc.[44]

4) Finally, "*Adaptability*" presupposed simple and continuous floors, movable partitions, and general mounting fixtures. One definition of adaptation is "a form or structure modified to fit a changed environment."[45] The thinking was that "adaptability" through all parts of a building meant that some parts should accommodate for an easy adaption whereas other parts should be exchanged. Therefore, the idea of generality for the structure and "interchangeability" for the fittings was imbedded in the concept of adaptability (fig. 5).

Looking at the concept of adaptability through KBS's more methodological three-level "categories of parts," we assume that only the function-related parts should be interchangeable whereas building-related and environment-related parts are general, and more or less fixed, allowing for "adaptability" of the whole. These "categories of parts," together with the four key

fig. 5 Spread from the catalogue *Arkitektur – Struktur* illustrating "classification by life" and "adaptability." Photo of catalogue by the author.

concepts described here, constitute the key points of KBS's "structure philosophy." The four concepts were by no means unique to KBS; instead they became more and more frequent in the international discussion of architecture and by the mid-1970s, they had become staple goods for any architect interested in flexible architecture.

If we return to the earlier discussion on KBS's study-trips to West Germany, Holland and England in 1963–64, we can follow some of the influences from these excursions in the 1968 exhibition *Architecture-Structure*. John Weeks' "indeterminate architecture" with its three categories – 1) where growth occurs through additions, 2) growth occurs through new construction, 3) growth does not occur – was similar to KBS's function-, building-, and environmental-related parts, for which a gliding scale towards increased generality is opposed to a diminishing level of adaptability.[46] Also the Candilis, Josic, and Woods proposal for the renewal of central Frankfurt from 1963, the same year as KBS visit in Germany, was featured in KBS's exhibition *Architecture – Structure*. It was one of two images that were to illustrate the new thinking of the "interchangeability" of parts. The other was a spread from a publication by the West German Planungsgruppe für Institutsbau in Baden-Württemberg, which KBS had visited on a study-trip in 1963[47] (fig. 6).

A direct reference to British structuralism in the exhibition *Architecture – Structure* was Archigram's *Plug-in City* from 1964 (the same year as KBS's trip to the UK). It was illustrating KBS's "environment-related parts" in a panel on "Classification of life." The *Plug-in City* was a mega structure into which one could connect and disconnect at will.[48] In KBS's vision of the environment-

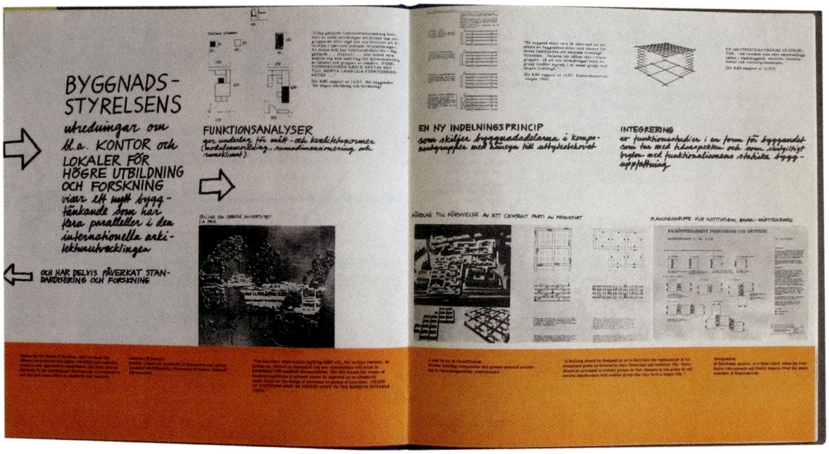

fig. 6 Spread from exhibition catalogue *Arkitektur – Struktur* that explains the significance of "functional analysis" with illustrations on the right hand page of Candilis, Josic and Woods proposal for Frankfurt and a publication from Planungsgruppe für Institutsbau. Photo of catalogue by the author.

related parts, it represented a structure that "together with other parts, constitute the whole environment."[49]

We have seen that there were parallel developments in government building agencies in Sweden, England, the Netherlands, West Germany, and the Nordic countries during the 1960s. The institutions exemplified in this study were all essentially developing organizations and building programs from a structuralist point of view. One can argue that KBS's structuralism was more pragmatic and technical then its international equivalents, with its emphasis on the economic advantage of structural thinking rather than the social and cultural benefits of participatory design and the liberty of material interchangeability. Also, looking at the buildings that KBS built under the umbrella of structuralism during the 1960s and 1970s, one could claim that this was the case. However, it is easy to see how KBS's belief in the government's (and the building industry's) endeavor towards rationalization and efficiency was in recognition of the humanistic foundation for structuralist ideas (figs. 7, 8).

In the light of the growing ambiguity of the discipline of architecture, the increasing difficulties of public policy-making and the escalating critique of the State, what was KBS's reason for launching an official architectural theory? What could be gained by publicly announcing working methodologies and architectural ideas? And, in 1968, at a time of great uncertainty – not least for architecture ideology – wasn't there a great risk that the philosophy would fail and that the chartered path would be heavily criticized? As we have seen, KBS's structural philosophy was clearly founded in architectural con-

fig. 7 The governmental office building complex Garnisonen in Stockholm, built by KBS, designed by Tage Hertzell and completed in 1972. Photo Holger Ellgaard, CC, 2014.

fig. 8 The Arrhenius Laboratory at Stockholm University, built by KBS and designed by Carl Nyrén, 1973. Photo Holger Ellgaard, CC, 2010.

ceptions that had obvious links to the international debates on re-humanizing architecture and other links with the contemporaneous national and international research and trends of the 1950s and 1960s. Yet it was, I argue, ultimately conceived as a response to the administrative and financial demands of the government, which thus overshadowed KBS's already weak social and humanist ambition.

Endnotes

1 The paper refocuses, expands and re-examines an earlier study by the same author "Architecture-Structure, 1968: A Manifesto for a Swedish Philosophy of Architecture," initially presented at the conference proceeding *Theory for the Sake of Theory II*, ed. Efe Duyan (Istanbul: Dakam, 2011), 52–65.

2 Henry A. Millon, "Architectural Principles in the Age of Humanism: Its Influence on the Development and Interpretation of Modern Architecture,"

in *Journal of the Society of Architectural Historians*, Vol. 31, No. 2 (May, 1972): 83–91.

3 Ibid. 84. Ezra Ehrenkrantz's book *The Modular Number Pattern: Flexibility through Standardization* (London: Tiranti) was published in 1956, and essentially sprung out of the research he had conducted as a Fulbright scholar at the modular construction section of the British Building Research Station. In the 1960s Ehrenkrantz developed School Construction Systems Development (SCSD) which became influential in various approaches of "systems construction." See *School Construction Systems Development*, report No. 1, published by School Planning Laboratory (Palo Alto: Stanford University, 1962).

4 Reyner Banham, "New Brutalism," originally published in *Architectural Review*, December 1955, reprinted in *October*, No. 136, Spring 2011: 19–28.

5 One version of the story of the origins of the term "New Brutalism" is that Swedish architect Hans Asplund coined it as he showed Villa Göth to British visitors, and the phrase then spread to the UK and was subsequently widely used. See Helena Mattsson, *Arkitektur och konsumtion: Reyner Banham och utbytbarhetens estetik* (Stockholm: Symposium, 2004) 72 and 274–275. Reyner Banham gave another version in "The New Brutalism" as he wrote in a footnote: "There is a persistent belief that the word 'Brutalism' (or something like it) had appeared in the English Summaries in an issue of *Byggmästaren* published late in 1950. The reference cannot be traced, and the story must be relegated to that limbo of Modern movement demonology where Swedes, Communists, and the Town and Country Planning Association are bracketed together as different isotopes of the common 'Adversary.'" Banham, "New Brutalism," 20.

6 Banham, "New Brutalism," 20.

7 Byggnadsstyrelsen, *Byggnadsstyrelsen: Byggnadsverk och verksamhet* (Stockholm: Byggnadsstyrelsen, 1983), 38.

8 Ibid. 37–39.

9 Nils Ahrbom, *Arkitektur och samhälle: funderingar över 50 års svensk arkitektur* (Stockholm: Arkitektur förlag, 1983).

10 KBS, *Byggprocess och verksplanering*. KBS-rapport, no. 10 (Stockholm: Byggnadsstyrelsen, 1966); KBS, *Office Building Investigation 1966*. KBS-rapport, no. 12E (Stockholm: Byggnadsstyrelsen, 1967); KBS, *Om byggnader för högre utbildning och forskning*. KBS-rapport, no. 16 (Stockholm: Byggnadsstyrelsen, 1967).

11 KBS, *Minnesanteckningar från Byggnadsstyrelsens resa till England 14–21 oktober 1964 för studier av organisation och utvecklingsarbete för statligt byggande*, KBS-rapport, no. 44 (Stockholm: Byggnadsstyrelsen, 1970).

12 KBS, KBS-rapport, no. 10.

13 Hughes, Jonathan, "'The Matchbox on a Muffin': The Design of Hospital in the Early NHS," in *Medical History*, 2000, 44: 21–56.

14 John Weeks, 1960 cited in Anders Ekholm, Nils Ahrbom and Peter Broberg, *Utvecklingen mot strukturalism inom arkitekturen* (Stockholm: Statens råd för byggnadsforskning, 1980), 96.

15 Anders Ekholm, "Internationell strukturalism," in Ekholm et al. *Utvecklingen*.

16 KBS, *Minnesanteckningar*.

17 KBS, *Systembyggnade*. KBS-rapport, no. 102. (Stockholm: Byggnadsstyrelsen, 1973).

18 KBS, *Architecture-Structure*, exhibition catalogue (Stockholm: Byggnadsstyrelsen, 1969).
19 Ibid.
20 *Acceptera* was an accompanying text to the preceding Stockholm exhibition of 1930 and authored by Uno Åhrén, Gunnar Asplund, Wolter Gahn, Sven Markelius, Gregor Paulsson, Eskil Sundahl.
21 KBS, *Architecture-Structure*.
22 Nils Ahrbom, "Svensk structuralism," in Ekholm et al. *Utvecklingen*, 160, 166. Nils Ahrbom left a professorship at the Royal Institute of Technology (Kungliga tekniska högskolan), KTH, Stockholm, in 1963 to head the newly-started Development Department at KBS.
23 Architectural historian Claes Caldenby makes a similar remark regarding the influences for the exhibition *Architecture – Structure*, saying that exhibition designer Allan Westerman (and museum director Bengt O H Johansson) to a large extent added the international references when making the exhibition. Claes Caldenby, ed., *Arkitektur i förändring* (Stockholm: Svensk Byggtjänst, 2000), 29–30. Although the making of the exhibition was by the hands of Johansson and Westerman, it is rather peculiar that Ahrbom disregards KBS's influences from the study-trips to "structuralist-minded" institutions and building sites, as described earlier.
24 KBS, *Office Building Investigation 1966*, KBS report no. 12E.
25 KBS, *Architecture-Structure*.
26 Ahrbom, *Arkitektur och samhälle*, 175.
27 Francis Strauven, *Aldo van Eyck: the shape of relativity* (Amsterdam: Architectura & Natura, 1998); Alan Colquhoun, *Modern Architecture* (Oxford: Oxford University Press, 2002).
28 Colquhoun *Modern Architecture*, 222.
29 Nils Ahrbom, "Given lägenhetsyta, variabel rumsindelning," in *Byggmästaren* 1934, no. 16, (Stockholm: Byggmästaren, 1934), p. 104–105.
30 Nils Ahrbom, "Spatial Design: Philosophy or Architecture?" from 1945, in Michael Asgaard Andersen, ed., *Nordic Architects Write: A documentary anthology,* (Abingdon, UK: Routledge, 2008).
31 Nils Ahrbom, "Den nya bygglådan" from 1955, in Ahrbom, *Arkitektur och samhälle*.
32 Strauven, *Aldo van Eyck*; Eric Mumford, *The CIAM Discourse on Urbanism, 1928–1960* (Cambridge, Mass.: MIT Press, 2000).
33 Oskar Hansen, "The Open Form in Architecture – The Art of the Great Number" in Oskar Newman, ed., *Dokumente der Modernen Architektur: CIAM '59 in Otterlo* (Stuttgart: Karl Krämer Verlag, 1961).
34 Torsten Frendberg, "Unikt projekt i Kallebäck," in *Arkitektur* 1959, no. 3 (Stockholm: Arkitektur förlag, 1959).
35 Erik Friberger, "Bostadskonfektion och individuell bostadsförsörjning," in *Byggmästaren*, 1937, no. 10. Stockholm: Byggmästaren.
36 Ahrbom "Svensk structuralism."
37 This is pointed out by architectural historian Johan Mårtelius, see Johan Mårtelius, "With Functionalism as the Hub," in Andersen, *Nordic Architects*; Quotes from Ahrbom, *Arkitektur och samhälle*, 172.
38 KBS, *Architecture-Structure*.
39 Habraken, John, 1972. *Supports: an alternative to mass housing*. London: The Architectural Press, 1972), pp. 59–60.
40 John Habraken, Description written in 2000 of the edited reprint of the

1972 English edition of the book *Supports* (online). Accessed August 25, 2011, available at www.habraken.com.

41 KBS, *Architecture-Structure*˙

42 SBI. *Måltypisering.* SBI-rapport no. 56 (Copenhagen: Statens Bygge forskningsinstitut, 1966).

43 KBS, *Architecture-Structure.*

44 KBS, *Incitamentsavtal.* KBS-rapport, no. 57 (Stockholm: Byggnadsstyrelsen, 1970); KBS, *Systembyggnade.* KBS-rapport, no. 102 (Stockholm: Byggnadsstyrelsen, 1973).

45 *Webster's New Universal Unabridged Dictionary* (New York: Random House and Barnes & Noble, 2003).

46 Anders Ekholm, "Internationell strukturalism," in Ekholm et al. *Utvecklingen.*

47 KBS, unpublished material from KBS study-trip to West Germany and the Netherlands in 1963, the Swedish National Archive.

48 Simon Sadler, *Archigram: Architecture without architecture* (Cambridge, MA: MIT Press, 2005).

49 KBS, *Architecture-Structure.*

Andres Kurg

Courtyards, Corners, Streetfronts: Re-Imagining Mass Housing Areas in Tallinn

In May 1978, at an exhibition of young architects in the foyer of the Academy of Sciences library in Tallinn, Estonian architect and artist Leonhard Lapin displayed his project "The City of the Living – The City of the Dead." The design inserted a cemetery into a public courtyard between existing prefabricated buildings of a kind that were typical of the residential districts constructed on the outskirts of Tallinn during the 1960s (fig. 1). The project proposed that garages be repurposed to function as tombs, with the cars inside acting as sarcophagi and the gravestones serving also as the apparatus of a children's play area. ("In this way, people would take better care of the area and parents would not allow their children to vandalize its equipment," mocked one reviewer.[1]) This grotesque scene, executed in the style of pop art, satirized the idea of a new urban micro-district that would provide everything necessary for daily life. In the same year Estonian writer Mati Unt published his celebrated novel, *Sügisball*, about life in one of the mass-residential districts of Tallinn, where Lapin was quoted as having said that this added cemetery would make the district entirely self-sufficient, so that "inhabitants would be able to remain in their neighborhoods forever without ever needing to cross a single thoroughfare."[2] The project referred to the courtyard visible from the living-room window of the apartment in which Lapin lived with his then-wife, artist Sirje Runge. In Lapin's design, several members of the architectural establishment had been buried in the courtyard – their names are shown on gravestones – and a corner of the courtyard has been set aside for the common

fig. 1 Leonhard Lapin, "The City of the Living – The City of the Dead," 1978. Display board, 100 × 100 cm Museum of Estonian Architecture.

grave of members of the Architects' Union. In this way, Lapin commented on the changed conditions of architects' work; in the context of mass-produced dwellings the role of the architect had faded, leaving him or her only to follow obediently the many restrictive building laws and regulations.

Although exceptional in the sharpness and directness of its critique, for the group of architects of which Lapin was a leading figure this interest in the courtyards and unused territories between prefabricated houses was nothing new. Two years earlier, Lapin's colleague Tiit Kaljundi had presented a proposal called "View of the New Visual Environment" at an exhibition of monumental art curated by Lapin in Tallinn Art Hall (fig. 2). In that work, Kaljundi imagined ways to "relieve the spatial-aesthetic inferiority of buildings" and to insert landscape gardens between the prefabricated houses of the new districts. Kaljundi's proposals included the agrarian landscaping of the courtyards, so that besides being visually attractive they would provide inhabitants with an opportunity to observe the various stages of growth: sprouting, growing, maturing and ripening. "The mechanized farming method necessary for this development would itself become part of the spectacle. The harvested crop would provide a food supply for birds which are of use to the urban environment."[3]

In this article, I examine the relationship between the Soviet (modernist) mass-housing districts and these unconventional projects in the context of other works by the group of young architects that came together in Estonia during the 1970s, a group that has retrospectively been called the Tallinn School. This loosely-knit circle of friends and colleagues posed their

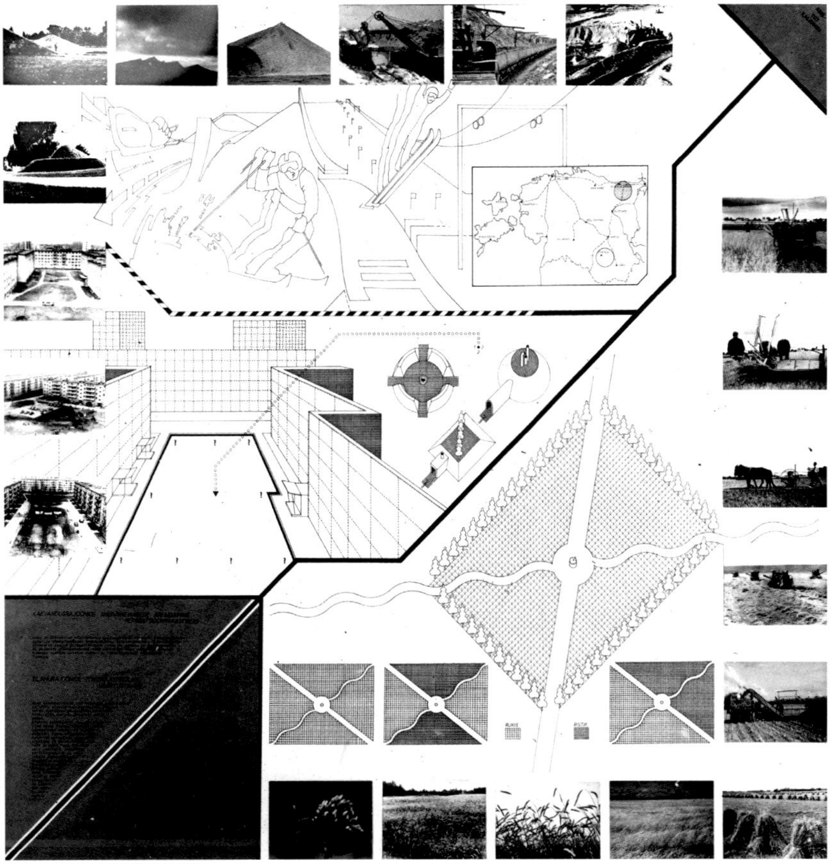

fig. 2 Tiit Kaljundi. "View of a New Visual Environment I," 1976. Display board, 100 × 100 cm. Item lost; reproduction from Tiit Kaljundi family archive. a) Redeveloping slag heaps in mining areas as recreational landscapes. b) Re-evaluation of residential areas as artificial landscapes. c) Agrarian landscaping in large cities.

critique of the surrounding environment in forms that differed radically from the professional approach of preceding generations, forms that ranged from tactics drawn from the contemporary art practices of the period – such as the "happenings" organized in the industrial fringes of the city – to seminars and conferences oriented toward the professional audience and polemical articles published in the cultural press. Their critique of mass construction and alienation in the new housing districts of Tallinn reached its highpoint with "Architectural exhibition 78" at the Academy of Sciences library, which displayed projects that addressed directly the prefabricated suburbs and the changed profession of the architect. A year later, during the congress of the Estonian Architects' Union, this critique bore fruit as Mart Port, the long-time head of the union and architect of several of the mass-housing areas (and whose name appeared on a headstone in Lapin's cemetery proposal), failed to achieve re-election while several members of the Tallinn School became members of the union's board.

Several retrospective accounts have underlined the position of these critical works as "pure ideas," demonstrating the emergence of architecture as art and of the architect as artist during this period.[4] Furthermore, these accounts have combined this idea with the idea of resistance to the Soviet regime through cultural forms, thereby implying that these works contributed directly to the struggle for national independence.[5] In those countries that were annexed to the Soviet Union during World War II the representation of cultural production as "dissident" has been widespread.[6] However, the application of such vocabulary to the given case is problematic. Dissidence implies withdrawal from state-supported structures and autonomous cultural production, a notion that is hard to sustain in the context of discussions and events that grew out from the established architects' professional organizations and institutions. The strategies sought by the architects of the Tallinn School were directed at actively reworking the socialist-modernist urban environment, rather than breaking entirely from it; their projects reverberated through and continued existing public discussions. It could be argued that it was the question of housing – including the built environment of the mass-housing estates – that provided a recognizable subject and common ground for communication with the public: questions on anonymity, homogeneity and lack of individuality were discussed by the wider public and the group's proposals for reworking these estates resonated with public expectations.

Mass Housing Areas in Tallinn

Modernist planning principles and industrialized mass-housing construction methods were reintroduced in the USSR from the mid-1950s onwards, following a series of top-down initiatives by the Communist Party and its First Secretary, Nikita Khrushchev. In a speech at the all-Soviet Conference of Builders, Architects and Workers in the Construction Materials in Moscow in 1954, Khrushchev launched the large-scale use of industrial construction methods that was to speed up building processes and reduce costs. This was followed in 1955 by a decree against decoration in architecture (being costly and otherwise excessive) and by decisions in the all-Soviet meeting of architects advocating the decentralization of cities in urban planning.[7] Against the previous forms and classical language of architecture, it was now the "social role of housing, new technical means of its construction and [raised] standards of comfort that took the role of aesthetic categories."[8] Indeed, from 1959 onwards special factories began to produce concrete panels for system-built

fig. 3 View of the Mustamäe residential area in Tallinn. Photograph from late 1970s. Museum of Estonian Architecture.

fig. 4 Five-story panel houses in Mustamäe. Photograph 1975. Museum of Estonian Architecture.

housing, the most widespread of which was a licensed system from France; the Camus-system.[9] This gave rise to the infamous mass-produced apartment blocks that spread throughout the Soviet bloc and have retrospectively come to signify the uniformity of state socialism.[10]

In Tallinn, the competition for the first of the new mass-housing districts, the suburb of Mustamäe, was announced in 1958.[11] It was to follow modernist planning principles: buildings would be orientated toward maximizing sunlight, services and shopping areas would be oriented around transportation hubs, and separate apartments would be provided for each family. The outcome was strongly influenced by the then popular models of neighborhood planning introduced in countries such as Sweden (esp. Vällingby by Sven Markelius, 1950–54) and the United Kingdom (Harlow by Sir Frederick Gibberd, 1947), which set the standards for these new Soviet micro-districts.[12] Following these models, the final plan of the Mustamäe district was divided into nine micro-districts of 7,000 inhabitants, each with a school, a kindergarten, a sports field and a multi-purpose center for retail facilities, all within walking distance of the apartment blocks (fig. 3). The plan and elevation of the Mustamäe apartment blocks was largely determined by the selection of prefabricated details from the newly-erected Tallinn housing factory. On the exterior, the seams joining the square concrete wall panels (each the size of one room) were left visible, leaving the houses with an overall "unfinished" character (fig. 4). Inside, the one and two-bedroom apartments aimed to provide 9 m^2 per inhabitant, with a kitchen of 4.5 m^2 and a 1.7 m^2 bathroom. The "extended living space" of the courtyards and common areas was intended to compensate for the tiny apartment spaces, including restaurants and cafes, workers clubs, childcare and retail facilities.[13] In 1962, Mart Port had predicted that "concepts like 'my apartment' and 'my house' will be replaced by words like 'our micro-district' and 'our city.'"[14]

As a replacement for the Soviet communal flats of the Stalin era, the industrialization of housing production was initially welcomed as a progressive course of events, promising better living standards and comfortable housing conditions for a wide segment of the population. Mustamäe became a milestone in the urbanization of Estonia: by 1959, more than half of the country's inhabitants lived in cities and the following decade saw a period of rapid increase in housing and public infrastructure and a corresponding change in the appearance of the cities. However, in the early 1970s there emerged a change in the discourse about mass-housing estates; they were now seen as lacking adequate service facilities, as being repetitive and thus monotonous in form and as ignoring the wider context of the city.

In 1973, leading architecture critic Leo Gens described Mustamäe as a solution that had enabled thousands of families to have a new, well-equipped apartment close to the center of Tallinn; but Gens simultaneously argued that it lacked what he called "human scale":

> It seems that we would have to plan micro-districts with variable buildings, green areas and intimate corners, that the new district could indeed become cozy. One needs to be bolder in adding architectural small forms, decorative sculptures, pools and fountains, to the green areas of the micro-districts. All this would bring something exceptional to every micro-district.[15]

For Gens it was possible to resuscitate the area by suitable additions, service structures and a "main street" which would gather together cultural institutions and smaller cafés and "where one could simply walk, looking at the vitrines and observing the passers-by."[16]

A more pessimistic attitude towards mass housing was taken by representatives of the emerging discipline of environmental psychology, which studied the ways in which the architectural environment affects the individual and social psyche of its inhabitants. Psychologist Mati Heidmets warned, in his articles on changes in the living environment, of a process he called "mustamäeization," whereby new towns give rise to a new kind of personality, with its specific ways of thinking and acting.[17] According to Heidmets, inhabitants of new towns no longer care for their surroundings and have lost the way of identifying themselves actively with their neighborhood, demonstrating instead passivity: "No wonder then, if for a third generation inhabitant of Mustamäe it is insurmountably difficult to hammer a nail into the wall, as already even his grandfather would have called a handyman from the housing committee for this."[18]

Heidmets laid much of the blame for this on the uniformity of the architecture:

> One hundred grey houses, all the same, do not cause the inhabitant warm feelings towards them, yet one grey house among a hundred red ones can do this. This means that from the viewpoint of identification, the continuity and uniqueness of the environment is important, but so is participation in its production.[19]

For Heidmets, the task of architecture and planning was to increase the possibilities for identification by adding diversity and idiosyncrasy to these areas, prioritizing recognizable images and landmarks.

The Tallinn School Architects

The new generation of architects, graduating in the early 1970s from the Estonian State Art Institute in Tallinn, emerged as a significant alternative voice in these discussions. After graduation, most were employed in the collective-farm design office EKE Projekt to work on the design of production and residential structures for agricultural farms. Founded in 1966, the EKE design office had by the mid-1970s grown into a large studio with around 1,000 employees, supported by contracts from clients in rural areas. Since collective farms were owned cooperatively, they could generate and retain profits which were in turn reinvested in the building of village centers, local kindergartens and schools, and even shared sanatoria and spas at seaside resorts. This gave architects working in the EKE office a certain autonomy from the state, an opportunity to make contracts with the construction companies of the collective farms and thus bypass the system of mass construction and prefabricated materials of the state housing factories.[20]

Parallel to their design work throughout the 1970s, several architects in this group published polemical articles in the cultural media on urban issues and the built environment, drawing attention to the forgotten heritage of the early twentieth century or discussing changes in contemporary world architecture.[21] They also worked on samizdat translations of works by contemporary Western architects, especially the leading postmodernist authors like Robert Venturi, Aldo Rossi and Leon Krier, but also closer colleagues from Finland.[22] Leonhard Lapin wrote reviews on avant-garde art and architecture from the early twentieth century, particularly Estonian functionalism and Russian suprematism.[23] Opposed to the narrow specialization of the previous generation, this group also actively sought dialogue and cooperation with other cultural fields. Tiit Kaljundi later observed:

> The traditional master-architect approach to design and corresponding self-assurance, was left in the background […] Leo [Lapin] declared from the outset that in order to do something in architecture, you should explore other fields.[24]

The group collaborated with writers, theater production, film and contemporary visual art; all were engaged as a means of organizing the environment and implementing a critique of the institution of architecture.

This was demonstrated by the exhibition of monumental art at Tallinn Art Hall in May 1976, where Lapin curated a room devoted to contemporary "experimental" practices. This space featured models and designs by his fellow architects, abstract paintings and proposals for kinetic sculptures, as well as schemas for the redevelopment of new town areas. Tiit Kaljundi's work "View of the New Visual Environment" (see above) on the decorative planting of agricultural crops in urban green spaces drew inspiration from contemporary land art. In the "X" shape formed by its crossing diagonals it was similar to Dennis Oppenheim's work from 1969, "Cancelled Crop," which harvested the grain in its raw stage to intervene in the cycle of production and consumption (the "X" shape thus signified the cancellation). In contrast, Kaljundi's project emphasized the unexpected juxtaposition of the micro-district courtyard with traditional agricultural methods of growing crops, as if making literal the erasure of the difference between the town and the country, a common slogan in Soviet official rhetoric.

Lapin's own project in the show featured a fantasy variation on a suprematist tower, "Monument to Tallinn," located at the center of a ring-road in Mustamäe (fig. 5). Planned to be 345 meters high, its aim was to visualize the city's history utilizing "audio-visual multimedia" on every story. At night it functioned as a gigantic suprematist tower, where "single elements sparkle and peel off into outer space. Unique spatial variations are regulated by computer." This project and the exhibition as a whole may also be understood

fig. 5 Leonhard Lapin, "A Monument to Tallinn," 1976. Exhibition display, gouache on wood, 100 × 100 cm. Museum of Estonian Architecture.

in the context of Lapin's statements on "synthetic architecture," where, countering the official doctrine concerning the synthesis of the arts, he called for architects to act themselves *as* artists.[25] He proposed not to bring the separate arts together in architecture, but to see architecture as a synthetic discipline that combined "philosophical ideas, sociology, psychology, research in theology and experiments in theater, the formal aesthetics of the visual arts, the endeavors of the scientific-technological world and industrial possibilities."[26] Thus, the new architecture was still industrial and mass-produced, yet it was painterly rather than mechanical in its variety "It approaches not so much the decorative arts as design […]"[27]

In the early 1970s especially, Lapin demonstrated a rather welcoming attitude towards technology and the machine. According to his ideas the mechanization and industrialization of the building process were not mistakes to be avoided, but had not yet been extensive enough. Writing in a popular cultural magazine in 1973, he called on the reader to pay more attention to the industrialization of the building process, as its aim – shifting the work from building site to factory – had not yet been realized. Architecture for him was the field that represented the machine age in its clearest and most radical form. Instead of an architecture that was produced by a machine, he looked ahead to an architecture that performed itself as a machine. Moreover, "in developing mass construction, architects should work out clear, comprehensive and human-centered principles of urban planning, that would reverse prejudices about the perspectivelessness of the technical city."[28]

The "Architecture Exhibition '78"

These diverging attitudes – the more conciliatory one represented by Kaljundi and the more radical one of Lapin – were displayed and extended at an architecture exhibition in 1978 in the Academy of Sciences library. The exhibited works were, formally, surprisingly different from one another; and because participants did not make any prior agreements on content, the divergent approaches of individual members occasionally became obvious. It is therefore relevant to take a closer look at a variety of examples.

The cemetery project by Lapin, which surprised the other participants as well as the wider public, caught the most attention and caused a small sensation in the writings of the establishment figures it referred to.[29] Its direct attack on the country's leading architects – not only the name of Mart Port, but also that of Port's closest collaborator Malle Meelak, which was recognizable on one of the tombstones – was unprecedented at the time. Lapin's work also offered a reference to the destruction of large scale housing projects in the West – an explosion (carried out as a suprematist composition) in one corner of the work referenced in Lapin's own words the demolition of mass housing in Pruitt-Igoe. However, he himself chose not to demolish the area but rather to *detourn* it through this bizarre intervention.

Other works from the exhibition had similar critical content. Architect Harry Šein showed allegorical black and white montage images of the four prefabricated housing areas in Tallinn, with a corpse and a vandalized car in front of a partly-ruined prefabricated apartment building in Mustamäe. The dystopian street scene had the appearance of a documentary image of the aftermath of a revolt, or of the degeneration of the area itself (in the author's own interpretation the corpse was an alcoholic sleeping on the street). In another image, other buildings are shown to be not so much deteriorating as becoming integrated with new structures – a Coliseum-like stadium, a (shopping) arcade, an open market (fig. 6).

fig. 6 Harry Šein, "Hills I–II (Mustamäe, Õismäe)," Exhibition display, photomontage, 100 × 100 cm. Item lost; reproduction from Harry Šein family archive.

Šein expanded on the ideas behind the exhibition in a longer article "Of emptiness, what else?"[30] published in the local cultural newspaper in the course of debate following the show. Describing a shift in environmental planning from the static order toward "a certain objective and dynamic regulation of the environment," he saw architecture as moving from the production of buildings toward the designing of human interactions.[31] An important notion for him was self-regulation: instead of a clearly defined spatial division within which the user could operate, he or she was now able to change his or her own micro-surroundings and decide upon her own patterns of behavior. This kind of self-regulation stood in opposition to centrally-controlled building regulations and standardized designs and gave the inhabitant some small measure of autonomy and space to actively realize her own identity. However, this also meant a change for the architect. Recounting the alienation of the inhabitants in the new towns, Šein wrote:

> The dwellers feel every day that they are not able to participate in the design of the living environment, nor are they able to manipulate it during use. The more complete is the habitation when we move into it, the more we uphold the initial prohibitions and taboos, the less it will be a home for us. […] We can survive without people's architects, more important is that people themselves could be architects.[32]

Among all the members of the Tallinn School, Šein's approach came closest to the views of the environmental psychologists, who lamented the passivity of the dwellers in the new housing areas and called for their participation in order to increase the possibilities for identification with their living quarters.

Tiit Kaljundi's display at the exhibition in the Academy of Sciences library placed the question of freedom of choice in the context of the small town: How was the consciousness of the inhabitants of small towns to be raised so that they would not leave for larger cities and yet be offered comparable diversity? Analyzing the existing architecture of the small towns, Kaljundi showed photographs of facade-screens facing onto the main street, making the buildings behind them appear larger and more imposing than in actuality (fig. 7). (This was inspired by the recent works of Robert Venturi and Denise Scott Brown on American vernacular architecture.[33]) This architecture of appearances was one way of relieving the inferiority of smaller cities, but Kaljundi's own solution pointed to a different kind of approach; toward buildings that would value "activities, as well as the overall architectural image."[34] Examples of this kind of work included recent buildings by his colleagues that had been built in some smaller Estonian towns: a sanatorium in Pärnu by Vilen Künnapu and the Rapla KEK construction company office by Toomas Rein. In addition, Kaljundi referenced the "Instant city" project by Archigram, which transports "colorful cultural events" from town to town. Kaljundi thus combined a semantic approach that regards architecture as language (drawn from the works of Venturi) with late-modernist micro-environments and pop-utopias. The ways of identifying with the environment indicated by Heidmets appear here simultaneously both as a legible symbolism and as events of the kind proposed by Šein (his "design of human interactions").

Architect and artist Jüri Okas exhibited a black-and-white display board called "Monument to Leonhard Lapin in Räpina" (fig. 8). It presented a photo of a huge rusty container in the countryside near a small town in South-Eastern Estonia, onto which Okas had written instructions on how to redesign the object as a monument: "inscribe surname into pressed soil, level, press down and sow grass." Lapin's name also appeared on the container as graffiti, together with "Alice," "Malle," "Räpina" and "T-Rex." Borrowing his

fig. 7 Tiit Kaljundi, "The Questions of the Small Town," 1978. Exhibition display, collage, photo, ink on cardboard, 100 × 100 cm. Courtesy Tiit Kaljundi family.

aesthetic approach from the conceptual art of the period, Okas presented the discarded industrial relic as a monumental structure, similar to those Robert Smithson had documented in a North American context, as examples of the entropic blending and piling up of the environment.

A year later (1979), Okas brought this approach to the context of mass housing in Tallinn, showing on an *intaglio* print based on a photomontage a series of instructions for intervening in an empty corner formed at the meeting point of two standardized dwellings. This piece, called "A Corner Solution," consisted of a huge pile of mud or gravel that was to be poured into the corner space between the houses, reaching a height of five stories at its uppermost point (fig. 9). On top of this were to be added sheets of steel and chromed rods. In winter the pile could be made of snow. In this ironic approach to combining the aesthetics of Western land-art with generic local prefabricated houses,

Okas presented his own vision for the completion of these places: the entropic "other" rising among the systematic order of the buildings.

The work corresponded to Okas' interests in banal and inconspicuous architectural objects. Since the early 1970s he had photographed structures that often related to the "surplus" of industrial society; the infrastructure that worked for everyday comfort but went unnoticed or remained invisible. His interventions in the architectural context may be seen as an alternative to both the official criticism of Mustamäe represented by Gens, which demanded coziness, decorative sculptures and fountains, and the approach demonstrated by environmental psychology, which demanded legible symbols and architectural variety.

The Aftermath of the Exhibition

Reception to the exhibition was largely mixed. Among the architectural elite it received opposition to its sharp irony, but it was praised in equal measure for expanding the boundaries of architecture and breaking existing stereotypes.[35] Seemingly presented as a survey exhibition, it showed instead projects by one group of like-minded young colleagues; works that did not insist on being built but were conceptual objects intended as a critical commentary and an engagement with public debate. In this way the group fought those architects who simultaneously occupied established positions of power while also pretending to represent the interests of all architects – primarily those on the board of the Architects' Union. The broader cultural public however responded more positively: the critique of the environment resonated with positions that had also been spelled out by writers, film-makers and sociologists. The exhibition additionally marked a shift in professional culture, including architectural discussion topics that had until then been excluded from the professional realm.

Among the reviews of the exhibition and the public responses written in the guestbook, there appeared to be a division between the comments of those who assessed the show according to the standards of a traditional architecture exhibition – which is obliged to present exemplars of achievement in architectural design – and those who saw it as part of a critical debate concerning issues of architecture, urbanization and the role of the architect. The former saw the exhibition as a preparatory exercise for the building of actual houses. This was reflected in guestbook comments such as "Great talkers are shitty doers (People's architect)"[36] and "It is interesting that architects are still making jokes;" and in an article in the cultural weekly *Sirp ja Vasar* by architect Paul Härmson, who saw the architects as "personalities still in search of their own way."[37] On the other hand, there were comments from those

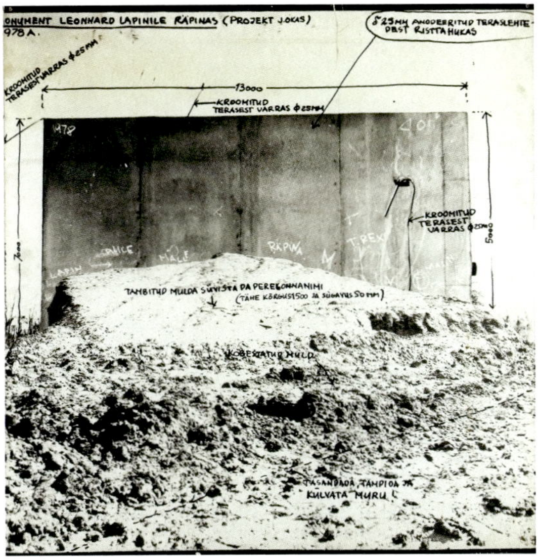

fig. 8 Jüri Okas, "Monument to Leonhard Lapin in Räpina," 1978. Display board, 100 × 100 cm Museum of Estonian Architecture

fig. 9 Jüri Okas, "A Corner Solution," 1979. Intaglio, 52 × 60 cm. Courtesy of the artist.

who saw the exhibition itself as significant. One such comment in the guestbook said, "Extremely relevant exhibition – only not to get tired," another one added "Hooray! Long-live the angry ones," and in a published review, writer Mihkel Mutt wrote of the importance of experiencing the individuals' works as part of a public exhibition: "In addition to an ordinary contact between the work and the viewer, […] in seeing art within a group […] there exists a series of contacts between the viewers themselves." This collective experience also allowed him to understand that "there is something different in the air."[38]

Following the shift in power within the Architects' Union in 1979, in 1980 its activities broadened towards an increasing dialogue with the public. In April 1980 its youth section organized a "Tallinn seminar" that focused critically on urban planning and the development of the city, with presentations from the representatives of fields like ecology and psychology, but also from several influential writers and critics, raising discussion of the built environment beyond the narrow specialist field of planners and architects. In 1981 the Architects' Union started to publish the journal *Ehituskunst* (Building art), which became the main channel of communication for this new approach to architecture and the built environment, publishing articles on contemporary architectural issues side-by-side with historical accounts and essays. The editorial column in the first issue, which was devoted to "environment architecture," understood the environment now in an entirely new sense that demonstrated its alliance with the increasingly popular postmodernist trends of the West: "forgotten categories like traditionalism, historical image, symbol, metaphor, humor, ornamentation and house-on-the-street have reappeared in recent years."[39] Whereas modernist architecture saw as its goal an ideal environment to be achieved by subsuming the existing one, the new environmental architecture set out from what already existed by adding to it and perfecting it.

Conclusion

In many ways, contrary to the later postmodern projects, these examples from the second half of the 1970s demonstrate a younger generation of architects engaging with the socialist-modernist environment, critiquing mass-housing production while refusing to turn their backs on the overall ethics of modernism. Projects like Lapin's monument in Mustamäe or his Tallinn skyline used avant-garde aesthetics to counter the dullness of official building production, without thereby completely contradicting the dominant Soviet system. Such works blurred the boundaries between withdrawal outside and engagement within that system. Equally, Lapin's views on mass housing were balanced on the border of official endorsement and dissident withdrawal. Mechanization had been the Soviet Union's official doctrine for achieving utopia, promising a better living standard, increased mobility and shorter working hours; but it was at best only ever partially realized and in many cases, such as in the new towns, only in an inverted form.

In contrast, projects like Lapin's cemetery or Okas' "A Corner Solution" demonstrated a greater degree of ambiguity in their approach towards the environment, displaying the ironic aspects of uniform building production and the simplistic and populist solutions to that uniformity of production – adding fountains and flower-beds between the huge prefabricated panel structures. Instead of the pragmatic architectural decisions characteristic of the work of planning professionals, these architects and artists drew their ideas from more ambiguous conceptual art practices, which suggested neither straightforward and practical solutions nor legible symbols for identification. Unlike Šein, Lapin and Okas preferred not to dismantle or destroy the existing built environment, instead they proposed to detourn or deterritorialize it through the insertion of what had so far been excluded from socialist (and in this case also modernist) urbanity.

The activities of this group of architects were also significant in extending the discussion into the public sphere, thereby producing a new public engagement with issues that existed apart from the officially endorsed discussions. Countering the dominant discourse of the governing architectural elite, they produced their alternative discourse – partly appropriating the dominant terms and formats, but also extending them and investing them with new meanings. This included not only verbal language, but also the form of exhibitions and various methods of representation. Of course, the architects also depended on the official institutions: as members of the Architects' Union they could hold events under the organization's auspices; and working in a cooperative design office provided access to means and materials while potentially affording greater autonomy than a state design office. By concentrating critique around issues of housing, the living environment and everyday urban spaces – the corners and courtyards of prefabricated housing areas – these architecture exhibitions played a significant role in the production of a new public, which was simultaneously reinforced by parallel discussions in other segments of the society.

Endnotes

1 Mati Unt, "Arhitektuurinäitus," *Sirp ja Vasar*, June 9, 1978, 8.
2 Mati Unt, "Sügisball," *Looming* 9 (1978), 1433. Translated as: Mati Unt, *The Autumn Ball* (Tallinn: Perioodika, 1985).
3 Text on the display board, Museum of Estonian Architecture, EAM Fk 672.
4 See: Krista Kodres, "Müüdiloojad ja teised," Ehituskunst 5 (1991), 3–14.
5 Leonhard Lapin, Avangard. Tartu Ülikooli filosoofiateaduskonna vabade kunstide professori Leonhard Lapini loengud 2001, aastal (Tartu: Tartu Ülikooli kirjastus, 2003), 235.
6 See: Sirje Helme, Jaak Kangilaski, Lühike Eesti kunsti ajalugu (Tallinn: Kunst, 1999).

7 Julia Kosenkova, "Predstavleniya o celostnom organizme goroda v period izmeneniya tvorcheskoj napravlennosti sovetskoj arhitektury," in *Estetika ottepeli: novoe v arhitekture, iskusstve, kul'ture*, ed. Olga Kazakova (Moscow: ROSSPEN, 2013), 15–75 (p. 27).
8 Nina Krainyaya, "Estetika tipovoi zastroiki 1960-h gg. glazami ee proektirovshika," in *Estetika ottepeli*, 76–80.
9 "Le Havre: Ilôt N17, système Camus," Fiche DOCOMOMO, accessed March 20, 2016, http://www2.archi.fr/DOCOMOMO-FR/fiche-havre-n17-va.htm.
10 See: Pedro Ignacio Alonso and Hugo Palmarola, *Panel* (London: Architectural Association Publications, 2014).
11 Triin Ojari, "Modernismi parameetrid: Mustamäe kujunemisest," Kümme. Eesti Arhitektuurimuuseumi aastaraamat (Tallinn, Eesti Arhitektuurimuuseum, 2000), 49–64 (p. 61).
12 An important influence on Soviet planning was the fifth UIA congress in Moscow in July 1958, an accompanying exhibition on contemporary planning in the West and subsequent publications. See: B. Vasil'jev et al., *Goroda-sputniki. Harlou, Vizensho, Vellingbi. Iz opyta gradostroitel'stva za rubezhom.* (Leningrad: Gosudarstvennoe izdatelstvo literatury po stroitelstvu, arhitekture i stroitel'nym materialam, 1958).
13 Triin Ojari, "Elamispind. Modernistlik elamuehitusideoloogia ja Mustamäe," Kunstiteaduslikke Uurimusi 2 [13] (2004), 42–65 .
14 Mart Port, "Pärlid ja kommikarbid. Mõtisklusi arhitektuurist," *Rahva Hääl*, May 23, 1962.
15 Leo Gens, "Mustamäe," *Noorus* 11 (1973), 67–68.
16 Ibid.
17 Mati Heidmets, "Mustamäestumise tagamaadest," *Sirp ja Vasar*, August 4, 1978.
18 Ibid.
19 Mati Heidmets, "Linn inimeses," *Looming* 4 (1978), 630–639 (p. 635).
20 Mart Kalm, "The Oasis of the Industrialised Countryside in Soviet Estonia," *Industry and Modernism. Companies, Architecture, and Identity in the Nordic and Baltic Countries during the High-industrial Period*, ed. Anja Kervanto-Nevanlinna (Helsinki: Finnish Literature Society 2007), 352–371.
21 Vilen Künnapu, "Keeruline arhitektuur," Sirp ja Vasar, May 5, 1973.
22 "Soome ja Eesti arhitektide ühine sümpoosion 'Kunst ja ehitamine' / 'Taide ja rakennus'" (Common symposium of Finnish and Estonian architects "Art and Construction", October 14, 1979. [Manuscript in Jüri Okas' collection]
23 See: Leonhard Lapin, Kaks kunsti. Valimik ettekandeid ja artikleid kunstist ning ehituskunstist 1971–1995 (Tallinn: Kunst, 1997).
24 Tiit Kaljundi, "The Chronicles of the Tallinn School (answers to a questionnaire)," in *Environment, Projects, Concepts: Architects of the Tallinn School 1972–1985*, ed. Andres Kurg and Mari Laanemets. (Tallinn: Eesti Arhitektuurimuuseum, 2008), 313–314.
25 Leonhard Lapin, "Kunstide süntees kaasaegses arhitektuuris – sünteetiline arhitektuur," *Kunst* 45 (1/1974).
26 Ibid.
27 Ibid.
28 Leonhard Lapin, "Masinaajastu ja kunst," *Kultuur ja Elu* 9 (1973), 56.

29 Protocols of the Board Meetings of the Estonian Architects' Union, Estonian State Archives (ERA) f. R-1951, n. 1, s. 227, l. 81.
30 Harry Šein, "Tühjusest, millest siis muust," *Sirp ja Vasar*, August 25, 1978.
31 Ibid.
32 Ibid.
33 The transposition of Venturi's ideas to the Soviet Estonian context was discussed at the time by Veljo Kaasik. See: Veljo Kaasik, "Mida arvata Venturist?" Arhitektuur. Kogumik ettekandeid, artikleid, vastukajasid, dokumente ja tõlkeid uuemast arhitektuurist, ed. Leonhard Lapin (Tallinn, 1979), 72–75. [Manuscript in Museum of Estonian Architecture].
34 Text on the display board, held by the architect's family.
35 Tõnu Karu, "Arhitektuurinäitus," Sirp ja Vasar, June 9, 1978, 8.
36 "Väljavõtteid arhitektuurinäituse (22.05–6.06 1978) külalisteraamatust" (Excerpts from the guestbook of the Architectural exhibition), *Arhitektuur. Kogumik ettekandeid, artikleid, vastukajasid, dokumente ja tõlkeid uuemast arhitektuurist*, ed. Leonhard Lapin (Tallinn, 1979) [Manuscript in Museum of Estonian Architecture].
37 Paul Härmson, "Kas tõesti tühjusest?" Sirp ja Vasar, June 23, 1978, 9–10.
38 Mihkel Mutt, "Arhitektuurinäitus," Sirp ja Vasar, June 9, 1978, 8.
39 V. K. (Vilen Künnapu), "Keskkonnaarhitektuuri suundumusi. 7 projekti," in *Ehituskunst* 1 (1981), 40.

Axel Zutz

"Complex Projects": Landscape Architecture as the Integrating Discipline

This chapter discusses the planning and realization of two different types of open urban space in the former German Democratic Republic (GDR) from the perspective of the theory and history of garden art and landscape development. Landscape architecture played an integral role in these developments that in the terminology of GDR planning were addressed as "complex projects." Landscape architects had not only the task of creating an aesthetically pleasing design; they also had to address different cultural, political and daily needs. Typical issues in planning and realization were the complexity and interdependence of functionality and symbolic meaning. Other subjects included the relation between buildings and open space, scale and territory, public use and control, and last but not least matters of power, history, utopian vision and reality.

The idea of the "Komplexprojekt" was born with the master classes of the Berlin Bauakademie in the beginning of the 1950s, following the model of the Bauhaus. Complex designs comprised interdisciplinary teamwork and integrated realization. With the beginning of this type of design strategy at the Bauakademie, landscape architect Reinhold Lingner (1902–1968) assembled a team of younger colleagues including Hubert Matthes (born 1929) and Erhard Stefke (1931–2016), who became responsible for the projects that will be discussed in this chapter.[1]

In many East German development projects, such as the monumental boulevards in the most important cities that – as with the Stalinallee in

East Berlin – were erected in the first years after the war, the standard was that landscape architects were involved in the planning process of complex projects from the very beginning. Stalinstadt (begun in 1950) is an important reference as this had not yet been the case from the outset, but later it became the usual approach. One reason for this integration of landscape architecture was to have a better survey of landscape potentials, plants and surfaces.

The principle of complex projection was then continued until the end of the GDR. "Well-kept greens are part of the socialist environment. They affect the residential milieu and have a positive influence on the patterns of behavior, and on habits of the citizens,"[2] stated the programmatic booklet *Grünanlagen im Wohngebiet* (Green Spaces in the Residence Area), published by a collective of the GDR Bauakademie Berlin in 1975 (fig. 1). This chapter follows the implementation of such socialist environments and discusses two examples that illustrate different urban contexts and strategies.

The first example deals with the 25-hectare Ernst-Thälmann-Park housing complex in the Berlin district Prenzlauer Berg. First designs for this project date from 1978, and it was built between 1983 and 1986. It is a completely newly built residential area with flats for 4,000 inhabitants and educational, cultural, and sports facilities that were erected on the site of a former gas plant within a 1900-era area. The area was developed in conjunction with a 16-hectare landscape park planned around a monument to the prewar labor leader Ernst Thälmann. The second example is one of the most important squares of central Berlin, the Gendarmenmarkt in the GDR-era Platz der Akademie, a listed ensemble of monumental late-baroque and classicist buildings. This public space was redesigned between 1979 and 1984.

Both examples are designs by landscape architect Hubert Matthes, who from 1977 to 1980 was department head for the planning of green space in the city administration of East Berlin.[3] Both projects are exceptional because of their experimental, progressive and representative character – yet with universal meaning, as they served as role models for the entire GDR.

Ernst-Thälmann-Park: Housing, Monumentality and Political Meaning

The site of the Ernst-Thälmann-Park development had been occupied since 1872 by the fourth of seven Berlin gas plants, and comprised six gas tanks. Three original tanks were destroyed during the Second World War; three surviving tanks dated from 1889, 1896 and 1900. The inventory of Berlin monuments *Bau- und Kunstdenkmale in der DDR, Hauptstadt Berlin I* listed the gas tanks in 1983 as "characteristic buildings," though they were not officially protected as historic monuments.[4] In the 1970s, gas from the Soviet Union had

fig. 1 Cover *Grünanlagen im Wohngebiet*. Bauakademie der DDR 1975.

replaced Berlin city gas, and so the Central Committee (ZK) of the Socialist Unity Party of Germany (SED) decided to close down the gas plant in 1981 and build a park on the location.[5]

When Hubert Matthes made his first drawings for the new park in 1978 (fig. 2), his design fitted into the strategy of the contemporaneous general development plan (Generalbebauungsplan) by the office of the chief architect of Berlin, Roland Korn (born 1930), that discussed proposals for green open spaces in the inner-city district. Matthes designed the project in an optimistic, festive, peppy and swinging style: a "culture and leisure park" not only for the surrounding district but for the whole of East Berlin. It was also a project utilized in a certain Cold-War competition with West Germany's federal horticulture show planned in West Berlin for 1985. Matthes' first concept covered the entire block of 30.65 hectares, with the park at a size of 26 hectares. In addition to the park, connections to other green spaces were to be established.

At first, the three remaining gas tanks and one of the adjoining administration buildings were to be included in the design.[6] The architects made several proposals to use the former tanks for studio, circus or disco activities or as a technical museum, solarium, greenhouse or planetarium. Preservationists and the public wanted to keep the former gas containers, but the request to list them as monuments was not successful. Instead, a number of designs were developed that included a new central monument with political meaning which in the end was placed close to a traffic connection frequently used by SED leaders (the Protokollstrecke).

Then, in February 1981, the SED Central Committee demanded the integration of housing into the project, as new apartments were needed to reach the goals of the GDR's housing program. In April 1981, the SED party congress decided to change the initial designs accordingly. The housing project was scheduled to be completed for the hundredth birthday of Ernst Thälmann (1886–1944), a German communist leader killed on Hitler's orders in 1944. In February 1982, SED chairman Erich Honecker decided with no further discussion that Soviet artist Lew Kerbel (1917–2003) was to be commissioned for a monument to Thälmann in the center of the park.[7] Kerbel was well known for large-scale monuments; in 1971, he had sculpted the monumental head of Karl Marx for Karl-Marx-Stadt (today Chemnitz), and in 1981 he designed a similarly monumental Lenin sculpture in Havana.[8] When completed, Kerbel's head of Thälmann was 13.5 meters tall, 13 meters wide and weighed 50 tons; the sculpture was to be surrounded by a paved plaza of 3,800 square meters. Kerbel's commission provoked protests by GDR artists, who felt cheated.[9] It also prefigured a number of further planning decisions for the park, as Kerbel insisted that conifers instead of the usual linden trees should be planted[10] and urged that a "wall" be built at the back of the monument, which implied a certain deployment of buildings and influenced the general layout of the space.[11]

After the selection of Kerbel and the final decision of the GDR council of ministers to build the Thälmann-Park district, a design competition was organized in early 1982 by the Aufbauleitung Sonderbauvorhaben with its director Erhardt Gißke (1924–1993) to determine the urban, architectural and landscape layout for the park and eight hundred and fifty apartments.[12] One second prize and two third prizes were awarded. Receiving second prize was the collective of architect Helmut Stingl (1928–2001), which then had no landscape architect on the team. Thus, when Stingl was commissioned with the project and became general planner (Generalprojektant) for the complex in January 1983,[13] he was asked to be more precise about landscaping. In the Berlin town-planning administration, nevertheless, there had been ongoing lobbying by Matthes and his landscape architects for the project. After Matthes left Berlin to teach in Weimar in 1980, Erhard Stefke took over, having been employed in the department since 1978.

In April 1983, the magistrate of Berlin decided to build the park.[14] The last steps of the design process were developed in cooperation with the garden administration of the city of Berlin and the VEB Wohnungsbaukombinat. The combination of housing and landscape architecture that was built on the site was a new type of residential park (Wohngebietspark) that – with exception of the culture center and a planetarium – was no longer designed

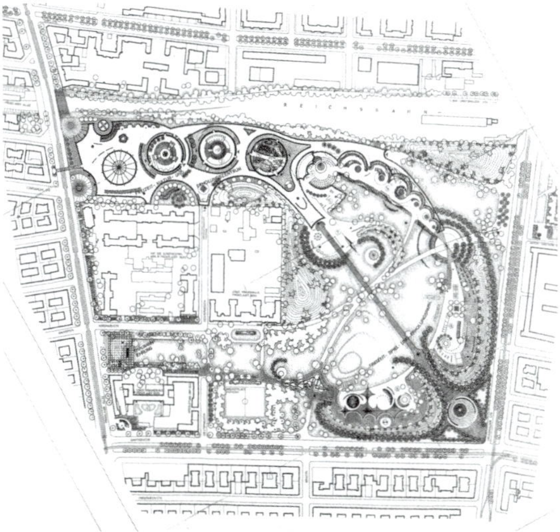

fig. 2 First ideas by Hubert Matthes from 1978 for a "culture and leisure park" with no housing. Scientific Collections Institut für Raumbezogene Sozialforschung (IRS) C_23_08_05.

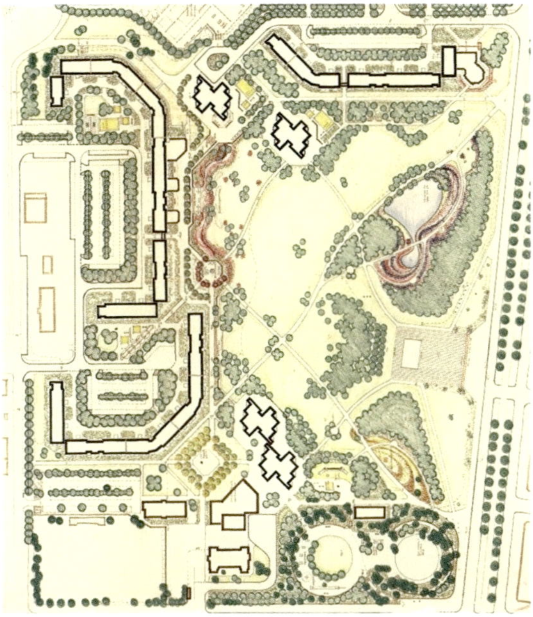

fig. 3 Plan of the residential park with the monument by Erhard Stefke of 1983. IRS Scientific Collections C_23_08_08.

to have general significance for the city of East Berlin as a whole (fig. 3).[15] A document written to prepare the economic investment summarizes the project:

> The construction of 1,342 flats on this area not only improves the environmental conditions of the citizens of our capital, but at the same time is a distinctive contribution to solving the problem of housing and developing the city center. In the center of the densely populated district Berlin-

> Prenzlauer Berg, a park will be built for the leisure and recreation of the citizens. [...] the ensemble of monument, park and housing is an expression of the growing strength of socialism.[16]

With no explicit mention of the historic gas tanks, the text also provided a definition of "the historical political meaning of the place":

> The function and urban-architectural design of the "Ernst Thälmann Park" form a comprehensive ensemble including the parts of the former gasworks which are worth preserving. [...]
>
> The starting point for the design of the new residence building and the "Ernst-Thälmann-Park" is the "Ernst-Thälmann-monument". [...] The monument, park and new residence buildings are connected in a harmonious unity of highly artistic town planning quality. The "Ernst-Thälmann-monument" by its monumentality and political meaning is the predominant element of the comprehensive composition.[17]

The investment program also named key design features of the gardens: the monument, a rhododendron grove with pond and flower garden for the Ernst Thälmann Pioneer Organization, a rose garden, "sophisticated playgrounds" and sports facilities south of the railway route.[18] The investment comprised forty-thousand cubic meters of new topsoil, the thirteen-hundred square meter rose garden, sixteen-hundred square meter rhododendron grove and thirteen-hundred square meter pond, a fifty-thousand square meter lawn, the eight-hundred-fifty square meter flower garden, two hundred and thirty conifers, and over three thousand broadleaf trees.[19]

One of the key features that later became a cause for public disapproval was, however, not mentioned: the demolition of the historic gas tanks; the official (unwritten) justifications for this course of action were the toxic ground and the costs of restoration. The public did not welcome the demolition of historic monuments: a hundred and sixty protest notes and letters from prominent experts including Ewald Henn, chief of the Association of German Architects (BDA), authors (Bernd Wagner), professors (such as Dietmar Kuntzsch of the Kunsthochschule Weißensee) and monument preservationists (such as Ludwig Deiters) were sent to the institutions in charge.[20] Leaflets, protest cards, badges and buttons made by students and preservation activists informed citizens about the planned demolition and appealed to them to join the protest. But the state institutions, supported by the police and the state security, prevailed and the three historic gas tanks were demolished on July 28, 1984.

When the park and housing estate were officially opened on April 15, 1986,

fig. 4 Ernst-Thälmann-Park, the finished project in 1986. *Ernst-Thälmann-Park* (Bauakademie der DDR 1986), XIII.

the development comprised 1,336 high quality flats for four thousand inhabitants in eight WBS70 slab buildings and four tower buildings of twelve, fifteen and eighteen floors (fig. 4). Social infrastructure included a culture center, an indoor swimming pool, two kindergartens, a school with a sports hall, shops and three restaurants. A special feature was the planetarium equipped with top modern technology by Carl-Zeiss-Jena; landscape architecture around the planetarium was again designed by Stefke.

The landscaping of the park was realized by the gardening combine VEB Landschafts- und Grünanlagenbau Mühlhausen, which carried out planting and maintenance together with inhabitants mobilized in so-called economic mass initiatives for the improvement of their environment. Compared with the first designs, the park was reduced to a size of 16 hectares and, in the end, served as a public residential area park. Following the ideas of architect Martin Wagner[21] and the modern town-planning models of the Weimar period (executed, for example, by landscape architect Leberecht Migge), the park was designed for all age groups,[22] included modern and ambitious playgrounds (as compared to the usual GDR standards), and also had a pond as an "ecological" design element. Still, the green space of the park does not form a harmonious unity or continuing connection with the neighboring residential area; it is accessible from all directions and upon entrance is divided into different spaces. A single spectacular sightline exists in the panorama view from the street to the monument and towards the housing slabs behind it, but from within the park it is almost impossible to see the monument; thus it is visible to passing drivers but invisible to the majority of inhabitants and park users.

This observation may also indicate something about the limits of complex design projects of this scale rooted in the ideas of a political leadership disconnected from the people and their local history. The gas tanks on the site had been real monuments of local significance. But instead of integrating them into the park a distanced hero worship of Thälmann was celebrated by Kerbel's work in a Stalinist way, with the sculpture staged to be seen from a traffic connection frequently used by SED leaders. The demolition of the tanks as monuments of work and technics was pushed through against local opposition. The lack of integration of GDR artists into the design of the monument may be seen as another aspect in the disconnected attitude of political decision making.

Nevertheless, the Ernst-Thälmann-Park became a popular housing area in the city center of East Berlin. Due to its quality and its good original condition, it is the first ensemble of modular-construction building with precast concrete slabs to be listed in Germany – in 2014 – and is protected as an ensemble including the park; a significant step in the appreciation of late GDR architecture and town planning (fig. 5).[23]

Platz der Akademie: History "*à la* Schinkel"

In a complex project of a different type, realized almost parallel to the urban-yet-more-peripheral landscape and housing project Thälmann-Park, the meaning of history and built heritage was much more important: the redesign of the historic Gendarmenmarkt (Platz der Akademie) square from 1976 to 1986. This "most beautiful square of Berlin"[24] is part of the baroque Friedrichstadt expansion that had been planned around 1700. The square covers three blocks of the regular grid of the city enlargement and measures three hundred twenty-five by one hundred fifty meters.

From 1700, two churches and surrounding graveyards were placed at the north and south of the site, with the middle field kept free as a parade ground and market. This former military use of the square provided the name Gendarmenmarkt. From 1770, the market was transformed into a baroque architectural square with a "French comedy house" by architect Jan Boumann in the middle field, flanked by two almost symmetrical churches by Carl von Gontard and Georg Christian Unger that, by order of King Friedrich II, were crowned by seventy-eight meter tower domes. Through these interventions, the square became a place for absolutist representation; the church domes were built for the impressive scenery alone with nothing in it. In 1802, a new national theater by Carl Gotthard Langhans replaced the comedy house, but

fig. 5 Ernst-Thälmann-Park and two of the listed buildings today. Photo Axel Zutz 2014.

was destroyed by fire in 1817. Karl Friedrich Schinkel then constructed the now famous Konzerthaus between 1818 and 1821. Schinkel disliked the domes (terming them *geschmacklos*) and made an unbuilt proposal for a Greek agora that should integrate them.[25] After the 1848 revolution with its manifestations and riots, the Gendarmenmarkt became a highly symbolic place after a hundred thousand participants joined the burial commemoration of a hundred eighty-eight dead citizens on the square.

In the second half of the nineteenth century, the square was turned into a place of bourgeois representation and decoration. A public initiative succeeded in erecting a monument to the poet Friedrich Schiller, in order to represent revolutionary demands,[26] and in 1871 the monument by Reinhold Begas was placed in the square, surrounded by lawn and decorative plants.[27] In 1895 (figs. 6, 7), a decorative garden layout was installed that covered most of the square, but around 1920 a more functional design reduced the number of plants and decorations. Since 1928, several architects have made proposals for a new design of the Gendarmenmarkt and the surrounding blocks, but none of the modernist ideas for greater unity and strength of the ensemble were realized.[28] During the years of national socialism, design proposals were made to use the site for parking and demonstrations in the context of the 1936 Summer Olympics (fig. 8). The middle field was paved and the Schiller monument was removed (the official reason was a lack of structural safety).

fig. 6 Gendarmenmarkt, Berlin. Plan by Garden Director Hermann Mächtig 1895. Landesdenkmalamt Berlin.

fig. 7 Gendarmenmarkt as a decorated garden around 1900. Period postcard.

After the Second World War, the theater, domes and churches were in ruins, and because of other priorities initiatives to redesign the square were postponed. In 1946, then again in 1956, municipal-planning chief Richard Ermisch (1885–1960) and architect Günther Zimmermann (biographical dates unknown) respectively proposed the demolition of the churches intending to give the square a new, strong frame that was meant to link to a style of "national tradition" paradigmatically recognized in Schinkel's theater. These proposals were not realized, nor were others of later years that were intended to open the block grid of the Friedrichstadt and place isolated single buildings in a landscape of parks surrounded by inner-city expressways.[29] In 1950, the square was renamed Platz der Akademie. In 1967, at last, the saving of the ruins began.

Then in 1976 the ninth SED party congress, the Central Committee, the Berlin head of the SED and the city council of East Berlin decided to rebuild the square with its three monumental buildings, as well as the historic, fram-

fig. 8 Modernized Gendarmenmarkt with car parking after 1936. Period postcard.

ing blocks around the square, on the basis of the baroque grid. As in the case of Thälmann-Park, a number of programmatic statements were issued regarding the design and the sociopolitical meaning of the project. Taking up older ideas from the 1920s, the three parts of the square interrupted by the grid of streets would be treated as one surface. The magistrate's decision stated that

> The area of the square which includes the two towers slightly in front of the theater will underline the impression of the monumental buildings by a clearly structured pavement without use of other sculptural elements.[30]

A document regarding the sociopolitical targets of the urbanistic situation in the city center stated that the square should create a "top ranking communication zone" for pedestrians coming from the central areas for demonstrations at the Marx-Engels-Forum and the Unter den Linden axis.[31] Planning principle no. 9 (of 10) emphasized that

> The whole surface should be designed as a pedestrian zone which stresses the architectural qualities of the monumental buildings and may realize flexible functions following the social-political targets.[32]

fig. 9 Reconstruction model of 1976 for the Platz der Akademie (Gendarmenmarkt). Scientific Collections IRS.

The urban-planning concept specified that an architectural square of metropolitan importance should be designed with "a single paved surface that should open multiple possibilities to use the square" (fig. 9).[33]

The designs for the square were made by the landscape architect Matthes. After 1980, the younger landscape architect Andreas Naumann replaced Matthes.[34] Architect Manfred Prasser (born 1932), employed in the combine *Volkseigener Betrieb Baumontagekombinat Ingenieurhochbau, Magistrat von Berlin, Aufbauleitung Sonderbauvorhaben* (IHB), was appointed as general planner (Generalprojektant, or Komplexarchitekt).

Prasser and Matthes were united by a long partnership. In 1968, they had designed Berlin Alexanderplatz (destroyed in 2006) and the park near Berlin's television tower (Fernsehturm, 1970, today renovated in part). In their Platz der Akademie design, the symmetric composition of the three monumental buildings was combined with a homogeneous pavement surface, which produced a kind of unitary tableau for the entire square for the first time. Prasser wanted to give the square a "tender frame" with "fine lines and steps."[35] The pattern of the pavement was also meant to provide a grid for planting trees in the middle of precast ground slabs. Matthes had the idea of designing "halls made of trees" (*Baumsäle*) and thought of cubically trimmed lindens similar to the famous, late-baroque Brühl's Terrace in Dresden.[36] But as the effort of trimming linden trees was thought to be too great, Globe Norway maples (*acer platanoides "Globosum"*), which are much smaller than lindens, were planted on the north and south sides of the square.[37] Public seating was designed by Naumann in a classicist manner "*à la* Schinkel," with lantern bases, benches and bollards made in colored, nudged pebble concrete – by GDR standards, this was a very pronounced effort.

In 1984, the square got its new leveling and surfacing, constructed by GDR "building soldiers," conscripts who had refused to bear arms.[38] A number of new buildings were also constructed, filling wartime gaps left in the line of facades surrounding the square. These new buildings were decorated with precast slabs with neo-Renaissance patterns and art noveau mosaics.[39] The monument to Schiller that had been removed in 1936 was initially not to be set up again, but in 1986, after the surfacing had been finished, the monument was returned from West Berlin to its former position in front of the theater. Step by step, the restoration and reconstruction of the three main buildings also succeeded. In 1983, the "French Dome" was reopened, in 1984 the new concert hall was inaugurated and at last in 1996, after Germany's reunification and the end of the GDR, the reconstruction of the "German Dome" was finished.

The new design of the square by Matthes, Prasser and Naumann marks a turning point regarding the handling of historic quarters in East German cities (fig. 10).[40] This urban reconstruction project, in connection with modern landscape architecture, may be seen as a counter-approach to the town planning models of the 1960s and 1970s. It is an example of a switch back to the historical layout of cities and of the appreciation of their qualities. At the same time, the re-enhancement of the old structures meant a change of scale towards traditional urban space and the individual. This trend reversal was no specific Eastern phenomenon: the West Berlin garden heritage administration began to reconstruct the first historic squares in this period.[41] The development of pedestrian zones is another east-west-parallel.

But there are some specific East German aspects. The change was more radical, compared with the models of town planning in the 1970s with their open composition and metaphors of progress. The design of the square was no simple reconstruction of an old structure but, with the exception of the monumental buildings, a completely new approach regarding surfaces and surrounding facades. A reconstruction of the late nineteenth-century Wilhelminian design was no option for the socialist planners; instead, they were looking for Prussian Enlightenment-era references.[42] Schinkel's classicism became the leading motive. Matthes' playful landscape architecture added a layer of trees as a relativizing aspect to the powerful architectures of Schinkel and Gontard but also followed Schinkel's agora idea of a clearly arranged urban space. The intimate zones under the trees offered a new quality of open space in the historical center of East Berlin. The project marks the rediscovery of public "urban" space after the "murder of the city"[43] in the first period after the war. Combined with Naumann's benches, lanterns and bollards, the Matthes redesign produced a kind of neo-historistic modernism

fig. 10 The reconstructed place with the postmodern buildings decorated with precast slabs (right), the paved surface around 1984 and new buildings from the 1990s. Photo Axel Zutz 2012.

of a unique, complex and comprehensive piece of art. The Platz der Akademie is an outstanding example that shows how urban planning tasks in socialist Germany could be tackled using the resources of history.[44]

Complexity, Design and Power

The two complex projects of Ernst-Thälmann-Park and the Platz der Akademie mark different approaches and relations in terms of the influence of political power, the relevance of history, design, urban environment and the scale of planning. In terms of power and ideology, the Platz der Akademie development is exceptional, as the historic ensemble with its two churches is closely linked with the history of the kings of Prussia. The remaking of the site was led predominately by the city administration; the SED party did not play a dominant role. In this case, national cultural heritage, the meaning of the 1848 revolution, and Schiller as a representative of bourgeois rights offered a strategy to link the redesign of the square with a socialist narrative, but with the restoration of the monumental architecture of the Prussian state and the creative interpretation of cultural history with (post)modern artifacts, the links to Schiller and the 1848 revolution became less important.

The Ernst-Thälmann-Park development, in contrast, illustrates the continuity of older ideas about socialist urban ensembles. The development staged the personal cult of Thälmann as a socialist working-class hero while important local monuments of the history of technology and production were demolished. The monument by Kerbel was a mere political gesture separate from the residence buildings. Its disconnection from the people and the real local history characterizes state-party bureaucracy in its blind self-orchestration and indicates early signs of the end of the GDR.

In terms of environment, both projects mark an increasing awareness of healthier living conditions. Thälmann-Park redeveloped a poisoned industrial territory within a 1900-era neighborhood. Its design stands in the tradition of landscape and peoples' parks, and it resumed patterns of postwar modernism together with monumental sculpture in the style of socialist realism. With this combination, the project aimed to represent a working-class tradition and the power of the SED government. The Platz der Akademie project also had an environmental dimension, as it improved the system of green spaces in the inner city and reduced vehicle traffic. Its design combined references to classicism with its baroque-modernist grid, which linked to the cultural heritage of "good" Prussian traditions with postmodern public furniture. Elements of nineteenth-century neo-Renaissance and Berlin art noveau facades completed the eclectic variety of details.

Both examples are models for the construction of life and society in "complex" projects in which landscape architecture played an important part. The Thälmann-Park development combined modern sculptural architecture with a beautiful "natural" landscape without streets or cars. It offered a better integration of daily needs for the individual with shopping, leisure, restaurants, sports, education and playgrounds. The design of the green provided the frame for all these elements. The new Platz der Akademie also offered, with its attractive pedestrian zone, space for individual retreat or communication linked to the scale and tradition of the European city. The design of the greenery enhanced the basic structure and quality of the square.

Regarding town-planning history, a major distinction can be identified between these projects. Whereas the Thälmann-Park development with its high-rise "modern" buildings implemented a completely new residential area in an older 1900-era neighborhood, the reconstruction of Platz der Akademie is an example of a postmodernist approach toward adapting a large-scale revitalization project to the pattern of the old city structure.

Since 1989, both projects continued to receive a high degree of recognition. In both cases, citizen initiatives have strived to save the public green space and the structures and designs from GDR times. Thälmann-Park has been listed as a monument; inhabitants and users do not want the neighborhood to be changed, and oppose densification schemes in order to keep the green space. In the case of the Gendarmenmarkt, an initiative of urban intellectuals has successfully defended the GDR heritage against plans to redesign the square.[45] Similar discussions can be traced to other high-prestige GDR projects – at this moment including the area around the television tower in the heart of the historically old and Eastern city – but that is another story.[46]

Endnotes

1 I would like to dedicate this chapter to Erhard Stefke, who died on January 21, 2016.

2 *Grünanlagen im Wohngebiet: Gestaltung und Pflege von Grünanlagen in unseren Wohngebieten. Grundsätze, Anregungen, Beispiele*, ed. Bauakademie der DDR, Institut für Städtebau und Architektur (Berlin: Institut für Städtebau und Architektur, 1975), 6, 18. This translation and all subsequent translations by the author.

3 After 1980, Matthes became professor at the Hochschule für Architektur und Bauwesen in Weimar (today the Bauhaus Universität Weimar).

4 Heinrich Trost, *Die Bau- und Kunstdenkmale in der DDR. Teil: Hauptstadt Berlin 1* (Berlin: Beck, 1987), 411.

5 Florian Bielefeld, Dirk Moldt, Petra Schröck, Brotfabrik Berlin (eds.), *Gasometer sprengt man nicht!* (Berlin: Brotfabrik Berlin, 2014), 67.

6 Study of the urban planning department, March 1979, quoted from Thomas Flierl, "'Thälmann und Thälmann vor allen.' Ein Nationaldenkmal für die Hauptstadt der DDR (1996)," in Flierl, *Berlin: Perspektiven durch Kultur. Texte und Projekte* (Berlin: Theater der Zeit, 2007), 37–98 (p. 78).

7 Flierl, "'Thälmann und Thälmann vor allen,'" 79; Bielefeld, Moldt, Schröck, *Gasometer sprengt man nicht!*, 75.

8 Bielefeld, Moldt, Schröck, *Gasometer sprengt man nicht!*, 74.

9 Flierl, "'Thälmann und Thälmann vor allen,'" 83; Bielefeld, Moldt, Schröck, *Gasometer sprengt man nicht!*, 76–78.

10 Heidrun Günther, *Gartenhistorisches Gutachten Landschaftsarchitektur in Ost-Berlin. Ernst-Thälmann-Park 1978–1986* (Berlin: Landesdenkmalamt Berlin, 2002), 19.

11 Flierl, "'Thälmann und Thälmann vor allen,'" 81–82.

12 Bielefeld, Moldt, Schröck, *Gasometer sprengt man nicht!*, 99.

13 Flierl, "'Thälmann und Thälmann vor allen,'" 83.

14 Bielefeld, Moldt, Schröck, *Gasometer sprengt man nicht!*, 100.

15 See Werner Rietdorf and Horst Baeseler, ed. Bauakademie der DDR, Institut für Städtebau und Architektur, *Freizeitanlagen. Grundlagen, Anregungen, Beispiele für die Planung und Gestaltung und Baudurchführung* (Berlin: Verlag für Bauwesen, 1979), 92–106.

16 *Dokumentation zur Investitionsvorbereitung 'Ernst-Thälmann-Park' Berlin*, April 1983, Institut für Raumbezogene Sozialforschung, Wissenschaftliche Sammlungen, Nachlass von Helmut Stingl, 3.

17 *Dokumentation zur Investitionsvorbereitung 'Ernst-Thälmann-Park' Berlin*, 7.

18 Ibid.

19 *Ernst-Thälmann-Park in der Hauptstadt der Deutschen Demokratischen Republik, Berlin*, ed. by Bauakademie der DDR (Berlin: Bauinformation, 1986), 53.

20 Bielefeld, Moldt, Schröck, *Gasometer sprengt man nicht!*, 123–125.

21 Martin Wagner, *Das sanitäre Grün der Städte. Ein Beitrag zur Freiflächentheorie* (Berlin: Heymann, 1915).
22 See Johann Greiner and Helmut Gelbrich, *Grünflächen der Stadt: Grundlagen für die Planung. Grundsätze, Kennwerte, Probleme, Beispiele* (Berlin: Verlag für Bauwesen, 1972).
23 See the listing, accessed August 2016, http://www.stadtentwicklung.berlin.de/denkmal/liste_karte_datenbank/de/denkmaldatenbank/daobj.php?obj_dok_nr=09030002.
24 Laurenz Demps, *Der schönste Platz Berlins. Der Gendarmenmarkt in Geschichte und Gegenwart* (Berlin: Henschel, 1993).
25 See Adalbert Behr and Alfred Homann, *Das Schauspielhaus in Berlin* (Berlin: Verlag für Bauwesen, 1985), 110; Laurenz Demps, *Der Gensd'armen-Markt: Gesicht und Geschichte eines Berliner Platzes* (Berlin: Henschel, 1987), 292.
26 See Michael Bienert, "Schiller. Der Freiheit ein Museum! Vor 250 Jahren wurde Friedrich Schiller geboren – Ortstermin in Weimar, Marbach und Berlin," in *Der Tagesspiegel*, 9 November 2009, accessed August 2016, http://www.tagesspiegel.de/kultur/schiller-der-freiheit-ein-museum/1629912.html.
27 Jörg Kuhn, "Gartenkunst und Denkmal (Teil 1). Von der 'Verwässerung der Denkmalidee,'" in *Botschaften zur Gartendenkmalpflege. Festschrift für Klaus-Henning von Krosigk. Ein bunter Strauß von Aufsätzen und Essays von Gartendenkmalpflegern und Freunden zum Abschied aus dem Landesdenkmalam*t, ed. Landesdenkmalamt Berlin and Deutsche Gesellschaft für Gartenkunst und Landschaftskultur e.V. (Berlin, Petersberg: Imhof, 2011), 143–145.
28 Demps, *Der Gensd'armen-Markt*, 437.
29 See Werner Durth, Jörn Düwel and Niels Gutschow, *Architektur und Städtebau in der DDR*: 2 *Aufbau. Städte, Themen, Dokumente* (Frankfurt a. M., New York: Campus, 1998); Simone Hain, *Archäologie und Aneignung. Ideen, Pläne und Stadtfigurationen. Aufsätze zur Ostberliner Stadtentwicklung nach 1945* (Erkner: Institut für Regionalentwicklung und Strukturplanung IRS, 1996).
30 Magistratsbeschluss 4.28.1976, quoted after Behr, Homann, *Schauspielhaus*, 132.
31 Aufbauleitung Sonderbauvorhaben Berlin, *Platz der Akademie Studie*, Berlin 1976, 1.
32 Ibid., 2.
33 Ibid., 11; Aufbauleitung Sonderbauvorhaben Berlin, *Platz der Akademie, Freifläche und Erschließung Platz der Akademie, IVE Berlin I. Baustufe 1978, Dokumentation zur Investitionsvorentscheidung*, Berlin 1978, 3.
34 Naumann (born 1955) later became Professor of Landscape Architecture in Erfurt.
35 "Zärtliche Fassung," interview by the author with Hubert Matthes and Manfred Prasser, summer 2010.
36 Matthes used an earlier idea from 1859, when a Berlin administrator proposed to plant the square with linden alleys or linden groups (Lindenlauben); in Demps, *Der Gensd'armenmarkt*, 351.
37 In East and West, in a kind of fashion typical for the 1980s, this species was often used in pedestrian zones, yards, city centers, spa-resort parks, terraces and parking lots. This variety of maple will not grow taller than four

meters, whereas trimmed linden trees will reach a height of six to eight meters.

38 Information given to the author by Andreas Naumann. This pavement was used in East Berlin on several occasions, for example, in the Ernst-Thälmann-Park and near the Deutsches Theater in central Berlin.

39 See Florian Urban, "Erker im Plattenbau. Die DDR entdeckt die historische Stadt," in eds. Frank Betker, Carsten Benke and Christoph Bernhardt, *Paradigmenwechsel und Kontinuitätslinien im DDR-Städtebau* (Erkner: Leibniz-Institut für Regionalentwicklung und Strukturplanung IRS, 2010), 127–145.

40 There are a number of further examples; for example, the reconstruction of the residence district at Arkonaplatz in central Berlin.

41 See *Botschaften zur Gartendenkmalpflege.*

42 See Helmut Meier and Walter Schmidt (eds.), *Erbe und Tradition in der DDR. Die Diskussion der Historiker* (Berlin: Akademie Verlag, 1988).

43 Wolf Jobst Siedler, *Die gemordete Stadt* (Berlin: Herbig, 1964).

44 For further explanations, see Axel Zutz, "Modern-postmoderne Landschaftsarchitektur im Zentrum der Hauptstadt: Der Gendarmenmarkt / Platz der Akademie," in *Deutschland Archiv*, 45:4 (2012), 641–654, accessed August 2016, http://www.bpb.de/geschichte/zeitgeschichte/deutschlandarchiv/147742/landschaftsarchitektur-im-zentrum-berlins.

45 In 2009 and 2010, the building commission of the senate of Berlin and the garden-preservation board discussed the redesigning of the Gendarmenmarkt. See Veranstaltungen, Öffentlich planen, Gendarmenmarkt, Senatsverwaltung für Stadtentwicklung und Umwelt, accessed August 2016, http://www.stadtentwicklung.berlin.de/planen/staedtebau-projekte/gendarmenmarkt/de/veranstaltungen.shtml. In summer 2010, twenty-three thousand signatures for the preservation of the 1984 design were collected. In reaction to this, the administration organized a public vote. The majority voted for "no change – keep it as it is." See Gendarmenmarkt, Variantenabstimmung zur Bepflanzung des Gendarmenmarktes, Senatsverwaltung für Stadtentwicklung und Umwelt, accessed August 2016, http://www.stadtentwicklung.berlin.de/planen/staedtebau-projekte/gendarmenmarkt/de/abstimmung/index.shtml.

46 See Axel Zutz, "Der Park am Fernsehturm. Entwurfsgeschichte, Elemente und Verfasser," in Paul Sigel and Kerstin Wittmann-Englert (eds.), *Frei-Raum unter dem Fernsehturm: Historische Dimensionen eines Stadtraums der Moderne*, (Berlin: Theater der Zeit, 2015), 94–120; accessed August 2016, http://stadtdebatte.berlin.de/.

Andreas Kalpakci

UIA, R. Buckminster Fuller, and the Architectural Consequences of "Total Environment"

Architecture for a "Total Environment"[1]

From May 19–26, 1968, the International Union of Architects (UIA), the world representative of the architectural profession,[2] held its fifth Seminar on Industrial Architecture in Detroit, USA.[3] Organized by Louis Rossetti (1895–1983),[4] the seminar explored how to connect industrial facilities with their surroundings. The seminar had also the latent task of connecting architects with industry stakeholders. This was the first time that UIA organized a public event in the US: seventy architects from seventeen countries on both sides of the iron curtain visited factories (fig. 1) and met with local labor unions, government officials and business corporations.

R. Buckminster Fuller (1895–1983), who was among the speakers at the seminar, prophesied the coming of an epoch in which industrialization would make of the planet's resources the final limit to mankind's inhabitation possibilities, discharging all internal political borders as arbitrary conventions. "I simply find a whole world society," Fuller pointed out: "no exceptions, whether Russia, or the United States, no exceptions."[5] At the same time, this unprecedented liberty would come with the responsibility of "taking care of all of humanity": if industrialization were to permit the mobilization of all of the finite resources of "Spaceship Earth,"[6] then the possibility of liberating mankind from all the divisions internal to its social body would also be within reach. As he stated elsewhere, "industrialization is the first religion / that is realistically universal."[7] Drawing from terminology in use among cyberneti-

fig. 1 The 57-acre Chrysler Corporation Sterling Stamping Plant built in Detroit by the firm Giffels and Rossetti Inc., in *Review of the International Union of Architects*, 52 (November 1968), 4. Image credit: UIA. In the photograph it is difficult to distinguish where the factory ends and where the surroundings begin.

cians such as Hasan Ozbekhan (1921–2007),[8] Fuller named this planetary horizon the "total environment,"[9] announcing that its epoch had arrived. As UIA's *Review* later reported, Fuller held his fellow participants "breathless for four hours."[10] How did this come to be?

UIA had organized five Seminars on Industrial Architecture throughout the 1960s. Although the seminar was hosted every time in a different place and by a different national chapter, a number of prominent international participants were present on several occasions. Architects including Jean Fayeton (1908–1968) from France,[11] Walter Henn (1912–2006) from West Germany,[12] Nikolaï Kim (1913–2009) from the USSR,[13] and Jean-Pierre Vouga (1907–2006) from Switzerland[14] were among the seminar's most assiduous contributors, and either held international reputations as experts in this new field or were in positions of control within their respective national bureaucracies. These seminars were less ceremonial than the periodic UIA congresses, but were nonetheless official. Seminars, as a well-established organizational form in the field of postwar international organizations, were tasked to gather participants from different countries and organizations to discuss a subject of common expertise and to exchange knowledge, convene resolutions and collaborate on policy recommendations.[15]

Even in this special context, Fuller was known for his verbosity and extenuating lectures. Yet, apart from his contribution, the fifth seminar was clearly committed to a very practical agenda. Fuller might have acted as the event's provocateur, an idealist whose cosmopolitan views appealed to the

fig. 2 Advertisement of the French firm Minangoy Poyet, in *Review of the International Union of Architects*, 38 (May 1966), iii. Image credit: UIA. An ad for roofing products illustrates an example of postwar industrial buildings.

internationalism of UIA, which in turn tolerated his presence. However, the fact that the Detroit seminar was part of an ongoing series indicated that the field of industrial architecture was still in the making: the seminar's conclusions addressed the projective need for legislation about the "proper direction and control of industrial development," and for the creation of new interprofessional committees.[16] In other words, the roles of the ingenuous provocateur and of the uncompromising gatekeeper were not that well-defined.

Crisis of Industrial Building

From the AEG turbine factory to the Fagus factory to the Montreal silos celebrated in *Vers une Architecture*, industrial buildings had a past as aesthetic metonymies of modern architecture: their photographs became the preferred instruments for the international mobilization of avant-garde architects after the First World War. Differently from these origins however, industrial architecture at the end of the 1950s was developing into a field of its own. It possessed many unprecedented characteristics: from the machinery that new facilities accommodated, including nuclear reactors in thermal power stations, to the size and the infrastructure that served them, industrial architecture was growing staggeringly in complexity (fig. 2), which was reflected in the growing number of specialists around the drawing table, and in its institutionalization as a field of professional and academic expertise nested between planning, architecture and engineering. Moreover, the asymmetry in the industrial development of postwar countries and the fact that industrial architecture was sensitive information in a period of growing geopolitical confrontation further isolated this subject among only a specialized niche.

In the 1950s, industrial architecture did not receive within the UIA the same systematic attention that was being given to the industrialization of mass housing. The field emerged when pressure for postwar reconstruction subsided in 1959 with the events of UIA's fifth congress in Moscow. As architects gradually withdrew from the role of necessary emissaries of the political visions for reconstruction, adversaries with greater technical competencies could have easily threatened their positions on articulated expert teams of postwar planning agencies, institutes, and firms. "Co-ordination or Stagnation," warned the title of an article published in 1958 for the first issue of the British journal *Industrial Architecture*. The article advocated the modernization of the building industry by "methods of organization which apply to other industries, particularly the younger industries" including the chemical and aircraft industries. The latent logic of this discussion was that, by adopting the "language common to all" in the world of industrial production, the profession could avoid stagnation, eventually rescuing its legitimacy: this reasoning, however, lead to the ambiguous conclusion that all architecture could, in differing degrees, be recognized as "industrial," although in fact only the building types strictly defined as "Industrial Architecture" were the source of this new preoccupation.[17]

Building on these pre-existing developments, the Seminar on Industrial Architecture set to reposition the field as one among many specialized subjects within architecture. Industrialization had been part of UIA's agenda since the union's foundation in 1948, when the first congress introduced the international study of industrial production of building elements for housing projects in the context of postwar reconstruction. The seminar instead aimed to problematize specifically industrial facilities.

Its first summit on this special focus took place in 1960 in Kazimierz, Poland, on the theme "Architecture at the Service of Industry" and at the initiative of the UIA Polish section.[18] The seminar unfolded as a sequence of seven speeches, which spanned from the new tendencies in the organization of industrial production to the pressing issue of the architect's position in engineering works, and the concern for pollution within and around production sites. Jean Fayeton opened the seminar showing chemical factories, oil refineries and works of the French Commissariat à l'Énergie Atomique, to argue that architects are alone in defending "human values in front of economic or technical interests." A delegate from East Germany observed that the purpose of using colors in factories was to increase workers' visual capacity and reduce their fatigue. Walter Henn argued that in comparison with Europe, where industrial architecture was focused on offering services to workers and their communities, American factories were planned solely to achieve productivity through the future expansion and transformation of buildings. Delegates from the UK, Romania, Poland and Italy illustrated recent realizations in their countries, while Swedish delegate Ralph Erskine (1914–2005) concluded the seminar with a presentation on "factories and industrial communities in Scandinavia."

Aside from individual contributions, however, the premise of the seminar resided between these different approaches, since "its objective was to confront the points of view of architects of the different countries of the East and the West in front of the problems of Industrial Architecture."[19] This comparison showed that industrial architecture was problematic, because of significant differences across countries, which were interpreted as indications of the crisis of industrial architecture as a building type planned to serve productivity rather than society. Instead, a more or less hidden message of the seminar was that industrial architecture ought to provide optimal working conditions and a carefully planned relationship between the workplace and its surrounding neighborhood, city and region.

The seminar tested these preliminary conclusions at the margins of its schedule.[20] First, participants completed a questionnaire, which asked them whether it would be "opportune to create a working group to elaborate a Charter of Industrial Urbanism and Architecture (similar to the Athens Charter of the CIAM)." Second, the majority of participants proposed to institute a permanent UIA commission on industrial architecture, to parallel those that already existed for school buildings, public health and other subjects.

The responses to both proposals were negative:[21] paradoxically, however, opportunities to overturn this unfavorable verdict then grew steadily. The UIA's interest in the seminar increased in the coming years despite those early rejections, as UIA's General Secretary Pierre Vago (1910–2002) along with the UIA Executive Committee intervened to actively maneuver the initiative from behind the scenes.[22] After the seminar in Kazimierz, UIA's *Review* would dedicate special issues to exhaustively covering the results of all future seminars.[23] The stakes were high.

Fuller's Decade

In 1961, the sixth UIA Congress was held in London under the title "New Techniques and New Materials," as praise for industrialization. In a 1998 memoir, Dennis Sharp (1933–2010) recalled how the aluminum-sheet pyramids of UIA's pavilion (fig. 3) related to the congress euphoria: "the buildings were meant to be an advertisement for the kind of technology architects (particularly British architects and producers) were interested in at the time: quick built temporary modern structures in this case based on space frame grid construction."[24] The congress had the merit of generalizing the question of industrialization beyond the discussion of building types or "an isolated technical process," problematizing it as an issue of architectural education, of regional adaptation, of professional capability, of humanization and of the moral imperative of improving worldwide living standards.[25]

This optimism was met with reasoned critiques: for example, Jerzy Hryniewiecki (1908–1989) argued that building techniques were primitive when compared to other branches of production.[26] However, industrialization found unexpected supporters who were ready to expound upon its positive consequences. R. Buckminster Fuller arrived at the congress as a wild card, and contributed to it as an impromptu guest speaker.[27] From this pulpit, Fuller presented a "proposal" for repurposing the UIA so as to target precisely the weaknesses that Hryniewiecki and other critics identified in the building industry: he called this ten-year plan the World Design Science Decade, an initiative that he launched from Carbondale, Illinois,[28] aimed at an inventory of the planet's resources, at rearranging industrial systems to increase their efficiency and at readdressing all the results of industrialization to a social cause. Fuller believed that "making the world's totally available resources serve one hundred percent of an exploding population may only be accomplished by a boldly accelerated design evolution," and he argued that such an evolution did not depend upon political ideologies, but relied instead on systems design: "it is a task which can only be accomplished by the world's architects, inventors and scientists/artists," he concluded. With the aim of recruiting architecture students, who could fully invest their talents in this project better than embedded professionals, Fuller proposed to transform the UIA into a center for the coordination of the world's architecture schools: all research results would then be computed and monitored through an electronic scale model of the planet (fig. 4).[29]

In 1962, the UIA declined Fuller's "proposal" of organizational reform, approving nevertheless the broader pedagogical initiative. Thereafter, the union provided Fuller with platforms to address students and convene exhibitions of their projects.[30] Under these conditions, Fuller's research group in Carbondale, the World Resources Inventory, embarked in a multivolume project to equip students with a collection of surveys, theoretical essays, procedural instructions and design tactics so that they could immediately step into

fig. 3 Theo Crosby, the Headquarters Building at the sixth UIA Congress in London in 1961. Image credit: Architectural Association. Notice the 132 prefabricated aluminum pyramids on the roof.

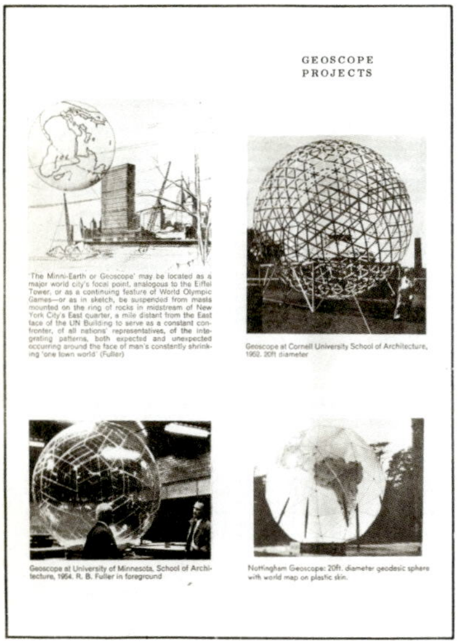

fig. 4 "Geoscope Projects," in John McHale (ed.), *World Design Science Decade 1965–1975: The Ten Year Program*, vol. 4 (Carbondale: Southern Illinois University, 1965), 31. Image credit: Fuller Estate. For the display and control of world resources, Fuller proposed UIA to use a machine of his own invention, which he called the "minni-earth," i.e. a geodesic sphere used as a cybernetic planisphere.

redesigning systems. The Decade initiative thus charted the consequences of industrialization for architecture: it dislodged architecture's object as the simple response to a client's brief, reframing it as "comprehensive design"; it displaced architecture's site from building on a specific place to mobilizing resources and industries at a planetary level, terming it the "ecological context";[31] and it responded to the crisis of the architect's role not through camouflage or by adopting an external logic, but by conceiving an organizational diagram that would reskill architects with plentiful knowledge, exceeding that which any other profession could have ever possessed.

In comparison to this vigorous universalism, however, UIA stood in a fragile political and organizational equilibrium,[32] and the Seminar on Industrial Architecture, which unfolded in parallel with Fuller's Decade, charted a different outline of architecture's response to the expansion of industrialization, in which the profession of architecture should firmly be rooted as its point of departure.

The Tihany Resolution

Presided by Eugène Beaudouin (1898–1983), the second UIA seminar took place in Brazil in 1962 as a threefold celebration of Brasilia being built, of Brazil's industrialization, and of UIA's organizational capabilities.[33]

Commenting on the first seminar, Jan Zachwatòwicz (1900–1983) argued that the architect was the only professional responsible for both standardized industrial building in its context as well as for those who work in it. It is in this act of mediation that the architect could claim a role in industrial architecture.[34] In continuation with this position, the second seminar "Architecture of Industry in Mankind's Service," reversed the agenda introduced in Kazimierz.[35] Instead of comparing buildings across the East-West divide, the seminar was arranged as groups working in parallel on systematized complementary issues: the planning of industrial zones, architecture and structure, prefabrication, industrial buildings in developing countries and working conditions.

Delegates disagreed on details. Nikolaï Kim's discussion of integrating small-sized factories into a single body with shared services was criticized as a solution possible only within a planned economy. To some, the distinction between industrial and developing countries was not "a distinction of kind, but only one of degree,"[36] as if industrialization was a predefined ladder, whereas others thought that developing countries were likely to do better than industrial countries since the former could profit from the latter's past mistakes.[37] All delegates agreed however on definitions: the factory was not "merely an instrument of production." Beaux-Arts trained architect Jean Demaret (1897–1967) argued that the factory was "one of the greatest manifestations of our epoch" (fig. 5).[38] The architect "should be the chief coordinator of the squad," concluded Kim, referring to "elaborate studies by Soviet sociologists and economists."[39] Whether the premise was "History" or historical materialism, the conclusion was the same: the scales of industrialization might have been unprecedented, but industry was just another part in the

fig. 5 The spherical laboratory for the acceleration of electrons built in Toulouse by the *Beaux Arts* trained architect Camille Montagné, in *Review of the International Union of Architects*, 19 (January 1963), 3. Image credit: UIA. This photograph opens the section that the *Review* dedicated to the second seminar, and is a good representation of industrial architecture as Fayeton understood it: architects ought to overcome both functionalism and the grammar of styles, so as to resolve the unprecedented scale of these new tasks as a composition of abstract geometries.

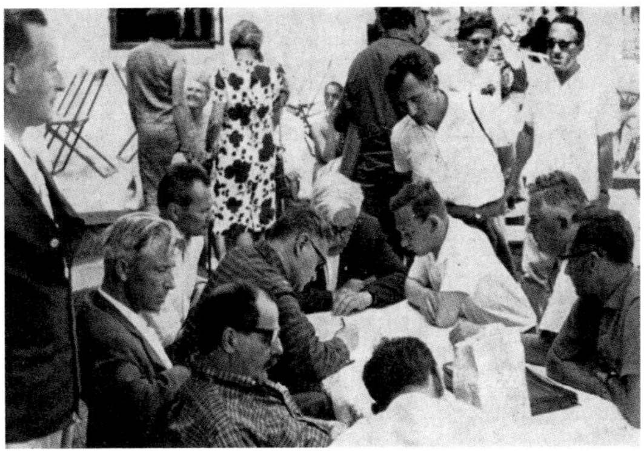

fig. 6 Conference of the chairmen of the working groups – i.e., Georges Candilis (France), Walter Henn (West Germany), Constantin Kartachev (USSR), Mieczyslaw Pietraszun (Poland), George Heery (USA), and Paul Waltenspuhl (Switzerland) – at the third seminar in 1966 in Tihany, Hungary, in *Review of the International Union of Architects*, 30 (December 1964), 13. Image credit: UIA.

vast program of modern architecture. The only response was neither camouflage, nor reskilling, but the drafting of a new social contract.

Although the seminar resulted in an organizational disaster that caused deep resentment among UIA officials,[40] its setup indicated that a first attempt was made to internalize industrial architecture as a subject for international collaboration. The Polish section had once again drafted a charter, and left to the forthcoming seminar the task to finalize it.[41] On this front, UIA could now fulfill its mandate, and act as the mediating center between East and West, developed and developing, machine and human.

The third seminar, held in 1964 in Hungary (fig. 6), indeed achieved the adoption of a Charter of Industrial Architecture.[42] While not having an explicit theme, the 1964 seminar addressed industrial architecture on a more abstract level and at a larger scale. East and West were denoted by their use of materials – "western countries are developing the use of prefabricated steel structures, whereas socialist countries are mainly using reinforced concrete."[43] The works of the town-planning group chaired by George Candilis (1913–1995) identified the issue of the factory's "surroundings" and the interrogative of "large undertakings."[44]

The Tihany Resolution, as the charter was titled,[45] described industrial building as a field put in motion on one end by the evolution of technics and the progress of science, but nested on the other end among complex and fragile equilibria: the "genius peculiar to each nation," the chosen site for an implantation, the workers' psychophysical well-being, the flexibility of program requirements, the plasticity of spatial composition. The resolution assigned to the architect the "harmonization of problems resulting from the implantation of various categories of industry with all other factors of urban and regional development."[46] The architect ought to introduce preoccupations, examine repercussions, deal with problems, and be the spokesman of human values. The bottom line was that industrial architecture could have been possible if only the architect would have stabilized the field of industrial building by addressing all of its scales, all at the same time. In 1965, "after an animated discussion," the UIA Executive Committee decided to accept and diffuse the resolution.[47]

In Defense of Large Undertakings

The fourth seminar, in 1966, was themed after the "large undertakings for energy, traffic, and sanitation" that were under construction in Switzerland at the time.[48] "The civilization of the future," argued seminar organizer Jean-Pierre Vouga, "will be more dependent on a geographic structure of networks and upon the design of vast schemes in support of day-to-day activities."[49] Next to built examples like the Lavey Dam, Switzerland, participants also discussed ambitious initiatives like the Transhelvetischen Kanal, a project of continental scale aiming to establish a navigable route between the Mediterranean and the North Sea by connecting the Rhine and Rhône Rivers on Swiss territory.

However, the seminar served also to study in detail how to translate into practice the capacity for harmonization stipulated by the Tihany Resolution. Fayeton discussed the case of thermal power stations. First, he argued, the architect assists the team in "finding the most economical and harmonious spatial organization," by giving "plastic meaning to all the forms" arranged

fig. 7 Aerial view of the dam in Zeltingen, West Germany, in Charles-Édouard Geisendorf et al. (eds.), *L'Architecte et l'Urbaniste en Face des Grands Travaux de l'Énergie, du Trafic et de l'Assainissement* (Lausanne: Bulletin Technique de la Suisse Romande, 1966), 35. Image credit: *Bulletin Technique de la Suisse Romande*. The architect's "harmonizing" role in the works of the Moselle translated in the attempt to account for the landscape. Hydroelectric power stations were developed as horizontal rather than as vertical volumes, and they were completed with a roof terrace to relate with their surroundings: yet these were small details in comparison to the scale of the finished works. Note for example the size of the dam in Zeltingen and of the power station on its right end compared to the community next to it.

into "a coherent composition." Second, the architect continues beyond the building because, for example, "the machinery" – i.e., turbo alternators and the handling apparatus – "is also important enough to be treated as an element of architecture": machines should be revealed using color "to create a visual order and strengthen the plastic signification."[50] Henn more candidly confessed that "it was not always easy for them [architects] to stand up against the many engineers" and authorities, and even when they succeeded their task was just to check that "ugly forms were avoided." His work for the transformation of the Moselle River into a navigable waterway was an example of this compromise: a gigantic infrastructure presented as a landscape project (fig. 7).[51] Compromises aside, there was still one aspect of industrial architecture that the seminars had all-but neglected until 1966: the problem of the environmental effects of industrialization.

The fourth seminar, then, acknowledged pollution mostly as a local phenomenon. Spatial displacement of polluting facilities was considered the

fig. 8 View of the Thermal Power Station of Chavalon-sur-Vouvry, Switzerland, in UIA, Charles-Édouard Geisendorf et al. (eds.), *L'Architecte et l'Urbaniste en Face des Grands Travaux de l'Énergie, du Trafic et de l'Assainissement* (Lausanne, Bulletin Technique de la Suisse Romande, 1966): 44–45. Image credit: *Bulletin Technique de la Suisse Romande*. The power station is on the foreground, overlooking the Rhône delta and Lake Geneva on the background.

optimal solution, if coordinated within a regional plan that divided residential from industrial zones: this was offered as a solution that architects were capable of adopting.

An example of this discourse was the thermal power station of Vouvry in Switzerland, where the decision to go for the production of electricity through the combustion of heavy oil was taken on the assumption that the siting of the power station on an alpine peak, higher than any inhabited area, would have kept all pollutant away from the population (fig. 8). In the logic of a "total environment," however, the solution of spatial displacement would have been irrelevant, since the very cause of Vouvry's pollution was its choice to use oil as an energy source, not in its position in space. Nevertheless, it was not at all clear how the professional architect was supposed to respond here. The Tihany Resolution did not offer answers to these kinds of problems. Nor did the discussion at the seminar seem to grasp this dialectic, since pollution and the use of energy were tackled as separate issues: urban sanitation and sewage works on one hand, hydroelectric and thermal power generation on the other.[52]

fig. 9 Group photograph at the fifth seminar in 1968 in Detroit, in *Review of the International Union of Architects*, 52 (November 1968), 10. Image credit: UIA. From left to right: Horace Huckle (UK), R. Buckminster Fuller (USA), Ernest Groosman (Netherlands), American Institute of Architects President Robert Durham (USA), Marc-Joseph Saugey (Switzerland), and Louis Rossetti (USA).

Detroit

In light of all past shortcomings, the fifth seminar, held in 1968 in Detroit, attempted to chart "The Effect of Industrial Architecture on Man and the Environment." So, while previous seminars had reached out to discuss how the industrial building was part of different fields – its immediate surroundings, industrial zones, territorial developments, regional plans – the fifth seminar introduced the notion of "environment" to chart its consequences, above all pollution. With the prospect of establishing a UIA Commission on Industrial Architecture, the seminar set out to reconcile two logics: the gradual work of theorizing industrial architecture as the result of "harmonization" and the logic of Fuller's call for the reform of the entire industrial cycle on the premise of a "total environment" (fig. 9).

This combination of a technocratic agenda with the global vision of R. Buckminster Fuller followed a certain strategy. In 1968, Fuller was no longer foreign to international circles. Although the World Design Science Decade was drawing to a premature end,[53] his travels and buildings had received international recognition, which culminated in 1967 with the US Pavilion at the Montreal Exhibition. Although Fuller in 1968 was presenting the same logic as in 1961, he had in the meantime become an institution in his own right. His presence at the seminar was therefore not that of a provocateur, but rather of an expert along with all other participants. What he brought to the table was precisely the capability that all others could not have, embedded as they were in their professional competencies and responsibilities. His presentation to the 1968 seminar therefore tackled issues of a global scale once more: commenting on how little time remained before the regeneration of life would stop due to the pollution in the atmosphere – an image that echoed Rachel Carson's 1962 book, *Silent Spring*[54] – Fuller rushed to confirm: "I am perfectly confident that I am going to be able to submit to you enough of

fig. 10 Vignette, in *Review of the International Union of Architects*, 58/59/60 (December 1969), 27. Image credit: UIA. This vignette, published in the last issue of the *Review*, commented on UIA's reorganization by asking: "who is the imbecile who appointed an architect with the project of a dam?" With one absurd example, the vignette questioned the whole enterprise of theorizing industrial architecture anew, as if to say that architects should put their time into fields that needed their competencies, and that industry was clearly not one of them.

the generalized principles which are operative so you will find interconnections. You will understand general systems theory in the very biggest way," he announced.[55] On these premises, the fifth seminar inaugurated the UIA Commission on Industrial Architecture, and officially proclaimed Detroit as its headquarters. The seminars had thus reached their second goal, after the Tihany Resolution had marked the completion in 1965 of the first goal. No less ceremoniously, the seminar added systems theory to the repertoire of skills for the architect faced with industrial architecture.

The history of the Seminars on Industrial Architecture within the UIA illuminates the study of architecture in the context of the competition between state-socialist and capitalist countries in the Cold War period. The seminars were strategically deployed in order to enable international discourse among professional architects, and to diminish the influence that central issues of the East-West divide had on it. An agenda of jointly agreed resolutions and the treatment of new issues like environmental protection and systems theory were not alone in building bridges across the East-West divide, but did stress the professional ethics of architects and – not least – underlined and justified the necessity of the UIA as an international platform.

In this context, the seminars had been as much of a novelty as Fuller's Decade. The "harmonization of the Tihany Resolution was certainly a different approach from the "retooling" of the Decade: the resolution was presented after cumulative observations, whereas the Decade was introduced as a new frame of reference. The internationalism of each was also different, since Fuller's cosmopolitanism disregarded political boundaries and ideologies as arbitrary conventions, whereas the UIA tried to work within them. However, they both attempted to engage in the intellectual project of redirecting industrial building from a mere response of productivity to questions for social therapy: either by addressing "human values," or by advocating benefits for "100 % of humanity," they both mobilized individuals to theorize architecture anew.

Yet this achievement was short lived. From the mid-1960s, UIA began to suffer from internal problems deriving from the antagonism of student organizations that lamented the union's machinations as bureaucratic, and from the critique of developing countries that accused the UIA of serving only industrialized societies. On top of that, the global unrests of 1968 unsettled the institutional context which the UIA was part of. Thus, by the time that the commission had been created, the organizational structure around it was forced to change.[56] In 1969, at the tenth UIA Congress in Buenos Aires, Argentina, new officials were elected and the very idea that industrial architecture could belong to the architect's imagery was derided (fig. 10): UIA arose from this catharsis with a new geographical ambition for regional promotion instead of solely East-West dialogue, and with a new architectural agenda that had been liberated from industrialization as a necessary premise, while nonetheless retaining industry's effects on society as among its main concerns.

Endnotes

1 This paper draws on the research for the author's dissertation project "Making CIAM: The Organizational Techniques of the Moderns, 1928–1959" conducted at the gta Institute, Zurich, under the supervision of Prof. Laurent Stalder. The research was made possible by a grant from the Swiss National Science Foundation.

2 Scholarship in English about UIA is scarce; for a historical overview of UIA, sometimes incorrect, see UIA, *L'UIA, 1948–1998* (Paris: Les Éditions de l'Épure, 1998).

3 For a list of participants and reports, see "5th Seminar on Industrial Architecture: Detroit (U.S.A.) May 19–26, 1968," *Review of the International Union of Architects*, 52 (1968), 3–32.

4 Rossetti was well established in the field of industrial architecture in Detroit, second perhaps only to Albert Kahn.

5 For the transcript of Fuller's speech, see R. Buckminster Fuller, "UIA Seminar," Stanford University Libraries: R. Buckminster Fuller Collection, M1090-S8-b61-f5UIA-Seminar (May 5, 1968).

6 His notion is further developed in R. Buckminster Fuller, *Operating Manual for Spaceship Earth* (Carbondale: Southern Illinois University Press, 1968).

7 Fuller, *Untitled Epic Poem on the History of Industrialization* (Highlands: Jonathan Williams, the Nantahala Foundation, 1962), 178.

8 Generalizing from all the instances of planning (corporate, economic and urban), Ozbekhan theorized planning as a "system" included in a "meta-system" that was the "total environment: this combined all 'human/social, life/nature and thing/technology centered environments.'" Hasan Ozbekhan, "Toward a General Theory of Planning," in *Perspectives of Planning: Proceedings of the OECD Working Symposium on Long-Range Forecasting and Planning, Bellagio, Italy, October 27–November 2, 1968*, ed. Organization for Economic Co-Operation and Development (Washington, D.C.: OECD Publications Center 1969), 47–158 (p. 111).

9 Ozbekhan and Fuller were both part of the *Ekistics* network. However, while Ozbekhan theorized "total environment" as part of a generalization of planning, Fuller used the term in a common-sense way. At the Detroit seminar, Fuller gave his definition of "environment" in response to Nikolaï Kim, who spoke "about the many different ways in which you could talk about the environment [...] My definition of environment is everything that isn't me." Fuller, "UIA Seminar," 70.

10 Louis A. Rossetti, "Introduction," *Review of the International Union of Architects*, 52 (1968), 4–6 (p. 5).

11 Jean Fayeton was an expert in the architecture of thermal power stations, who served France as Chief Architect of Civil Buildings and National Palaces.

12 As the Director of the Institute of Industrial Architecture in Brunswick, Walter Henn began an international study of industrial architecture in 1955 that resulted in *Industriebau*, four volumes published between 1961 and 1966.

13 A student of Moisei Ginzburg in the 1930s, Nikolaï Kim acted from 1961 to 1986 as Deputy Scientific Director and Chief Architect of the Central Research Institute of Industrial Buildings in the USSR, where at the same time he also served as Board Secretary of the Union of Architects.

14 From 1960 to 1972, Jean-Pierre Vouga was Cantonal Architect in Vaud Canton. A convinced supporter of an architecture intended as international relations, he wrote of UIA that it let "the language of architecture triumph over that of propaganda." Jean-Pierre Vouga, "La Naissance de l'UIA," *Review of the International Union of Architects*, 49 (May 1968), 6–7.

15 See, for example, the Housing and Community Planning Seminar that the United Nations organized in 1954 in New Delhi; Tom Avermaete and Maristella Casciato, *Casablanca Chandigarh: A Report on Modernization* (Zurich: Park Books, 2014), 310.

16 Rossetti, "Introduction," 6.

17 Worthy of note are the two attempts by the author, Denis A. Birchett, at a definition of the subject: "one definition of industrial architecture could be 'that form or type of architectural expression which derives from the detailed nature of the industry concerned'. Another definition could be that 'industrial architecture is all architecture which by its scale and nature needs to be produced by the use of industrial methods.' To the former definition belongs perhaps a study like an oil refinery or an atomic station; to the latter definition a schools production programme, or a

housing scheme." Denis A. Birchett, "Co-Ordinate or Stagnate," *Industrial Architecture: The 'FIRST' Industrial Architecture Magazine*, 1 (spring 1958), 22–25 (p. 23).

18 The seminar took place from October 3–9, 1960. The organizer was the Industrial Section of Stowarzyszenie Architektów Polskich (SARP). For a list of participants and reports, see "Nouvelles Des Sections: Pologne: Premier Séminaire d'Architecture Industrielle," *Review of the International Union of Architects*, 5 (November 1960), 37–38.

19 Ibid.

20 Two discussions were held outside of the seminar, at an exhibition of student projects from Warsaw and at the gathering that drew up the seminar resolutions. Jan Zachwatowicz, "Séminaire International de l'Architecture Industrielle," *Review of the International Union of Architects*, 6 (December 1960), 8–9.

21 A new charter seemed superfluous, since CIAM appeared to address the subject exhaustively. CIAM, however, postulated only the separation of residential and industrial areas via a green belt, without discussing the industrial building. Ibid., 8; Le Groupe CIAM-France, *La Charte d'Athènes, avec un discours liminaire de Jean Giraudoux* (Paris: Plon, 1943), 147–162. Moreover in 1959 and 1961 the UIA Executive Committee voted down the creation of a new and ninth working commission because with the waning of postwar reconstruction, that organizational form entered a deep crisis; UIA, "La vie de l'U.I.A," 1 (February 1960), 5, 9.

22 Pierre Vago served as the UIA General Secretary from its foundation in 1948 to its tenth congress in 1969. Vago's interest in the seminars was mostly due to their organizational form – he was searching to replace the ceremonious world congresses and the inconclusive commissions with alternatives capable of drafting resolutions in partnership with influential stakeholders; Pierre Vago, *Une vie intense* (Bruxelles: Archives d'Architecture Moderne, 2000).

23 Directed by Vago and financially supported by UNESCO, the *Review* published sixty issues between 1960 and 1969.

24 See UIA, *L'UIA, 1948–1998*, 109. For more on the pavilion, see Theo Crosby, "International Union of Architects Congress Buildings, South Bank, London," *Architectural Design* (November 1961), 484–506.

25 For the resolutions taken by the sixth congress, see James Maude Richards, "Conclusions du VIe Congrès International des Architectes," *Review of the International Union of Architects*, 10 (October 1961), 17.

26 "The Effect of Industrialisation on Architecture: Summary of the Report by Jerzy Hryniewiecki," *Review of the International Union of Architects*, 10 (October 1961), 15.

27 *Architectural Design* editor Monica Pidgeon promoted and announced Fuller's participation. John McHale, "Richard Buckminster Fuller," *Architectural Design* (July 1961), 290–322.

28 Fuller's involvement with universities began in 1948 and was consolidated at the Department of Design created in 1955 at Southern Illinois University in Carbondale.

29 Fuller called this machine a Geoscope or "Minni-Earth," as "it would seem to hover above the earth as an independent asteroid." Fuller, "Proposal to the International Union of Architects," in *World Design Science Decade 1965–1975: Phase I (1963) Document 1 Inventory of World Resources:*

Human Trends and Needs, ed. John McHale (Carbondale: World Resource Inventory, Southern Illinois University, 1963), 1.

30 The history of Fuller's "Proposal" and other speeches to UIA is well documented in Joachim Krausse, *Your Private Sky: Discourse R. Buckminster Fuller* (Baden: Müller, 2001).

31 The Decade initiative postulated that "the only design context for all of our major problems is the global context." Recycling metals, using renewable energy sources, reforming the food cycle, and instituting centers to monitor pollution and waste were all tasks that followed from the premise of the planet as mankind's "total environment" with finite resources. John McHale, ed., *World Design Science Decade 1965–1975: Phase II (1967) Document Six: The Ecological Context: Energy and Materials* (Carbondale, Illinois: World Resource Inventory, Southern Illinois University, 1967), 6, 8.

32 On UIA's international standing, see Miles Glendinning, "Cold-War Conciliation: International Architectural Congresses in the Late 1950s and Early 1960s," *The Journal of Architecture*,14:2 (April 1, 2009), 197–217, accessed 12 December 12, 2014, doi:10.1080/13602360802704869. The congresses of 1959 in Moscow and of 1963 in Havana caused international controversy and internal friction.

33 The seminar took place in October between Rio de Janeiro and Brasilia. For a list of participants and reports, see "Brazil: On the 2nd Seminar of Industrial Architecture – 1962," *Review of the International Union of Architects*, 19 (January 1963), 3–22.

34 Jan Zachwatowicz, "Séminaire International de l'Architecture Industrielle," *Review of the International Union of Architects*, 6 (December 1960), 9.

35 "IInd Seminar of Industrial Architecture," *Review of the International Union of Architects*, 16 (September 1962), 41–42.

36 "Brazil: On the 2nd Seminar of Industrial Architecture – 1962," 17.

37 Ibid., 7.

38 Ibid., 13.

39 Ibid., 7.

40 The alleged cause for this reception was the indifference of the Brazilian section. Vouga, "IInd Seminar of Industrial Architecture," *Review of the International Union of Architects*, 17–18 (December 1962), 35.

41 "Brazil: On the 2nd Seminar of Industrial Architecture – 1962," 21.

42 The seminar took place from June 1–10, 1964, in Budapest and Tihany, under the leadership of Jeno Szendroi. For a list of participants and reports, see "Hungary: The Third International Seminar on Industrial Architecture," *Review of the International Union of Architects*, 30 (December 1964), 6–15.

43 Ibid., 11.

44 International Union of Architects, *Final Report of the Sixth Congress of the International Union of Architects, London, 3rd–7th July 1961* (London: Cement and Concrete Association, 1962), 181.

45 After the indication of the sources, it is assumed that the Tihany Resolution was the published and reworked version of the unpublished Polish Charta. "Hungary: The Third International Seminar on Industrial Architecture," 9.

46 Note that these "other factors" did not include resource distribution, pollution or the planetary scale. Ibid., 15.

47 "Report on the Meeting of the Executive Committee in Torremolinos," *Review of the International Union of Architects*, 32 (March 1965), 27.

48 The seminar took place from May 16–21, 1966, in La Tour-de-Peilz. For a list of participants and reports, see Charles-Édouard Geisendorf, et al., eds., *L'Architecte et l'Urbaniste en Face des Grands Travaux de l'Énergie, du Trafic et de l'Assainissement: Conférences et Exposés* (Lausanne: Bulletin Technique de la Suisse Romande, 1966).

49 "IVth Seminar on Industrial Architecture," *Review of the International Union of Architects*, 40 (September 1966), 26.

50 Ibid., 24.

51 Ibid.

52 Ibid., 21–22.

53 As the sixth and last volume of the series was published in 1967, the departures of McHale and Fuller from Carbondale, in 1968 and 1969, respectively, brought the project to an end.

54 Rachel Carson, *Silent Spring* (Boston: Riverside Press, 1962).

55 Fuller, "UIA Seminar," 59.

56 Robert Matthew, "The Reorganization of the U.I.A.," *Review of the International Union of Architects*, 58/59/60 (December 1969), 12–13.

Piotr Bujas, Alicja Gzowska

New Agencies: Convergent Frameworks of Research and Architectural Design

The 1960–1980 period witnessed the formation of a transitional professional framework in architecture that contributed to the new geopolitical setting, mediated the crisis of hitherto prevailing forms of practice and design tasks, and redefined the scope of competences and the very role of the discipline. The key shift from an object-based to a process-based model of architectural knowledge production was affected by the emergence of new organizational forms and operational strategies. Institutions and agencies of the new kind – from dominant, state, interdisciplinary research institutes to nongovernmental organizations,[1] informal groups, intelligences and transnational policies – occupied a central position in this transition. Although the actors differed widely in character, they enabled and encouraged an unprecedented scale of cooperation and exchange in multilateral systems related to architecture.[2] The development of intensive transnational collaboration resulted in the formation of the current internationally influenced, yet localized discipline and architectural practice, which is "turning experiments in design into experiments in organizational process, decision-making and cross-disciplinary practice."[3]

In this article, we make an attempt to group and categorize the agencies, taking into consideration the types and operational modes adopted by them, and thus propose a provisional taxonomy of exchange frameworks in international architectural practice. The categories elaborated in the article together with their respective sets of examples also form a presentation of a new research perspective on the analysis of architectural culture in Central Europe.

Our proposal is a response to the growing number of analyses of individual companies and their activities.[4] Despite the absence of thorough comparative studies on the subject, the formative role of these institutions and their similarities have already been raised in a recent debate concerning the polarization of architectural production and the Cold War.[5] Until recently, the problems of interactions in culture (including material culture) in a geopolitical context have been discussed within a comparative approach investigating the relations between the main superpowers (the US and the USSR) and their zones of influence, or considered from a internal perspective of Central European countries.[6] Consequently, approaches tended to underline differences due to the use of nationally focused methodologies or historically oriented categories and their entrenchment of Cold War regional divides by cross-border and system comparisons.[7] At present, owing to the influence of postcolonial theories and studies starting from multidirectional, transnational and regional characteristics,[8] the revised and updated transfer-studies model is rising in importance.[9] The model is sensitive to the reciprocal character of exchange[10] and the differing degrees and qualities of flows – not only institutional flows but informal forms of exchange such as the dissemination of models and knowledge.[11] Despite its precision, the transfer-studies formula – elaborated primarily in connection with policies and diplomacy – is only applicable to a limited extent to the understanding of the logic of processes of production and knowledge exchange in Central European architectural agencies and the effects of their activity.[12] The limitations have therefore generated a growing interest in theories stressing the advantage of going beyond the bipolar setting toward multifaceted research strategies, such as entangled history[13] and attempts at applications of the Actor Network Theory model.[14] In these strategies, the emphasis is shifted from object-based to process-oriented (action-oriented) methodologies by replacing the descriptive approach specific to the humanities with an extended analysis of the changing network dynamics of phenomena, which in "transgressing the confinement to national boundaries" lays the conceptual groundwork for conceptual history.[15] According to the historians and sociologists Michael Werner and Bénédicte Zimmermann, the main advantage of this approach lies in the possibility of extent and in-depth analysis, and an understanding of "not only interconnectedness in history, but also how this interconnectedness generates meaning in different contexts."[16]

Applying the approach to the convergence of frameworks of postwar agencies – which is the subject of this article – makes possible not only their description, but also an analysis of actors and processes which led to their emergence and influenced their duration or change in time as well as their scope of influence and effects.[17] Therefore, our focus here is on the operational modes of selected institutions, which offers a means to outline both their methods of functioning and their role in supranational circulation and networks. As much as the groupings and categorizations proposed below seem to present a unified character, institutions belonging to one category often differ significantly in their status and specialization, hence in the effects of their activities.

Design Institutes

Planning institutions – or, rather, design institutes, playing a dominant role in the system – were established to address the needs of reconstructing postwar Europe and were associated with the realization of large-scale state investments, which due to their high degree of complexity and scope of coordination exceeded the capacities of small prewar design offices. The interdisciplinary teams organized in these institutes were focused on supplying optimal, practical solutions based on the current state of knowledge. On both sides of the Iron Curtain, state design offices such as the Soviet Mosprojekts, Energoprojekt in Yugoslavia, the Bulgarian Technoexportstroy, the Dutch Rijksgebouwendienst, or the Greater London Council not only specialized in a holistic preparation and realization of urban and architectural designs for cities and regions, but also worked on planning-development strategies, audits and standard designs. Gradually, a majority of the institutes started to provide consulting services, and became intermediaries between construction companies and research institutes and for developing exports. This was the case with Poland's Miastoprojekt Kraków, which employed their experience of the construction of Nowa Huta – a greenfield, socialist city – to prepare, for example, the master plan of Baghdad (1967 and 1873) (fig. 1), the General Housing Program for Iraq (1976–1980) (fig. 2), and other complex projects which included in the regional plan of Tripolitania (1979–1989).[18] Although the agencies varied in size and profile (for example, the operational mode of Miastoprojekt Kraków was based on research and historical studies and supported by academic practice), they played a pivotal role as nodes of exchange and interdisciplinarity applied to transfer economies. The characteristic of their frameworks of exchange was an emphasis on practical aspects of their activity: providing design services, contracting expert workforces for project coordination and disseminating their methods (for example, localized planning, regional strategies based on context studies, and knowledge management).

fig. 1 Miastoprojekt-Kraków office in Baghdad, in the foreground boards presenting the master plan of Baghdad, Iraq, late 1960s. Photo courtesy of Andrzej Mój.

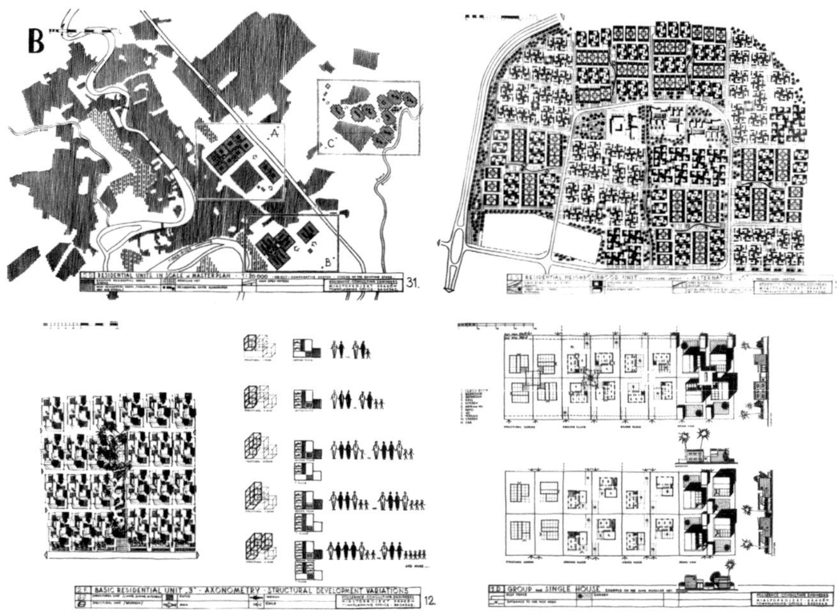

fig. 2 Miastoprojekt-Kraków, The Residential Neighborhood Units model for the Baghdad City – scales, composition, alternatives and structural developments, Iraq, 1966–7. Photo courtesy of Miastoprojekt-Kraków Archive.

Research Institutes

Another equally active framework for the architectural network in Europe was composed of various types of research institution such as the Hungarian Institute for Building Science (ETI), the German Federal Institute for Materials Research and Testing (BAM), the Russian Research Institute of Building Physics (NIISF), and the Research Center for Civil Engineering in Bratislava (VUIS),[19] which were established to address new demands of mass housing,

fig. 3 Thin rubber membrane model used in search for optimal shape of one-pillar structure in BISTYP laboratories, Warsaw, Poland, pic. By W. Stasiak, *Inżynieria i budownictwo*, No. 4, 1963.

fig. 4 BISTYP [Architecture: Maciej Krasiński, Jerzy Hryniewiecki, Ewa Krasińska. Construction: Wacław Zalewski, Andrzej Żórawski, Stanisław Kuś], "Supersam" supermarket in Warsaw, Poland, 1960–1962. Photo courtesy of Paweł Giergoń.

standardization and urban planning. For instance, Poland's BISTYP (Office for Research and Standard Projects of Industrial Architecture), besides studies and standard designs (primarily of industrial plants), was mainly concerned with scientific and experimental research in structural engineering, and with innovative construction methods and techniques, their optimization and application (fig. 3). In close collaboration with architects, BISTYP engineers developed several pioneering structures (such as the Supersam supermarket in Warsaw, 1962), as well as suitable building standards, nomenclature and repeatable, efficient methods of construction (for example those developed during the construction of several factories roofed with thin prefabricated shells) (fig. 4). Research at BISTYP related to research-based design formulas emerging since the mid 1960s ran parallel to studies conducted in the US, for example, on cybernetic support for serial systems (Berkeley University[20] and the L. March studio at MIT) or to research-by-design conducted within large corporate office frameworks, for example at C.A. Dioxiadis.[21] Research unit status and the convergence of specializations of individual institutes, academic units and design institutes encouraged the establishment of official exchanges on the grounds of state agreements on international technical and scientific cooperation, resulting in the creation of an influential system outside the prevailing tracks of architectural production. Study tours, internships, scholarships and conferences were accompanied by the circulation of produced knowledge: a circulation of textbooks, norm guides and other publications – frequently not only of technical but also of theoretical character. Such publications were produced at institutes including VÚVA Brno (the Research Institute for Building and Architecture),[22] which attempted to accord as much importance to their main activity of supporting industrialization and standardization of construction as to the theoretical and experimental research on architecture and urban planning; for example through the publication of a series of design handbooks drawing on prominent international sources originating both in the West and the USSR.

Groups and Collectives

Informal grassroots transfer, mediated by groups and collectives and very often difficult to trace, was crucial for the convergence of the architectural culture between the East, the Center and the West. As their role changed after the Second Word War and the emphasis in practice shifted, architects teamed in structures such as Arbeitsgruppe 4, KADER, Team 10 and RGZ (Radna Grupa Zagreb) to work together on designs, participate in architectural competitions and collaborate with other groups or students. They also developed co-working methods based not only on comparatively regular meetings and the sharing of tasks, but also on correspondence and publications. The mode of organization was frequently formed in response to official constraints and conventions, thus becoming the model of alternative practice. A significant example is offered by the KS 100 collective, established by Juliusz Żórawski in Kraków as a reaction to conditions of state supervision and the centrally imposed doctrine of socialist realism in the early 1950s (fig. 5). Żórawski is ranked among a few iconic architects of Polish prewar modernism, although his works on the theory of building architectural form and on a consistent system of spatial explanation remain largely unknown internationally.[23] His theoretical contribution was particularly important due to his advanced use of *Gestalt* theory in architecture, which paralleled the work of Rudolf Arnheim and such methodologies as the formal analysis of Christopher Alexander.[24] Due to ideological discrepancies, Żórawski and his work were rejected by dominant professional circles cooperating with the Communist regime. Several of his competition designs, though awarded first prizes, were rejected

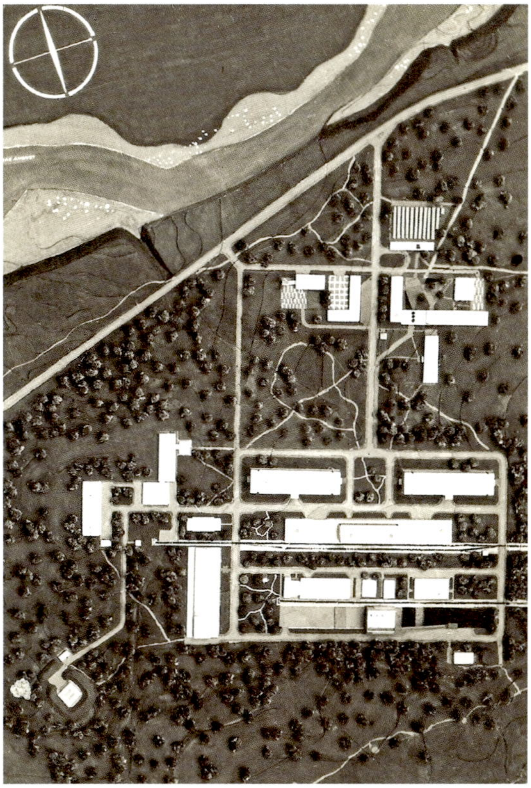

fig. 5 KS100 Collective, competition entry for leather industry plant "Podhale" in Nowy Targ, Poland, 1950–1952. Photo courtesy of Krystian Seibert.

or abandoned. The formula of the collective was supposed to allow Żórawski to cooperate with state-employed architects as well as with students, while the team was supposed to remain anonymous in design competitions, which was essential in the face of the rejection or abandonment of the implementation of his several winning projects. Unfortunately, the team's work results, criticized by the Party Advisory Committee, did not stand a chance of being realized, remaining a record of efforts in continuation and development of late international modernism under communist conditions.

Professional Associations

Networks formed by organizations of professional architects, creating an actual platform for local individuals and networks, were invaluable in the context of international architectural exchange. Congresses and seminars, lectures and exhibitions organized by the most prominent of the associations, the International Union of Architects (UIA), but also by mutually cooperating associations of architects from individual countries (including *Bund Deutscher Architekten* (BDA), the Association of Czechoslovak Architects

fig. 6 Representatives of the Polish Architects Association (right), and the Czechoslovak Architects Association (left) signing the cooperation agreement, Katowice, Poland, 1971. *Architektura*.

(SAČSSR), the Union of Architects of Yugoslavia (UAY), the Association of Polish Architects (SARP)) encouraged the extension of these networks, the establishment of international cooperation and the exchange of staff (fig. 6). Thematic seminars (for example, the UIA Seminar on Industrial Architecture organized since 1960), project confrontations producing wide-ranging conceptual projects (including the periodic Warsaw Confrontations organized in Poland) and competitions (including the competition for the theater in Novi Sad, co-organized by SARP and UAY, and the international competition for the reconstruction of Skopje) were also important for the network. The confrontational and networking character of the competitions stimulated acquisition commissions in an open, international circulation and also constituted an administrative framework for building collective know-how through the exchange of knowledge and expertise in the case of the implementation of selected projects.

Professional associations were also concerned with the documentation and popularization of local architecture as well as the organization of events and competitions (fig. 7). A majority of the associations were involved with or commissioned the publication of professional journals (partly or entirely published in foreign languages), and translations and reprints of currently discussed texts and projects. Editors exchanged texts, prepared occasional materials and press releases for foreign journals. State-dependent associations participated in the official politics of international exchange by organizing or coordinating study visits, internships and traineeships on the grounds of international agreements, initiating and supporting scholarship programs while frequently implementing an informal agenda. This created an organizational framework for network cooperation, new initiatives, the exchange of standards or education through international exchanges and symposia.

fig. 7 W. Lebiediew and his Moscow team, competition entry for Gocław District in Warsaw, Warsaw Confrontations contest. *Architektura* 1976.

Educational Institutions

Schools of design and related initiatives were crucial mediators in the production of competence and of professionals prepared to employ new work methods in the discipline's extended field, such as research economy.[25] Although they partially adapted the strategies of knowledge transfer and workforce mobility from research institutions, they specialized in scholarship programs dedicated to a growing number of students, which enabled travel and complementary education. They also became the environment for initiating research on methods of knowledge dissemination and assisted in the popularization of particular methodologies and solutions.[26] The supra-nationality of mechanisms organizing their activity is demonstrated by, for example, courses on design for tropical zones conducted on both sides of the Iron Curtain. Such postgraduate courses were first organized in postcolonial urban centers: the AA School of Architecture, founded by the London Architectural Association in 1954, was followed four years later by the International Course on Building (ICB–BIE, later transformed into the Institute for Housing Studies, IHS), organized by the Bouwcentrum in Rotterdam, and subsequent years saw the formation of a series of similar courses (for example, at the University of Liverpool in 1967 and the Development Planning Unit UCL, 1971). In an analogous approach, Eastern Bloc initiatives were represented by the postgraduate course on Urban and Regional Planning for Developing Countries at the Szczecin University of Technology in Poland, organized by Piotr Zaremba in 1966. Although the program drew on the experience of the aforementioned establishments – including the principles of tropical architecture[27] as well as Otto Königsberger's method of action planning and the concept of planning as research, mediated with the local government, experts and technologies –[28] its original contribution stemmed from the professional experience of Polish specialists in adapting methods elaborated by the so-called Polish school of urban planning[29] to foreign conditions. The focus of Zaremba's course on planning and urban planning – topics only marginally tackled by analogous courses in the UK and the Netherlands which concentrated primarily on architecture and problems of form and material adjustment to tropical climates – led to the creation of a competitive and complementary educational offer based on a shared knowledge basis supplied with the specific experience of the Polish teaching staff.[30] The practice and principles of the institutions frequently went well beyond their educational mission and became an instrument for consulting and for the initiation of actual projects. Thus, an educational institution served as a knowledge-exchange platform, parallel to the state-controlled exchange agents,[31] facilitating also connections and cooperation with non-socialist countries (for example, Mexico) (fig. 8).[32]

Networks and Intelligences

The least researched category of our provisional taxonomy is based on types of transfer and the adaptation of tools developed during the Second World War for application to internal exchange networks of the state or the market and then, since the outbreak of the Cold War, connected with the defense and the military as well as with technological forecasting on both sides of the East-West dichotomy. It comprises military, industrial, academic think-tanks emerging from RAND (military-academic think-tank originated from a US Military Forces project with the same name) and working since the 1940s in the US, and nonprofit networks of civil and expert support,[33] mediating transfer that was both official and classified; for example, the multilateral exchange of project and equipment documentation.

Such agencies, geared to fast, deliberative problem-solving, had a decisive impact on decisions related to the distribution and development of certain technologies and expertise. Since the 1960s, special COMECOM (Council for Mutual Economic Assistance) units, such as the Council Committee for Cooperation in Planning and the Council Committee for Scientific and Technical Cooperation, dedicated to strategic planning, had cooperated with state foreign-trade central agencies, for example, POLSERVICE, the Polish institutional exporter of expert labor. The postwar formation of horizontal-transfer channels of know-how, academic and specialist labor was greatly influenced by the establishment of various non-military subjects, including

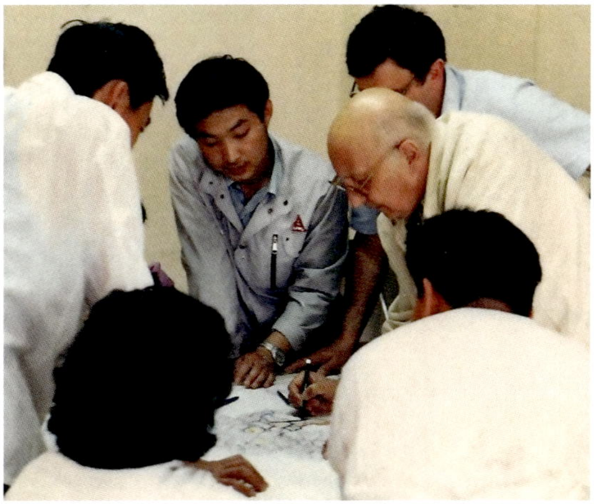

fig. 8 Piotr Zaremba with students from Tsing Hua University during workshops on development planning for Chinese provinces, Beijing, China, 1984. Photo courtesy of the Zaremba Family.

private business enterprises, to provide services to the specializing nodes of state controlled and military networks (logistics, telecommunications). An example that falls into this category in Hungary is TESCO (the International Organization for Technical-Scientific Cooperation), state-founded in 1962 for the purposes of institutionalization and mediation of the export of knowledge, technology and staff exchange. The organization, still currently in operation, was responsible for exporting to fifty-seven countries, for contracting eighty-five hundred experts from the leading companies and institutions, and for integrating branches and dimensions of construction, planning and technological export (including VÁTI and IPARTERV). In addition, TESCO provided training and managed scientific cooperation with UN agendas such as the Industrial Development Organization (UNIDO), the Food and Agriculture Organization (FAO), the Development Program (UNDP) and the International Atomic Energy Agency. Techniques which had previously determined the success of forecast adaptation and that of operations research on the functioning of Cold War networks were applied two decades later to the reality of searching for new markets and to the "marketing" of knowledge (fig. 9).

The methodology and the ensuing categorization of agencies discussed here may help to clarify their various dimensions, frame their scope of actions, and provide insight into processes of a different nature and different effects (figs. 10, 11). It also indicates a number of useful tools for verifying the hypothesis that operational modes actively adopted by individual institutions and actors do not suggest a functional differentiation between the Western and the Eastern sides of the scene; this results from similar relations in the network and a number of previously undocumented influences. In addition,

fig. 9 PARTERV company, power plant constructed within TESCO labor exchange framework in Sousse, Tunisia, 1970s. Photo courtesy of TESCO Archive.

this perspective may help to answer questions concerning the extent to which the profile of the institutions and agencies was generally affected by a well-crafted strategy, long-term practice or external control. One should also remember that the institutionalization of architectural culture was a means of disciplinary control and, consequently, that transfer and related activities were subjugated to political and economic decisions on, for example, a mandated topic or the outcome of research.[34] It should also be kept in mind that not every cooperation was necessarily defined by the forms of exchange described above; they could also produce a negative, undisclosed transfer (for example, one consisting of the reproduction or imitation of standards) and divergent results.[35]

The significance of these issues may be demonstrated by the operational modes of intelligences and state-private networks, which justify the claim that certain mechanisms of the Eastern Bloc economy – owing to the cooperation – simulated an "internalized" capitalism, including the internal circulation of foreign currencies between foreign-trade central agencies and the government. Some authors have also suggested the appropriation of propaganda techniques for the purposes of economic intelligence during the period in which the two blocs competed in their access to and cooperation with countries of the Non-Aligned Movement, and later during the period of economic competition and debt-payment policy in the 1980s.[36] The models that were elaborated under Western conditions might be considered as a laboratory that prototyped (economic) state-private networks after the political-transformation period in CEE and European Union countries. This first selection of hypotheses stresses the need for further and broader research and for continued exchange among researchers. However, the increasing activity of Central European networks is likely to make it only a matter of time.

fig. 10 Scheme of the agency types and profiles. Piotr Bujas, Alicja Gzowska.

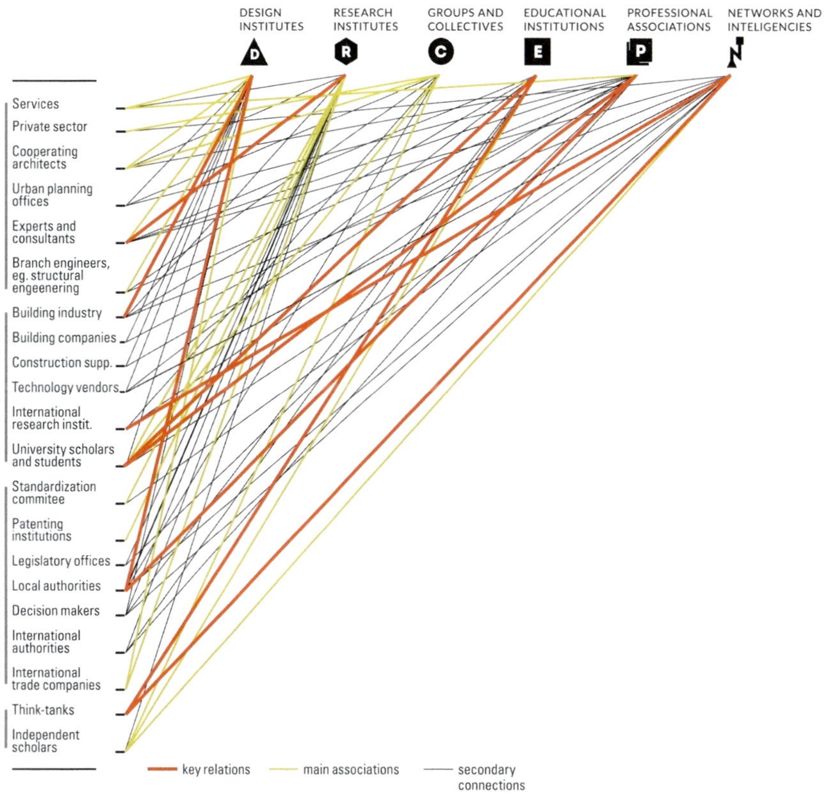

fig. 11 Scheme of the agency types and profiles. Piotr Bujas, Alicja Gzowska.

Endnotes

1 Such as consultancy firms, charities, university centers, scientific associations, think-tanks, etc.

2 Diane Stone, "Transfer Agents and Global Networks in the 'Transnationalization' of Policy," *Journal of European Public Policy*, 11:3 (June 2004), 545–566.

3 Iris Meder, et al., ed., *Lifting the Curtain. Architekturnetzwerke im Mitteleuropa* (Salzburg, Wien: Müry Salzmann, 2015), 46.

4 See Dafne Berc, Dubravka Sekulić, Piotr Bujas and Łukasz Stanek, symposium presentation, "South of East-West: Post-Colonial Planning, Global Technology Transfer, and the Cold War," Berlage Institute, November 9–10, 2010: http://www.south-of-eastwest.net/index.php?id=2; Stanek, "Miastoprojekt Goes Abroad: The Transfer of Architectural Labour from Socialist Poland to Iraq (1958–1989)," *The Journal of Architecture*, 17:3 (2012) 361–386; Alicja Gzowska, "An Institution for Structural Innovation: Office for the Study and Design of Industrial Building Types (BISTYP) in Postwar Poland," in *Nuts & Bolts of Construction History: Culture, Technology and Society*, eds. Robert Carvais, André Guillerme, Valérie Nègre and Joël Sakarovitch, 2 (Paris: Picard, 2012), 281–288; Markéta Žáčková, "'*Byl sice jistý plan* [...]'." *Výzkumný ústav výstavby* a *architektury* (*VÚVA*) a*experimentální bytová výstavba přelomu padesátých* a *šedesátých let dvacátého století*," *Notebook for Art, Theory and Related Zones 17*, (2014), 20–49.

5 The European Architectural History Network biannual conferences have been the platform for the debates since 2010; see programs available at http://www.eahn.org/, accessed March 8, 2016.

6 Cold War International History Project, info at https://www.wilsoncenter.org/program/cold-war-international-history-project, accessed on March 8, 2016.

7 On "methodological nationalism," see Jani Marjanen, "Undermining Methodological Nationalism: Histoire croisée of Concepts as Transnational History," in *Transnational Political Spaces: Agents – Structures – Encounters*, eds. Mathias Albert, et al. (Frankfurt a.M., New York: Campus, 2009), 239–263; Michael Werner, Bénédicte Zimmermann, "Beyond Comparison: Histoire Croisée and the Challenge of Reflexivity," *History and Theory*, 45 (February 2006), 33–35.

8 Including the notion of competitive internationalism, which might be considered an adaptation of Pierre Bourdieu's social theory to transnational production of culture; see Alan Dingsdale, *Mapping Modernities – Geographies of Central and Eastern Europe* (London: Routledge 2002), esp. "Spatial Modernity and the Communist Project," 99–147. See also Ákos Moravánszky, *Competing Visions: Aesthetic Invention and Social Imagination in Central European Architecture, 1867–1918* (Cambridge, Mass.: MIT Press, 1998).

9 Walter L. Hixson, *Parting the Curtain: Propaganda, Culture and the Cold War* (New York: St. Martin's Press, 1997); Michael David-Fox, "The Iron Curtain as Semi-Permeable Membrane: The Origins and Demise of the Stalinist Superiority Complex," in *Cold War Crossings: International Travel and Exchange Across the Soviet Bloc, 1940s–1960s*, eds. Patryk Babiracki and Kenyon Zimmer (College Station: Texas A&M University Press, 2014);

Knowledge Through the Iron Curtain project, detailed info at http://www.helsinki.fi/aleksanteri/kic/background.htm, access on March 8, 2016.

10 Peter Romijn, Giles Scott-Smith and Joes Segal, eds., *Divided Dreamworlds? The Cultural Cold War in East and West* (Amsterdam: Amsterdam University Press, 2012).

11 Diane Stone, discussing types of transfer, points out that "there are different degrees of transfer: straightforward copying of policy, legislation or techniques as well as various forms of emulation, synthesis and hybridization, and inspiration." She also claims that the "objects of transfer can include policies; institutions; ideologies or justifications; attitudes and ideas; and negative lessons. Transfer can take place across time, within countries and across countries." Stone, "Transfer Agents and Global Networks," 546, 548. See also David Dolowitz and David Marsh, "Who Learns What from Whom: A Review of the Policy Transfer Literature," *Political Studies*, 44:2 (June 1996), 343–357.

12 Simo Mikkonen and Pia Koivunen, eds., "Beyond the Divide: Introduction," in *Beyond the Divide: Entangled Histories of Cold War Europe* (New York: Berghahn Books, 2015), 3.

13 Werner, Zimmermann, *Beyond Comparison*, 31–33.

14 For example, MACOSPOL project http://www.medialab.sciences-po.fr/projets/macospol, accessed on March 8, 2016.

15 Marjanen, "Undermining Methodological Nationalism," 241–242, following the original understanding of *Begriffsgeschichte* as the study of modes in which "ideas, movements, translations of concepts transcends confines and trigger historical innovation that form transnational discourses." Reinhardt Koselleck, *Begriffsgeschichten: Studien zur Semantik und Pragmatik der politischen und sozialen Sprache* (Frankfurt a.M.: Suhrkamp, 2006).

16 Werner, Zimmermann, *Beyond Comparison*, 239–240.

17 Diane Stone distinguished the following operational modes: diffusion, transfer, convergence and learning; see Stone, "Transfer Agents," 546 and on.

18 Stanek, "Miastoprojekt," 362–376.

19 *An International Directory of Building Research Organizations* (Washington, D.C.: National Academy Press, 1989).

20 See for example Christopher Alexander, *Notes on the Synthesis of Form* (Cambridge, Mass: Harvard University Press, 1964).

21 Meder, et al., *Lifting the Curtain*, 68.

22 Žáčková, "'*Byl sice jistý plan,*'" 22–23.

23 Juliusz Żórawski, *O budowie formy architektonicznej* (Warsaw: Arkady, 1962).

24 Andri Gerber, "Notes on the Analysis of Form: Christopher Alexander and the Language of Patterns," in *Explorations in Architecture: Teaching Design Research*, eds. Urs Staub and Reto Geiser (Basel, Boston: Birkhäuser, 2008), 122.

25 Avigail Sachs, "The Postwar Legacy of Architectural Research," *Journal of Architectural Research*, 62:3, (February 2009), 53–64.

26 For example, TU Berlin courses.

27 Jane Drew and Maxwell Fry, *Tropical Architecture in the Dry and Humid Zones* (London: Batsford, 1964).

28 Judith Hopfengärtner, "Critical Knowledge Transfer: Teaching on

Planning and Building in Developing Countries at Architecture Schools in Germany," presentation at the symposium "South of East-West."

29 For example, Bolesław Malisz's Threshold analysis; see: Bolesław Malisz, *Zarys teorii kształtowania układów osadniczych* (Warsaw: Arkady, 1981).

30 Piotr Bujas, Alicja Gzowska, "Socialist Development Aid? Training, Research and Educational Activities in Architecture and Planning for Developing Countries in People's Republic of Poland," submitted for publication.

31 Gzowska, Bujas, "Szczeciński kurs urbanistyki dla krajów rozwijających się. Geneza, rola i znaczenie," presentation at the conference "Piotr Zaremba – polityk, urbanista, pamiętnikarz" (Szczecin University of Technology, 7–9 October 2013).

32 Halina Orlińska, "The 20th Anniversary of the Postgraduate Course of Town and Country for Developing Countries," *Town and Country Planning Research*, 10 (1985), 29.

33 For example, OSRD (the Office of the Scientific Research and Development), established "to consult with the military on technological advances and strategic practices [...]" and "to design the problem, criteria, objectives, and a series of possible conclusions through simulations, quasi-experimentation, and operational gaming [...]" "The processes used in system analysis would come to be known as 'forecasting.'" Beatriz Colomina, Annemarie Brennan and Jeannie Kim, *Cold War Hothouses: Inventing Postwar Culture from Cockpit to Playboy* (New York: Princeton Architectural Press, 2007), 56, 61.

34 Sachs, "The Postwar Legacy."

35 Diane Stone sees particular reasons for divergent results in the "lack of shared vision; network disunion; defection" as well as in "internal determinants; e.g. bureaucratic resistance; political inertia – absence of coordinating and consensus-making in networks;" see Stone, "Transfer Agents," 562–563.

36 Colomina, Brennan, Kim, *Cold War Hothouses*, 65, 89.

Appendix

Notes on Contributors

Mirko Baum is a practicing architect and has been Professor for Construction and Design at the RWTH Aachen from 1993 to 2013. He was born in the Czech Republic and studied architecture at the Technical University in Prague. He was a founding member of the architects' commune Školka SIAL in Liberec, and after his emigration to Germany in 1974 he worked in renowned practices such as Kraemer, Sieverts und Partner and the office of Josef Paul Kleihues. He served as a guest lecturer at the Academy of Fine Arts and the Technical University in Prague and was a guest professor at the University of Kassel. Since 1996 Mirko Baum has published and edited a series of reports on Constructional Design. His other publications include *Brennpunkt Dessau* (2001) and *Straße am Ende der Welt. Über Architektur und andere Dinge* (2007). He also has been present in public media programs on topics such as Music and Architecture.

Ljiljana Blagojević, Ph.D., is an architect and architectural scholar. Her authored books include *Itinereri: Moderna i Mediteran, tragovima arhitekata Nikole Dobrovića i Milana Zlokovića* (2015), *Novi Beograd: osporeni modernizam* (2007), *Modernism in Serbia: The Elusive Margins of Belgrade Architecture, 1919–1941* (2003), *Moderna kuća u Beogradu, 1920–1941* (2000) and, in co-authorship with Krunoslav Ivanišin and Wolfgang Thaler, *Dobrović in Dubrovnik: A Venture in Modern Architecture* (2015). Dr. Blagojević practices architecture, publishes and lectures internationally. Her research articles were published by *StadtBauwelt*, *Perspecta*, *The Journal of Architecture*, *Architektúra & Urbanizmus*, *Prostor*, *arq-Architectural Research Quarterly* etc. She co-authored and co-curated the presentation of Serbia at the elenventh International Exhibition of Architecture in Venice, 2008.

David Crowley is professor at the School of Humanities at the Royal College of Art, London, where he runs the Critical Writing in Art & Design MA. He is the author of various books including *National Style and Nation-State: Design in Poland* (1992), *Warsaw* (2003) and editor, with Susan Reid, of three edited volumes: *Socialism and Style. Material Culture in Post-War Eastern Europe* (2000); *Socialist Spaces. Sites of Everyday Life in the Eastern Bloc* (2003); and *Pleasures in Socialism: Leisure and Luxury in the Eastern Bloc* (2010). Crowley has also curated exhibitions including "Cold War Modern" at the Victoria and Albert Museum in 2008–2009, "The Power of Fantasy. Modern and Contemporary Art from Poland" at BOZAR, Brussels, 2011; "Sounding the Body Electric. Experimental Art and Music in Eastern Europe" at Muzeum Sztuki, Łódź, 2012 and Calvert 22, London 2013; and "Notes from the Underground. Art and Alternative Music in Eastern Europe 1968–1994" at Muzeum Sztuki, Łódź, 2016.

Kenny Cupers is Associate Professor in the History and Theory of Architecture and Urbanism at the University of Basel. His research centers on questions of human and material agency, the epistemology and geopolitics of modernism, and design as a technique of social intervention. He is the author of *The Social Project: Housing Postwar France* (2014), winner of the International Planning History Society European book prize and the SAH Spiro Kostof Award, amongst other prizes. Other publications include *Use Matters: An Alternative History of Architecture* (2013) and *Spaces of Uncertainty* (2002, with Markus Miessen).

Igor Demchenko is a postdoctoral fellow at the Kunsthistorisches Institut in Florenz. He received a PhD in architectural history from Massachusetts Institute of Technology in 2015; his doctoral dissertation explored the restoration of medieval Islamic monuments in Soviet Central Asia. His research focuses on the influence of state ideology on architectural production and historic preservation in the colonial context. His work was supported by the Swiss Government Excellence Scholarship, the Kunsthistorisches Institute in Florenz, the Canadian Center for Architecture, the Aga Khan Program for Islamic architecture, and the Dumbarton Oaks Research Library.

Cornelia Escher is an architecture historian and curator. She is a postdoctoral researcher at the University of Konstanz and holds a doctoral degree from ETH Zurich. From 2011 to 2013, she was a researcher at the Institute for the History and Theory of Architecture at ETH Zurich. Her research and publications focus on architecture in the nineteenth and twentieth century with a special interest in its global dimensions and its intersections with the sciences as well as artistic practices. She has published articles in international journals and has been a member of the editorial team of ARCH+ from 2009 to 2011. She was part of the curatorial teams of exhibitions such as "Atelier Bow-Wow" (ETH Zurich, 2013) and "Megastructure Reloaded" (Former State Mint, Berlin 2008).

Judith Hopfengärtner studied architecture at TU Karlsruhe, EPF Lausanne and at the Bartlett School of Architecture, UCL, where she received her Diploma. She taught design at the University of Karlsruhe (KIT) and earned an MAS in History and Theory of Architecture at the Institute gta of the ETH Zurich with research on Aldo Rossi's teachings at the ETH Zurich and his influence on Swiss architects. She was assistant to the Chair for the Theory of Architecture at ETH Zurich 2010–2015 and is co-editor of *Aldo Rossi und die Schweiz. Architektonische Wechselwirkungen* (Zurich, gta, 2011, with Ákos Moravánszky).

Andreas Kalpakci is a fellow of the Doctoral Program in History and Theory of Architecture at the gta Institute at ETH Zurich. His dissertation project "Making CIAM, 1928–1959: The Organizational Techniques of the Moderns" analyzes CIAM as an international organization for understanding how post-war CIAM influenced the institutionalization of modernism. Kalpakci holds a Master of Science in Architecture from the Accademia di Architettura di Mendrisio and a Master of Environmental Design from the Yale School of Architecture, where he studied as a Fulbright grantee. Kalpakci's research interest consists in understanding macrohistorical phenomena of institutional maintenance and change that intersect architecture with science, technology, and international relations.

Karl R. Kegler is Professor for the History and Theory of Urbanistics and Architecture at the Hochschule München / University of Applied Sciences Munich. From 2011 to 2015, he was postdoc and senior assistant at the Institute gta of the ETH Zurich. Prior to that, Kegler worked as a scientific researcher and lecturer at several university institutions and has co-authored and edited numerous books on the history of architecture and on science and technology studies. Publications and research interests include the intellectual history of planning and architecture, popular culture and literary studies. He has published *Wege zu einer neuen Baukunst* (2000), *Utopische Orte. Utopien in Architektur- und Stadtbaugeschichte* (2004) and *Deutsche Raumplanung* (2015) on the history and theoretical basis of regional planning in Germany.

Andres Kurg, PhD, is a researcher and head of the Institute of Art History, Estonian Academy of Arts, in Tallinn. His research explores the architecture and design of the Soviet Union in the late 1960s and 1970s in relation to technological transformations and changes in everyday life as well as its intersections with alternative art practices. He studied art history at the Estonian Academy of Arts and architectural history at University College London. He has published articles in *AA Files*, *ArtMargins*, *Journal of Architecture*, *Home Cultures* and contributed to many collected volumes and exhibition catalogues. In 2008 he co-edited *Environment, Projects, Concepts: Architects of the Tallinn School 1972–1985*. He recently co-curated "Our Metamorphic Futures. Design, Technical Aesthetics and Experimental Architecture in the Soviet Union 1960–1980" in Vilnius National Gallery of Art and Estonian Museum of Applied Art and Design (2011–12), a project funded by a grant from the EU "Culture" program. In 2015 he was a guest scholar at the Getty Research Institute in Los Angeles.

Torsten Lange is postdoctoral assistant at the Guest Lectureship for the Theory of Architecture at ETH Zurich. He received his Diploma in Architecture from the Bauhaus University Weimar and his Master in Architectural History from the Bartlett School of Architecture/UCL, and earned his Ph.D. with the thesis "*Komplexe Umweltgestaltung* [complex environmental design]: architectural theory and the production of the built environment in the GDR, 1960–1990" (UCL, 2015). His research focuses on postwar architecture and urbanism, especially in socialist European countries, and examines theories of production, labor, and materiality as well as alternative forms of architectural practice. His work has been published in *ARCH+*, *archimaera*, *The Journal of Architecture*, and *East Central Europe*, and in edited volumes such as *Industries of Architecture* (Routledge, 2016).

Martin Maleschka is an architect and photographer working and living in Cottbus, Germany. While studying Architecture at Brandenburg University of Technology, he developed a keen interest in photography and in the architectural art of the German Democratic Republic – a passion that stems from having grown up in the socialist model city of Eisenhüttenstadt. In 2006, he began uploading photos of architectural art on various image-hosting websites, and since then has built up the most comprehensive photographic collection of architectural art in East Germany with more than 10,000 images published to this day. His work has been exhibited in a number of solo shows. At the moment, he is working on a guidebook for architectural art in East Germany.

Tamás Meggyesi has been Full Professor of Urban Design at Budapest Technical University since 1991. From 1962, he worked as a researcher at the Chair for Urban Design at the Technical University, where he also received his Diploma in Architectural Design in 1960. He was the Founding Professor of the Institute for Urban Planning of the Mihaly Pollack Technical High

School in Pécs, Hungary. He has won numerous urban design competitions and was awarded with the Ybl-prize and Széchenyi prize. He has published extensively on urbanism, including books such as *The Exterior Space* (2003), *Paths of Twentieth Century Urbanism* (2005), *Urban Morphology* (2009).

Ákos Moravánszky is Professor Emeritus of the Theory of Architecture at the Institute gta of ETH Zurich, where he taught between 1996 and 2016. He studied architecture in Budapest and received his Ph.D. in Vienna. He was a Research Fellow at the Zentralinstitut für Kunstgeschichte in Munich, and the Getty Center in Santa Monica. From 1991 until 1996 he was appointed Visiting Professor at M.I.T. in Cambridge, Mass. The main areas of his research and publication activities are the history of East and Middle European architecture in the nineteenth and twentieth centuries, the history of architectural theory, and the iconology of building materials and constructions. He is the author of *Competing Visions: Aesthetic Invention and Social Imagination in Central European Architecture, 1867–1918* (Cambridge, Mass., 1998) and *Lehrgerüste. Theorie und Stofflichkeit der Architektur* (Zurich, 2015).

Hashim Sarkis is an architect, educator and scholar. He received his BArch and BFA from the Rhode Island School of Design in 1987, his MArch with distinction from the Harvard University Graduate School of Design (GSD) in 1989, and his PhD in architecture from Harvard University in 1995. Sarkis established the Higher School of Studies in Boston and Beirut in 1998, prior to which he worked for several design firms including with Rafael Moneo in the *Souks* project of Beirut. From 1995 to 2014, Sarkis was on the faculty of the Harvard University Graduate School of Design, where he taught design studios and the history and theory of architecture. Between 2002 and 2014, he was the Aga Khan Professor of Landscape Architecture and Urbanism in Muslim Societies at the GSD and also directed the GSD's Aga Khan Program. In 2014, he was appointed Dean of the School of Architecture and Planning at MIT.

Erik Sigge is an architectural historian, preservationist, and currently a PhD candidate in History and Theory of Architecture at the School of Architecture, KTH Royal Institute of Technology in Stockholm, Sweden. He is the founding editor, with Helen Runting and Fredrik Torisson, of the journal *LO-RES*. Erik is a member of the research environments "Architecture in Effect: Rethinking the Social in Architecture" and "Scandinavian Research Network for Welfare and Architecture". He received a Bachelor degree in Integrated Conservation of the Built Environment at the University of Gothenburg, Sweden, and a

Master degree in Historic Preservation at the GSAPP, Columbia University, New York. Erik was earlier Director of Educational and Cultural Programs at Scandinavia House in New York City, where he led the public programs of The American-Scandinavian Foundation.

Daniela Spiegel is an art and architectural historian. From 2004 to 2013 she was a Research Associate at the Technical University of Berlin, Department of Building Archeology. Since 2013 she has been working as a research associate at the Bauhaus University Weimar, Department of Heritage Conservation and Architectural History. Her 2008 Ph.D. thesis examined fascist new towns in Italy, *Die città nuove des Agro Pontino im Rahmen der faschistischen Staatsarchitektur* (2010). Together with Harald Bodenschatz she led a research project about urban design in the era of Mussolini, *Städtebau für Mussolini* (2011). Her Habilitation Project and current research focuses on GDR holiday architecture in a comparative European context.

Axel Zutz is a graduate in landscape planning at the Technical University Berlin and a Ph.D. candidate in the field of theory and history of landscape development; his dissertation was funded by the Hans Böckler Foundation of the Federation of German Trade Unions. Zutz's research focuses on garden-, environmental-, and planning histories of the twentieth century. He was a scientific assistant at the Brandenburg State Office for the Preservation of Monuments and State Archaeological Museum, and has been involved in the research project "Die Niederlausitz und die südliche Lubuskie. Eine Kulturlandschaft im Zentrum Europas" (Niederlausitz and southern Lubuskie. A cultural landscape of central Europe) coordinated by the Chair for the History of Technology (Prof. Dr. phil. habil. Günter Bayerl) at the Brandenburg University of Technology Cottbus-Senftenberg. Zutz has extensively published on the history of landscape and planning within the German Democratic Republic.

Index